Applied Demand Analysis

Applied Demand Analysis

MANOJ KUMAR DASH
Institute of Technology and Science
Ghaziabad (Uttar Pradesh)

BIJAYA KUMAR PANDA
P.G. Department of Economics,
Berhampur University
Berhampur (Orissa)

SERIALS PUBLICATIONS
NEW DELHI (INDIA)

First Published – 2010

ISBN: 978-81-8387-325-3

Published by

SERIALS PUBLICATIONS
4830/24, 1st Floor, Ansari Road
Darya Ganj, New Delhi-110002 (India)
Phone : 23245225. Fax : 91-11-23272135
E-mail: serials@satyam.net.in

CONTENTS

ABBREVIATIONS

ADS	—	Addilog Demand System
AIDS	—	Almost Ideal Demand System
AIDM	—	Asymptotically Ideal Demand Model
CDDS	—	Cobb-Douglas Demand System
CDS	—	Complete Demand System
CEDS	—	Constant Elasticity Demand System
CES	—	Consumer Expenditure Survey
CPI	—	Consumer Price Index
CPIAI	—	Consumer Price Index for Agriculture laborer
CPIIW	—	Consumer Price Index for Industrial Worker
CPIRL	—	Consumer Price Index for Rural Labour
CPIUNME	—	Consumer Price Index for Urban Non-Manual Employees
CSO	—	Central Statistical Organisation
DAIDS	—	Dynamic Almost Ideal Demand System
DADS	—	Direct Addilog Demand System
DLDS	—	Double Logarithmic Demand System
DLES	—	Dynamic Linear Expenditure System
DTLS	—	Direct Translog Demand System
ECM	—	Error Correction Model
ELES	—	Extended Linear Expenditure System
FIML	—	Full Information Maximum Likelihood

GAIDS	—	Generalized Almost Ideal Demand System
HLES	—	Hierarchic Linear Expenditure System
IADS	—	Indirect Addilog Demand System
ILO	—	International Labour Organization
ITDS	—	Indirect Translog Demand System
LA\AIDS	—	Linearised Almost Ideal Demand System
LDS	—	Linear Demand System
LES	—	Linear Expenditure System
LIDS	—	Linear Incomplete Demand System
MBS	—	Marginal Budget Share
MPC	—	Marginal Propensity to Consume
MPTCE	—	Monthly Per capita Total Consumer Expenditure
MPCE	—	Monthly Per capita Consumer Expenditure
MSE	—	Mean Square Error
NSE	—	Nasse Expenditure System
NSSO	—	National Sample Survey Organisation
PCAIDS	—	Proportionally Calibrated Almost Ideal Demand System
PDS	—	Pearce Demand System
QES	—	Quadratic Demand System
QUAIDS	—	Quadratic Almost Ideal Demand System
RDS	—	Rotterdam Demand System
SMLM	—	Simulated Maximum Likelihood Method
SURE	—	Seemingly Unrelated Regression Estimate
TDS	—	Translog Demand System
VECM	—	Vector Error Correction Model
WCPCS	—	Working Class Family Livings Survey

NOTATIONS

p	=	Price vector
$\hat{p}$	=	Vector of logarithm of prices
q	=	Vector of quality purchased
y	=	Total expenditure (Scalar-proxy variable for income)
y^*	=	Real expenditure
$\tilde{y}$	=	Real income
w_i	=	Budget share.
w_i^*	=	Subsistence budget share
μ	=	Marginal budget share vector
λ	=	Lagrangian multiplier
$u(q)$	=	Direct utility function
$u^*(y, p)$	=	Indirect utility function
$c(u, p)$	=	Cost function
$q_i(y, p)$	=	Marshallian demand function
$h_i(u, p)$	=	Hicksian demand function
u_i	=	Marginal utility vector
q_y	=	Income slope vector
λ_y	=	Income response of marginal utility of income (scalar)
λ_p	=	Price slope vector marginal utility of income

γ_{ij}	=	Committed quantity coefficient
α_i	=	Intercept term of AIDS
β_i	=	Marginal budget share coefficient
θ_i	=	Household size coefficient
θ_i^*	=	Preference coefficient
ϕ	=	Income flexibility
m	=	Household size
U	=	Negative Definite Matrix (Second order derivatives of the U.F.)
$\hat{p}$	=	Diagonal Matrix of prices
$\hat{q}$	=	Diagonal Matrix of quantities
$\hat{w}$	=	Diagonal Matrix of budget shares
Q_p	=	Price slope matrix
Q_p^*	=	Utility-compensated price slope matrix
Q_p^{**}	=	Marginal-utility-of-Income-compensated price slope matrix
H	=	Uncompensated price elasticity matrix
H^*	=	Utility-compensated price elasticity matrix
H^{**}	=	Marginal-utility-of-Income compensated price elasticity matrix
θ	=	Uncompensated price response matrix (For differential budget share form of demand equations)
Γ	=	Slutsky substitution matrix
Z	=	Demand shift variables matrix
η_{oj}	=	Expenditure elasticity
η_{ij}	=	Uncompensated cross-price elasticity

η_{ii}	=	Uncompensated Own-price elasticity
η_{is}	=	Size elasticity
η_{if}	=	Preference elasticity
n_{ij}^{*}	=	Compensated cross-price elasticity
n_{ii}^{*}	=	Compensated own-cross-price elasticity
n_{ij}^{**}	=	Marginal-utility-of-income compensated cross-price elasticity
n_{ii}^{**}	=	Marginal-utility-of-income compensated own-cross-price elasticity
δ_{ij}	=	Kronecker delta
$\ln(P^{*})$	=	Stone Price Index
P^{**}	=	Frisch Price Index
P	=	Divisia Price index
A(p)	=	Cost of subsistence
B(p)	=	Cost of bliss
S	=	Vector of stocks

PREFACE

The studies on complete demand systems are of recent origin, even though applied work in consumer demand has a long history. Since 1960s, there has been a growing body of literature on complete demand system (CDS) which involves the simultaneous estimation of complete set of demand equations for every commodity purchased by the consumer. Interest in complete demand system arises out of both theoretical and practical reasons. Stone (1954), Houthakker (1960), Barten (1964) and Theil (1965) have laid the foundation of this approach. With the increasing availability of NSS data in detail for many commodities of household budget for a large number of years as well as increasing access to better computing facilities, many researchers are now engaged in the estimation of complete demand system. By now, a variety of complete demand systems have been proposed for econometric use. All of these demand systems pay strong allegiance to neoclassical demand theory and most of them introduce theoretical as well as particular restrictions, especially some form of separability, in order to simplify the demand system and to reduce the number of parameters to be estimated.

The consumer expenditure data used in the study is the all-Orissa and all-India average Monthly Per Capita Consumer Expenditure (MPCE) on nine broad commodity groups and the corresponding monthly per capita total consumer expenditure (MPCTE), published in different NSS reports from 42nd round (July, 1986-Jan, 1987) to 61st round (July, 2004-June,2005) on consumer expenditure. The retail price data consistent with NSS commodity classification and its rounds used for estimating LES and AIDS and their variants is the time-series of consumer price indices for industrial workers and agriculture labour compiled and released by the Labour Bureau, Ministry of Labour, and Government of India. The consumer price indices for agriculture labourer and industrial worker have been used for estimating demand pattern in the rural and urban sectors respectively of Orissa and all India.

Current research in applied demand analysis has been addressing the twin issues of degree of non-linearity of the Engel curves, and the ability to capture the price effects approximately by the demand system. Further, in addition to income and prices, the role of demographic variables like household size and composition; dynamic aspects like past level of consumption, consumer tastes and preferences etc. are also being emphasized. Continuous efforts are being made to modify and generalize the existing demand systems to incorporate the above developments. The recent focus has been in the estimation of Linear Expenditure System (LES) and Almost Ideal Demand System (AIDS) and their variants and generalisations. While the focus has been on variant and generalisation of Linear Expenditure System (LES) and Almost Ideal Demand System (AIDS), a very few researchers have estimated their variants and generalisations. There is no such specific studies on complete demand system for Orissa and a very few regional studies has been done so far in India. Considering such aberrations, the present study is the modest venture to fill this gap by estimating the two most popular complete demand systems like Linear Expenditure System and Almost Ideal Demand System along with some of their variants to explore the demand patterns in the backward state like Orissa in particular and in the developing country like India in general.

Now econometrics studies on household consumption expenditure occupy prime place in the formulation of perspective plans and government policy making. Demand forecasting for various items of consumption is made, given a certain growth pattern of the economy, a projected growth in population, its rural-urban consumption, and distribution consumption expenditure etc. For estimating the consumption demand for different goods and services, econometric estimation of expenditure elasticities become an imperative necessity. The success of government programmes depends on correct estimation of the various demand functions for different consumption goods. For estimation of Poverty line, determination of consumption baskets at different levels of expenditure is essential. The current interest in demand analysis also extends to welfare application and other diverse areas such as computation of true cost of living indices, calculation of optimal commodity taxes, estimation of cost of a child etc. All these are very useful for current and future policy formulations.

1

INTRODUCTION

INTRODUCTION

In the history of demand analysis two threads related but separable can be discerned: first, the work of economists interested in the discovery of general laws governing the operation of markets and second, the works of those interested in the psychological laws governing the behaviour of the consumer called consumer preferences. The dichotomy continues to characterise the subject as computing opportunity and skills have expanded, empirical research has produced more sophisticated demand equations, and at the same time theoretical economists have enormously increased their knowledge of the mathematics of preference relations. While these two activities have not always been in balance, the great strength of empirical demand analysis has been the existence of strong theoretical foundations, which could be drawn upon or modified for the empirical analysis. This interplay between the theory and empirics has been perhaps more fruitful in demand analysis than in any other area of the theory of consumer behaviour.

Econometrics analysis of household consumption expenditure has come to occupy an important place in applied econometrics. The initial efforts in this area were focused on the estimation of Engel curves from cross-sectional household budget data. The extensive literature available for the estimation of income effects from budget data prompted by the classic works of Allen and Bowley (1935); Wold and Jureen (1953) and Prais and Houthakker (1955)[1], income elasticities have by now come to occupy an important place in policy formulation and demand projections. Some efforts were also made to estimate the demand function of single commodity or commodity group from time-series data using single equation approach (Schultz, 1935 and Stone, 1954). The single equation approach concentrates on the demand for a particular commodity or commodity group paying much attention to its specific characteristics. However, this approach is often not fully consistent with the theory of consumer behaviour. Wald (1940), Frisch (1959) and Stone (1954) have bridged the gap between the well structured preference theory and the applied demand analysis.

The studies on complete demand systems are of recent origin, even though applied work in consumer demand has a long history. Since 1960s, there has been a growing body of literature on complete demand system (CDS) which involves the simultaneous estimation of complete set of demand equations for every commodity purchased by the consumer. Interest in complete demand system arises out of both theoretical and practical reasons. Stone (1954), Houthakker (1960), Barten (1964) and Theil (1965) have laid the foundation of this approach. With the increasing availability of NSS data in detail for many commodities of household budget for a large number of years as well as increasing access to better computing facilities, many researchers[2] are now engaged in the estimation of complete demand system. By now, a variety of complete demand systems have been proposed for econometric use. All of these demand systems pay strong allegiance to neoclassical demand theory and most of them introduce theoretical as well as particular restrictions, especially some form of separability, in order to simplify the demand system and to reduce the number of parameters to be estimated for these models.

There are two broad approaches to Complete Demand System (CDS). The first one consists of specifying a functional form for utility function, maximizing it subject to the budget constraint and solving for the demand equations. The derived demand functions are estimated by using full information maximum likelihood (FIML) or Zellner's Seemingly Unrelated Regression Estimation (SURE) method. Application of duality in demand analysis has established one-to-one correspondence among the direct utility function, indirect utility function and cost/expenditure function showing that the latter two, under specific conditions, contain the same information about preferences as that of the direct utility function. Therefore, the alternative approach to the utility maximization includes the derivation of the demand functions directly from a specified indirect utility function using Roy's identity and indirectly from a cost/expenditure function using Hotelling's theorem or Shephard's lemma. The popular complete demand systems coming under this category are the Linear Expenditure System (LES) and its variants and generalisations; the Direct Addilog Demand Systems (DADS) and Indirect Addilog Demand Systems (IADS); Double Logarithmic Demand System (DLDS), the Translog Demand System (TDS) and its variants and generalisations, the Almost Ideal Demand System (AIDS) and its variants and generalisations.

The complete demand systems can be broadly classified as additive and non-additive. The additive demand systems are restrictive in the sense that they do not allow inferior goods and impose severe restrictions on price effects. In reaction to the criticisms of additive models, a class of 'non-additive' models has come into existence. These classes of flexible models claim dual purpose: provides better description of observed behaviour than the restrictive additive models and allows empirical verification of consumer theory. But the flexible demand systems are more data demanding and create problems when there is no enough variation in data. The most familiar models of this type are Nasse Expenditure System (NSE); Translog Demand System (TDS) and its variants and generalisations; and Almost Ideal Demand System (AIDS) and its variants and generalisations.

In the second approach, demand functions are specified without any reference to the existence of the utility function and theoretical restrictions such as adding-up, homogeneity and symmetry are, generally, imposed as restrictions on parameters in the estimation procedure. The most familiar models of this type are the Rotterdam Demand System (RDS); Frisch Demand System (FDS); Pearçe Demand System (PDS); Constant Elasticity Demand System (CEDS) and Quadratic Expenditure System (QES). This approach is also consistent with the theory of consumer behaviour since the fulfillment of theoretical restrictions implies that the demand equations have been generated from a hypothetical utility function.

Even though the introduction of theoretical restrictions reduce the number of parameters of demand equations, severe limitations still stem from the large number of parameters contained in these demand systems. The assumptions of additivity of preferences (Pigou, 1910 and Houthakker, 1960) and separability (Leontief, 1947 and Sono, 1960) provide a means of alleviating these limitations. The additive utility function, in spite of its restrictive consequences, has been very popular, particularly for broad commodity groups, because of its simplicity of specification and estimations as well as less data demanding. Further, restrictions on the additive utility functions with Frisch's want independence assumption enables the estimation of a complete set of direct and cross-price elasticities from income elasticities, expenditure weights, and money flexibility (Frisch, 1959). The money flexibility coefficient can be computed if the direct price elasticity for a want-independent commodity or group of commodities is reliably known. The assumption of separability is more popular in complete demand systems that encompass a large number of commodities.

Complete demand equations have been estimated for India and their results have been extensively used in planning and policy. While the focus has been on Linear Expenditure System (LES), a very few researchers[3] have estimated its variants and generalisations. The recent focus has been on the Almost Ideal Demand System (AIDS) and its variants and generalisations.

A very few studies[4] have estimated AIDS and its variants and generalisations. Recently Murty (2005) has estimated LES and AIDS with demographic specification using consumer expenditure data of the first five quinquennial rounds (27th to 50th rounds). For the convenience of exposition of complete demand system, instead of relying on the results of earlier studies, he has estimated the two demand systems for seven commodity groups using the pooled time-series of cross-section data of the above five quinquennial rounds.

The availability of National Sample Survey (NSS) data for different rounds of consumer expenditure has led to a number of studies on patterns of household consumption and demand. However, a majority of these studies are confined to Engel curve analysis.[5] But the studies based on complete demand system are scanty both at the national as well as regional level. The complete demand system has been applied both for the estimation of the parameters and for testing the validity of theoretical postulates. A majority of the studies on complete demand system deals with the estimation rather than testing theoretical postulates. These studies are mostly used the mean level of time-series data. On the other hand, estimation of complete demand system from time-series of cross-section data has the advantage of large variation in total expenditure and it involves aggregation over consumers. It is also worth mentioning that a very few comprehensive studies[5] on complete demand system have been reported for developing countries like India. This study is an endeavor to estimate the Linear Expenditure System (LES) and the Almost Ideal Demand System (AIDS) along with some of their variants from the NSS time-series and pooled time-series of cross-section data of Orissa and all-India from 42nd round (1986-87) to 61st round (2004-05) with a view to bring out the structural features relating regional dualism (rural and urban) etc. and for testing the validity of theoretical postulates.

The plan of exposition of this chapter is as follows: Section-1 is the introduction. The scope and broad objectives of the study are expressed in Section-2 and Section-3 respectively. Section-4 deals with the methodology which includes the NSS sample design, its published information and description of commodity groups; the models and computer software used in the study. The hypothesis formulated for the study is presented in Section-5. The organisation of the study is explained in Section-6. Finally, the chapter ends with the limitations of the study in Section-7.

SCOPE OF THE STUDY

Household budgets have been often studied for a variety of purposes such as computing cost of living indices, demand forecasting, demand patterns, measuring level of poverty, disparity in living standards, cost-benefit analysis of optimal tax theory, welfare analysis etc. Demand analysis is generally based on aggregate time-series and pooled time-series of cross-section data but occasionally and more recently, on cross-section or even panel data. Cross-section household data are generally used for constructing cost of living indices and Engel curve analysis, which reflects the consumption pattern and the living standards of the household. Cross-section data is also used for measuring the level of poverty and disparities in the level of living. Continuous cross-section and panel data on household budgets are helpful in studying dynamic aspects of consumer behavior. The scope of the study is limited to time-series data for estimating the Linear Expenditure System (LES) and Almost Ideal Demand System (AIDS) and their variants.

Household budget data are being collected in every round of NSS beginning from the 1st round through 28th round. After 28th round, the NSSO had decided to conduct household expenditure survey in every five years beginning from 27th round instead of each round. But after lapse of 13 years to build up time series data, NSSO again carried out its annual consumer expenditure survey in each round from 42nd round onwards on a reduced scale. Since, time series data on consumption expenditure from 28th round to 41st round is not available, the scope of the study is limited to the data set collected and published by the NSSO from 42nd round (1986-87) to 61st round (2004-05).

It is hard to limit the horizon of the study on household demand as there are number of factors such as household size and its composition, occupational structure, social class, regional affiliation of the household etc., which effect household demand patterns. These factors as well as its sub-factors are either quantitative or qualitative in nature. The household size and its composition always influence the household demand patterns. Two households with same income and household size but differing in their composition not necessarily have the same standard of living. Hence, the demand patterns vary from household to household due to variation of household size and its composition. It is difficult to study the demand pattern of the households taking into account all the factors. Hence, we have limited the scope of the study by including household size ignoring its composition as an explanatory variable in the demand systems.

Both the LES and AIDS models can be made flexible by allowing its parameters to vary with the change in demographic features, dynamic behavior related to past levels of consumption, the shift in taste and preference of the consumer, prices etc. Accordingly, we have different variants of these models. The scope of the study is limited to the estimation of LES and its variants incorporating separately the average household size and a time variable as an additional variable and also a non-additive variant of it (Nasse Expenditure system) by making its committed quantity parameters as function of prices. Further, its scope is also limited to the estimation of AIDS with demographic specification and AIDS with and without theoretical restrictions.

Due to non- availability of time-series of consumer price indices for Orissa and all India prior to 1985-86, most of the earlier demand studies in India are based on wholesale price indices. Since, time series of consumer price indices for Orissa and all India are now available for the calendar and financial years, this study is based on financial year consumer price indices for some rounds and calendar year price indices for some other rounds according to their period of survey. But the duration of most of the NSS rounds exactly coincides with the agricultural year (1st July to 30th June) for which consumer price indices are not available. Therefore, the scope of the study is limited for using the financial year consumer price indices for those rounds whose period of survey coincides with the agricultural year.

OBJECTIVES OF THE STUDY

The principal objectives of the study are:

(i) To estimate the LES model and its variants which includes the Linear Expenditure System (LES-1); a variant of LES incorporating household size by demographic translating procedure to examine the operation of economies and diseconomies of scale in household consumption (LES-2); another variant of LES incorporating linear time trend to show the change in demand of different commodities due to change in the taste and preference of the consumers over time (LES-3) and a non-additive variant of LES popularly known as Nasse Expenditure System (NES) by making its committed quantity parameters as function of all prices using time-series of consumer expenditure data of NSSO at the level of nine broad commodity classifications. The parameter estimates along with the expenditure, uncompensated price, size and preference elasticities estimated from above four models separately for rural and urban sectors of Orissa and all India are also analysed in the study.

(ii) To estimate six variants of the AIDS model viz., the linear approximation of the AIDS model with demographic specification abbreviated as AIDS-1 to examine the operation of economies and diseconomies of scale in the consumption of different items which has a direct bearing on the demand for different commodities; the linear approximation of the AIDS model without any restriction abbreviated as AIDS-2 (or simply LA\AIDS); a variant LA\AIDS with only homogeneity restriction imposed (AIDS-3); another variant LA\AIDS with both homogeneity and symmetry restrictions imposed (AIDS-4); the fifth variant of LA\AIDS model with 'no household size' and 'no cross price effects' named as AIDS-5 and finally, the sixth variant of LA\AIDS model with explicit additivity restriction imposed i.e. 'no household size' and 'no price effects' (AIDS-6) using time-series of consumer expenditure data of NSSO at the level of nine broad commodity classifications. The parameter estimates along with the income/ expenditure, uncompensated price and size elasticities estimated from above six models separately for rural and urban sectors of Orissa and all India are analysed and the validity of different restrictions are tested in the study.

(iii) To test the validity of theoretical restrictions like homogeneity (no money illusion), symmetry (equality of cross-substitution effects) and both homogeneity and symmetry as well as other 'a priori' restrictions like 'no economies of scale or household size effects', 'no cross price effects' and 'no price effects' (explicit additivity).

(iv) To examine the inter-income-group variations in the consumption pattern of different food and non-food items among three segments of the population viz., bottom 30 percent (low income group), middle 40 percent (middle income group) and top 30 percent (high income group) separately in the rural and urban sectors of Orissa and all India using time-series of cross-section consumer expenditure data of NSSO at the level of twelve broad commodity classifications.

(v) To examine the inter-sectoral variations in consumption patterns separately for Orissa and all-India as well as inter-temporal variations in consumption patterns separately for rural and urban sectors of the state and the country using time-series of consumer expenditure data of twenty NSS rounds

(1986-87 to 2004-05) at the level of twelve broad commodity classifications.

(vi) To compare the performance of LES and its three variants as well as LA\AIDS and its five variants separately in both rural and urban sectors of Orissa and all-India.

(vii) To ascertain the most plausible demand system on the basis of the overall performance of LES and AIDS models using the economic 'a priori', statistical and econometric criteria.

METHODOLOGY

The present study is based on the household budget data collected by the National Sample Survey Organisation (NSSO) from 42nd (July 1986- June 1987) to 61st (July 2004-June 2005) rounds of its enquiry. This section provides a brief description about the NSS data collection and its sample design, the description of major commodity groups, the database and the consumer price indices used in the study.

DESCRIPTION OF NATIONAL SAMPLE SURVEY ROUNDS FOR DATA COLLECTION

The National Sample Survey Organisation was set up in 1950 and it is the primary agency for collecting data on various socio-economic characteristics along with household consumer expenditure on a nation-wide basis. The consumer budget enquiry forms an integral and perhaps the important part of an overall programme of the NSS to conduct national socio-economic enquiries to provide data needed for planning of national development. In India, the data on consumer expenditure has been collected every year through a series of repetitive surveys called rounds. Data on household consumer expenditure are being collected in every round of the NSS beginning from the first round (October 1950-March1951) through 28th round (1973-74). After the 26th round of the survey, the governing council of NSSO had decided that the survey on consumer expenditure to be undertaken once in every five year beginning from the 27th round. Thus, the first quinquennial survey on consumer expenditure was conducted in the 27th round (October 1972 - September 1973), the second quinquennial survey in 32nd round (July 1977-June 1978), the third quinquennial survey in 38th round (January-December, 1983), the fourth quinquennial survey in 43rd round (July 1987-June 1988), the fifth quinquennial survey in 50th round (July 1993-June 1994), the sixth quinquennial survey in 55th round (July 1999-June 2000) and the seventh quinquennial survey in 61st round (July 2004-June 2005). To meet some specific ad-hoc requirements, a survey on consumer expenditure was also conducted in the 28th round outside this quinquennial programme.

Consumer expenditure inquiry on a reduced scale (except quinquennial round) is carried out every year from 42nd round (1986-87) onwards with a view to build up a time series of consumer expenditure data. Some of these reduced scale annual surveys spread over a full year and some others over six months but the quinquennial surveys spread over a period of one year coinciding with the agricultural year. Until the eleventh round, the duration of NSS rounds varied from 3-8 month and the gap between any two successive rounds ranged from one to four months. Further, until the 7th round the reference period was not uniform and varied from one week to one month. From the 7th round onwards the reference period has been uniformly made 30 days preceding the date of enquiry for all the commodities. From 14th round onwards, the survey period was made one year coinciding with the agriculture year to eliminate seasonal fluctuation. Entire survey period of one year was divided into 4 sub-rounds each of 3 months duration coinciding with four agricultural seasons. This is done with the motive of removing seasonal fluctuations from the data. The seasonality in the purchase of durable and semi-durable items might cause underestimation of monthly consumer expenditure data. However, the extent of this downward bias can be minimized by dividing each round into four sub-rounds of three months duration to eliminate seasonality bias. This procedure is known as moving sampling method. The detail particulars like the duration of the round, reference period, size of sample and number of sample households covered from 42nd to 61st rounds in rural and urban sector of Orissa and all India is described in *Table-1.* Estimates of consumption expenditure presented in this study are based on one month reference period.

The surveys have been conducted on the basis stratified random sampling with at least two independent and interpenetrating sub-samples. Within each sub-sample in rural areas, villages and households are the first and final stage units respectively. In case of urban area, towns, census block and household are the first, second and final stage units respectively. The four big cities viz., Bombay, Madras, Calcutta and Delhi form a separate stratum. The incorporation of independent and interpenetrating sub-samples enables us to have an idea of the magnitude of the sampling and non-sampling errors for NSS estimates; the closer the sub-sample estimates the smaller is the margin of error.

BRIEF DESCRIPTION OF THE SAMPLE DESIGN OF NSSO

The NSS have been following multi-stage stratified sampling. In recent rounds, the villages have been taken as first-stage units in the case of rural India and urban blocks as first-state units in case of urban India. The households constitute second stage units for both the rural and urban India. The entire rural and urban sectors of India have been divided into a number of strata and an appropriate number of villages or urban blocks are selected from each stratum with probability proportional to the size of the selected unit. Form each selected village or urban block; some households (ten or twelve on the average) are selected as second-stage units.

During 27th round, India was divided into 66 agricultural regions and each region was again sub-divided into a number of stratums with almost the same rural population. The total number of rural stratums in India during 27th round was 392. Two independent sub-samples of 24 villages each were selected systematically with equal probability in each stratum after arranging the stratum in a serpentine order. All the households

Table 1
Survey and Reference Periods, Sample Size and Household Covered During 42nd to 61st NSS Rounds in Rural and Urban Sectors of Orissa and all India

				India				Orissa				
				Sample Size		Household		Sample Size		Household		
Round	Report No.	Reference Period	Survey Period	Rural Villages	Urban Blocks	Rural	Urban	Rural Villages	Urban Blocks	Rural	Urban	No of Income Class
42	365	30 days	July 1986 to June 1987	8379	4628	12237	6736	168	60	463	566	12
43	Vol.15	30 days	July 1987 to June 1988	8874	4743	12564	6753	177	60	482	558	12
44	Vol.14	30 days	July 1988 to June 1989	7458	6459	13764	9879	216	120	432	524	12
45	Vol.16	30 days	July 1989 to June 1990	7387	7128	14503	14241	287	255	568	510	12
46	Vol.17	30 days	July 1990 to June 1991	4578	3452	12543	6783	360	184	716	368	12
47	Vol.18	30 days	July to Dec. 1991	4373	2511	8642	5005	196	60	388	120	12
48	397	30 days	Jan. to Dec. 1992	4321	2419	8324	4805	192	52	382	104	12
49	399	30 days	Jan. to June 1993	4882	2791	75036	44367	201	63	3187	1005	12
50	401	30 days	July 1993 to June 1994	6951	4650	69206	46148	335	104	3338	1037	12
51	436	30 days	July 1994 to June 1995	8536	5536	16244	10519	342	112	758	236	12
52	440	30 days	July 1995 to June 1996	7643	4876	14499	9959	289	89	656	228	12
53	442	30 days	Jan. to Dec 1997	5479	4687	13725	17385	212	47	924	719	12
54	448	30 days	Jan. to June 1998	5058	1755	19,936	6,983	216	36	860	144	12
55	453	30 days	July 1999 to June 2000	3070	2074	35492	24316	242	46	912	213	12
56	476	30 days	July 2000 to June 2001	4321	3423	21649	35624	248	174	997	991	12
57	481	30 days	July 2001 to June 2002	6381	9297	25505	37123	344	228	1376	911	12
58	484	30 days	July to Dec. 2002	4675	3498	18687	13982	190	67	760	268	12
59	490	30 days	Jan. to Dec.2003	6553	3757	26143	14870	243	64	972	254	12
60	505	30 days	Jan. to June 2004	4755	2669	18975	10656	211	56	840	224	12
61	508	30 days	July 2004 to June 2005	7999	4602	79298	45346	384	120	3836	1187	12

Source: Reports of National Sample Survey Organisation, Ministry of Statistics and Programme Implementation (GoI) and Sarvekshena (GoI), Vol.15-18.

in a sample village were divided into three sub-stratums on the basis of their means of livelihood as (i) self employed in non- agriculture (ii) rural labour and (iii) others. On an average, 12 sample households were selected from a sample village which includes two households from sub-stratum-1, five households from sub-stratum-2 and another five households from sub-stratum-3. But in case of urban areas, towns with population less than 50 thousand formed sub-stratum-1 and the remaining cities (except Calcutta, Delhi, Bombay and Madras) formed sub-stratum-2. From each stratum urban blocks were selected circular systematically with probability proportional to the size of the block. All the blocks are again divided into two independent interpenetrating sub-samples. All the households in a block are divided into two sub-stratums (i) self-employed in manufacture and (ii) self-employed in other activities. On the average 12 households were selected with 6 households from each sub-stratum. Almost the same procedure was adopted in 32nd and 38th rounds in the selection of households which constitute the second stage units for both the rural and urban India.

In 43rd round, some significant changes have been made in the sample design. In the rural sector, the household in the sample village were first grouped into two sub-strata: sub-stratum-1 and sub-stratum-2. Sub-stratum-1 consists of 8 or 10 relatively most affluent households depending on whether the sample village had less than eighty or more households. If more than 10 households qualify to form affluent households, only 10 of them will be included in sub-stratum-1 and remaining are grouped as sub-stratum-2. Two sample households were selected from sub-stratum-1 circular systematically with a random start. In case of sub-stratum-2, before selection of the sample households, all households were regrouped into three means of livelihood classes viz. self-employed in non-agriculture, rural labour and others categories of households. The others categories of households were again regrouped into five land ownership classes, households possessing (a) less than one 1 acres (b) 1 to 2.49 acres, (c) 2.5 to 4.99 acres, (d) 5 to 9.99 acres, and (e) 10 acres and above. Eight households were selected circular systematically with a random start, after arranging the households belonging to different groups in a continuous manner.

In the urban sector also, two sub-strata of households were formed in each sample block. In all the cities with population of 10 lakh and more and households with Rs.1000/- or more per capita expenditure (MPCE) constituted sub-stratum-1 and the remaining households constituted sub-stratum-2. On the other hand, in the towns with population less than 10 lakh, households with MPCE level Rs.800/- or more constituted sub-stratum-1 and the remaining households constituted sub-stratum-2. For selection of sample households, all the households of sub-stratum-2 were first grouped into four means of livelihood classes, namely (i) self-employed (ii) regular wage/salaried (iii) casual labour and (iv) others. The households of the group-i and group-ii were again regrouped on the basis of three MPCE levels. Then, four sample households from sub-stratum-1 which constitute most affluent households and 6 households from sub-stratum-2 which constitute the non- affluent households were selected circular systematically after arranging the households by means of their livelihood i.e. first self-employed in non-agriculture followed by rural labour then others categories of households in sub-stratum-2. Almost the same procedure with little modification in the selection of households which constitute the second stage units was adopted for both the rural and urban India during the 50th and 55th rounds. In urban sector, households with monthly per capita expenditure Rs.1200 and more in 50th round and Rs.1500 and more in 55th round (in cities with population ten thousand and more) and also households with monthly per capita expenditure Rs.1000 and more in 50th round and Rs.1200 and more (in towns with population less than ten thousand) were placed in second-stage stratum-1 and the rest in second-stage stratum-2 in 55th round.

During the 61st round (the seventh quinquennial survey on consumer expenditure) some major changes have been made in the formation of second stage stratum (SSS) in a sample village/block. In each sample village/block, households were grouped into three second stage stratums. In the rural sector, SSS-1 consists of 10 relatively most affluent households of the sample village. If more than 10 households qualify as affluent households only 10 of them (most affluent) are included in second stage stratum-1 (SSS-1). The remaining households of the sample village having principal earning from non-agriculture activity constitute SSS-2. The rest of the households constitute SSS-3. Similarly in the urban sector, all the households of a sample block are grouped into three second stage stratums on the basis of two cut-off points (A and B) of the monthly per capita consumption expenditure. A is the higher cut-off point determined by the top 10 per cent of the households in a NSS regional with MPCE more than A and B is the lower cut-off point determined by the bottom 30 per cent of the households in a NSS regional with MPCE less than B. So, these cut-off points will vary from one NSS region to another. In a sample block, households with MPCE more than A are grouped under SSS-1; households with MPCE equal to or less than A but equal to or more than B are grouped under SSS-2 and finally households with MPCE less than B are grouped under SSS-3. A sample of ten households, two households from SSS-1 and four households each from SSS-2 and SSS-3 are selected circular systematically with a random start separately for the rural and urban sectors.

For collecting data on consumption, the adoption of a reference period always involves a difficult choice. A short reference period (i.e. one day) gives unstable data. And long reference period can introduce a good amount of recall error into the data. Annual series of consumer expenditure survey up to 49th round have used uniform reference period of last thirty days for all item of consumption. In the sixth quinquennial survey (55th round), one half of the sample households surveyed through schedule type-1, which had thirty days of reference period. The sample households surveyed through schedule type 2, the reference periods were 'last seven days'. To avoid the problem of using two schedule types and inconsistency of data collected for two reference periods during 55th round, the double reference period of 'last thirty days' for non-durable goods and 'last one year' for some durable goods was again introduced during 61st round. In all quinquennial surveys up to 43rd round (1986-87), the double reference period of 'last thirty days' and 'last one year' has been used for three categories of items like clothing and bedding; footwear and durable goods and from the 50th round onwards, the double reference period is used for two more categories in addition to the above three categories viz., educational expenses; and medical care (institutional). For all other items of consumption, the reference period is 'last thirty days' (except the sixth quinquennial survey).

PUBLISHED INFORMATION OF NSSO

Detailed information on household consumer expenditure is collected for almost all the items of consumption; including quantity and value of the items consumed, but very little has been published. The NSS reports and 'Sarvekshna' issued by the Government of India furnish data on consumer expenditure on various consumption items. The per capita total expenditure for 30 days is classified into twelve expenditure classes. The classification is formulated in such a way so as to obtain approximately 5 per cent of the population each in the first two and last two classes and 10 per cent each in the middle eight classes. It becomes very difficult to combine rural distribution with urban distribution of income. Therefore, the NSSO formulated four (comparable) expenditure levels for comparing rural and urban results from 43rd round onwards.

For each income class, the standard NSS table provides the estimates of average number of persons; per thousands distribution of households, persons, number of adult males, adult females and children by monthly per capita expenditure on broad group of items and percentage of expenditure on food and non-food items to total expenditure and per capita quantity and value of consumption of different cereals and some other selected items by per capita expenditure classes. This information is available separately for all states, union territories and also for all India. The data are also published separately for rural and urban sectors of the states as well as all India.

DATABASE OF THE STUDY

The consumer expenditure data used in the study consists of all-Orissa and all-India average monthly per capita consumer expenditure (MPCE) on nine broad groups of items and the corresponding monthly per capita total consumer expenditure (MPTCE), separately for rural urban households. The expenditure data has been taken from different NSS reports form 42nd round (July, 1986 to Jan, 1987) to 61st round (July, 2004-June, 2005) of surveys excluding the 49th and 60th rounds for which the consumer price indices are not compatible. The period covered is, therefore, from July 1986 to June 2005. For each round of the NSS survey, we have estimated the average monthly per capita expenditure of all the expenditure classes for each item of consumption to generate item-wise time-series data. For 61st round, we have estimated the average monthly per capita expenditure for three population groups based on ranking by the level of monthly per capita total expenditure MPTCE viz., low income group (the bottom 30 per cent of the population); the middle income group (middle 40 per cent of the population) and high income group (the top 30 percent of the population) separately for the rural and urban sector of the state of Orissa and for all India.

The nine broad specific items considered here are cereals and its substitutes; pulses and its products; milk and its products; edible oil and fats; meat, fish and egg; other food items, clothing (which including clothing and beddings); fuel and light; other non-food items. The other food items and the other non-food items are the residual categories. The former includes vegetables and fruits; sugar and gur; salt and spices; beverages and processed food etc. while the latter consists of expenditures on transport; medical care; education; recreation; rents and taxes etc. and also expenditure on durables such as utensils, ornaments household equipments, furniture etc. It should be mentioned that the items other than the residual items are fairly standard items for which the NSSO regularly publishes expenditure estimates. However, for some of these items like pulses and its products; meat, fish and egg; edible oil and fats; pan, tobacco and intoxicants etc.; the observed budget shares are frequently small. Yet this grouping of items has been retained essentially because of the fact that such a grouping is considered in most of the disaggregated studies based on consumer expenditure data (see, for example, Bhattacharya and Maitra (1970); Radhakrishna, Murty and Shah (1979); Coondoo and Majumder (1987); Meenakshi and Ray (1999) and Murty (2005)).

CONSUMER PRICE INDEX (CPI)

On account of the importance of the Consumer Price Index (CPI)[6], the International Labour Organisation (ILO) had set general guidelines and standards for compilation of consumer price Indices by all the member countries. In principle and practice, Consumer Prince Index (CPI) measures the changes over time in the general level of prices of goods and services that a reference population acquire, use or pay for consumption. There are four different Consumer Price Indices (CPI) brought out in India on monthly basis viz. CPI for Urban Non-Manual Employees [CPI(UNME)], CPI for Industrial Workers, [CPI(IW)], CPI for Agricultural Labourers [CPI(AL)] and CPI for Rural Labourers [CPI(RL)] which has been compiled and released at national level. While the first one CPI (UNME) is compiled and released by the Central Statistical Organisation (CSO), Ministry of Statistics and Programme Implementation (GoI) on monthly basis since 1961 and the rest three indices are compiled and released by the Labour Bureau, Ministry of Labour (GoI) on monthly basis since 1960.

The Labour Bureau compiles the CPI for industrial workers [CPI(IW)] on monthly basis for a number of goods and services which varies between 120 to 160 (as the consumption basket varies from centre to centre) collected from 261 markets in 76 centres covering 20 states of the country. The various goods and services are classified into six main item groups (i) food (ii) pan, supari, tobacco and intoxicants (iii) fuel and light (iv) housing (v) clothing (vi) miscellaneous items. The base year of this index is 1982 and the weights of the index are based on the estimates generated from the data collected through the Working Class Family Living Survey (WCFLS) conducted during 1981-82. The Labour Bureau also compiles the CPI for Agricultural Labourers [CPI(AL)] and Rural Labourers [CPI(RL)] on monthly basis using the retail price of 260 different goods and services collected by the NSSO from fixed markets of 600 sample villages spread over in 20 states of the country. The various goods and services are grouped into four main groups, namely (i) food items (ii) fuel and light (iii) clothing, bedding and foot wear (iv) other non-food items. The base year for both the indices is 1986-87. The weights for both the indices are based on the estimates generated from the data collected through household consumer expenditure survey conducted by NSSO in its thirty eight round (1983). The Labour Bureau released its [CPI (RL)] series for 20 states and all-India since November, 1995.

The indices are worked out using Laspeyres' weighted aggregate method. First the price relative of each item for each village is worked out. A simple average of village-wise price relatives is calculated at the zonal level for each state. The zonal price relatives are weighted to arrive at the average state level price relatives. The state index is calculated as the weighted average of the state level price relatives, the weights being the proportion of consumption expenditure as determined by consumer expenditure survey of the NSSO of rural agricultural labour/rural labour households. The all India index is then worked out as the weighted average of the state index numbers, weights being the estimated consumption expenditure of the rural agricultural labour/rural labour households in each state as a proportion of total of such expenditure for all the states for which the index is being compiled separately. The weights of various CPI series for the states and for all India at group and sub-group levels has been calculated and released by the Labour Bureau for the industrial workers with base 1982 and for agricultural labourers and rural labourers with base 1986-87.

The retail price data used in the present analysis in the time-series of consumer price indices for industrial workers with base 1982 and agricultural labourers with base 1986-87 compiled and released by the Labour Bureau for different financial and calendar years, separately for Orissa and all India. Since, the consumer price index series for agricultural years which coincides with the period of most of the NSS rounds are not available; we have used the financial year consumer price indices series as the proxy for agricultural year consumer price indices for deflating expenditure data of some NSS rounds for which the period of survey coincides with agricultural year, and calendar year consumer price indices for deflating expenditure data of some other rounds for which the period of survey coincides with a calendar year. To maintain consistency between different financial years and the periods of NSS rounds, we have not considered the expenditure data for 49th and 60th rounds and the price index of 1995-96 while compiling these indices so that the retail price-series consistent with the NSS rounds can be obtained. Since, the price indices released by the Labour Bureau for some of the specific commodity groups are not the same for the commodity groups considered in the analysis, we have complied the indices for such item groups using the weighted diagram released by Labour Bureau separately for industrial workers and agricultural labourers for Orissa and all India. In this manner, the price index series for all the nine specific item groups considered in the study has been compiled and checked for consistency separately for rural and urban sectors of Orissa and all India as no other satisfactory up-to-date retail price series is readily available. The price index series, thus, compiled separately for rural and urban sectors of Orissa and all India may be taken as the proxy for the actual retail price movement in the state as well as in the country. It is also pointed out that the retail price-series so constructed are assumed to be applicable to households belonging to different levels of monthly per capita expenditure, an assumption which is not strictly valid because some amount of price differential is known to exist across different MPCE classes. Finally, the price index series so compiled for industrial workers are used for deflating the urban expenditure data and for agricultural labourer to deflate the rural expenditure data for the state as well as for the country.

DESCRIPTION OF MAJOR COMMODITY GROUPS

The expenditure incurred by a household on domestic consumption during the reference period is the household's consumer expenditure. Household consumer expenditure is the total of the monetary values of consumption on various group of items namely food; pan, tobacco and intoxicants; fuels light; clothing; foot wear; miscellaneous goods and services and durable goods. The consumption may be out of (i) purchases made in cash and credit during the reference period; (ii) home-grown stock; (iii) goods received in exchange of goods and services; (iv) any other receipt of goods like gift, charity, borrowing and free collection. The consumption out of purchases is evaluated at the purchase price. The consumption out of home-grown product is evaluated at ex-farm or ex-factory prices but the value of consumption of goods out of gift, charity, loans, goods received in exchange of goods and services and free collection is imputed at the average local price. It is pertinent to mention here that consumption expenditure of a household on food items like cereals and its substitutes; pulses and its products; milk and its products; edible oil and fats; meat, fish and egg; vegetables and fruits; sugar and gur; salt and spices; beverages and processed food etc. relates to actual consumption by the household and also by the guests. *Table* 2 provides a brief description of the broad food and non-food items and the individual items included under each broad item groups.

Cereals and its substitutes constitute a major share of household's food consumption are usually a person's staple food in our country. Cereals that include rice, wheat, maize, jowar, bajra etc. and their products do not include the consumption of cereals by livestock belonging of the household. But sometimes, by choice or due to scarcity, a person may consume little or no cereal. The food requirement is partially or wholly met by consuming such food items which could be treated as substitutes for cereals. Tapioca, jackfruit seeds, mahua etc.are consumed in some parts of the country as substitutes for cereals where as potato and sweet potato consumed as substitutes for cereals are not included as substitutes of cereals but included under vegetables. Gram includes gram products such as sattu obtained by frying and powdering of gram and besan made out of gram is not included in cereals but included in other pulse products. Milk and its products include ghee, butter, curd etc. Milk used for the preparation of sweets at home is not included in milk products. Edible oils used for toilet purposes by the household are not included. Oilseeds are sometimes purchased or grown by the household for extracting edible oil for consumption; the value of oilseeds so used is included in edible oil. Consumption of garlic and ginger is accounted in spice but not in vegetables. But green chillies are included in vegetables. Beverages, refreshment and processed food, another group of food items includes tea, coffee, mineral water, soft drinks, fruit juice, green coconut water etc. It also includes other beverages such as cocoa, biscuits, cakes, pastries, pickles, sauce, jam, jelly, sweets and other salted refreshments not prepared at home. Refreshments prepared at home are not included. But food purchased in the form of cooked meal is included under processed food.

Under non-food items, miscellaneous good and services (or other non-food items) are a residual category covering all items other than pan, tobacco and intoxicants; fuels light; clothing; footwear and durable goods. It includes among other things such as expenditure on education, medical care, entertainment, conveyance, consumer taxes and cess. The items like spectacles, torches, locks, umbrellas, rain coats, gas lighters etc. named as 'minor personal effects' or 'goods for personal care effects' is a sub-group of miscellaneous items. These are not included in durables but included in miscellaneous good and services. The expenditure on other consumer services, another item of this group includes the expenditure on domestic servants, cooks, attendants, sweepers, ironing charges, tailors, priests, barbers and beautician, telephone charges, postal charges, repair charges etc. Another sub-group of miscellaneous items is sundry articles which includes electric bulbs, tube lights, batteries, earthen wares, glass wares, plastic goods such as buckets, water bottle, coir and rope, washing soap, other washing detergents, incense sticks, room refreshers, insecticides etc. Entertainment expenditure which includes expenditure on cinemas, theatres, melas, fairs, picnics, charge for hiring video cassette, subscription to dish antenna and cable TV facilities etc. and education expenses such as expenditure on book, journal, newspaper, paper, pen, pencil, magazine, novels, and fees paid to educational institutions are also included in miscellaneous expenditure.

Table 2
Description of Major Commodity Groups

Items	*Description*
Cereals and it substitutes	Rice (all varieties), wheat (all varieties) and their products, jowar and its products, bajra, maize, barley, small millets, ragi, other cereals.
Pulses and its products	Arhar (tur), moong, masur, urd, gram (split), khasari, peas, soyabean, other pulses and its products.
Milk & its products	Liquid milk, milk (condensed & power etc), ghee, butter, curd, lassi, other milk products.
Edible oil and fats	Mustard oil, groundnut oil, coconut oil, till oil, linseed oil, palm oil, rapeseed oil, sunflower oil, oil seeds & its products, vanaspati, margarine etc.
Meat, fish and egg	Mutton, beef, fork, buffalo meat, other meat, poultry, other birds, egg, egg products, fish (fresh & dry) etc.
Other food items	Vegetables, fruits, nuts, sugar, gur, salt, spices, beverages, refreshments and processed food, pickles, jams and jellies etc.
All food items	Item 1+ item 2 + ...+ Item 6.
Clothing	Mill made cotton, handloom cotton, khaddar, hosiery, woolen, silk, rayon, bedding & uphoistery.
Fuel & light	Coke, fire wood, chips, electricity, dung cake, kerosene, matches, charcoal, other oils used for lighting, candle, gobar gas, other fuel and light.
Other non-food items	Amusement and sports, education, medicine, toiletries, sundry goods, services, conveyance, ceremonials, rent for domestic use, garage rent, consumer taxes and cess.
All non-food items	Item 8 + Item 9 + Item 10.

Note: Compiled from the NSSO description of major commodity groups.

Occasional payments as donations are not included here. Another item is the conveyance which includes expenditure incurred on account of journeys undertaken and transportation of goods made by any means of conveyances. In case of owned conveyance, the cost of fuel for power-driven transport and animal feed for animal driven carriages is also included. Medical expenses which include the expenditure on medicines, payment to doctors and nurses etc. and all clinical charges are also included in miscellaneous expenditure. The distinction between institutional and non-institutional medical expenses lies whether the expenses were incurred on medical treatment as a patient of a medical institution (institutional) or otherwise (non-institutional). Another item is rent which includes house and garage rent, residential land rent etc.

MODELS

Both the LES and AIDS models can be made more flexible by allowing their parameters to vary with the variables like household size and its composition, past levels of consumption, price of other commodities, consumer's taste and preferences etc. In this study, we have estimated two widely used demand systems viz., LES and LA\AIDS along with their variants using time-series of consumer expenditure data for eighteen rounds (from 42nd to 61st excluding 49th and 60th rounds), average household size and consumer price indices of nine broad food and non-food items separately for rural and urban sectors of Orissa and all India.

The estimable form of LES model and its variants with their stochastic specifications are as follows:

(i) the simple Linear Expenditure System (LES-1) in budget share form whose additive stochastic specification is:

$$\text{LES-1:} \qquad w_{it} = v_{it}\gamma_i + \beta_i\left(1 - \sum_{j=1}^{n} v_{jt}\gamma_j\right) + u_{it}$$

$$i = 1, 2, ..., n \ \ and \ t = 1,\ 2, ..., T$$

(ii) the budget share form of the Linear Expenditure System incorporating household size with the marginal budget share parameters (LES-2), the additive stochastic specification of which is:

$$\text{LES-2:} \qquad w_{it} = v_{it}\gamma_i + \left(\beta_i + \theta_i m_i\right)\left(1 - \sum_{j=1}^{n} v_{jt}\gamma_{jt}\right) + u_{it}$$

$$i = 1, 2, \ldots, n \text{ and } t = 1, 2, \ldots, T$$

(iii) the budget share form of the Linear Expenditure System replacing the budget share by a linear time trend (LES-3), the additive stochastic specification of which is:

$$\text{LES-3:} \qquad w_{it} = v_{it}\gamma_i + \left(\beta_i + \theta_i^* t\right)\left(1 - \sum_{j=1}^{n} v_j\gamma_j\right) + u_{it}$$

$$i = 1, 2, \ldots, n \textit{ and } t = 1, 2, \ldots, T$$

(iv) the additive stochastic specification of the Nasse Expenditure System (NES) in budget share form is:

$$\text{NES:} \qquad w_{it} = v_{it}\gamma_i(v) + \beta_i\left(1 - \sum_{j=1}^{n} v_{jt}\gamma_j(v)\right) + u_{it}$$

$$i = 1, 2, \ldots n \textit{ and } t = 1, 2, \ldots, T$$

$$\text{with} \qquad \gamma_i(v) = \sum_{j=1}^{n} \gamma_{ij}\left(v_{jt}/v_{it}\right)^{1/2}$$

The effect of the increase in the household size on the consumption of a particular good must thus be viewed in the context of allocating expenditure among all goods. The direction of the effect of increase in the household size on the consumption of the *ith* good cannot be inferred from the direction of the effect of such a change on the marginal budget share parameter, β_i. Indeed, there is no presumption that the increase in the household size will increase rather than decrease β_i, since changes in β_i regardless of the direction, implies a reallocation of the expenditure among the goods but leaves the total expenditure unchanged.

The estimable form of LA\AIDS model and its variants with their stochastic specifications are as follows[8]:

The additive stochastic specification of the estimable LA\AIDS model with demographic specification (AIDS-1) in budget share form is given by

$$w_{it} = \alpha_i^* + \beta_i \log\left(\frac{y_t}{P^*}\right) + \sum_j \gamma_{ij} \log p_{jt} + \theta_i \log m_t + v_{it}$$

Further, the additive stochastic specification of the simple estimable LA\AIDS model (AIDS-2) in budget share form is given by

$$w_{it} = \alpha_i^* + \beta_i \log\left(\frac{y_t}{P^*}\right) + \sum_j \gamma_{ij} \log p_{jt} + v_{it}$$

The additive stochastic specification of AIDS-3 and AIDS-4 models are nothing but the above AIDS-2 model constrained with homogeneity restriction and both homogeneity and symmetry restrictions respectively. The other additive stochastic specification of the estimable LA\AIDS model with 'no cross price effects' restriction (AIDS-5) in budget share form is given by

$$w_i = \alpha_i^* + \beta_i \log\left(\frac{y_t}{P^*}\right) + \gamma_{ii} \log p_i + v_i$$

Finally, the additive stochastic specification of the estimable LA\AIDS model with 'explicit additivity' restriction (AIDS-6) in budget share form is given by

$$w_{i/t} = \alpha_i^* + \beta_i \log\left(\frac{y_t}{P^*}\right) + v_{it}$$

where '*y*' is per capita household expenditure; β_{ij}, v_{ij} and θ_i denotes the effect of income, price and household size respectively on budget share. The use of household size, *m*, as deflator for '*y*' follows Weisskoff (1971) and Sener (1977). Although, empirically not the most plausible form, our approach is justified because of non-availability of published data on household composition. It is better to include average household size as an additional explanatory variable rather than ignoring its effects altogether.

COMPUTER SOFTWARE

We have used econometric software, LIMDEP (Version-7) for estimating the parameters of the LES, AIDS and their variants. We have also developed programs through an integrated spread sheet package– LOTUS SMARTSUITE (Version-9) to compute expenditure and uncompensatory price elasticities and some test statistics separately for the LES, AIDS and their variants.

HYPOTHESIS

The hypotheses formulated for the present study are as follows:

(1) There are significant inter-income-group variation in the consumption patterns of different food and non-food items in the rural and urban sectors of Orissa and all India.

(2) There are significant inter-sectoral variation in the consumption patterns of different food and non-food items in Orissa and all India.

(3) There are significant inter-temporal variation in the consumption patterns of different food and non-food items in both the rural and urban sectors of the state and the country.

(4) The marginal budget shares are positive. These shares are higher for different food items and lower for different non-food items for rural households than their urban counterparts in the state and the country.

(5) The expenditure/income elasticities are less than unity for different food items, and more than unity for

different non-food items in both rural and urban sectors of the state and the country.

(6) The expenditure/income elasticities are higher for different food items and lower for different non-food items for rural households than their urban counterparts in the state as well as in the country.

(7) The own-compensatory price elasticities of the different food and non-food items are negative.

(8) The own-compensatory price elasticities of rural households are higher for different food items and lower for different non-food items than their urban counterparts in the state as well as in the country.

(9) Size coefficients and elasticities are positive for the food items but negative for the non-food items i.e. different food items exhibit economies of scale and different non-food items exhibit diseconomies of scale in both rural and urban sectors of the state and the country.

(10) Marginal effect of taste changes and preference elasticities are negative for different food items but positive for different non-food items in both rural and urban sectors of the state and the country.

ORGANIZATION OF THE STUDY

The study is structured into seven chapters. Chapter-1 is the introduction which deals with the scope, objectives, methodology and the hypotheses formulated for the study. This chapter also provides a brief description of NSS methodology and sample design for data collection and a brief account of the database and consumer price indices used in the study. Chapter-2 provides a brief up to date review of some important national and international studies on different complete demand systems based on cross-section, time-series and pooled time-series of cross-section data. Chapter-3 briefly outlines the static theory of consumer behavior along with its duality aspect relevance to our analysis. The theoretical (general) and the particular restrictions of demand functions, the problem of aggregation across individuals and commodities and the implication of separability on the income and price effects have been analysed in this chapter. Chapter-4 deals with the theoretical analysis of different types of utility and non-utility based, additive and non-additive and the recently developed flexible functional form of complete demand systems. This chapter also provides a brief account of different variants and generalisations of the Linear Expenditure System (LES), the Translog Demand System (TDS) and the Almost Ideal Demand System (AIDS). The specification, estimation and empirical analysis of the Linear Expenditure System (LES) along with its three variant is examined in Chapter-5. This chapter also provides a brief account of inter-income group, inter-sectoral and inter-temporal variation in consumption patterns in the states vis-a-vis in the country. Chapter-6 deals with the specification, estimation and empirical analysis of the Almost Ideal Demand System (AIDS) along with its variants. The AIDS model and its variants are estimated with and without imposing the neoclassical restrictions like additivity, homogeneity and symmetry and the other 'a priori' restrictions like 'no cross-price effects' and 'no price effects' to test the validity of these theoretical restrictions. Finally, the summary and findings of different chapters are presented in Chapter-7. The hypotheses formulated for the study are tested on the basis of the findings of the study, and the policy of implication of demand analysis is also narrated in this chapter.

LIMITATION OF THE STUDY

The NSS data suffers from certain limitations. Srinivasan, Radhakrishnan and Vaidyanathan (1974) express certain doubts about the validity of NSS data. Thus, the study possesses all the inherent limitation of NSS data. Price variation in the NSS data creates serious problems in the estimation of quality variation in the consumption pattern. In family budget studies, the average price paid is generally taken as measure of its quality. Thus, it is supposed that higher the price better is the quality of the commodity.[9] The study does not take into account the seasonal effect of price variations which is important because higher price may not be index of better quality but may be the seasonal change in quantity demanded.

The consumption of certain items like liquor and tobacco is frowned upon by certain sections of households. Also quite often, the head of the household is not aware that some members of the household are regular and causal consumer of such items. The consumption estimates of these socially unacceptable items therefore, are likely to be downward biased.[10]

As an alternative to expenditure data, one may use the quantity data in the estimation of demand function. But this has its own problems because it is difficult to pool the quantity data owing to the heterogeneity of the items consumed. Another problem of quantity data is that it is not possible to express consumer services in quantity terms. Hence, we have used the consumption expenditure data in our study to avoid the above problems.

NOTE

1. For details see Brown and Deaton (1972) for an excellent survey on econometric studies of household expenditure; and Bhattacharya (1975) and Panda (1996) for Indian studies on consumer behaviour.
2. For international studies on Complete Demand System refer Wold and Jureen (1953); Stone(1954); Deaton (1980,1986,1987,1988,1990&1997); Deaton and Muellbauer (1976); Pollak and Wales (1969,1970,1979,1980 & 1992), Pashardes(1993); Lewbel (1987,1991 &1995); Moshini(1995) and Buse (1994). For the Indian studies on Complete Demand System see Radhakrishna and Ravi (1992); Meenakshi (1996); Murty (1997, 1998, 1999); Meenakshi and Ray (1999) and Murty (2005).
3. See Chern and Wang (1994); Barten (1969); Yoshihara (1969); Parks (1969); Goldberger and Gamaletsos (1970); Radhakrishan and Ravi (1992); Grewe (1998); Coondoo and Majumder (2000) and Murty (2005) for the variants and generalisation of LES.
4. See Ray (1980, 1982); Blanciforte and Green (1983); Bollino (1986); Eales (1992); Decostar and Frederic (1998); Meenakshi and Ray (1999), Coondoo and Majumder (2000); Alston, Chalfant and Piggott (2001) and Murty (2005) for the variants and generalisation of AIDS.
5. Refer the studies of Radhakrishna and Murty (1973); Murty (1978) and Ray (1982, 1991).
6. See Brochure on Consumer Price Index for Urban Non-Manual employees, Jan.-June 2006 and Consumer Price Index Labour Bureau, Government of India for consumer price indices.

7. See Zellner (1962) and Greene (2000) for details on the estimation of seemingly unrelated regression equations (SURE).
8. For detail refer Section-6.3 and Table-6.1 of Chapter-6.
9. For details refer Prais and Houthakker (1955).
10. See Sukhatme and Sukhatme (1970), Srinavasan (1977) and Minhas, (1988).

2

REVIEW OF STUDIES ON COMPLETE DEMAND SYSTEMS

INTRODUCTION

The empirical analysis of consumer behavior has always held a central position in applied econometrics and many standard techniques now developed were in response to practical problems involved in analysing and interpreting the demand data. An equally central position in economic analysis is held by the theory of consumer behavior which has provided a structure and language for model formulation and data analysis. Demand analysis is, thus, in the rare position in econometrics of possessing long interrelated pedigrees on both theoretical and empirical sides. Although the systematic econometric exercise relating to consumer behaviour started in 1930s, hardly any attempt was made in India prior to 1950. The lack of interest in consumer studies in India can be attributed to the general stability of consumption pattern and the non-availability of relevant data on household consumption. Since the inception of five year plans in the country, the income of the people has increased considerably leading to a higher demand for different commodities. This might have also caused readjustment in the demand for different goods. All these developments necessitated a study of consumer behaviour in India. The availability of data on household consumption on a nation-wide basis since the setting up of the National Sample Survey Organisation (NSSO) in 1950 has stimulated interest in consumer behaviour studies.

Narrowly defined, demand analysis is a small subset of the areas of consumer behaviour, referring largely to the study of commodity demands by consumers, most usually based on aggregate time-series data but occasionally, and more recently, on cross-sectional or even panel data of household consumption expenditure. The links between conventional demand analysis based upon single equation and simultaneous equation system, and the recent demand systems such as linear expenditure system and its variants, almost ideal demand system and its variants and other demand system satisfying the property of separability and aggregation has been established. The strength of consumer demand analysis has been its close articulation of theory and evidence and the theoretical advances (particularly duality) which has permitted a more intimate relationship between the theory and the interpretation of the evidence. It is not possible to study applied demand analysis without keeping statistics and economic theory simultaneously in view.

During the last half century, a few studies on consumer behaviour have been conducted in India. These studies differ not only in their scope but also in their sources of the database. Almost all consumer studies in India are based on cross-section NSS data on consumption expenditure collected by NSSO during its various rounds. Non-availability of time-series consumption expenditure data during 29th round to 41st round and also non-availability of satisfactory time-series of consumer price indices has discouraged researchers to work on complete demand systems based on time-series data. However, very few researchers have estimated different complete demand systems from cross-section, time-series and pooled time-series of cross-section data. The regional/state level studies are scanty in India and particularly for the state like Orissa. Keeping this in view, an attempt has been made in this chapter to provide an upto date review of the literature on the theory of demand and empirical estimation of complete demand systems both at international and national level.

This chapter is organised into seven sections. Section 1 is the introduction. Section 2 examines various approaches for restricting a large number of commodities in the consumer's utility maximization problem to a relatively smaller number by commodity grouping which will be manageable for empirical estimation. Section 3 provides a brief review of single demand equations versus system of demand equations. Since, the focus of this study is for the estimation of Linear Expenditure System and Almost Ideal Demand system and their variants, a brief review of studies on Linear expenditure system with its variants and generalisations is presented in Section 4 and Almost ideal Demand System with its variants and generalisations is narrated in Section 5. Section 6 presents a brief review of literature on other demand systems with their variants and generalisations. Finally, Section 7 is the concluding remarks of this chapter.

COMMODITY GROUPING AND SEPARABILITY

In the standard utility maximization problem[1], a consumer makes budget allocation decisions on a large number of goods with different relative prices. The solution to this problem gives the quantity demanded of each good as a function of its price, prices of other goods, and the consumer's income. However, when the number of goods involved is too large, the consumer's allocation problem becomes complex for the empirical analyst. The problem of finding theoretically appealing approaches for reducing a large number of goods to a relatively small and more manageable number has attracted and continues to attract the attention in the demand literature. The literature proposes two alternative approaches: one that groups commodities based on the behavior of their relative prices- the composite commodity theorem; and another that makes assumptions about the consumer's preferences-separability and two-stage budgeting.

Hicks (1936) and Leontief (1936) have proposed the composite commodity theorem which asserts that if a group of prices move in parallel, then the corresponding group of commodities can be treated as a single good. The price and quantity indices of the commodity groups are used to derive an expenditure function that satisfies the usual properties of expenditure functions (increasing in utility and prices, concave in prices, and linearly homogenous). The usefulness of the composite commodity theorem in constructing commodity groups for empirical analysis is limited (Deaton and Muellbauer, 1980). The source of limitation is that relative prices fluctuate considerably in practice. Also, it would be difficult to justify the aggregation problem involved. For example, a relatively volatile price of meat would prevent it being grouped with other foods whose prices are relatively stable.

Strotz (1957) proposed the concept of a utility tree[2] which allows consumers to break a decision into multiple steps. A closely related concept is two-stage budgeting, which hypothesizes that consumers first allocate total expenditure to broad groups of commodities (the first stage) and then allocate each group expenditure to the individual commodities in that group (the second stage). Weak separability is both necessary and sufficient condition for the second stage of two-stage budgeting [3]. Several studies attempt to empirically test the restrictions imposed by separability within flexible demand systems[4]. These studies derive functional relationships that must hold between goods that belong to the same group and goods that belong to other groups, expressed in terms of price and expenditure elasticities. They have tested whether these relationships are supported by data or not.

Lewbel (1996) in an attempt to circumvent some of these limitations developed a generalized composite commodity theorem, which is an extension of original Hicks-Leontief idea. The generalized composite commodity theorem relaxes the assumption of perfect correlation among group prices and instead allows for less than perfect co-movement among intra-group prices. It assumes that the distribution of an individual commodity's price is independent of the composite group price, and tests for the generalized composite commodity theorem based on co-integration relationships between each of the good's prices and the price indices of groups to which they belong. Interesting applications of Lewbel's generalized composite commodity theorem are by Davis (2003) and Reed et al. (2005).

Davis (2003) has extended Lewbel's bivariate Engel-Granger test to a multivariate framework, while Reed et al. (2005) applied the generalized composite commodity theorem to nonlinear demand systems. In contrast to the composite commodity theorem which relies on an external factor (namely, the constancy of relative prices) to define commodity groups. Separability defines commodity groups using consumer preferences themselves. If preferences are weakly separable, then commodities can be partitioned into groups so that preferences within groups can be described independently of consumption in other groups. This implies that a sub-utility function can be defined for each group, so that the values of each of the sub-utility function can be added to give total utility.

However, there are a number of problems associated with the tests mentioned above. One of the problems, as mentioned by Lewbel, is that weak separability restrictions require group prices which depend on the parameters of the individual's utility function. Also, separability restrictions are difficult to test due to the multicollinearity of aggregate price data. A more important problem with both the tests for separability and commodity groupings is that they have been developed in the context of time-series data. Their applicability in the context of cross-sectional or panel data is limited. Since, the studies based on pooled time-series of cross-section data, follow the 'traditional' approach of maintaining the assumption of weak separability among broad food groups or any other broad consumption goods. The food items that are closely related to be grouped together into composite food commodities, where a group comprises items that are close substitutes.

STUDIES ON SINGLE DEMAND EQUATION

There are two distinct approaches to the estimation of demand equations. The first and original approach concentrates on the demand for a particular commodity or a commodity group.

The second approach developed almost entirely since 1970s, involves the simultaneous estimation of complete demand systems containing a demand equation for every commodity or commodity group purchased by consumers. In the single demand equation context, homogeneity is the strongest restriction. Imposing homogeneity before estimation implies that the demand is a function of relative prices and real total expenditure. Such analysis basically deals with the measurement of elasticities. The requirement that demand systems should satisfy the adding-up property which has been ignored and perhaps unimportant because these early studies considered only a fraction of the total budget[5] and concentrated on the choice of explanatory variables pragmatically with the goal of getting better model fits.

The single equation approach to demand analysis has lost its popularity with the introduction of utility-based demand system-the linear expenditure system (LES) by Stone (1954). The derivation of LES imposes theoretical restrictions of adding-up, homogeneity, and symmetry. One limitation of the LES is that it does not include inferior and complement goods. All goods must be substitutes which obviously make it a too restrictive functional form except for cases where commodities are grouped into broad categories, so that it is reasonable not to expect inferiority or complementarity among them. While the imposition of the theoretical restrictions helps to generate degrees of freedom, it also forces the analyst to take theoretical restrictions as given (because these restrictions are embedded in the model). An interesting alternative is one that allows restrictions to be tested empirically. The second approach to the estimation of system of demand equations[6] covering all current expenditure made by the consumer has drawn the attention of the researchers after early 1970s[7]. This approach enables us to use of various single equation and cross-equation restrictions as implied by the theory of consumer behaviour in the formulation as well as estimation of demand systems because most of the theoretical restrictions on the demand equations are cross-equation restrictions. The functional forms of some important studies based on single equation approach are:

Schultz (1938) had estimated the linear demand functions for agricultural products treating per capita consumption as a linear function of the prices of the product relative to a general price index and an annual time trend. He has estimated the demand function for a number of farm products like wheat, sugar, potatoes, barley, corn, oats and hay for United States over the period 1896-1914. He found that the demand for agricultural products were price inelastic with absolute values being less than unity.

Prais and Houthakker (1938) had estimated semi-logarithmic demand functions for different food items like tea, coffee, margarine etc. for the middle-class British families in 1938. He found that margarine was essentially independent of income. The income elasticity of tea was significantly lower than that of coffee suggesting that coffee was more of a luxury commodity than tea for middle-class British families. Condensed milk was apparently an inferior commodity with negative income elasticity. Their result was consistent with other later studies.

Fox (1958) estimated a long-term specification of demand for farm products in United States. His approach was based on inverse demand function in which the demand functions are solved for prices. He included a new variable that could lead to a shift in the demand curves. The estimates of the parameters were used to make inference about price and income elasticities of demand. Fox also found that the demand for veal, chicken, apple and sweet potatoes were income elastic and are responsive to economic factors like price and income. In general, the estimated demand for farm products are price inelastic as concluded by Schultz and Stone earlier.

Stone (1964) had estimated the log-linear specification of demand functions for some food items like fresh milk, condensed milk, butter, margarine, tea, coffee, beer etc. for United Kingdom over the 1920-38. He found that fresh milk is price inelastic but income elasticity is positive. The cross-price elasticities indicate that beef is a substitute and cream is a complement for fresh milk. The trend coefficient had shown a slight increase in per capita consumption after allowing price effects. The demand for condensed milk is elastic but it is an inferior commodity. Butter is more like fresh milk in terms of own-price and income elasticities. The demand for margarine is highly inelastic with somewhat negative income elasticity. Butter, chocolate and confectionary are substitutes while cakes and biscuits are complements. The demand for tea, coffee and beer are substitutes. In general, demand for most of the food items are both price and income inelastic.

Houthakker (1965) had estimated the log-linear specification of demand functions for food, clothing, rent and durable for eight European countries like United States, United Kingdom, Canada, Belgium, France, Italy, Netherlands and Sweden over the period 1948-59. He found that price elasticities were not as consistent as those of income elasticities. Many price elasticities have wrong sign. He also found that food items are income inelastic and declined as the average income rises.

Several studies have been conducted in the area of applied demand analysis. Most of the studies were based on single-equation estimation for aggregate or disaggregate goods. Such studies are Hogarty and Elzinga (1972), Johnson and Oksanen (1974, 1977), Labys (1976), McGuiness (1980 and 1983), Duffy (1983), Ornstein and Hanssens (1985), Ahtola et al. (1986), Adrian and Ferguson (1987), Godfrey (1988), Atkinson et al. (1990), Johnson et al. (1992), Lee and Tremblay (1992), and Blaylock and Blisard (1993).

STUDIES ON LINEAR EXPENDITURE SYSTEM WITH ITS VARIANTS AND GENERALISATIONS

Static complete demand system expresses the relationship between budget shares, prices, and total expenditures as a contemporaneous relationship. Early research in the analysis of static complete demand system was initiated by Stone (1954), who included a set of equations, one for each commodity group in the system, and then estimating the equations simultaneously. The estimation of the static complete demand system is important in identifying the interdependence among commodities, specifying the effects of changes in the price of certain commodity on the demand for other commodities. Various functional forms have been used in estimating the demand systems. One such functional form is the linear demand system and another one is the double-log or constant elasticity demand system. Each of these is a straight generalisation of single demand equation. One of the most widely used functional forms is the Linear Expenditure System.

Issues relating to model specification and testing of theoretical restrictions like homogeneity and symmetry of complete demand system dates back to the early efforts by Barten (1969) and Deaton & Muellbauer (1980). Barten (1969) rejected homogeneity using the likelihood ratio obtained from the maximum likelihood estimation. Deaton and Muellbauer (1980) developed the AIDS model, rejected homogeneity based on F-tests. Deaton and Muellbauer assumed that the rejection of homogeneity is a symptom of dynamic misspecification.

Stone (1954) has developed a popular demand system known as the linear expenditure system (LES) which has a wide range of applications in applied demand analysis. He has derived a set of linear demand equations maximizing the Stone-Geary utility function (first proposed by Klein and Rubin, 1947-48) subject to the budget constraint. He derived the linear demand equations by imposing the general restrictions and the particular restriction of additivity. The LES has certain limitations, viz., linearity of the Engel curves, inelastic price-quantity demand curves, and incapable of incorporating complementary and inferior commodities. In spite of above limitation, it has extensive empirical application because of linearity and parsimony of the estimated parameters. Nevertheless, the uneasiness with some of its strong restrictions like the proportionality between price and income elasticities, and necessity goods becoming luxury ones as higher incomes paved the way for the development of new models of complete demand system.

Rudra (1964) and Paul and Rudra (1964) fitted the simplest forms of the linear Expenditure system (LES) to time-series data of domestic consumption in India. They fitted LES to NSS data from the 8th through 14th round for six commodities groups-Food grains, milk products, other food, clothing, fuel and light and other non-food. With regards to prices, they constructed price index series for each commodity group by averaging the official indices of wholesale prices of constituent items over the periods covered by different NSS rounds. The LES fitted to the data set fairly well, but the expenditure elasticities obtained from it were found to be different from the usually accepted cross-section estimates obtained from different NSS rounds. This led the researchers to raise series of doubts on the validity of cross- sectional elasticities for the purpose of demand projections.

Bhattacharya (1967) re-examined the Paul-Rudra computation of elasticities analyzing separately the rural and urban estimates as well as the pooled rural-plus-urban estimates. In each case, the half simple-wise estimates and the corresponding combined sample estimates were analysed separately. The price series, however, were the same in each case. It was shown that while using Stone's two stage iterative procedures for estimating the parameters of LES, Paul and Rudra had been misled by the agreement between the results of consecutive cycle and had stopped after a few cycles. Bhattacharya continued the iteration for many cycles and obtained the better estimates of the parameters. He considered three commodities groups such as food grains, other food and non-food items and used the prices indices based on official wholesale prices mentioned above. The result indicates extreme sensitivity of the estimates to changes in price data. This suggests that owing to limitation of data, the estimates of the parameter of LES were associated with wide margins of uncertainty.

Joseph (1968) made interesting comparisons of demand projections based on the constant elasticity Engel curves with those based on LES. The former takes no account of the shifts in the Engel curves resulting from changes in relative prices over time. Also projections from the Engel curves were shown to vary with the choices of the base period and also of the period to which the cross-section elasticity referred. In fact, for some items the estimated constant elasticity varied markedly over NSS rounds. It was suggested that unless the interval between the base period and the forecast period is very short, the projections form LES would be superior to those based on constant elasticity Engel curve. Joseph (1968) also carried out other interesting exercises such as fitting the LES to data set relating to sections of the population in specific size-classes of per capita total consumer expenditure, and also fitted generalized forms of the LES in which the parameters are assumed to be linear functions of time.

Pollak and Wales (1969) and Pollak (1970) introduced habit effects into complete demand system. They incorporated habit effects in Linear Expenditure System (LES) by assuming that the necessary quantity of each good is proportional to consumption of that good in the previous periods. They concluded from their habit formation analysis that past consumption influences current preferences and hence current demand, and a higher level of past consumption of a good implies a higher level of present consumption.

Radhakrishna and Murty (1972) fitted the LES to data of nine commodity groups from NSS 8th round through 14th round. The twelve per capita expenditure brackets were grouped to obtain three broad expenditure ranges: lower, middle, and higher and the fit was carried out separately for these ranges as well as for the overall averages. Many interesting results were obtained. Thus, the committed expenditure increased with rising expenditure levels, particularly in the rural sector, while marginal budget shares for most of the food items moved in the opposite direction.

Murty and Murty (1980) estimated the LES for nine commodity groups separately for three different income groups. They found that the non-linear model used by Iyengar and Jain (1972) and their estimation from LES lead broadly the same conclusions. Murty (1980) estimated the Rotterdam demand system on four commodity groups imposing the homogeneity and symmetry condition. One striking feature of the estimates is that the expenditure elasticities are quite insensitive to the model specification. However, the same symmetry and additivity restrictions have some effect on these estimates.

Coondoo and Majumder (1985) have fitted three different models namely LES, SNAM and modified version of SNAM and compared the performances of these three models empirically on fairly disaggregated nine commodity groups. The basic data for the analysis was the time-series of cross-section estimates of total consumer expenditure separately for rural and urban India from 7th to 20th round of NSS during the period 1953-54 to 1973-74. For each round, the estimates of average per capita expenditure for three groups of population, namely the poorest 30 percent, the middle 40 percent and the richest 30 percent have been used. The price data used in this study are the same as that of the study by Radhakrishna, Murty and Shah (1979). The results of their study revealed that the modified SNAM has the best empirical performance for both the rural and urban sectors. Furthermore, this model overcomes another limitation of LES i.e. exclusion of inferior and complementary goods.

Majumder (1986) fitted two demand systems viz. LES and AIDS to NSS time- series consumption expenditure data from the 7th through 28th round for nine commodity groups separately for the rural and urban sectors. The price data used in the study are same as those used by Radhakrishna, Murty and Shah (1979). The results of the study reveal that AIDS performed better than LES on the whole. Because of the large number of parameters, AIDS have greater explanatory power and the elasticities computed from AIDS are not restricted as in LES. For finer level of disaggregation of commodities both the LES and AIDS might turnout to be unsatisfactory.

Nayga (1995) has estimated the meat demand system using the CES data collected during 1992. He adopted simple selection approach to estimate the Linear Expenditure System. He observed that beef and pork expenditures are positively related to household size. He observed that age is significantly influencing the expenditures on various meat products. He also found that expenditure on beef initially increases with age and then declines.

Grewe (1998) estimated a set of demand equations for food which allow for extended families as one form of household composition to another. Using the exact form of the indirect utility function and the expenditure function, he calculated household equivalence scales which show the cost to the household of an additional member for each of seven age-sex categories. The data used to estimate the demand equations is drawn from the Indonesian Susenas Survey of Household Consumption during 1990. He has estimated the Linear Expenditure System (LES) with demographic specification and has shown the advantages of this familiar specification which is parsimonious in the number of parameters estimated. He has defined the indirect utility function and the expenditure function that are necessary for the calculation of theoretically valid household equivalence scales. The demand equations are estimated individually using maximum likelihood method corrected for the presence of heteroscedasticity in the data.

Raper, Wanzala and Nayga (2002) analyzed food expenditures and subsistence quantities of poverty status and non-poverty status of U.S. households using linear expenditure system that postulates subsistence quantities to be linear combinations of demographic variables. The data collected by the CES during 1992 were used in the study. The Heckman's (1979) two-step procedure has been applied to estimate the demand system. The study deals with the analysis of expenditure elasticities, own-price elasticities, and subsistence quantities for each income group across nine aggregate food commodity groups. They found that the estimates of expenditure, own-price elasticity and subsistence quantity differ across income groups.

Murty (2005) examined the usefulness of the popular Linear Expenditure System vis-à-vis the two other flexible models namely, the Nasse Expenditure System, a generalisation of the linear expenditure system itself, and the Almost Ideal Demand System for seven broad commodity groups separately for the rural and urban sectors of India. He has used the published NSS data of five quinquennial rounds over the period 1972-94. The Empirical results indicate wide variation in marginal budget share and demand elasticities across income groups, rural-urban sectors and alternative model specifications. The results also show that the flexible models, which are theoretically superior, gave unacceptable positive price responses for some commodities and violated second order condition of utility maximization.

Kao, Lee and Pitt (2006) examined the issues on the estimation of consumer demand equations subject to binding non-negative constraints. They proposed computationally feasible specifications of complete demand systems and applied the simulated maximum likelihood (SML) method for estimating the demand systems. Their study indicates the econometric implication of the SML estimates which can avoid high-dimensional integration problems. As contrary to the simulation method of moments, the simulated pseudo-likelihood methods require the simulation of quantities demanded subject to non-negativity constraints. The SML approach requires only simulation of the likelihood function. The SML approach avoids solving for simulated demand quantities because the likelihood function is conditional on observed demand quantities. The results provide empirical evidence on the importance of this approach for taking into account the possible cross-equation correlations in disturbances.

This Linear Expenditure System has been estimated in a number of studies for various countries such as Stone (1954) and later Stone, Brown and Rowe (1965) for Britain; Pallinck (1964) for Belgium; Leoni (1967) for Italy; Parks (1969) for Sweden; Pollack and Wales (1969) for USA; Yoshihara (1969) for Japan; Van Brookhaven (1971) for Belgium; Solari (1971) for Denmark France, Italy, Norway, United Kingdom and Switzerland, Sanz-Ferror (1972) for Belgium; Sanz-Ferror (1973) for Spain; Deaton (1975) for Britain; and Paul and Rudra (1964); Bhattacharya (1967); Joseph (1968); Radhakrishna and Murty (1980) and Murty (2005) for India. This is due to its relative simplicity from the point of view of its estimation and interpretation. This model has also been used in a number of studies to explore the inter-country variations of demand patterns (Parks, 1969; Baschet and Debreu, 1971; Goldberger and Gamaletsos, 1970; Theil, 1971; Solari, 1971 and Barten, 1973).

STUDIES ON ALMOST IDEAL DEMAND SYSTEM WITH ITS VARIANTS AND GENERALISATIONS

There have been numerous empirical studies of demand systems (Barten, 1969; Christensen et al., 1975; Deaton & Muellbauer, 1980) using static demand models. Efforts in applied demand analysis during late 1970s have centered on specifying demand equations that allows non-linear Engel curves and non-separable preferences and also allows inferior commodities into the analysis. Almost Ideal Demand System (AIDS) is one of such functional form proposed by Deaton-Muellbauer (1980). This model has overcome most of the limitations of the earlier demand systems and hence, the adjective is 'almost ideal'. The AIDS model is the first order approximation in any demand system and it perfectly aggregates over consumers without forcing linearity on the Engel curves. Like the linear expenditure system, the AIDS model can be made more flexible and analytically more reliable by allowing the intercept term, α_i of the share equations expressed as a linear function of the other explanatory variables like the demographic characteristics, dynamic behaviour related to past consumption, change in consumers taste etc. as suggested by Deaton (1980).

Deaton and Muellbauer (1980) proposed the Almost Ideal Demand System (AIDS) model. It is one of the most popular demand systems in applied demand analysis for a number of reasons. First, it is derived from a specific cost function and thus corresponds to a well defined preference structure which is convenient for welfare analysis. These so-called PIGLOG preferences also have the property of consistent aggregation from the micro to the macro level, while allowing non-linear Engel curves. Second, the functional form of the preferences is 'flexible' in the sense that it can be thought of as a local second-order approximation to an unknown preference structure. Third, it overcomes one of the limitations of LES i.e. exclusion inferior and complementary goods. Fourth, homogeneity and symmetry restrictions depend only on estimated parameters and so are easily imposed and/or tested. Finally, Deaton and Muellbauer (1980b) suggested a linear approximation of the non-linear AIDS model, which works well if prices are collinear using British data. They have found that the parameter estimates from its non-linear and linear variants did not vary much.

Ray (1980) extended the Almost Ideal Demand System (AIDS) by incorporating family size explicitly and estimated the demand system using the procedure suggested by Barten (1964). He estimated the model using non-linear full information maximum likelihood method for nine disaggregated commodity groups first on pure time-series and then on pooled cross-section data collected by NSSO (1957-76). Within and across, equation restrictions are imposed and tested. This study assumes static preferences.

Ray (1982) also extended AIDS model incorporating family size as an explanatory variable through Barten scaling. The extended model is popularly known as 'Household AIDS'. He estimated the model by using non-linear disaggregated group of commodities first on pure time series data and than on pooled cross-section data collected by NSSO (1957-76). Within and across, equation restrictions are imposed and tested. Separate models were estimated for urban and rural data and also for unrestricted and restricted (with homogeneity imposed) equations.

Blanciforte and Green (1983) have made the Almost Ideal Demand System (AIDS) dynamic by incorporating habit effects and tested the homogeneity and symmetry restrictions with more dynamic generalisations. They have used the time-series of cross-section budget data over the period from 1971 to 1982. They accepted the hypothesis of the presence of habit effects in consumption. Moreover the high degree of autocorrelation found in the AIDS model can be corrected by rightly specifying the model incorporating habits. Blanciforte, Green and King (1986) analyzed U.S. consumer behavior over the period 1948-1978, using static and dynamic forms of the linearised Almost Ideal Demand System (LA\AIDS) and the Linear Expenditure System (LES). They have used the data of annual aggregate personal consumption expenditures on eleven commodity groups including clothing and a four-commodity breakdown of food expenditures and estimated the models with prices and total expenditures as independent variables, both with and without the imposition of homogeneity.

Bollino (1986, 1987) has estimated and statistically tested a generalised version of AIDS (GAIDS). Evidence from Italian household data suggests rejection of AIDS and its variants with demographic specification. Frequently in empirical demand analysis, the problem arises due to the presence of a 'constant term' in a given theoretically plausible demand system. The most commonly known 'translating' procedure which redefines expenditure as the overhead cost is to be incorporated into the 'committed quantities'[8] of the demand system. From a theoretical viewpoint, translated systems may not satisfy the non-negativity condition for all possible price-expenditure situations. Empirically it seems plausible to confine the attention only to a sub-region of all possible price-expenditure situations depending upon the characteristics of data. In addition, relevance of committed quantities can always be ascertained in a probabilistic sense for any translated demand system nested to its original counterpart. He has also estimated AIDS in several of his recent empirical demand studies using both the aggregate time-series and the pooled budget data Italian households over the period from 1973 to 1983.

Bollino and Violi (1989) generalised the AIDS model which nests the Lewbel (1989) demand system. Estimation and statistical testing based on Italian household budget data suggests rejection of both homogeneity and symmetry in favour of the GAIDS even when demographic effects are considered. It is evident from the recent empirical consumer demand literature that the search for increasingly flexible functional forms is a continuous process. By redefining expenditure in terms of overhead costs, the ' translating' procedure, which can be interpreted as introducing 'committed quantities' into the basic model, has led from the original AIDS to GAIDS and from the original Translog to the generalized Translog (GTL). In these studies, they presented a generalized model, GAITL, which nests both the generalised versions of the AIDS and Translog which leads a further generalisation of the Lewbel (1989) demand system. They provided empirical evidence based on a time-series of cross sections of Italian household budget data for the period 1973-1987, focusing upon the crucial comparison between our novel result and previous findings appeared in the literature.

Eales (1992) proposed a new demand system called as Inverse Almost Ideal Demand System (IAIDS). The IAIDS model estimated from the time-series data of National Accounting Statistics from 1971 to 1989 retains all of the desirable theoretical properties of the AIDS model with the exception of consistent aggregation. An empirical issue is whether a linear approximation will work as well for the IAIDS as it has done for the AIDS model, since quantities are not as highly correlated as prices. An application to U.S. meat demand demonstrates that the linear approximation of the IAIDS is excellent which enhances the ease and range of application.

Eales and Unnevehr (1993) developed the inverse AIDS (IAIDS) model in order to test the endogeneity of prices and quantities in the U.S. meat demand system. They found that IAIDS had all the desirable theoretical properties of the AIDS, except aggregation from the micro to the market level. The study used cross-section data of U.S. meat demand and found that both prices and quantities are endogenous within the entire meat market.

Kastens and Brester (1996) estimated U.S. per capita food demand systems using an absolute price Rotterdam model [9], a first-differenced LA\AIDS and LA\AIDS models, and a first-differenced double-log demand system. They have estimated out-of-sample forecasts of annual U.S. per capita food consumption data over the period 1923 to 1992 as the basis for model selection. They concluded that models imposed with more parametric restrictions provided better forecasts than models with less number of parametric restrictions, and found the double-log demand system is a superior forecaster among alternate models. Most of the demand studies ignored formal testing procedures like unit-roots and co- integration tests needed for establishing a dynamic specification. Some studies that used unit-roots and cointegration tests to formulate dynamic specification to estimate food demand systems include Balcombe and Davis (1996); Karagiannis et al. (2000) and Fraser and Moosa (2002). Balcombe and Davis (1996) They estimated the LA\AIDS model using the consumption expenditure data of Bulgaria. They argued that the conventional estimation of the LA\AIDS should be done within the framework of contemporary time-series methodology. The study applied canonical co-integrating regression procedure to estimate the demand system, and found that homogeneity and symmetry conditions hold in the case of the dynamic LAIDS model.

Fan, Lee, and Hanna (1996) estimated the linear LA\AIDS model for thirteen categories of consumption items using the data obtained from the Consumer Expenditure Survey (CES) of the U.S. Bureau of Labor Statistics over the period 1980 to 1990. A new price index was constructed using the Consumer Price Index and the American Chamber of Commerce Cost of Living Index, where the latter index was accounted for regional price variations.

Chamber and Newman (1997) used the AIDS model as a representation of long-run demand in both discrete time and continuous time error correction models framework. Out-of-sample forecasts were estimated to generate forecasts of budget shares beyond the sample period. Their earlier study used RMSE and MAE criteria to determine the continuous time adjustment mechanisms, based around fully modified estimates of the long-run preference parameters which provide a remarkably accurate method of forecasting budget shares.

Banks, Blundell, and Lewbel (1997) introduced a model of consumer demand that is consistent with the observed expenditure patterns of individual consumers in a long time-series of expenditure surveys and is also able to provide a detailed welfare analysis due to shifts in relative prices. A non-parametric analysis of consumer expenditure patterns suggests that Engel curves require quadratic terms in the logarithm of expenditure. While popular demand systems such as the Translog and the Almost Ideal Demand Systems do allow flexible price responses within a theoretically coherent structure in which the expenditure share Engel curves are linear in the logarithm of total expenditure. They derived the complete class of integrable quadratic logarithmic expenditure share systems and a specification from this class is estimated from a large pooled data set of U.K. households. Models that fail to account for Engel curvature are found to generate important distortions in the patterns of welfare losses associated with a tax increase.

Decoster (1998) proposed the micro simulation models for indirect taxation in order to make these models policy relevant. A possible solution for this econometric problem is the separability and the closely related notion of two-stage budgeting. Weak separability is applied to the Almost Ideal Demand System (AIDS), its quadratic extension (QUAIDS) and the Rotterdam model. The two-stage budgeting demand systems were estimated from Belgian time-series data and were evaluated by means of a comparison of their elasticities (both partial and total); goodness-of fit measures and their forecasting accuracy. Though the rank three QUAIDS model does not dominate others in every respect (at least for time-series data), it has nice theoretical properties, which can on their own be a justification for the use of the system. The study intends to evaluate the performance of three two-stage demand systems for 32 commodities, which are to be used in a static micro simulation model for indirect taxes (see Decoster, 1995). Due to the fact that the demand systems did not dispose of a long-time series of Belgian individual household data (like the UK Family Expenditure Survey data) to capture precise price effects, estimation was done on aggregated time series data.[10.] Before the systems to be used for forecasting, income effects are to be reestimated in the future on budget survey data and linked to the price effects estimated from time-series data. Another approach would be to find an optimal combination of micro (on budget survey data) and macro (on time-series of cross-section data) estimations using a minimum-distance estimator. Evaluation of the three two-stage demand systems has been done by means of a comparative study of goodness-of-fit measures, the elasticities and the forecasting performance of the models.

Feenstra (1999) computed an exact Price Index for the estimation of the Almost Ideal Demand System. The Almost Ideal Demand System has been evaluated using the expenditure shares data at two points of prices for comparison i.e. at their simple and geometric mean. The increasing number of surveys on individual or household level budget data including socio-economic variables has raised the interest for the analysis of consumer behavior.

Fan and Lewis (1999) used data from the consumer Expenditure Survey (CES) over the period1980-1992; the Consumer Price Index, and the American Chamber of Commerce Researchers Association price index to analyze the budget allocation pattern of African-Americans for thirteen commodity goods. The budget allocation patterns for African-Americans were compared to those for Asian-Americans, Caucasian-Americans and Hispanic- Americans. Several demographic variables and dummy variables for ethnicity were included in a linear AIDS model estimation. Annual total expenditures were used as a proxy for household income. Demand functions that constitute a complete demand system specify the allocation of total expenditures among all the goods contained in a consumer's budget set. Demand systems have been used mainly in conjunction with time-series data, because they specify the demand for a good as a function of total income and the prices of all goods in a system as changes in the price of commodities are usually observed over time. Demand systems used in recent empirical research include those based on flexible functional forms, such as the Translog, Rotterdam, and Linear Almost Ideal Demand System (LA\AIDS).

Eales and Unnevehr (1999) proposed a new demand system called the Inverse AIDS (IAIDS). This Inverse AIDS (IAIDS) retains all of the desirable theoretical properties of the AIDS model with the exception of consistent aggregation. An empirical issue is whether the linear approximation of AIDS will work as well for the IAIDS, since quantities are not highly correlated as prices. An application of IAIDS to U.S. meat demand by using Consumer Expenditure Survey data of USA from 1970 to 1996 demonstrates that the linear approximation of the IAIDS is also excellent which enhanced the ease and range of application.

Karagiannis and Mergos (2000) presented a dynamic specification of the LAIDS based on recent developments in cointegration techniques and error correction models. The study used Greek meat consumption data over the period 1958-1993, and it was found that the proposed formulation performed well on both theoretical and statistical grounds, as the theoretical properties of homogeneity and symmetry were supported by the data. They also found beef and chicken to be luxuries while mutton-lamb and pork were necessities. All meat items were found to be substitutes to one another except chicken and mutton-lamb, and pork and chicken.

Perali and Chavas (2000) developed an alternative econometric methodology to estimate a system of censored demand equations. Their study was based on cross-section data collected from Colombian urban households. They have followed a two-step procedure for estimation. In the first step, they have used the Tobit model and introduced the methodology by specifying the AIDS model modified according to a translating and scaling demographic transformation. In the next step, they have used the jackknife technique to estimate demand equations in unrestricted form and recovered the demand parameters imposing the cross-equations restrictions by using minimum distance estimation procedure

Liu and Chern (2000) specified a functional form which is a crucial task in demand analysis. Four food demand systems for twelve aggregated food items in urban China are estimated and compared using province level data over the period 1992-1999. The results show the expenditure elasticities especially for food grains are different based on the functional form chosen. They investigated the predicting performance of the models showing high expenditure elasticities for food grains in China. They are motivated by the previous findings of their other studies on food demand in China using the linear approximate almost ideal demand system (LA/AIDS).

Chern (2000) compared the performance of four demand systems viz., LES, QES, AIDS and LA/AIDS. Since, the shortcomings of the LA/AIDS have been extensively investigated (Buse, 1994; Hahn, 1994; Moschini, 1995); there has been more attempts to estimate the original AIDS model. He argued that, the estimated expenditure elasticities imply that as urban Chinese household income increases, they consume more aquatic products, poultry and milk. Based on the high own-price elasticities of these three food groups, traders need to be cautious in instituting a price policy in order to maintain their profitability. These elasticities need to be used cautiously to investigate the potential impact of the long-term trend of income and prices on China's domestic agriculture as well as international trade. He concluded that in terms of forecasting/predicting accuracy, the LES and QES are more preferable than the LA/AIDS and AIDS, no matter whether it is considered from *ex post* simulation or from *ex ante* prediction.

Karagiannis and Velentzas (2000) estimated a dynamic specification of an error correction model of the LAIDS[11]. In the estimation of U.S. meat demand systems, often time-series properties of data and the potential dynamic specification were ignored by the earlier studies. They found that the proposed formulation performed well on the basis of theoretical and statistical criteria as the theoretical properties of homogeneity and symmetry were supported by the data. The role of time-series properties of the data (unit-roots and co-integration) in the dynamic specification of the AIDS model was investigated, and the elasticity estimated from both static and dynamic models are compared. They found that beef and chicken were luxuries while mutton-lamb and pork were necessities. All meat items were found to be substitutes to one another, except chicken and mutton-lamb, pork and chicken.

Fisher, Fleissig and Serletis (2001) compared three locally flexible functional forms viz., the Generalized Leontief, the Basic Translog, the AIDS with three effective globally regular functional forms namely, the Full Laurent model, the QUAIDS, the GEF and two globally flexible functional forms i.e. the Fourier model and the Asymptotically Ideal Model (AIM)). Their comparison is based on criteria such as the Alkaline Information criterion, the Bayesian-Schwartz information criterion, and the elasticities of substitution and out-of-sample forecasts. Using the quarterly US private consumption data, prices and expenditures from 1960 to 1991, they found that global flexible functional forms perform better than locally flexible functional forms. They derived the correct formula for the AIDS model elasticities, when the Tornqvist or two modified versions of the Stone's index are used to linearise the model. We find that these three indices, along with Stones (widely used) price index, do not yield satisfactory results. The use of those linearization exacerbates lead to misclassification of goods as complements and the estimated elasticities found to be different from those of the full non-linear AIDS model. In other words, the linear approximations of AIDS do not adequately approximate the original non-linear AIDS.

Guha (2001) estimated the dynamic version of AIDS model incorporating the past levels of consumption as proposed by Pollak (1970). She has examined the habit-forming effects on nine commodity groups in the rural areas of four states of India viz., Punjab, Gujarat, West Bengal and Tamil Nadu using AIDS model. She found that habit effects are significant in all the states. She used the time-series data ranges over 4 quartiles over the period 1972-73 to 1987-88 that is 1972-73, 1977-78, 1983-84, and 1987-88. The empirical results show that habit formation hypothesis are accepted for all states and it is predominant in case of Northern and Western India when compared with the Southern and Eastern India. Thus, it can be concluded that in general habit-forming effects are significant and plays an important role in determining future consumption level. Hence, such effects should be incorporated while estimating demand systems.

Labeagaa and Jordi (2002) estimated demand system with individual heterogeneity by using household level cross-section data. The main goal of their study is to assess the importance of controlling individual unobservable effects and measurement errors when analysing demand patterns at the microeconomic level. They provided empirical evidence of the demand for non-durable goods using a panel of households from the Spanish Continuous Family Expenditure Survey. The functional form they used is the Almost Ideal System. They described how heterogeneity among consumers and measurement errors affects inferences on expenditure and price effects. They could not reject the presence of correlated unobserved heterogeneity that could bias pooled estimates. In general, income effects show a downward bias and price effects an upward bias in their study.

Epstein and Rubinfeld (2002) proposed a new variant of AIDS, the so-called Proportionally Calibrated Almost Ideal Demand System (PCAIDS). This new model has the same logic as AIDS but it incorporates a number of restrictions that make all the elasticity values depend on a single parameter and on a set of revenue market shares. Making use of that property, PCAIDS merger simulation can be performed for the estimation of the aggregate market price elasticity, an estimation of the own-price elasticity of a single product variety and a vector of market shares for the different varieties that are sold in the market.

Menezes , Carlos and Azzoni (2002) have estimated the two-stage budget shares from two Brazilian Budget Consumption Research conduced in 1987/88 and 1995/96. In the first study, income, own and cross price elasticities were calculated for Brazilian staple food basket. Following Edgerton (1997), they assumed that preferences are weakly separable and that price indices are good approximations to true cost-of-living indices, which are precisely the assumptions needed to justify estimation of the model. This study was conducted in two steps. At the first step they applied the LAIDS model for eight groups of consumption goods and service, which cover all consumption expenditure. At the second step they applied the LA\AIDS model on eleven staple foods, which covered around 90 per cent of all food expenditure. Then the two-stage budget technique was used to calculate between group elasticities and total elasticities for staple food basket.

The elasticity significant intervals were calculated using delta method. The results indicated that the elasticities are in conformity with the economic 'a priori' criteria. All income elasticities are positive and significant as well as the own price elasticities are all negative as expected. They have also calculated the elasticities for two income groups: the richest and the poorest. Brazil has a high incidence of income inequality. Therefore, it is expected that the income and price elasticities must be different between the richest and the poorest. It was found that the income elasticity is higher for the poorest than the richest for all staple food baskets. Moreover, the own price elasticities are much higher for the too poorest than too richest for the most important staple food items like rice and beans. Eventually, these results help to understand better the household consumption habits in Brazil and highlight the consumption differences between poor and rich Brazilian.

Fraser and Moosa (2002) incorporated a stochastic trend and seasonality into the LA\AIDS model using Harvey's structural time-series methodology. They estimated the demand system for meat in U.K. using three versions of the LA\AIDS model viz., deterministic trend and deterministic seasonality; stochastic trend and deterministic seasonality; and stochastic trend and seasonality. The study concluded that the structural time-series model with stochastic trend and seasonality performed better in terms of model diagnostics, goodness-of-fit, and out-of-sample forecasting. They have used out-of-sample forecasts to perform the Ashley, Granger, and Schmalensee test (1980) for model selection.

Wang and Bessler (2003) have estimated the Rotterdam, LA\AIDS and Vector Error Correction (VEC) models for meat demand using quarterly data of expenditure on meat in U.K. They have estimated the out-of-sample forecasts and conducted the Diebold and Mariano test (1995) for model selection. They concluded that VECM performed better in forecasting as compared to LAIDS and Rotterdam models. The evaluation of forecasting accuracy via measures of point estimates is a well established practice in the forecasting literature. The mean error (ME), the error variance (EV), the mean square error (MSE), and the MAE are often used for evaluating forecasting performance. The usual practice for choosing among alternative forecasting models has been to select a model that has the lowest accuracy measure without assessing its sampling uncertainty.

Kebede (2003) has examined the combined effects of changes in prices, income and different household compositions on the basis of number of adult and young members, and male and female members. They used Quadratic Almost Ideal Demand System (QUAIDS), since this demand system provides a unified framework for analysing the combined effects in a systematic fashion. The 'outlay equivalent method', which was used with single demand equations in various studies, was applied to the demand system. Underlying preference structures for classifying goods into different groups is also examined by conducting alternative tests of separability in preferences. Panel/longitudinal data were used to control the household level heterogeneity.

Dong, Gould and Kaiser (2004) extended the Amemiya-Tobin approach to demand system estimation using an AIDS specification. In Amemiya-Tobin approach, demand (share) equations are derived from a non-stochastic utility function and latent expenditures (shares) are hypothesized to differ from observed expenditures due to errors of maximization across the consumer, errors of measurement of the observed shares, or random disturbances that influence the consumer's decisions[12]. To account for these differences, error terms were added to the deterministic shares. The technique was applied to expenditure survey data collected from Mexican households during 1998. They have estimated twelve commodity demand models using simulated maximum likelihood procedures. Demographic characteristics such as household size, location, age, and number of children were also included in the model. They found significant impact of household size and composition on demand elasticities.

LaFrance (2004) has estimated the integrability of the linear approximation of Almost Ideal Demand System (LA\AIDS) including closed form solutions for the expenditure function, and generating a new method to nest the rank and functional form of a quadratic price independent generalized linear incomplete demand system. The purpose of his study was to completely clarify Slutsky symmetry, and the structural implications of integrability for the LA\AIDS. He identified the parameter restrictions that are consistent with integrability Two possible cases are found: (i) the log income coefficients vanish, so that the demands are homothetic, and the matrix of log-price coefficients is symmetric; and (ii) the matrix of log-price coefficients has rank one and is proportional to the outer product of log-income coefficients. Both cases are highly restrictive, the former with respect to income and the latter with respect to prices. Moreover, the non-homothetic case is non-linear in the parameters, eliminating the apparent advantage of the LA\AIDS in estimation. However, both cases admit closed form solutions for the expenditure (and indirect utility) functions. In addition, previously unknown relationships among LA\AIDS and the Linear Incomplete Demand System (LIDS) and the Linear Expenditure System (LES) are identified. Box–Cox transformations to nest rank and functional form in the quadratic price independent generalized linear incomplete demand system follow immediately from these relationships.

Dhar and Foltz (2005) used a quadratic AIDS model to estimate demand for various milk products. Scanner data over the period 1997-2002 were used in the study. They analysed the impact of labeling information and found that consumers are willing to pay significant premiums for such labels.

Jaffry, Taylor and Pascoe (2005) have estimated the own price, cross price and scale flexibilities for nine key fish species consumed in Spain. A market delineation study had previously identified three separate fish groups. For each group, long-run inverse demand relationships were estimated using the Inverse Almost Ideal Demand System (IAIDS). The demand model was developed using the Vector Error Correction Model (VECM) approach. Johansen's multivariate approach was used to obtain estimates of the long-run steady state relationships (vectors) among the budget shares, fish quantity consumed and total fish expenditure. The species generally had correct signs for own price flexibilities. Cross price flexibilities were significant and also negative. This implies the species within the groups were substitutes, confirming the results of the previous market delineation analysis. The scale flexibilities suggested that fish are generally a luxury good, although some species (e.g. hake, cuttlefish, squid and tuna) may be considered necessities in the Spanish market.

Gould and Villarreal (2006) have estimated the Quadratic Almost Ideal Demand System. Their study is a comprehensive analysis of total food expenditures based on a sample of urban Chinese households. A fractional logit analysis is used to analyze the relative allocation of FAFH and FAH expenditures. Not surprisingly, they found that household income is a primary determinant of such allocation, and that the percentage of income devoted to food decreases with increased income. They also found that as income increases, the share of total food expenditures associated with FAFH increases. The QUAIDS model used here is based on the original specification of Banks et al. (1996, 1997). They have also estimated a disaggregated demand system incorporating demographic variables. They found statistically significant substitution effects between foods. The choice of the QUAIDS specification was found to be the most plausible one as the likelihood ratio test indicated that this specification added significant explanatory power to the model as compared to the traditional AIDS specification. Using the QUAIDS specification they obtained reasonable elasticity estimates when compared to other analyses of food demand by Chinese households.

Taylor (2006) experimented with four popular theoretically plausible consumer demand systems to the same cross-sectional data set that combines expenditure data from the quarterly BLS consumer expenditure surveys with price data that are collected quarterly in cost-of-living surveys conducted by ACCRA. Six broad categories of expenditure on food consumed at home, housing, utilities, transportation, health care and miscellaneous items that exhaust total expenditure are analyzed. The four demand systems investigated are the Almost Ideal Demand System, the Linear Expenditure System, and the Indirect and Direct Addilog models. Despite absolute differences in magnitudes that in some instances are rather large, there is substantial agreement in the rank-orderings of elasticities. In general, the largest elasticities (for both own-price and total expenditure) are for transportation, miscellaneous, and housing expenditures, while the smallest elasticities (again for both own-price and total expenditure) are for food and utility expenditures. Engel's Law for food is confirmed in all instances.

A quadratic extension of this model (QUAIDS) has also been proposed by Blundell, Pashardes and Weber (1993) and further refined by Meenakshi and Ray (1999). There are several other versions of AIDS model like generalised AIDS, (Bollino, 1987); inverse AIDS (Eales and Unnevehr, 1994), Dynamic AIDS (Blanciforte and Green, 1983). The QUAIDS is called rank two demand system. Recent empirical analysis on micro data, however, suggested that demand systems should be rank three which implies that they should be able to include a greater variety of shapes of the Engel curves than rank two models[13]. A complete class of integrable rank three quadratic logarithmic expenditure share systems has been developed for the estimation of demand systems. Recently, several demand studies[14] have confirmed the appropriateness of QUAIDS in modeling preferences.

STUDIES ON OTHER COMPLETE DEMAND SYSTEMS WITH ITS VARIANTS AND GENERALISATIONS

The demand system discussed so far underlie a number of general restrictions like adding-up, homogeneity, symmetry etc. derived from consumer theory as well as particular restrictions like additivity imposed a priori on the structure of preferences. These restrictions are treated as part of maintained hypothesis with the specification of the models (like LES, IAS etc.) and in some adhoc manner in other models (like RDS, LDS etc.). The need for testing the empirical validity of these restrictions is treated in a behavioral framework like TDS and

AIDS models. Thus, the choice is not easy and perhaps depends on the purpose for which the model is being estimated. If the demand model were to form part of a larger macro-economic model, then a priori assumptions may also be incorporated. On the other hand, if the purpose is ex-post description or mere forecasting, perhaps, adhoc specifications will be sufficient. This section provides a brief review of the static and dynamic analysis of other complete demand systems, its variants and generalisation not covered in section 2.4 and 2.5.

The Rotterdam model of differential demand equations owes its origin to Theil (1965) and Barten (1967, 19680 and may be considered as one among the best models for testing the empirical validity of the neoclassical postulates. The model has been applied for various countries. Barten (1969) found that (i) aggregation and negativity restrictions were satisfied. The empirical validity of the symmetry condition was found to be questionable. Further tests using the same model were carried out by Byron (1968, 1970 and 1970). These studies seem to suggest the rejection of theoretical restrictions. However, Deaton (1974) suggests that these rejections may be due to the inappropriate use of asymptotically valid test criteria.

Deaton (1974) has estimated a nine commodity model for the U.K. using national accounts data for the period 1900-70. The symmetry restrictions could not be rejected whereas homogeneity appeared inconsistent with the empirical evidence. The additivity assumption has been uniformly rejected. Theil using the U.S. data and Parks using the Swedish data found symmetry was acceptable but did not test homogeneity and additivity. Results of 'systems estimation' on Indian budget data using this model by Murty (1980) are broadly similar.

Attempts were also made to compare the performance of the Rotterdam model with other models like LES and IAS. Parks (1969) for instance estimated the RDS with symmetry condition imposed, the LES and indirect addilog demand system (IAS). The results show that the performance of RDS was relatively better followed by the LES and IAS. Similar results were obtained by Theil (1975). Similarly, the performance of these were compared by Yohihara (1969) for Japan; Somermeyer et al. (1962) for Holland; and Radhakrishna et al (1979) and Radhakrishna and Murty (1981) for India. The results of these comparisons, however, did not lead to same conclusions as that of Parks. For instance, the results of Parks, Yoshihara and Theil suggest that the LES performs much better than both direct and indirect addilog demand systems; while that of Radhakrishna and Murty (1981) suggest that the indirect addilog model gives better fit to cross-section data.

The dynamic approach to demand system[15] dates back to the study of Pope et al. (1980) which used a flexible demand specification[16] to test for homogeneity conditions and habit formation effects. The study applied Box-Cox transformations to four meat demand relations in order to allow for more flexible functional forms. The lagged terms were included in the model to measure habit persistence. Maximum likelihood techniques were used to estimate the parameters and homogeneity conditions tested using likelihood ratio tests. The study rejected double log and linear functional forms as well as homogeneity on the basis of likelihood ratio tests.

Chavas (1983) developed a method for investigating structural change in economic relationships in the context of a linear model. It is assumed that the parameters can change randomly from one period to the next. His main objective is to investigate the structural change in U.S. meat demand and to identify the determinants of such structural changes that occurred during 1970s for beef and poultry but not for pork.

Gao and Spreen (1994) have estimated price and expenditure elasticities and the effect of demographic variables on demand for meat using the USA household food consumption survey data during 1987-88. A hybrid demand system, which combines a modified generalized addilog system and the Rotterdam demand system, was developed and used as the analytical framework. The results suggested that region, ethnic background, household size, urbanization, health information, female household head, employment status, and proportion of food expenditure on away-from-home consumption were found to be the significant household characteristics and socio-economic variables. The findings of the study supports the claim of other meat demand studies that both health concerns and convenience as the reasons for the changes in consumer preference in favor of poultry and fish.

Moschini and Daniele (1994) derived a general elasticity representation of necessary and sufficient conditions for direct weak separability of the utility function. He has used the Rotterdam model in the empirical analysis and to test few separable structures within a complete U.S. demand system emphasizing food items. They have observed some important implication of separability assumptions about food and meat demand.

Park and Rodney (1996) have analyzed twelve food commodity groups according to household poverty status. They have used the Food Consumption Survey data collected during 1987-88. Heckman's two-step procedure was used for the estimation of system of demand equations to account for bias arises due to zero expenditure on some item groups by the households. The second step of estimation involves the estimation of the linear expenditure system. Parameter estimates were used to obtain subsistence expenditures, own-price elasticities and expenditure elasticities. Own-price elasticities were similar between the income groups for most of the commodities. However, income elasticities were consistently higher for the lower-income groups.

Byrne and Capps (1996) used the two-step decision process for the estimation of the food-away-from-home demand system. They have estimated the demand system using a generalization of the Heien and Wessells (1990) approach. Household information gathered by the National Panel Diary Group was used for the analysis. Marginal effects were corrected by untangling the impact of respective variables on the inverse Mill's ratio. The expenditure and participation probability elasticities were similar to previous studies. The estimated income elasticities suggested that the food-away-from-home is a necessity good for U.S. society.

Nayga (1996) studied the impact of household characteristics on away-from-home wine and beer weekly expenditures in U.S.A. applying the Heckman (1979) two-step procedure to the data extracted from the Consumer Expenditure Survey (CES) during 1992. He observed that higher income households without children and headed by an older, white and highly educated individual spends more on wine away from home than others.

Yen, Kan and Su (2002) have estimated the censored systems of household oil and fat demand equations with a two-step procedure using the cross-sectional U.S. data of Food Consumption Survey during 1987-1988. They have estimated the translog demand model[17] without including the demographic characteristics. They found that own-price and total expenditure elasticities were close to unity, and compensated elasticities indicated net substitution among the products.

Yen, Lin and Smallwood (2003) have estimated the censored translog demand system for foods by quasi-maximum-likelihood estimation method using the food consumption data of the food stamp receiving households in the United States collected through the National Food Stamp Program Survey (NFSPS). They found that their estimation procedure results remarkably close parameters and elasticity estimates to those of the simulated-maximum-likelihood procedure. Among food items, pork and fish were found to be price elastic but all other food products were found to be price inelastic. The cross-price effects were less pronounced than own-price and total food expenditure effects.

Piggott (2003) introduced a new demand system, the Nested PIGLOG model, nesting thirteen other demand systems including five new demand systems. This new model and its nested forms were applied to U.S. food demand that includes food-at-home, food away-from-home, and alcoholic beverages. He found that although nested tests and out-of-sample forecasting performance favor generalizing models to a certain degree, statistically insignificant improvements to in-sample-fit and even poorer out-of-sample forecast accuracy undermine further generalizations. They compared the price and income elasticities between food-away-from-home and food-at-home and found that food-away-from-home was price and income elastic whereas food-at-home was price and income inelastic.

CONCLUSION

This chapter reviewed the literature on some restrictive particular restrictions of complete demand system along with some important studies on Linear Expenditure System; the Almost Ideal Demand System and other complete demand systems with their variants and generalisations. All of these demand systems pay strong allegiance to neoclassical demand theory and most of them introduce theoretical as well as particular restrictions, especially some form of separability, in order to simplify the demand system and to reduce the number of parameters to be estimated. The developments in the literature on econometric tests for the restriction like separability have focused mainly on time-series applications. The LES and AIDS models have been the most widely used functional forms for estimating price and expenditure elasticities.

The unrealistic assumptions of LES that budget shares are linear in expenditure, linearity of the Engel curves, proportionality between price and income elasticities and that expenditure elasticities are constant regardless of the point in the expenditure spectrum, incapable of incorporating complementary and inferior commodities limits its scope in empirical analysis. In spite of the above limitations, it has extensive empirical application because of linearity and parsimony of the estimated parameters. Nevertheless, the uneasiness with some of its strong restrictions like the proportionality between price and income elasticities, and necessity goods becoming luxury ones at higher incomes paved the way for the development of new models of complete demand system like Translog and Almost Ideal Demand System and its generalisation and variants.

The above review on complete demand systems reveals that the national level studies on demand systems are scanty. A very few researchers have estimated the LES and AIDS using NSS consumer expenditure data. The studies on complete demand systems are also scanty at regional/state level. No such specific study on complete demand system has been done so far either using the time-series or time-series of cross-section data of the recent rounds of NSS consumer expenditure data (i.e. 42nd to 61st) and especially for the state like Orissa. Considering such aberrations, the present study is the modest attempt to bridge this gap by estimating the most popular complete demand systems like Linear Expenditure System and Almost Ideal Demand System along with some of their variants to explore the demand patterns in the backward state like Orissa and in the developing country like India.

NOTE

1. The neoclassical economists made different assumptions on the measurability of utility and functional forms (additivity vs non-additivity). For a lucid exposition, see Stigler (1954).
2. See Strotz (1957, 1959).
3. See Deaton and Muellbauer (1980).
4. Refer the studies of Eales and Unnevehr (1988), Moschini (1992), Moschini *et al.* (1994), Nayga and Capps (1994), Edgerton(1997), and Carpentier and Guyomard (2001).
5. See Deaton and Muellbauer, 1980.
6. One is interested in complete demand system rather than each demand equation taken individually from it because the system as a whole provides important information on the degree and nature of interrelationship of the demand equations of the system. For details refer Lau (1976) and Thomas (1987).
7. Refer some of the important empirical studies on complete demand system such as Clements and Johnson (1983), Thom (1984), Uri (1986), Clements and Selvanathan (1987, 1991), Duffy (1987), Penm (1988), Selvanathan (1988, 1989, 1991), Heien and Pompelli (1989), Jones (1989), Tegene (1990), Yen (1994), Nelson and Moran (1995), Blake and Nied (1997), and Andrikopoulos, Brox and Carvalho (1997). Most of the above studies have estimated the AIDS model for empirical analysis.
8. See Samuelson (1947-1948).
9. See Theil (1965) and Barten (1966)
10. It is also possible to estimate price effects on a single household budget survey. For details refer Deaton (1987 and 1990).
11. See Wales and Woodland (1983).
12. See Christensen et. al. (1975).
13. See for example, Lewbel (1991), Blundell, Pashardes and Weber (1993) and Banks, Blundell and Lewbel (1997) and Banks et al. (1997).
14. The quadratic AIDS model has been estimated for a number of developed countries. Such studies include Abdulai (2002) who applies this model

to food expenditure data for Switzerland; Moro and Sckokai (2000) for Italian food expenditure data; Banks et al. (1997) and Blundell and Robin (1999) for expenditure data on broad consumption goods from the U.K.; Fisher et al. (2001) for U.S. aggregate consumption data; Abdulai and Aubert (2004) for Tanzanian food expenditure data, Meenakshi and Ray (1999) for Indian food expenditure data, Gould and Villarreal (2006) for food expenditure data from urban China, and Molina and Gil (2005) for aggregate consumption data of Peru.

15. A demand system is said to be a 'flexible functional form' if it is capable of providing a second order approximation to the behaviour of any theoretically plausible demand system at a point in the price-expenditure space.
16. Deaton and Muellbauer (1980) have found that the parameter estimates did not very much between the non-linear estimation and the linear version of AIDS. Pashardes (1993) argued that Stone's approximation of the price index leads to bias in parameter estimates of AIDS. The bias will be more serious for micro-level data than the aggregate time series data like ours.
17. Refer to the studies of Pope et al., (1980); Chavas (1983); and Kastens et al., (1996). They have examined the dynamic specification of AIDS either including lagged variables or using the differencing approach without formal testing for such dynamic specifications.

3

THE STATIC THEORY OF CONSUMER BEHAVIOUR

INTRODUCTION

Since 1950s, applied econometricians have been estimating systems of demand equations which have been explicitly or implicitly derived from the theory of utility maximization. Most of such studies have used the traditional specification of utility as a function of quantities consumed and have derived demand functions by manipulating the first order conditions of utility maximization subject to a budget constraint.[1] The structure of such derived demand equations has been analysed by Slutsky (1915) and Hicks (1936). Their investigation has established the familiar result that utility maximization implies the symmetry and negative semi-definiteness of the matrix of substitution terms. However, over the same period of time, demand theorists have increasingly used duality tools so that direct utility function is now frequently discarded as an analytical tool. The considerable power of the new methods in economic theory can be gauged from the work of Gorman (1776) and Barten (1977).

A wide range of problems can be handled with great elegance and simplicity using the tools of duality. The use of duality allows a considerable increase in the flexibility with which the empirical demand equations can be specified and permits a much more intimate relationship between theory and applications. The duality approach solves many of the problems of the traditional approach. We can go from preferences to behaviour in one step and also from behaviour to preferences in one step. The formulation of preference-consistent demand functions becomes straightforward and a clear route is open for the incorporation of empirical evidence into knowledge of preferences. The central concept in duality approach is the cost function (sometimes called the expenditure function). If we level the indifference curves by some arbitrary scaled utility indicator 'u', so that higher indifference curves always have a higher 'u' value, then we can measure the minimum cost of attaining that indifference curve at any price vector 'p'. We write this function as $c(u, p)$ which is an increasing function in 'u' and 'p', homogeneous of degree one and also concave in 'p' (Diewert, 1974).

The literature has also focused on the integrability problem, i.e. the conditions under which arbitrarily given demand function can be derived from a utility function.[2] This has established the important proposition that if the demand function has a symmetric, negative semi-definite substitution matrix, then there exists a utility function corresponding to that demand function. A byproduct of this proposition is that the marginal rate of substitution approach (Allen and Hicks, 1934), the demand function approach (Cassel, 1918) and the revealed preference approach[3] (Samuelson, 1947; Houthakker, 1950, and Uzawa, 1971) are logically equivalent to the classical theory of preference.

Applied demand research has prompted the work on aggregation of commodities. The Leontief-Hicks composite commodity theorem states that commodities whose prices move together can be lumped together as a single commodity without affecting the consistency conditions (Leontief, 1936 and Hicks, 1936). The grouping of commodities has also been suggested on the basis of separability (Leontief, 1947; Sono,1960; Strotz, 1957; Gorman,1959 and Pearce, 1964).

The question of the existence of a community scale of preferences has also received some attention (Gorman, 1953; Pearce, 1964 and Muellbauer, 1975, 1976). It has been shown that even if the behaviour of a group of consumers is consistent with preference theory, the group averages may not necessarily be consistent with preference theory; neither the symmetry conditions nor separability may hold at the macro level even though they may hold at the micro (consumer) level. Muellbauer (1975) has attempted to establish consistency between micro and macro data by defining macro aggregates instead of group averages for a representative consumer. In this chapter, an attempt has been made to recapitulate the theoretical developments and also to provide a brief summary of those aspects of the theory used in applied demand analysis.

This chapter is organised into seven sections. Section 1 is the introduction. Section 2 deals with the derivation of some common forms of complete demand functions. Section 3 analyses the indirect utility function, decomposition of price effect and the neoclassical restrictions on compensated demand functions. The features of the dual cost function are examined in Section 4. Section 5 provides a brief explanation on separability and some popular types of separability. The implications of additivity in direct and indirect utility functions are analysed in Section 6. The problem of aggregation is examined in Section 7. Finally, Section 8 is the concluding remarks of this chapter.

DERIVATION OF COMPLETE SET OF DEMAND FUNCTIONS

We begin by restating the classical theory of consumer demand, adopting the convenient matrix notation introduced by Barten (1964) and Theil (1965) and its later developments by Barten, (1966) and Theil (1967).

Let q_i denote the quantity purchased of good i ($i = 1, \ldots n$), p_i denote the price of good $i (i = 1,\ldots,n)$, and y denote income. All these variables are positive. We define the n×1 quantity vector q and the n×1 price vector p by

$$q = (q_1, ..., q_n)' \text{ and } p = (p_1, ..., p_n)'.$$

Given *p* and *y*, the consumer selects *q* to maximize the value of his utility function, $u = u(q)$ subject to the budget constraint, $p'q = y$.

The utility function will have certain classical properties. First, it is repeatedly differentiable. Denote the first derivatives (the marginal utilities of the goods) by $u_i = \frac{\partial u}{\partial q_i} \quad (i = 1, ..., n)$

and the second derivatives by $u_{ij} = \frac{\partial u_i}{\partial q_j} = \frac{\partial^2 u}{\partial q_i \, \partial q_j}$

$(i, j = 1, ..., n)$. We define the n × 1 marginal utility vector, u_q

where $u_q = \frac{\partial u}{\partial q} = (u_1, ..., u_n)'$ and the n × n second derivative matrix, *U* by

$$U = \frac{\partial u_q}{\partial q'} = \begin{pmatrix} u_{11} & \cdots & u_{1n} \\ \vdots & & \vdots \\ u_{n1} & \cdots & u_{nn} \end{pmatrix}$$

It will be assumed that $u_i > 0$ (i = 1,....,n), so that marginal utilities are everywhere positive. Further, it will be assumed that the symmetric matrix *U* is negative definite everywhere. This assumption not necessarily ensures that the constrained maximum problem has a unique solution for *q* as a function of *y* and *p*, an assurance that we shall rely on. Incidentally, it implies $u_{ii} < 0$(i=1,....,n) so that there is diminishing marginal utility to each good.

The constrained maximization of $u = u(q)$ subject to $y = p'q$ may be carried out with the aid of the Lagrangian multiplier. Thus, we consider the Lagrangian function as

$$\bar{u}(q,\lambda) = u(q) + \lambda(y - p'q)$$

where λ is the Lagrangian multiplier[4], and choose q and λ to find the maximum value of $\bar{u}(q,\lambda)$ without the constraint. Differentiating with respect to q gives,

$$\bar{u}_q = \frac{\partial \bar{u}}{\partial q} = u_q - \lambda p ,$$

While differentiating with respect to λ gives

$$\bar{u}_\lambda = \frac{\partial \bar{u}}{\partial \lambda} = (y - p'q)$$

When these derivatives are set equal to zero, we find

$$u_q = \lambda p, \; p'q = y \qquad (3.2.1)$$

which are the familiar set of $(n + 1)$ first order conditions in $(n + 1)$ unknowns of q and λ. That these conditions provides a maximum which is ensured by the negative definiteness of U, which further guarantees that (3.2.1) may be solved uniquely for q and λ as functions of y and p. We denote the solutions as q = q (y, p) and λ = λ (y, p). The n equations of the demand system, $q = q(y, p)$, namely $q_i = q_i(y, p) = q_i(y, p_1, ..., p_n)$ where (i=1,........,n) constitute the complete set of consumer demand functions. Each equation in the set gives the quantity demanded of each good '*i*' as a function of income and all prices. This set of demand functions is the main focus of the classical theory of consumer demand. When a particular functional form for $u = u(q)$ is specified, then one may be able to obtain the explicit functional form for $q = q(y, p)$, the parameters of the latter being related to those of the former.

COMPARATIVE-STATIC ANALYSIS OF DEMAND FACTIONS

In the spirit of generality which characterizes the classical approach, however, it is possible to proceed without specifying a particular utility function. General features of the complete demand system can be identified from the differentials of $q = q(y, p)$ and $\lambda(y, p)$ regardless of the specifications of $u = u(q)$.

Consider the *i*th demand function, $q_i = q_i(y, p)$; its slope with respect to income is $\partial q_i / \partial y$, and its slopes with respect to prices are $\partial q_i / \partial p_j \left(j = 1, \ldots\ldots, n\right)$. Similarly, the function $\lambda = \lambda(y, p)$ has income slope $\partial\lambda / \partial y$ and price slopes $\partial\lambda / \partial p_j \left(j = 1, \ldots, n\right)$. All of these slopes can be written in compact vector and matrix form. For the set of demand functions $q = q(y, p)$, we define the $n \times 1$ income slope vector q_y by

$$q_y = \frac{\partial q}{\partial y} = \left(\frac{\partial q_1}{\partial y}, \ldots\ldots\ldots, \frac{\partial q_n}{\partial y}\right)'$$

and the $n \times n$ price slope matrix Q_p known as 'Cournot price slope' matrix in the terminology of Frisch (1959, p.179) by

$$Q_p = \frac{\partial q}{\partial p'} = \begin{pmatrix} \frac{\partial q_1}{\partial p_1} & \cdots & \frac{\partial q_1}{\partial p_n} \\ \vdots & & \vdots \\ \frac{\partial q_n}{\partial p_1} & \cdots & \frac{\partial q_n}{\partial p_n} \end{pmatrix}.$$

Similarly, for $\lambda = (y, p)$, we denote the (scalar) income slope, λ_y as $\lambda_y = \frac{\partial\lambda}{\partial y}$ and the $n \times 1$ price slope vector, λ_p as

$$\lambda_p = \frac{\partial\lambda}{\partial p} = \left(\frac{\partial\lambda}{\partial p_1}, \ldots\ldots, \frac{\partial\lambda}{\partial p_n}\right)'.$$

We, further, introduce the differential of 'y' as dy and the differential p and q vectors as dp and dq where

$$dp = \left(dp_1,...,dp_n\right)' \quad and \quad dq = \left(dq_1,...,dq_n\right)'$$

(i) With this notation the total differentials of q = q(y, p) and λ = λ (y, p)) are expressed as

$$dq = q_y \; dy + Q_p \; dp \; and \; d\lambda = \lambda_y \; dy + \lambda'_p \; dp \qquad (3.2.2)$$

or still more compactly both the equations of (3.2.2) can be written as

$$\begin{pmatrix} dq \\ -d\lambda \end{pmatrix} = \begin{pmatrix} q_y & Q_p \\ -\lambda_y & -\lambda'_p \end{pmatrix} \begin{pmatrix} dy \\ dp \end{pmatrix} \qquad (3.2.3)$$

(ii) The total differentials of the first-order conditions, $u_q = \lambda p$ and $p'q = y$ are similarly expressed as

$$U \; dq = p \; d\lambda + \lambda \; dp \qquad and \qquad dy = p'dq + q'dp$$

or

$$\begin{aligned} U \; dq - p \; d\lambda &= 0 \;\; + \lambda \; dp \quad and \\ p'dq \;\; + \;\; 0 &= dy - q'dp \end{aligned} \qquad (3.2.4a)$$

or more compactly the two equation can be expressed as

$$\begin{pmatrix} U & p \\ p' & 0 \end{pmatrix} \begin{pmatrix} dq \\ -d\lambda \end{pmatrix} = \begin{pmatrix} 0 & \lambda I \\ 1 & -q' \end{pmatrix} \begin{pmatrix} dy \\ dp \end{pmatrix} \qquad (3.2.4b)$$

and expression which Barten (1966, pp.17) calls the 'fundamental matrix equation' of the theory of consumer demand.

Since both (3.2.3) and (3.2.4b) hold for any arbitrary values dy and dp, substituting (3.2.3) into (3.2.4b) and canceling the vector, (dq-dλ) from both sides of the equation (3.2.4c), we have

$$\begin{pmatrix} U & p \\ p' & 0 \end{pmatrix} \begin{pmatrix} q_y & Q_p \\ -\lambda_y & -\lambda'_p \end{pmatrix} = \begin{pmatrix} 0 & \lambda I \\ 1 & -q' \end{pmatrix} \quad \text{or}$$

$$\begin{pmatrix} q_y & Q_p \\ -\lambda_y & -\lambda'_p \end{pmatrix} = \begin{pmatrix} U & p \\ p' & 0 \end{pmatrix}^{-1} \begin{pmatrix} 0 & \lambda I \\ 1 & -q' \end{pmatrix} \qquad (3.2.4c)$$

The matrix equation (3.2.4c) is the 'fundamental matrix equation of the theory of consumer demand' in terms of partial derivatives (Barten, 1966, pp.18). The equation (3.2.4c) in conjunction with the budget constraint p'q = y provides the general features which a complete set of demand functions should possess regardless of the underlying utility function. The inverse of the pre-multiplying matrix on the right hand side of (3.2.4c) is given by

$$\begin{pmatrix} U & p \\ p' & 0 \end{pmatrix}^{-1} = \left(p'U^{-1}p\right)^{-1} \begin{pmatrix} \left(p'U^{-1}p\right)U^{-1} - \left(U^{-1}p\right)\left(U^{-1}p\right)' & U^{-1}p \\ \left(U^{-1}p\right)' & -1 \end{pmatrix} \qquad (3.2.5)$$

Thus, the solution of (3.2.4c) for the slope coefficients is given by equations (3.2.6a) and (3.2.6b) as follows:

$$\begin{pmatrix} q_y & Q_p, \\ -\lambda_y & -\lambda_p \end{pmatrix} = \left(p'U^{-1}p\right)^{-1} \begin{pmatrix} \left(p'U^{-1}p\right)U^{-1} - \left(U^{-1}p\right)\left(U^{-1}p\right)' & U^{-1}p \\ \left(U^{-1}p\right)' & -1 \end{pmatrix} \begin{pmatrix} 0 & \lambda I \\ 1 & -q' \end{pmatrix}$$

$$(3.2.6a)$$

or more compactly (3.2.6a) can be written as

$$\begin{pmatrix} q_y & Q_p \\ -\lambda_y & -\lambda'_p \end{pmatrix} = \left(p'U^{-1}p\right)^{-1} \begin{pmatrix} U^{-1}p & \left(p'U^{-1}p\right)\lambda U^{-1} - \lambda\left(U^{-1}p\right)\left(U^{-1}p\right)' - U^{-1}pq' \\ -1 & \lambda\left(U^{-1}p\right)' + q' \end{pmatrix}$$

$$(3.2.6b)$$

The blocks may be read off clockwise and then equating the corresponding block elements on the two sides of the equation (3.2.6b) and substituting (3.2.7) into(3.2.8), (3.2.9) (3.2.10), we have

$$\lambda_y = \left(p'U^{-1}p\right)^{-1} \qquad (3.2.7)$$

$$q_y = \left(p'U^{-1}p\right)^{-1} U^{-1}p = \lambda_y U^{-1}p \tag{3.2.8}$$

$$Q_p = \left(p'U^{-1}p\right)^{-1}\left(p'U^{-1}p\right)\lambda U^{-1} - \lambda\left(p'U^{-1}p\right)^{-1}\left(U^{-1}p\right)$$

$$\left(U^{-1}p\right)' - \left(p'U^{-1}p\right)^{-1} U^{-1}pq'$$

$$= \lambda\, U^{-1} - \lambda\, \lambda_y \left(U^{-1}p\right)\left(U^{-1}p\right)' - \lambda_y\, U^{-1}pq' \tag{3.2.9}$$

$$\lambda_p = -\left(p'U^{-1}p\right)^{-1}\left[\lambda\left(U^{-1}p\right) + q\right]$$

$$= -\lambda_y\left(\lambda U^{-1}p + q\right) = -\lambda\lambda_y \tag{3.2.10}$$

For most purposes, we substitute (3.2.8) into (3.2.9) and (3.2.10). This, further, simplify the solutions as

$$\lambda_y = \left(p'U^{-1}p\right)^{-1} \tag{3.2.11}$$

$$\lambda_p = -\left(\lambda q_y + \lambda_y q\right) \tag{3.2.12}$$

$$q_y = \lambda_y U^{-1} p \tag{3.2.13}$$

$$Q_p = \lambda\, U^{-1} - \lambda\, \lambda_y^{-1}\, q_y\, q_y' - q_y q' \tag{3.2.14}$$

Equations (3.2.11) to (3.2.11) provide the simplified income and price derivatives of the demand system, q = q(y, p) and the marginal utility of income function, $\lambda = \lambda(y, p)$ which will be used in the subsequent sections of this chapter.

NEOCLASSICAL RESTRICTIONS ON DIFFERENT FORMULATIONS OF DEMAND SYSTEMS

(a) Formulation-1 (General form)

The General restrictions/conditions of the complete set of

demand functions, $q = q(y, p)$ in terms of price and income derivatives (slopes) as well as price and income elasticities is obtained using the terminology of Frisch (1959) and then naming them accordingly.

i. Restrictions on Price and Income Derivatives

First, pre-multiplying (3.2.13) through by p′ gives the 'Engel aggregation' condition as

$$p'q_y = \lambda_y \ p'U^{-1}p = \lambda_y\lambda_y^{-1} = 1 \qquad 3.2.15a)$$

in view of (3.2.11). Alternatively, this condition implies

$$\sum_i p_i\left(\frac{\partial q_i}{\partial y}\right) = 1 \qquad (3.2.15b)$$

Second, post-multiplying the transpose of (3.2.14) throughout by 'p' gives the 'Cournot Aggregation' condition as

$$Q'_p p = \lambda\ U^{-1}p - \lambda\ \lambda_y^{-1} q_y q'_y p - qq'_y p$$

$$= \lambda\lambda_y^{-1} q_y - \lambda\,\lambda_y^{-1} q_y - q = -q.$$

in view of (3.2.8) and (3.2.15a)

So, $\quad q = -Q'_p p \qquad$ (3.2.16a)

Alternatively, this condition implies

$$q_j = -\sum_i p_i\left(\frac{\partial q_i}{\partial p_j}\right) \qquad (3.2.16b)$$

Third, since U^{-1} is symmetric, so is $\lambda\,U^{-1} - \lambda\ \lambda_y^{-1} q_y q'_y$ and also Q_p (in 3.2.14), we can find the 'symmetry' condition[5] as

$$\left(Q_p + q_y q'\right)' = \left(Q_p + q_y q'\right) \qquad (3.2.17a)$$

Alternatively, this condition implies

$$\left(\frac{\partial q_i}{\partial p_j}\right)+\left(\frac{\partial q_i}{\partial y}\right)q_j=\left(\frac{\partial q_j}{\partial p_i}\right)+\left(\frac{\partial q_j}{\partial y}\right)q_i \quad (i,j=1,2,...,n)$$

(3.2.17b)

Another familiar equation follows directly from the others and the budget constraint, and hence imposes no further restrictions. Post-multiplying (3.2.17a) through by p gives

$$Q_p\ p+q_y q'p=Q'_p p+q\ q'_y p=-q+q=0$$

in view of (3.2.15a) and (3.2.16a). Since, q'p=y, we find the 'homogeneity' condition as

$$Q_p\ p=-q_y y \qquad (3.2.18a)$$

Alternatively, this condition implies

$$\sum_j\left(\frac{\partial q_j}{\partial p_j}\right)p_j=-\left(\frac{\partial q_i}{\partial y}\right)y \qquad (i=1,2,\cdots,n) \quad (3.2.18b)$$

Equations (3.2.15), (3.2.16), (3.2.17) and (3.2.18) comprise the main content of the neoclassical theory of demand. They indicate restrictions connecting income and price derivatives which any complete set of demand functions must possess if it is derivable from maximization of any utility function. These restrictions, therefore, indicate the substantial reduction in parameters in a complete set of demand functions that are made available when a classical utility maximization process is postulated.

ii. Restriction on Price and Income Elasticities

Researchers are interested to interpret the above conditions in terms of elasticities rather than slopes so that it will be useful to restate the general conditions of demand functions in terms of elasticities. Consider the *ith* demand function, $q_i = q_i(y, p)$; its elasticity with respect to income and its elasticities with respect to prices are given below, where (j = 1,2,....,n). All of these elasticities may be written in compact matrix form as given below. Form the set of demand functions, q = q(y, p), we define then $n \times 1$ income elasticity vector 'η' given by η = $(\eta_{10}, \eta_{20}, \ldots, \eta_n)'$ and the n × n uncompensatory price elasticity matrix is denoted by H as

$$H = \begin{pmatrix} \eta_{11} & \cdots & \eta_{1n} \\ \vdots & & \vdots \\ \eta_{n1} & \cdots & \eta_{nn} \end{pmatrix}.$$

Direct definitions of the income elasticity vector, 'η' and the price elasticity matrix, 'H' become available if we define the $n \times n$ diagonal matrices of prices and quantities as,

$$\hat{p} = \begin{pmatrix} p_1 & 0 & \cdots & 0 \\ 0 & p_2 & \cdots & 0 \\ \vdots & \vdots & & \vdots \\ 0 & 0 & \cdots & p_n \end{pmatrix} \quad and \quad \hat{q} = \begin{pmatrix} q_1 & 0 & \cdots & 0 \\ 0 & q_2 & \cdots & 0 \\ \vdots & \vdots & & \vdots \\ 0 & 0 & \cdots & q_n \end{pmatrix}$$

Now, the income elasticity vector, 'η' and the price elasticity matrix, 'H' are

$$\eta = y\hat{q}^{-1} q_y \text{ and } H = \hat{q}^{-1} Q_p \hat{p} \qquad (3.2.19)$$

The total differential of $q = q(y, p)$ obtained in (3.2.2) is

$$dq = q_y \; dy + Q_p \; dp \qquad (3.2.20a)$$

which can be expressed in terms of logarithmic differentials and elasticities as

$$d\,(\log q) = \eta\,(d \log y) + H(d \log p) \qquad (3.2.20b)$$

Pre-multiplying (3.2.20a) throughout by $\hat{q}^{-1}$ and on further manipulation gives

$$\hat{q}^{-1} dq = \hat{q}^{-1} q_y \; dy + \hat{q}^{-1} Q_p \; dp$$

$$= \left(\hat{q}^{-1} q_y \; y\right)\left(y^{-1} \; dy\right) + \left(\hat{q}^{-1} Q_p \; \hat{p}\right)\left(\hat{p}^{-1} \; dp\right) \qquad 3.2.20c)$$

and on substitution of (3.2.19) into (3.2.20c) will just reproduce the equation (3.2.20b).

To proceed further, we denote the average budget shares by w_i as

$$w_i = \frac{p_i q_i}{y} \qquad (i = 1, 2, \ldots\ldots n)$$

which measures the proportions of income spent on the *n* goods. Les us define a n × 1 average budget share vector '*w*' as: $w = \left(w_1, w_2 \ldots\ldots, w_n\right)'$.

A direct definition of w become:

$$w = y^{-1}\ \hat{p}\, q = y^{-1} \hat{q}\, p \tag{3.2.21a}$$

These budget shares sum to unity:

$$\iota' w = \iota' y^{-1} \hat{p}\, q = y^{-1} \iota' \hat{p}\, q = y^{-1}\ p' q = 1 \tag{3.2.21b}$$

In view of p'q = y and 'ι' where ι = (1,1,.......,1)' denotes the n × 1 'sum vector'.

Now the neoclassical restrictions may be expressed in terms of the elasticities of the demand functions which are in terms of the coefficients in (3.2.20). First, Engel aggregation is shown by

$$w'\eta = \left(y^{-1}\ p'\hat{q}\right)\left(y\,\hat{q}^{-1}\ q_y\right) = p' q_y = 1 \tag{3.2.22a}$$

in view of (3.2.15a), (3.2.19) and (3.2.21a). Alternatively, this condition implies

$$\sum_i w_i\, \eta_i = 1 \quad (i = 1, 2, \ldots\ldots n) \tag{3.2.22b}$$

Second, the Cournot aggregation condition is given by

$$H' w = \left(\hat{p}\ Q_p'\ \hat{q}^{-1}\right)\left(y^{-1}\ \hat{q}\, p\right) = y^{-1}\ \hat{p}\ Q_p'\ p$$

$$= y^{-1}\ \hat{p}(-q) = -y^{-1} \hat{p}\, q = -w \tag{3.2.23a}$$

in view of (3.2.16a). Alternatively, this condition implies

$$\sum_i w_i \eta_{ij} = -w_j (j = 1, 2....., n) \qquad (3.2.23b)$$

Third, symmetry condition is manifested in

$$\left[\hat{w}(H + \eta\ w')\right]' = (H' + w\,\eta')\ \hat{w}$$

$$= \left[\hat{p}\ Q_p'\ \hat{q}^{-1} + \left(y^{-1}\ \hat{p}\,q\right)\left(y\,q_y'\ \hat{q}^{-1}\right)\right]\left(y^{-1}\ \hat{q}\,\hat{p}\right)$$

$$= y^{-1}(\hat{p}\ Q_p'\hat{p} + \hat{p}\,q q_y'\hat{p}) = y^{-1}\hat{p}\ (Q_p' + q q_y')\,\hat{p}$$

$$= y^{-1}\ \hat{p}\left(Q_p + q_y\,q'\right)\hat{p} = \hat{w}\left(H + \eta\ w'\right) \qquad (3.2.24a)$$

in view of (3.2.17a). Alternatively, this condition implies

$$w_i\left(\eta_{ij} + \eta_{i0}\ w_j\right) = w_j\left(\eta_{ji} + n_{j0}\ w_i\right) \quad \left(i, j = 1, ..., n\right) \qquad (3.2.24b)$$

Fourth, the homogeneity condition again follows by post-multiplying (3.2.24a) through by 'ι' and this gives

$$\hat{w}\left(H\iota + \eta\ w'\iota\right) = H'\ w + w\eta' w = H'w + w = 0 \qquad (3.2.25)$$

using $\hat{w}\iota = w$; (3.2.22a) and (3.2.23a). Since $w'\iota = 1$, equation (3.2.25) reduces to

$$H\iota = -\eta \qquad (3.2.26a)$$

Alternatively, this condition implies

$$\sum_j \eta_{ij} = -\eta_{i0}\ \left(i = 1, ..., n\right) \qquad (3.2.26b)$$

(b) Formulation-2 (budget share form)

Researchers are also interested to derive the above conditions of the demand functions in terms of the average budget shares rather than the quantities or the logarithms of quantities so that another restatement of these conditions may be useful.

Let us pre-multiply (dq = qy dy + Qp dp) throughout by $y^{-1}\hat{p}$, or equivalently (3.2.20b) by $\hat{w}$. We have

$$y^{-1}\ \hat{p}\ dq = y^{-1}\ \hat{p}q_y\ dy + y^{-1}\ \hat{p}\ Q_p\ dp \text{ or}$$

$$y^{-1}\ \hat{p}\ \hat{q}\ \hat{q}^{-1}\ dq = \hat{p}\ q_y\ y^{-1}\ dy + y^{-1}\ \hat{p}\ Q_p\ \hat{p}\ \hat{p}^{-1}\ dp \quad (3.2.27a)$$

This may be written as an alternate formulation of (3.2.27a)

$$\hat{w}\ d\ (\log q) = \mu\ d\ (\log y) + \theta\ d\ (\log p) \quad (3.2.27b)$$

where we have defined the n × 1 marginal budget share vector μ as

$$\mu = (\mu_1, \mu_2 ......, \mu_n)' = \hat{p}q_y = \hat{w}\eta$$

and the $n \times n$ price response matrix , θ as

$$\theta = \begin{pmatrix} \theta_{11} & \cdots & \theta_{1n} \\ \vdots & & \vdots \\ \theta_{n1} & \cdots & \theta_{nn} \end{pmatrix} = y^{-1}\ \hat{p}Q_p\ \hat{p} = \hat{w}\ H$$

$$\text{or } \theta = \hat{w}\ H = \begin{pmatrix} w_1\eta_{11} & \cdots & w_1\eta_{1n} \\ \vdots & & \vdots \\ w_n\eta_{n1} & \cdots & w_n\eta_{nn} \end{pmatrix}$$

Now, (3.2.27b) can be alternatively written as

$$w_i\ d\ (\log q_i) = \mu_i\ d\ (\log y) + \sum_j \theta_{ij}\ d(\log p_j)\ \ (i=1, 2, ..., n) \quad (3.2.27c)$$

$$\text{where } \mu_i = y^{-1} p_i \left(\frac{\partial q_i}{\partial y}\right) = w_i \eta_{io} \qquad (i, j = 1, 2, ..., n)$$

$$\text{and } \theta_{ij} = y^{-1}\ p_i\ p_j \left(\frac{\partial q_i}{\partial p_j}\right) = w_i\ \eta_{ij} \qquad (i, j = 1, 2, ..., n)$$

Here, μ, s measure the proportions of incremental income

spent on the '*n*' goods with given prices. The left hand side variable, $w_i\, d(\log q_i)$, has the following interpretation. Consider the total differential of the *ith* average budget share as

$$dw_i = d\left(\frac{p_i q_i}{y}\right) = \left(\frac{q_i}{y}\right) dp_i + \left(\frac{p_i}{y}\right) dq_i - \left(\frac{p_i q_i}{y^2}\right) dy$$

Multiply and divide the first term by p_i and the second term by q_i on the right hand side, we have

$$dw_i = \left(\frac{p_i q_i}{y}\right)\left(\frac{dp_i}{p_i}\right) + \left(\frac{p_i q_i}{y}\right)\left(\frac{dq_i}{q_i}\right) - \left(\frac{p_i q_i}{y}\right)\left(\frac{dy}{y}\right)$$

$$dw_i = w_i\, d(\log p_i) + w_i\, d(\log q_i) - w_i\, d(\log y) \qquad (3.2.28)$$

In many contexts, primary interest attaches to changes in the average budget shares, in response to changes in income and prices. As we see from (3.2.28), $w_i\, d(\log q_i)$ is just the 'endogenous component' of dw_i on the basis of which the consumer exercise choice. It, therefore, seems plausible to treat the $w_i d(\log q_i)$ as the dependent variables as is done in (3.2.27b), rather than treat the dq_i or the $d(\log q_i)$ as dependent variables as was done in (3.2.20a) and (3.2.20b), respectively. Theil (1967) refers as $w_i\,(d \log q_i)$ 'the quantity component of the change in the *ith* average budget share.

Restriction on Price and Income Elasticities

The neoclassical restrictions may be expressed again in terms elasticities on the basis of the coefficients in (3.2.27b).

First, Engel aggregation is shown by

$$\iota'\mu = \iota'\hat{w}\eta = w'\eta = 1 \qquad (3.2.29a)$$

in view of (3.2.22a). Alternatively, this condition implies

$$\sum_i \mu_i = 1 \qquad (3.2.29b)$$

Second, Cournot aggregation condition is shown by

$$\theta'\iota = H'\hat{w}\iota = H'w = -w \qquad (3.2.30a)$$

in view of (3.2.23a). Alternatively, this condition implies

$$\sum_i \theta_{ij} = -w_j \qquad (j=1,2,....,n) \quad (3.2.30b)$$

Third, symmetry condition is shown by

$$(\theta + \mu w')' = \left[\hat{w}(H + \eta\, w')\right]' = \hat{w}(H + \eta\, w') = \theta + \mu w' \quad (3.2.31a)$$

in view of (3.2.24a). Alternatively, this condition implies

$$\theta_{ij} + \mu_i\, w_j = \theta_{ji} + \mu_j\, w_i \qquad (i,\, j = 1,\, 2,\, ..,n) \quad (3.2.31b)$$

Fourth, homogeneity is shown by

$$\theta\,\iota = \hat{w} H \iota = -\hat{w}\eta = -\mu \qquad (3.2.32a)$$

in view of (3.2.26a). Alternatively, this condition implies

$$\sum_j \theta_{ij} = -\mu_i \qquad (i = 1,\, 2,....,n) \quad (3.2.32b)$$

INDIRECT UTILITY FUNCTION

Let us proceed to examine some utility aspects of the classical theory of demand. The demand functions $q = q(y, p)$ may be inserted into the utility function $u = u\ (q)$ to give maximum attainable utility as a function of y and p:

The function, u^* (y, p) is the indirect utility function as distinguished from the direct utility function $u = u(q)$. Denote the slope of the indirect utility function with respect to income as $\frac{\partial u^*}{\partial y}$ and its slopes with respect to prices as $\frac{\partial u^*}{\partial p_j}\ (j = 1,2,.....,n)$. We express these, in the spirit of the notation used earlier as

$$u_y^* = \frac{\partial u^*}{\partial y} \quad and \quad u_p^* = \frac{\partial u^*}{\partial p} = \left(\frac{\partial u^*}{\partial p_1},...,\frac{\partial u^*}{\partial p_n}\right)'$$

Applying the chain rule of differentiation, we have

$$u_y^* = u_q' q_y \quad and \quad u_p^{*'} = u_q'\, Q_p \qquad (3.3.1a)$$

By virtue of the first order conditions of utility maximization, we have $u_q = \lambda p$ or $u'_q = \lambda p'$ which on substitution into (3.3.1a), we have

$$u_y^* = \lambda\ p' q_y \quad and \quad u_p^{*'} = \lambda\ p'\ Q_{p'} \qquad (3.3.1b)$$

which in turn imply

$$u_y^* = \lambda \qquad and \qquad u_p^* = -\lambda\ q \qquad (3.3.1c)$$

since, $p'q_y = 1$ and $p'Q_p = -q'$.

The most attractive property of this utility function is that the demand functions can be derived form it using 'Roy's identity' which is

$$q = -(u_p^* / u_y^*) \qquad (3.3.2a)$$

Alternately, it implies

$$q_i = -\frac{\partial u^*}{\partial p_i} \Big/ \frac{\partial u^*}{\partial y} \qquad (i = 1, 2, \ldots\ldots\ldots\ldots n) \qquad (3.3.2b)$$

This is an important result for which one can directly specify an indirect utility function; derive the demand functions simply by differentiating the indirect utility function, avoiding the intricate steps involved in the maximisation of a direct utility function.

The Lagrangian multiplier, λ has now been identified as the marginal utility of income, so that the function $\lambda = \lambda(y, p)$ gives the marginal utility of income as a function of income and prices. Thus, the slope of the marginal utility of income with respect to income is λ_y and the vector of its slopes with respect to prices is λ_p. It will be convenient to denote the income elasticity of the marginal utility of income by

$$\eta_{\lambda y} = \left(\frac{\partial \lambda}{\partial y}\right)\left(\frac{y}{\lambda}\right) = \lambda_y\ \lambda^{-1}\ y \text{ since } \frac{\partial \lambda}{\partial y} = \lambda_y \qquad (3.3.3a)$$

and its reciprocal, the income flexibility[6] is given by

$$\phi = \frac{1}{\eta_{\lambda y}} = \lambda_y^{-1}\ \lambda\ y^{-1} \text{ or } \phi\ y = \lambda_y^{-1}\ \lambda \qquad (3.3.3b)$$

We shall have frequent occasions to replace $\lambda_y^{-1}\lambda$ by its equivalent, ϕ y. The marginal utility of income is positive but declines with income since u_q and p are positive. So λ is positive as per equation, $u_q = \lambda p$. Since U is negative-definite, so is U^{-1}. Hence $\lambda_y = \left(p' U^{-1} p\right)^{-1}$ is also negative; it then follows that $\eta_{\lambda y} < 0$ *and* $\phi < 0$.

DECOMPOSITION OF PRICE EFFECT

Let us examine the two compensation principles for a price change upon quantities demanded: (i) in the sense of keeping utility unchanged and (ii) in the sense of keeping marginal utility of income unchanged.

The total differential of $u = u^*(y, p)$ is

$$du = u_y^* \, dy + u_p^* \, dp = \lambda \, dy - \lambda \, q' \, dp = \lambda\left(dy - q' \, dp\right) \qquad (3.3.4)$$

in view of (3.3.1c). The total differential of $\lambda = \lambda(y, p)$ is

$$d\lambda = \lambda_y \, dy + \lambda_p' \, dp = \lambda_y \, dy - \left(\lambda \, q_y + \lambda_y \, q\right)' \, dp \qquad (3.3.5)$$

in view of (3.2.12). Setting $du = 0$ in (3.3.4) gives the income change

$$(dy)^* = q' \, dp \text{ as } \lambda \neq 0 \qquad (3.3.6)$$

which will compensate for a price change dp, in the sense of keeping utility unchanged. Alternatively, setting $d\lambda = 0$ gives the income change as

$$d\lambda = \lambda_y \, dy - \left(\lambda \, q_y + \lambda_y \, q\right)' \, dp = 0$$

or $\lambda_y \, dy = \left(\lambda \, q_y + \lambda_y \, q\right)' \, dp$ *or* $dy = \lambda_y^{-1}\left(\lambda \, q_y + \lambda_y \, q\right)' \, dp$

(3.3.7)

in view of (3.3.7) for $d\lambda = 0$ gives the income change as

$$(dy)^{**} = \left(\lambda\lambda_y^{-1} q_y + q^1\right) dp = \left(\phi y q_y + q\right)' dp \qquad (3.3.8)$$

which will compensate for a price change dp, in the sense of keeping marginal utility of income unchanged.

With these two concepts of compensation as represented in (3.3.6) and 3.3.8), the two decompositions of the effects of price changes upon quantities demanded are as follows. Recall that the total differential of the demand functions $q = q(y, p)$ is

$$dq = q_y\, dy + Q_p\, dp = q_y\, dy + \left(\lambda\, U^{-1} - \lambda\, \lambda_y^{-1} q_y\, q_y' - q_y\, q'\right) dp \tag{3.3.9}$$

in view of (3.2.14). Given a prices change dp if accompanied by an income change such that the level of utility is unchanged. The response of quantity change to such a utility-compensated price change can be obtained by substituting (3.3.6) into (3.3.9). So we have,

$$(dq)^* = q_y\, (q'\, dp) + Q_p\, dp = \left(Q_p + q_y\, q'\right) dp = Q_p^*\, dp \tag{3.3.10}$$

where

$$Q_p^* = Q_p + q_y\, q' = (\lambda\, U^{-1} - \lambda\, \lambda_y^{-1}\, q_y\, q_y' - q_y\, q') + q_y\, q'$$

$$= \lambda\, U^{-1} - \phi\, y\, q_y\, q_y'$$

The symmetric matrix Q^*_p may be referred to as the utility compensated (or slutsky) price slope matrix of the demand functions and its (*i, j)th* element is

$$\left(\frac{\partial q_i}{\partial p_j}\right)^* = \left(\frac{\partial q_i}{\partial p_j}\right) + \left(\frac{\partial q_i}{\partial y}\right) q_j = \lambda\, u^{ij} - \phi\, y \left(\frac{\partial q_i}{\partial y}\right)\left(\frac{\partial q_j}{\partial y}\right) \tag{3.3.11}$$

which measures the response of the quantity demanded of the *i*th good to a change in the price of the *jth* good when that price change is accompanied by an income change which just maintains the same level of utility. The total effect of a price change, $\left(\frac{\partial q_i}{\partial p_j}\right)$, has thus been decomposed into a substitution effect, $\left(\dfrac{\partial q_i}{\partial p_j}\right)^*$, and an income effect, $-\left(\dfrac{\partial q_i}{\partial y}\right) q_j$. On the Hicks-Allen definition, goods '*i*' and '*j*' are classified as substitutes, independent, or complements according as $\left(\dfrac{\partial q_i}{\partial p_j}\right)^* = \left(\dfrac{\partial q_j}{\partial p_i}\right)^*$ is positive, zero, or negative.

Alternatively, given a price change *dp* if accompanied by an income change, $dy = (dy)^{**} = (\phi y q_y + q)' dp$, such that marginal utility of income remains unchanged. The response to such a marginal-utility-of income-compensated price change can be obtained by substituting (3.3.8) into (3.3.9). So we have,

$$(dq)^{**} = q_y (\phi\, y\, q_y + q)'\, dp + Q_p\, dp$$

$$= (Q_p + q_y\, q' + \phi\, y\, q_y\, q_y')\, dp = Q_p^{**}\, \mathrm{dp} \tag{3.3.12}$$

where

$$Q_p^{**} = (Q_p + q_y\, q' + \phi\, y\, q_y\, q_y') = (Q_p^* + \phi\, y\, q_y\, q_y')$$

$$= (\lambda\, U^{-1} - \phi\, y\, q_y\, q_y') + \phi\, y\, q_y\, q' = \lambda\, U^{-1}$$

in view of (3.3.10). The symmetric matrix Q^{**}_p may be referred to as the marginal-utility-of-income-compensated (Frisch)[7] price slope matrix of the demand functions and its *(i, j)th* element is given by

$$\left(\frac{\partial q_i}{\partial p_j}\right)^{**} = \left(\frac{\partial q_i}{\partial p_j}\right) + \left(\frac{\partial q_i}{\partial y}\right) q_j + \phi\, y \left(\frac{\partial q_i}{\partial y}\right)\left(\frac{\partial q_j}{\partial y}\right)$$

$$= \left(\frac{\partial q_i}{\partial p_j}\right)^* + \phi\, y \left(\frac{\partial q_i}{\partial y}\right)\left(\frac{\partial q_j}{\partial y}\right) = \lambda\, u^{ij} \tag{3.3.13}$$

where u_{ij} denotes the *(i,j)th* element of U^{-1}. The above equation (3.3.13) measures the response of the quantity demanded of the *ith* good in response to a change in the price of the *jth* good when the price change is accompanied by an income change which just maintains the same level of the marginal utility of income. The total effect of an uncompensated price change, $\left(\frac{\partial q_i}{\partial p_j}\right)$, has, thus, been decomposed into three terms: a specific substitution effect (SSE) $=\left(\frac{\partial q_i}{\partial p_j}\right)^{**}$, a general substitution effect (GSE) = $\left(\frac{\partial q_i}{\partial p_j}\right)^{*}-\left(\frac{\partial q_i}{\partial p_j}\right)^{**}$, and an income effect (IE)= $-\left(\frac{\partial q_i}{\partial y}\right)q_j$. Any two goods 'i' and 'j' might be reclassified as substitutes, independent, or complements according as $\left(\frac{\partial q_i}{\partial p_j}\right)^{**}=\left(\frac{\partial q_j}{\partial p_i}\right)^{**}$ is positive, zero, or negative; that is according as $u^{ij}=u^{ji}\gtreqless 0$ (Houthakker, 1960).

Schematically, the decompositions are indicated as:

$$\begin{aligned} Q_p &= \lambda U^{-1} - \phi y\, q_y\, q_y' - q_y\, q' \\ (TE) &= (SSE) + (GSE) \quad + (IE) \end{aligned} \tag{3.3.14}$$

Equation (3.3.14) is the more general decomposition of the price effect into specific substitution effect, general substitution effect and the income effect in which the Hicks-Allen substitution effect (3.3.11) is further decomposed into specific substitution effect and general substitution effect.

NEOCLASSICAL RESTRICTIONS ON COMPENSATED DEMAND FUNCTIONS

It is now instructive to consider the demand functions in terms of Q^*_p and Q^{**}_p. The total differential of the demand functions, originally expressed as

$$dq = q_y \; dy + Q_p \; dp \qquad (3.3.15a)$$

In view of the definitions of Q^*_p and Q^{**}_p, the above total differential of the demand functions (3.3.15a) can alternatively be expressed as

$$dq = q_y \, dy \left(Q^*_p - q_y q'\right) dp \text{ since } Q_p = \left(Q^*_p - q_y q'\right)$$

$$= q_y \; (dy - q'dp) + Q^*_p \; dp \qquad (3.3.15b)$$

The above total differential demand function in terms of Q^{**}_p can alternatively be expressed as

$$dq = q_y dy + \left(Q^{**}_p - q_y \, q' - \phi \, y q_y q'_y\right) dp$$

$$[\textit{Since } Q_p = \left(Q^{**}_p - q_y \, q' - \phi \, y q_y q'_y\right)]$$

$$= q_y \left(dy - q'dp\right) + \left(Q^{**}_p - \phi \, y q_y \, q'_y\right) dp$$

$$= q_y \left(dy - q'dp\right) + \left(Q^{**}_p - Q^{**}_p \, pq'_y\right) dp$$

where $Q^{**}_p p = \phi \; y \; q$, which is shown in (3.3.22a) below.

$$dq = q_y \left(dy - q'dp\right) + Q^{**}_p \left(dp - pq'_y \; dp\right) \qquad (3.3.15c)$$

While in (3.3.15a) q_y is the coefficient of the change in nominal income in (3.3.15b) and (3.3.15c), it is the coefficient of the change in a deflated income variable. While in (3.3.15a) and (3.3.15b), the last term refers to changes in nominal prices, in (3.3.15c) it refers to the change in deflated price. Note that $q' \, dp = (dy)^*$ is the income change required to maintain a given level of utility in the case of the price change *dp*. This means that *q′ dp* gives the change in a true cost of living index, so that *(dy - q′ dp)* gives the change in real income.[8]

i. Restriction on price and income derivatives

The restrictions linking price and income slopes are manifested again. Consider the equation (3.3.15b) which uses q_y and Q^*_p.

First, the Engel aggregation appears again as

$$p'q_y = 1 \tag{3.3.16a}$$

as in (3.2.15a). Alternatively, this restriction implies,

$$\sum_i p_i\left(\frac{\partial q_i}{\partial y}\right) = 1 \tag{3.3.16b}$$

Second, for Cournot aggregation, post-multiply $Q_p^{*'}$ by p to obtain

$$Q_p^{*'}p = \left(Q_p + q_y\ q'\right)'\ p = Q_p'\ p + q\ q_y' p = -q + q = 0 \quad \text{3.3.17a)}$$

in view of (3.2.16a) and (3.3.16a). Alternatively, this restriction implies,

$$\sum_i p_i\left(\frac{\partial q_i}{\partial p_j}\right)^* = 0 \qquad (j = 1, 2, \ldots\ldots\ldots, n) \tag{3.3.17b}$$

Third, the symmetry condition appears again as

$$Q_p^{*'} = \left(Q_p + q_y q'\right)' = Q_p + q_y q' = Q_p^* \tag{3.3.18a}$$

in view of (3.2.17a). Alternatively, this restriction implies,

$$\left(\frac{\partial q_i}{\partial p_j}\right)^* = \left(\frac{\partial q_j}{\partial p_i}\right)^* \quad (i,\ j = 1, 2, \ldots, n) \tag{3.3.18b}$$

Fourth, the homogeneity condition appears as

$$Q_p^* p = \left(Q_p + q_y q'\right) p = Q_p p + q_y\ q'p$$

$$= -q_y\ y + q_y\ y = 0 \quad \text{3.3.19a)}$$

in view of (3.2.18a) and $q'\ p = y$. Alternatively, this restriction implies,

$$\sum_j \left(\frac{\partial q_i}{\partial p_j}\right)^* p_j = 0 \tag{3.3.19b}$$

Another well-known result is that the utility-compensated own-price slope must be negative[9]:

$$\left(\frac{\partial q_i}{\partial p_i}\right)^* < 0 \quad (i = 1, 2, \ldots\ldots, n) \qquad (3.3.20)$$

Now, consider the modified total differential of the demand functions (3.3.15c) which uses q_y and Q^{**}_p. and. Once again the different condition associated with this differential of the demand functions are:

First, Engel aggregation appears as

$$p' q_y = 1 \qquad (3.3.21a)$$

Alternatively, this condition implies,

$$\sum_i p_i \left(\frac{\partial q_i}{\partial y}\right) = 1 \qquad (3.3.21b)$$

Second, for Cournot aggregation, post-multiply $Q^{**'}_p$ by p to obtain

$$Q^{**'}_p\ p = \left(Q^*_p + \phi\ y\ q_y\ q'_y\right)'\ p = Q^{*'}_p\ p + \phi\ y\ q_y\ q'_y\ p = \phi\ y\ q_y \qquad (3.3.22a)$$

in view of (3.3.17a) and (3.3.21a). Alternatively, this condition implies,

$$\sum_i p_i \left(\frac{\partial q_i}{\partial p_j}\right)^{**} = \phi\ y \left(\frac{\partial q_j}{\partial y}\right) \qquad (j = 1, 2, \ldots\ldots, n) \qquad (3.3.22b)$$

Third, symmetry condition is apparent from above

$$Q^{**'}_p = \left(Q^*_p + \phi\ y\ q_y\ q'_y\right)' = Q^*_p + \phi\ y\ q_y\ q'_y = Q^{**}_p \qquad 3.3.23a)$$

in view of (3.3.18a). Alternatively, this condition implies,

$$\left(\frac{\partial q_i}{\partial p_j}\right)^{**} = \left(\frac{\partial q_j}{\partial p_i}\right)^{**} \qquad (i, j = 1, 2, \ldots\ldots, n) \quad (3.3.23b)$$

Fourth, homogeneity appears as

$$Q_p^{**}\, p = Q_p^{**'}\, p = \phi\, y\, q_y \qquad (3.3.24a)$$

in view of (3.3.22a) and (3.3.23a). Alternatively, this condition implies,

$$\sum_j \left(\frac{\partial q_i}{\partial p_j}\right)^{**} p_j = \phi\, y \left(\frac{\partial q_i}{\partial y}\right) \qquad (i = 1, 2, \ldots\ldots, n) \qquad (3.3.24b)$$

Also, the marginal-utility-of-income-compensated own-price slope is negative:

$$\left(\frac{\partial q_i}{\partial p_i}\right)^{**} < 0 \qquad (i = 1, 2, \ldots\ldots, n) \qquad (3.3.25)$$

Once $Q_p^{**} = \lambda U^{-1}$ is negative definite, its diagonal elements are negative.

ii. Restriction on price and income elasticities

The above analysis of differentials and slopes may be translated into analysis of logarithmic differentials and elasticities. We will work with the same income elasticity vector, $\eta_0 = (\eta_{10}, \eta_{20}, \ldots\ldots, \eta_{n0})'$, but we now introduce two compensated price elasticity matrices as follows:

$$H^* = \begin{pmatrix} \eta_{11}^* & \cdots & \eta_{1n}^* \\ \vdots & & \vdots \\ \eta_{n1}^* & \cdots & \eta_{nn}^* \end{pmatrix} \quad \text{and} \quad H^{**} = \begin{pmatrix} \eta_{11}^{**} & \cdots & \eta_{1n}^{**} \\ \vdots & & \vdots \\ \eta_{n1}^{**} & \cdots & \eta_{nn}^{**} \end{pmatrix}$$

where $\eta_{ij}^* = \left(\frac{\partial q_i}{\partial p_j}\right)^* \left(\frac{p_j}{q_i}\right)$ *and* $\eta_{ij}^{**} = \left(\frac{\partial q_i}{\partial p_j}\right)^{**} \left(\frac{p_j}{q_i}\right)$.

The matrix definitions of the compensated price elasticities in terms of Q^*_p and Q^{**}_p are clearly

$$H^* = \hat{q}^{-1}\, Q_p^*\, \hat{p} \qquad \textit{and} \qquad H^{**} = \hat{q}^{-1}\, Q^{**}\, \hat{p}\,,$$

while in terms of 'H' and 'η' we can write

$$H^{*} = \hat{q}^{-1}\left(Q_p + q_y\ q'\right)\hat{p} = H + \eta\ w' \tag{3.3.26a}$$

and $H^{**} = \hat{q}^{-1}\left(Q_p^{*} + \phi\ y\ q_y\ q_y'\ \right)\hat{p} = \hat{q}^{-1}Q_p^{*}\hat{p} + \phi\ y\hat{q}^{-1}q_y\ q_y'\hat{p}$

$$= H^{*} + \phi\ \eta\ w'\ \hat{\eta} = H + \eta\ w' + \phi\ \eta\ w'\ \hat{\eta} = H + \eta\ w'\left(I + \phi\hat{\eta}\right)$$

using $\eta = y\ \hat{q}^{-1}\ q_y$ and $w = y^{-1}\ \hat{p}\ q$. (3.3.26b)

NEOCLASSICAL RESTRICTIONS ON LOGARITHMIC DIFFERENTIAL OF DEMAND FUNCTIONS

A restatement of the demand functions and restrictions in terms of H* or H** of is straightforward. The logarithmic differential of the demand functions, originally expressed as

$$d\ (\log q) = \eta\ \left(d\ \log\ y\right) + H\left(d\ \log\ p\right) \tag{3.3.27a}$$

may, in view of the definitions of H^* and H^{**}, alternatively be expressed a

$$d(\log q) = \eta\ \left(d\ (\log y) - w'\ d\ (\log p)\right) + H^{*}\ d\ (\log\ p) \tag{3.3.27b}$$

or as

$$d(\log q) = \eta\ \left[d(\log y) - w'\left(I + \phi\hat{\eta}\right)d(\log p)\right] + H^{**}\ d(\log p)$$

$$= \eta\ \left(d(\log y) - w'\ d(\log p)\right) + H^{**}\left(d(\log\ p)\ - \iota\ w'\ \hat{\eta}\ d\ (\log\ p)\right) \tag{3.3.27c}$$

The last equation (3.3.27c) is based on the fact that $H^{**}i = \phi\ \eta$, as shown in (3.3.31b) below. While in (3.3.27a), η is the coefficient of the logarithmic change in nominal income, in (3.3.27b) and (3.3.27b) it is the coefficient of the logarithmic change in a deflated income variable. While in (3.3.27a) and (3.3.27b) the last term refers to logarithmic changes in nominal prices, in (3.3.27c) it refers to logarithmic changes in deflated prices.[10]

The restrictions of the above model reappear as follows: First, Engel aggregation appears as:

$w'\eta = 1$ (for model-3.3.27b) (3.3.28a)

Also, $w'\eta = 1$ (for model-3.3.27c) (3.3.28b)

Second, the Cournot aggregation is

$$H^{*'}w = (H + \eta w')' w = H'w + w\eta'w = -w + w = 0$$

(for model-3.3.27b) (3.3.29a)

$$H^{**'}w = (H^* + \phi\eta w'\hat{\eta})' w = H^*w + \phi\hat{\eta}\, w\eta'w = \phi\, \hat{\eta}\, w = \phi\, \hat{w}\eta$$

(for3.3.27c) (3.3.29b)

Third, symmetry appears as:

$$(\hat{w}H^*)' = [\hat{w}(H + \eta w')]' = \hat{w}(H + \eta\, w') = \hat{w}\, H^*$$

(for model-3.3.27b) (3.3.30a)

$$(\hat{w}H^{**})' = (\hat{w}H^*)' + (\phi\, \hat{w}\,\eta\, w'\hat{\eta})' = \hat{w}H^* + \phi\, \hat{w}\,\eta\, w'\hat{\eta} = \hat{w}\, H^{**}$$

(for 3.3.27c) (3.3.30b)

Fourth, homogeneity appears as:

$$H^*\iota = (H + \eta w')\iota = H\iota + \eta\, w'\iota = -\eta + \eta = 0$$

(for model-3.3.27b) (3.3.31a)

$$H^{**}\iota = (H^* + \phi\eta\, w'\hat{\eta})\iota = H^*\iota + \phi\eta\, w'\eta = \phi\,\eta\, w'\eta = \phi\eta$$

(for-3.3.27c) (3.3.31b)

For each of the above formulations, equations linking the price and income slopes within and across demand functions have been established. Under any of the representations being considered here, the force of the neoclassical theory is to reduce the number of free 'coefficients' in a complete set of demand functions. The reduction arises as a consequence of the restrictions which link the price and income coefficients in any set of demand functions which has been generated in a classical utility maximization process. The reduction in parameters is not costless, of course. The dynamic considerations are being ignored, as are possible feedbacks from demand to prices and income.[11]

DUALITY AND THE COST FUNCTION

There are many different ways of representing preferences and great convenience can be obtained by picking the one which is most appropriate for the problem at hand. For the purposes of generating empirically useable models in which quantities are a function of prices and total expenditure, dual representations are typically most convenient. In this context, duality refers to a switch of variables, from quantities to prices, and to the re-specification of preferences in terms of the latter. Define the cost function (or expenditure functions) which is given by

$$c(u,p) = \left(\min_{q} pq;\ u(q) \geq u^{\circ}\right) \tag{3.4.1}$$

If 'y' is the total budget to be allocated, then 'y' will be the cheapest way of reaching whatever can be reached at 'p' and 'y' , so that

$$c(u,p) = y \tag{3.4.2}$$

The function can be shown to be continuous in both its arguments, monotonically increasing in 'u' and monotonically non-decreasing in 'p'. It is linearly homogeneous and concave in prices, and the first and second derivative exists almost everywhere. It is strictly quasi-concave if $u(q)$ is twice differentiable everywhere. [12] The empirical importance of the cost function lies due to its two important features. The first is the 'derivative property', often known as Shephard's Lemma[13]. By virtue of this property, whenever its derivative exists, then

$$\partial c(u,p)/\partial p_i \equiv h_i(u,p) = q_i \tag{3.4.3}$$

The functions are known as Hicksian demand functions, in contrast to the Marshallian demand function, q_i (y,p). The second feature is the Shaphard-Uzawa duality theorem, which allows a constructive recovery of the utility function from the cost function for given convex preferences. [14] Hence, all the information in $u(q)$ which is relevant to behaviour and empirical analysis is encoded in the function c (u,p) or put another way, any function c (u, p) with the desirable properties can serve as an alternative to $u(q)$ as a basis for empirical analysis. The direct utility function need not be explicitly derived; if the cost function is correctly specified, corresponding to given pattern of preferences. The following procedure is, thus, suggested in empirical analysis. Starting from some linearly homogeneous concave cost function c(u, p), derive the Hicksian demand functions h_i (u, p) by differentiation. These demand functions can be converted into Marshallian demands by substituting for '*u*' from the inverted form of (3.4.2). This is written as

$$u = u^*(y, p), \tag{3.4.4}$$

and the function (3.4.4) is known as the indirect utility function. (The original function $u(q)$ is the direct utility function and the two are linked by the identity $(u^*(y, p) \equiv u\{q_i(y, p)\}$ for utility maximizing demands q_i (y, p). Substituting (3.4.4) into (3.4.3) yields

$$q_i = h_i(u, p) = h_i\{u^*(y, p), p\} = q_i(y, p) \tag{3.4.5}$$

Of course, the demands corresponding to the original cost function may not fit the data or may have other undesirable properties. To build this back into preferences, we must be able to go from q_i (y, p) back to c(u, p). But, form Shephard's Lemma, $q_i = q_i$ (y, p) may be rewritten as

$$\partial c(u, p)/\partial p_i = q_i\{c(u, p), p\} \tag{3.4.6}$$

which may be solved for c(u, p) provided the integrability conditions are satisfied. These turn out to be equivalent to Slutsky symmetry, so that demand functions displaying symmetry always imply some cost functions.[15] If the Slutsky matrix is also negative semi-definite (together with symmetry and the integrability condition), the cost functions will be appropriately concave and it must represent the same preferences. This possibility of moving easily between preferences and demands, is of vital importance if empirical knowledge is to be linked to the theory of consumer behaviour.

An alternative and almost equivalent straight foreword procedure is to start from the indirect utility function u*(y, p) which must be homogeneous of degree zero in '*y*' and '*p*' and quasi-convex in '*p*'. The Shephard's lemma takes the form

$$q_i = q_i(y,p) = -\partial u^*(y,p)/\partial p_i \big/ \partial u^*(y,p)/\partial y \qquad (3.4.7)$$

A formula is known as Roy's identity (Roy, 1942). This is sometimes done in 'normalized' form. Clearly, u*(y, p) = u* (1,p/y) = u* (r) where r = p/y, the vector of normalized prices. Hence, Roy's identity is can be written in a convenient form as

$$w_i = \frac{p_i q_i}{y} = \frac{\partial u^* / \partial \log r_i}{\sum_j \partial u^* / \partial \log r_j} = \frac{\partial \log c(u,p)}{\partial \log p_i}, \qquad (3.4.8)$$

where the last equality follows from rewriting (3.4.3).

One of the earliest and best practical examples of the use of these techniques is Samuelson's (1947-48) derivation of the utility function, u(q) from the specification of the linear expenditure system suggested earlier by Klein and Rubin (1947-48). Working (1943) had suggested that a useful form of Engel curve was given by expressing the budget share of good '*i*', (w_i), as a linear function of the logarithm of total expenditure as

$$w_i = \alpha_i + \beta_i \ln(y) \qquad (3.4.9)$$

For parameters, α and β generally functions of prices and this form was supported in later comparative tests by Leser (1963). From (3.4.8), the budget shares are the logarithmic derivatives of the cost function, so that (3.4.9) corresponds to differential equations of the form

$$\partial \ln c(u,p)/\partial \ln p_i = \alpha_i(p) + \beta_i(p) \ln c(u,p) \qquad (3.4.10)$$

which provides a general solution of the form

$$\ln c(u,p) = (1-u)\ln a(p) + u \ln b(p) \qquad (3.4.11a)$$

where

$$\alpha_i(p) = (a_i \ln b - b_i \ln a)/(\ln b - \ln a) \text{ and } \beta_i(p) = b_i/(\ln b - \ln a) \qquad (3.4.11b)$$

for $a_i = \partial \ln(a)/\partial \ln(p_i)$ and $b_i = \partial \ln(b)/\partial \ln(p_i)$

(3.4.11c)

The form (3.4.11a) gives the cost function as a utility-weighted geometric mean of the linear homogeneous functions, *a(p)* and *b(p)* representing the cost functions of the very poor (u = 0) and the very rich (u = 1) respectively. Such preferences have been called the PIGLOG class.[16] A full system of demand equations within the Working-Leser class can be generated by suitable choice of the functions *b*(*p*) and *a*(*p*). For example, if

$$\ln a(p) = \alpha_0 + \sum \alpha_i \ln p_i + 1/2 \sum_k \sum_m \gamma^*_{ij} \ln p_i \ln p_j \quad \text{3.4.12a)}$$

$$\ln b(p) = \ln a(p) + \beta_0 \prod p_j^{\beta_j} \quad (3.4.12\text{b})$$

we reach the Almost Ideal Demand System (AIDS) of Deaton and Muellbauer (1980), which is given by

$$w_i = \alpha_i + \beta_i \ln(y/P) + \sum_j \gamma_{ij} \ln p_j \quad (3.4.13\text{a})$$

where

$$\ln(P) = \alpha_0 + \sum \alpha_i \ln p_i + 1/2 \sum_i \sum_j \gamma_{ij} \ln p_i \ln p_j$$

(3.4.13b)

and $\gamma_{ij} = 1/2\left(\gamma^*_{ij} + \gamma^*_{ji}\right)$ (3.4.13c)

A variation of the above cost function is to replace the geometric mean given in (3.4.11a) by a mean of order 'ε' and it is given by

$$\ln c(u,p) = (1-u)\ln a(p)^{\varepsilon} + u \ln b(p)^{1/\varepsilon} \quad (3.4.14)$$

with Engel curves, $w_i = \alpha_i + \beta_i \ln(y)^{-\varepsilon}$ (3.4.15)

This is Muellbauer's PIGL class. Equation (3.4.15) is an equivalent Box-Cox form which has recently appeared in the literature as the 'Generalised Working model.[17]

The duality approach also provides a simple demonstration of the generic properties of demand functions which have played an important role in the testing of consumer rationality. The budget constraint implies immediately that the demand functions add-up (trivially) and they are homogeneous of degree zero in prices and total expenditure together (since the budget constraint is unaffected by proportional changes in 'p' and 'y'). Shephard's Lemma (3.4.6) together with the mild regularity conditions required for Young's Theorem implies that

$$\frac{\partial h_i}{\partial p_j} = \frac{\partial^2 c}{\partial p_j \, \partial p_i} = \frac{\partial^2 c}{\partial p_i \partial p_j} = \frac{\partial h_j}{\partial p_i}, \quad (3.4.16)$$

For s_{ij}, the Slutsky substitution term is $\partial h_i / \partial p_i$. The matrix of such terms, 'S', is symmetric. Furthermore, since c(u, p) is a concave function of 'p', 'S' must be negative semi-definite. (Note that the homogeneity of c(u, p) implies that 'p' lies in the null space of 'S'). Of course, 'S' is not directly observed, but it can be evaluated using (3.4.6); differentiating with respect to p_j gives the Slutsky equation.

$$s_{ij} = \partial q_i / \partial p_j + \partial q_i / \partial y (q_j) \quad (3.4.17)$$

Hence, to the extent that $\partial q_i / \partial p_j$ and $\partial q_i / \partial y$ can be estimated econometrically, symmetry and negative semi-definiteness can be checked.[18]

SEPARABILITY

The importance of separability lies in reducing the number of parameters involved in a demand model. The conventional approach in most of the empirical work is to work with some form of separability and bridge the gap between theory and empirical demand models. Sono (1960) and Leontief (1947) proposed the basic concept separability[19], since then several types of separability have been proposed in the literature. Strotz (1957, 1959) and Gorman (1959) developed two-stage budgeting : at the first stage, the consumer allocates his income to broad groups on the basis of group price indices and at the second stage allocated the group expenditure to its specific items on the basis of their prices.[20] This concept has found wide application in applied demand analysis. Some important forms of separability are presented below:

WEAK SEPARABILITY

Weak separability is the central concept for much of the analysis. A utility function is said to be weakly separable in grouping of commodities if the marginal rate of substitution between any two commodities within a group is independence of quantities of commodities consumed from other groups.

Let q^A be some sub-vector of the commodity vector q so that $q=(q^A, q^{\bar{A}})$ without loss of generality. q^A is then said to be weakly separable if the direct utility function takes the form

$$u = u\left(u_A\left(q^A\right), q^{\bar{A}}\right), \tag{3.5.1}$$

$u_A(q^A)$ is the sub-utility (or felicity) function associated with q^A. This equation is equivalent to the existence of a preference ordering over q^A alone; choices over the q^A bundles are consistent and independent of the vector $q^{\bar{A}}$. Generally, preferences as a whole are said to be separable if q can be partitioned into $(q^A, q^B, \ldots\ldots, q^N)$ such that

$$u = u\left(u_A\left(q^A\right), u_B\left(q^B\right), \ldots, u_N\left(q^N\right)\right). \tag{3.5.2}$$

Since 'u' is increasing in the sub-utility levels, it is immediately obvious that maximization of overall 'u' implies maximization of the sub-utilities subject to whatever is optimally spent on the groups. Hence, (3.5.1) implies the existence of the group demands

$$q_i^A = q_i^A\left(y^A, p^A\right), \tag{3.5.3}$$

where, $y^A = P^A q^A$ while (3.5.3) has the same implication for all groups.

Tests of these forms of separability can be based on the restrictions on the substitution matrix implied by (3.5.3). If 'i' and 'j' are two goods in distinct groups, then the condition[21]

$$s_{ij} = \mu_{GH} \frac{\partial q_i}{\partial y} \cdot \frac{\partial q_j}{\partial y}, \tag{3.5.4}$$

for some quantity μ_{GH} (independent of '*i*' and '*j*') is both necessary and sufficient for (3.5.2) to hold. Equation (3.5.4) implies that commodities '*i*' and '*j*' belong to two different groups, then their compensated cross-price derivatives are proportional to the product of their income derivatives, and the constant of proportionality which will vary with groups. It may also be noted that if any empirical demand system has compensated cross-price effects fulfilling the above property, then its utility function, if it exists, confirms to weak separability specification. Hence, Equation (3.5.4) can be used to test separability.

Subgroup demand functions are only part of what the applied econometrician need from separability. Just as important is the question of whether it is possible to justify demand functions for commodity composites in terms of total expenditures and also in composite price indices. The Hicks (1936) composite commodity theorem allows this at the given prices with the assumption that there are no relative price changes within subgroups. Since there is no way of guaranteeing this, nor often even of checking it, more general conditions are clearly desirable. In fact, the separable structure (3.5.2) may be sufficient in many circumstances. Write, u_A, u_B, etc. for the values of the felicity functions and $c_A(u^A, p^A)$ etc. for the subgroup cost functions corresponding to the direct subgroup utility functions, $u_A(q_A)$. Then the problem of choosing the group expenditure levels $(y_A, y_B .... y_N)$ can be written as

$$\max u = u(u_A, u_B, ..., u_N) \tag{3.5.5a}$$

$$\text{subject to } y = \sum_R c_R(u_R, p^R) \tag{3.5.5b}$$

Write

$$c_R\left(u_{R,} p^R\right) = c_R(u_R, \bar{p}^R)\left\{c_R\left(u_R, p^R\right) / c_R\left(u_R, \bar{p}^R\right)\right\} \cdot \tag{3.5.6}$$

for some fixed prices $\bar{p}^R$. For such a fixed vector, $c_R\left(u_R, \bar{p}^R\right)$ is a welfare indicator quantity index, while ratio

$c_R\left(u_R, p^R\right)/c_R\left(u_R, \overline{p}^R\right)$ is a true (sub) cost-of-living price index comparing p^R *and* $\overline{p}^R$ using u_R is a reference (see Pollak,1975).

One final issue related to separability is worth noting. As pointed out by Blackorby, Primont and Russell (1977), flexible functional forms do not in general remain flexible under the global imposition of separability restrictions. Hence, a specific functional form which offers a local second-order approximation to an arbitrary utility function may not be able to similarly approximate, say, an arbitrary additive utility function once its parameters are restricted to render it globally additive. For example, Blackorby et al. show that weak separability of the translog implies either strong separability or homothetic separability so that the translog cannot model non-homothetic weak separability. The possibility of imposing and testing restrictions locally (say, at the sample mean) remains, but this is less attractive since it is difficult to discriminate between properties of the data generation process and the approximating properties of the functional form.

STRONG SEPARABILITY OR BLOCK ADDITIVE UTILITY SPECIFICATION

A utility function is strongly separable in grouping commodities if the marginal rate of substitution between two commodities '*i*' and '*j*' from two different groups does not depend upon the quantity consumed of any other commodity which does not belong to either of the groups to which commodities '*i*' and '*j*' belong.

Strong separability[22] restricts (3.5.2) to the case where the overall function is additive i.e. for some monotonic increasing '*f*'[23]

$$u = f\left(\sum_R u_R\left(q^R\right)\right) \tag{3.5.7}$$

If each of the groups q^R contains a single good, preferences are said to be additive, or that wants are independent. We deal with this case for simplicity since all the additional features over weak separability occur between groups rather than within them. The central feature of additivity is that any combination of goods forms a separable set from any other, so that (4) must hold without the G, H labels on μ_{GH} i.e. for some μ and for all i, j in different groups ($i \neq j$ under additivity)

$$s_{ij} = \mu \frac{\partial q_i}{\partial y} \frac{\partial q_j}{\partial y} \tag{3.5.8}$$

Condition (3.5.8) implies that if commodities '*i*' and '*j*' belong to two distinct groups, then their compensated cross-price derivatives are proportional to the product of their income derivatives, and the constant of proportionality, the constant, μ is invariant among the groups.

The budget constraint (or homogeneity) can be used to complete this for all *i* and *j*; in elasticity terms,[24]

$$\eta_{ij} = \varphi \delta_{ij} \eta_{i0} - \eta_{i0} w_j \left(1 + \varphi \eta_{j0}\right) \tag{3.5.9}$$

For some scalar φ, (uncompensated) cross-price elasticity η_{ij}, and total expenditure elasticity (η_{i0}). This formula shows immediately the strengths and weaknesses of additivity. Apart from the data w_i, knowledge of the (*n*-1) independent η_{i0}'s together with the quantity φ (obtainable from knowledge of one single price elasticity) is sufficient to determine the whole (n × n) array of price elasticities. Additivity can therefore be used to estimate price elasticities on data with little or no relative price variation, e.g. on cross-section, on short-time series, or in centrally planned economies where relative prices are only infrequently altered.[25]

PEARCE SEPARABILITY

A utility function is Pearce separable in grouping commodities if the marginal rate of substitution between any two commodities belonging to the same group is independent of the consumption of any other commodity belongs to inside or outside of that group. The underlying utility function is the following form:

$$u(q) = f\left\{ u^{A}\left[f^{1}\left(q^{1}\right) + f^{2}\left(q^{1}\right) \ldots \frac{f_{n1}^{1}\left(q^{1}\right)}{n} \right] \right.$$

$$u^{B}\left[f_{1}^{2}\left(q^{2}\right) + f_{2}^{2}\left(q^{2}\right) \ldots f_{n2}^{2}\left(q^{2}\right) \right]$$

$$\left. u^{N}\left[f_{i}^{n}\left(q^{n}\right) + f_{2}^{n}\left(q^{n}\right) \ldots f_{n3}^{n}\left(q^{n}\right) \right] \right\}. \tag{3.5.10}$$

The restrictions on the compensated cross-price effects in this case differ from weak separability only in that (3.5.2) holds also for the case, $r = s$, in which the commodities 'i' and 'j' come from the same group.

ADDITIVE UTILITY FUNCTION

We now examine the necessary modifications of the foregoing results obtained in the special case where the direct utility function $u = u\ (q)$ is additive that is when

$$u = u\left(q_{1}, \ldots, q_{n}\right) = \sum_{i=1}^{n} u^{i}\left(q_{i}\right) \tag{3.6.1}$$

each $u^{i}(q_{i})$ being a function of only the corresponding q_{i} (or independent of q_{j}). We refer to this feature as direct additivity (or 'want-independence' or 'preference independence').[26] The implications of additivity can be examined for the alternative representations of the demand functions developed in Sections 2.and 3.

The key to additivity is the diagonality of the second derivative matrix 'U'. If u(q) is directly additive, then the marginal utility of any good varies with the quantity of that good alone, so $u_{ij} = 0\ (i \neq j;\ i, j = 1,2,\ldots\ldots,n\ )$; thus 'U' is diagonal.

Then, U^{-1} is also diagonal; specifically

$$u^{ij} = \begin{cases} u_{ii}^{-1} & \text{if } i = j \\ \\ 0 & \text{if } i \neq j \end{cases} \tag{3.6.2}$$

Since $H^{**} = \phi\, \hat{w}^{-1} \hat{\mu}$ in any case, under direct additivity we have

$$H^{**} = \hat{w}^{-1} (\phi\, \hat{\mu}) = \phi\, \hat{w}^{-1}\, \hat{w}\, \hat{\eta} \; = \phi\, \hat{\eta} \qquad (3.6.3a)$$

where $\hat{\mu}$ is the diagonal matrix of marginal budget shares. Alternatively, this condition implies,

$$\eta_{ij}^{**} = \begin{cases} \phi\, \eta_i & \text{if } i = j \\ 0 & \text{if } i \neq j \end{cases} . \qquad (3.6.3b)$$

Since $H^{*} = H^{**} - \phi \eta\, w' \hat{\eta}$ in any case, under direct additivity we have

$$H^{*} = \phi\, \hat{\eta} - \phi\, \eta\, w'\, \hat{\eta} = \phi\, \hat{\eta}\, (I - \iota\, w'\, \hat{\eta}) \qquad (3.6.4a)$$

Alternatively, this condition implies,

$$\eta_{ij}^{*} = \begin{cases} \phi\, \eta_i\, (1 - w_i \eta_i) & \text{if } i = j \\ -\phi\, \eta_i\, n_j\, w_j & \text{if } i \neq j \end{cases} . \qquad (3.6.4b)$$

Since $Q_p^{**} = \hat{q}\, H^{**}\, \hat{p}^{-1}$ in any case, under direct additivity we have

$$Q_p^{**} = \hat{q}\, \phi\, \hat{\eta}\, \hat{p}^{-1} = \phi\, y\, \hat{p}^{-1}\, \hat{q}_y . \qquad (3.6.5a)$$

Alternatively, this condition implies,

$$\left(\frac{\partial q_i}{\partial p_j}\right)^{**} = \begin{cases} \phi\, y\, p_i^{-1} \left(\dfrac{\partial q_i}{\partial y}\right) & \text{if } i = j \\ 0 & \text{if } i \neq j \end{cases} \qquad (3.6.5b)$$

Since $Q_p^* = Q_p^{**} - \phi\, y\, q_y\, q_y'$ in any case, under direct additivity we have[27]

$$Q_p^* = \phi\, y\, \hat{p}^{-1}\, \hat{q}_y - \phi\, y q_y\, q_y' = \phi\, y\left(\hat{p}^{-1}\, \hat{q}_y - q_y\, q_y'\right)$$

$$= \phi\, y\, \hat{q}_y\left(\hat{p}^{-1} - \iota\, q_y'\right). \tag{3.6.6a}$$

Alternatively, this condition implies,

$$\left(\frac{\partial q_i}{\partial p_j}\right)^* = \begin{cases} \phi\, y\left(\dfrac{\partial q_i}{\partial y}\right)\left[p_i^{-1} - \left(\dfrac{\partial q_i}{\partial y}\right)\right] & \text{if } i = j \\ -\phi\, y\left(\dfrac{\partial q_i}{\partial y}\right)\left(\dfrac{\partial q_j}{\partial y}\right) & \text{if } i \neq j \end{cases} \tag{3.6.6b}$$

Since $H = H^* - \eta\, w'$ in any case, under direct additivity we have[28]

$$H = \phi\hat{\eta}\left(I - \iota\, w'\hat{\eta}\right) - \eta w' = \phi\hat{\eta} - \eta\, w'\left(I + \phi\hat{\eta}\right) \tag{3.6.7a}$$

Alternatively, this condition implies,

$$\eta_{ij} = \begin{cases} \phi\eta_i - \eta_i\, w_i\left(1 + \phi\, \eta_i\right) & \text{if } i = j \\ -\eta_i\, w_j\left(1 + \phi\, \mu_j\right) & \text{if } i \neq j \end{cases} \tag{3.6.7b}$$

Finally, since $Q_p = Q_p^* - q_y\, q'$ in any case, under direct additivity we have

$$Q_p = \phi\, y\hat{q}_y\left(\hat{p}^{-1} - \iota\, q_y'\right) - q_y q'$$

$$= \phi\, y\, \hat{q}_y\, \hat{p}^{-1} - q_y\left(q + \phi\, y q_y\right)' \tag{3.6.8a}$$

Alternatively, this condition implies,

$$\left(\frac{\partial q_i}{\partial p_j}\right) = \begin{cases} \phi\, y \left(\frac{\partial q_i}{\partial y}\right) p_i^{-1} - \left(\frac{\partial q_i}{\partial y}\right)\left[q_i + \phi\, y \left(\frac{\partial q_i}{\partial y}\right)\right] & \text{if } i = j \\ -\left(\frac{\partial q_i}{\partial y}\right)\left[q_j + \phi\, y \left(\frac{\partial q_j}{\partial y}\right)\right] & \text{if } i \neq j \end{cases} \tag{3.6.8b}$$

In summary, under any of the representations, the force of the additivity assumption is to reduce the number of free 'coefficients'. The price slope matrices Q_p, Q^*_p, and Q^{**}_p are expressible in terms of the income slope vector, q_y and the scalar income flexibility, ϕ. The price elasticity matrices H, H^* and H^{**} are expressible in terms of the income elasticity vector 'η' and 'ϕ'. Thus, a directly additive utility function would lead to substantial economies in parameterising a complete set of demand functions, beyond those obtained from the general utility function.

As noted by Houthakker (1960, p.248), direct additivity rules out the possibility of specific substitution effects with all $u_{ij} = 0$ for $i \neq j$; η_{ij}^{**} and $\left(\partial q_i/\partial p_j\right)^{**}$ are zero for $i \neq j$. Direct additivity rules out inferior goods with all η_{i0} and $\partial q_i/\partial y$ are positive. Further, direct additivity rules out the possibility of complementary goods with all η_{ij}^{*} and $\left(\partial q_i/\partial p_j\right)^{*}$ are positive for $i \neq j$.[29] In the light of these restrictions; direct additivity may be a plausible specification when goods are defined broadly, but not when one works with a finer classification of consumer expenditures. In the latter case, specific substitution effects, complementarities and inferiorities may well be present.

INDIRECT ADDITIVITY

The indirect utility function in normalized prices, $u^*(p/y)$ is said to be additive if it is a sum of 'n' functions, each involving only one ratio (p_i/y) which can be written as

$$u^*(p/y) = u^*(p_1/y) + u^*(p_2/y) + \dots\dots\dots + u^*(p_n/y) \quad (3.6.9)$$

The indirect additivity assumption implies strong restrictions on consumer behaviour namely that the cross-price elasticities are identical for all commodities and only depend on the commodity whose price has changed.[30]

AGGREGATION

The theory of consumer behaviour discussed so far deals with an individual consumer while data are generally available in aggregate form for a group of consumers. If the demand functions of individual consumers (micro demand functions) satisfy the theoretical restrictions, will these theoretical restrictions be carried to the demand function of a group of consumers (macro demand functions) that expresses the average demand for a commodity of the group as a function of prices and average income of the group? Is the functional form of the 'macro demand equation' exactly the same as micro demand function? These are important questions, which have to be addressed in the aggregation problem.

Generally, three approaches are currently popular for establishing correspondence between the theory of consumer behaviour and macro demand function.[31] The most commonly used approach in applied demand analysis is to ignore the problem altogether and assume that the macro demand functions confirm to the theory of consumer behaviour. The argument in favour of this approach can be seen in the observation made by Hicks (1956, pp.55): the preferences hypothesis only acquires a prima facie plausibility when it is applied to statistical average. To assume that the representative consumer acts like an ideal consumer is a hypothesis needs worth testing

In the second approach, the search is for suitable functional form such that the micro demand functions represented by a functional form would yield a macro demand function of exactly the same functional form as the micro demand functions and also satisfying all of its theoretical restrictions.

It has been shown that perfect aggregation is possible if the demand functions of all individual consumers are linear functions of total expenditure and the marginal propensity to spend on any commodity is the same for all individual consumers. That is the individual demand function for the ith commodity must of the form:

$$q_i^h = a_{0i}^h(p) + a_{1i}(p)y^h \qquad h = 1,2,\ldots,m \qquad (3.7.1)$$

Aggregating (3.6.1) over the 'm' consumers and dividing it by mean would give the macro function as:

$$\bar{q}_i = a_{0i}(p) + a_{1i}(p)\,\bar{y} \qquad (3.7.2)$$

If (3.7.1) satisfies all the theoretical restrictions, (3.7.2) will also satisfies these theoretical restrictions. It can be checked that the following demand system satisfies perfect aggregation.

$$p_i q_i^h = p_i c_i^h + b_i\left(y^h - \sum_j p_j c_j^h\right) \qquad (\text{h} = 1, 2, 3, \ldots, \text{m}) \qquad (3.7.3)$$

The macro demand function is of the form

$$p_i \bar{q}_j = p_i c_i + b_i\left(\bar{y} - \sum_j p_j c_j\right) \qquad (3.7.4)$$

The restriction that the demand functions are linear and the marginal propensity to spend on a commodity must be the same for all individual consumers is unlikely to be met in practice. In a recent approach pioneered by Muellbauer (1975, 1976), it has been shown that it is possible to aggregate non-linear Engel curves provided aggregate demand is expressed as a function of representative expenditure rather than mean expenditure. The representative expenditure depends on both the expenditure distribution as well as prices. Muellbauer has shown that satisfactory aggregation is possible provided the individual cost functions are of the form:

$$c(p,u^h) = b_0^h\left[b_1(p)^\alpha\left(1-u^h\right) + b_2(p)^\alpha u^h\right]^{1/\alpha} \qquad (3.7.5)$$

where α and b_0^h are the parameters, while the cost function of the representative individual is given by

$$c(p,u_0)=\left[\,b_1(p)^{\alpha}(1-u_0)+b_2(p)^{\alpha}\,u_0\right]^{1/\alpha} \tag{3.7.6}$$

and the special case represented by equations (3.7.5) and (3.7.6) is known as *price independent generalized linearity* (PIGL).When 'α' tends to zero, these cost function- (3.7.5) and (3.7.6) will approach

$$\ln c(p,u^h)=\ln b_0^h+(1-u^h)\ln b_1(p)+u^h\ln b_2(p) \tag{3.7.7}$$

$$\ln c(p,u_0)=(1-u_0)\ln b_1(p)+u_0\ln b_2(p) \tag{3.7.8}$$

for the individual and representative individual respectively. The logarithmic form (3.7.8) is very popular and known as *price independent generalized log-linear* (PIGLOG) cost function. The demand equations for individual and representative individual whose cost functions are of the PIGLOG can be derived using Shephard's lemma as

$$w_i^h=a_{0i}(p)+a_{1j}(p)\ln\left(y^h/b_0^h\right) \qquad (i=1,2,3......,n) \tag{3.7.9}$$

where w_i is the budget share of *ith* item for the *hth* individual and for the representative individual

$$\overline{w}_i=a_{0i}(p)+a_{1j}(p)\ln(y_0) \tag{3.6.10}$$

$$\text{where}\quad \overline{w}_i=\frac{\sum_h p_i q_i^h}{\sum_h y_h}\quad \textit{and}\quad \ln y_0=\frac{\sum_h y^h\ln\left(y^h/b_0^h\right)}{\sum_h y^h}$$

Note that in (3.7.10), *ln* (y_0) is the representative expenditure. It is homogenous of degree unity in the individual's income. Moreover, an equi-proportional change in incomes of all individuals leads to a proportionate change in arithmetic mean income, $\overline{y}$. Thus, if the distribution of total expenditures remains unchanged there exist a proportional relationship between representative expenditure and mean expenditure.

Hence, we can define an aggregate parameter k such that $y_0 = \kappa\,\bar{y}$ and (3.7.10) can be rewritten as:

$$\bar{w}_i = a_{0i}(p) + a_{1i}(p)\ln(\kappa\,\bar{y}) \qquad (3.6.11)$$

The above macro demand function can be estimated from grouped data. The simplicity will be lost and estimation procedure becomes intricate if the assumption of unchanged expenditure distribution is relaxed. However, some simplifications are possible if the income distribution can be approximated by the well known form such as log-normal distribution.[32]

CONCLUSION

The general restrictions are quite useful for the demand analyst in estimating demand systems as well as judging the consistency of consumption behaviour of individuals. In a system of '*n*' demand functions, the number of parameters to be estimated is '*n*' income responses and n^2 price responses. However, if the estimated parameters are to be consistent with theory, there will be considerable reduction of free parameters. The aggregation property gives (n+1) restrictions, homogeneity '*n*' restrictions, symmetry n (n-1)/2 restrictions and finally negativity '*n*' inequality restrictions. Thus, there will be only (n+1) (n+2)/2 independent responses which are to be estimated in a system of '*n*' demand functions.

Even though the introduction of theoretical restrictions reduce the number of parameters of demand equations, severe limitations still stem from the large number of parameters contained in these systems. The assumptions of additivity Houthakker, (1960), and separability (Sono, 1960 & Leontief, 1947) provide a means of alleviating these limitations. The additive utility function, in spite of its restrictive consequences, has been very popular, particularly for broad commodity groups, because of its simplicity of specification and estimations as well as less demanding data requirements. Further restrictions on the additive utility functions with Frisch's want independence assumption enables the estimation of a complete set of direct and cross-price elasticities from income elasticities, expenditure weights, and money flexibility (Frisch, 1959). The money flexibility coefficient can be computed if the direct price elasticity for a want-independent commodity or group of commodities is reliably known. The assumption of separability is more popular in complete demand systems that encompass a large number of commodities.

NOTES

1. The neoclassical economists made different assumptions on the measurability of utility (cardinal vs ordinal)and functional forms (additivity vs non- additivity). For a lucid exposition, see Stigler (1954).
2. See Uzawa (1971)
3. The revealed preference approach has been an intensive area of study in the recent past. It directly postulates rationality in terms of observed behaviour of the consumer and brings out properties of demand functions like homogeneity, symmetry and negative semi-definiteness of the substitution matrix.
4. The Lagrange multiplier is often called the shadow price or marginal utility of income.
5. Fulfilment of symmetry and negative-definiteness of the substitution matrix by the demand equations ensures the convexity of the underlying indifference surface. In contract to this, these conditions also enable us to integrate the demand functions into an indifference surface (integrability conditions). For a rigorous treatment of this condition, see Wold and Jureen (1953) and Hurwicz (1971).
6. Our terminology follows that of Barten (1966) and Theil (1967). Houthakker (1960) uses the term 'income flexibility' refer to $\lambda_y^{-1} \lambda = \phi y$. Frisch (1959) uses the term 'income flexibility' to refer our term $\eta_{\lambda y}$.
7. See Frisch (1959, pp.184) who introduces this type of responses to price in terms of elasticities.
8. A parallel interpretation in terms of maintaining a given marginal utility of income may be made for the deflated price terms. For a brief discussion of deflation of the kind being considered here and in the sequel, see Theil (1964, pp.77-83); for more detailed treatments, see Theil (1967, Chapter-7) and Kloek (1966, chapter- 5), and for related material Rajaoja (1958, Chapter-3).
9. For a concise proof, see Barten (1966, p.22).
10. See Stone (1953, p.277) utilize the formulation (3.3.27b); Barten (1964) utilizes the formulation (3.3.27c).
11. For details Thomas (1987), Chapter-2, pp.50.
12. For proofs and further discussions see Mc Fadden (1978), Diewert (1974, 1980) or, less rigorously, Deaton and Muellbauer (1980a).

13. See Shephard (1953) for the details.
14. See McFadden (1978) and Diewert (1974, 1980).
15. See Hurwicz and Uzawa (1971) for details.
16. See Muellbauer (1976)
17. See Tranvan Hao, Ironmonger and Manning (1983) and Tranvan Hao (1983).
18. See Griliches and Intriligator (1986, pp.1772-76).
19. See Geary and Moroshima (1973)
20. See de Janvry et al. (1972); George and King (1971)and Radhakrishna and Murty (1980)
21. Byron (1968), Jorgenson and Lau (1975) and Pudney (1981b) have used essentially this technique to find separability patterns between goods within a single period.
22. The two-stage budgeting for small changes in prices and income is consistent only if the utility function confirms to strong separability specification (Gorman, 1959).
23. Goldman and Uzawa (1964) have show that the underlying utility function is of the form (3.5.7).
24. The relationship presented in (3.5.9) is suggested by Frisch (1959) and Houthakker (1960).
25. Another important use of separability in general and of additivity in particular is as a vehicle for the structuring and interpretation of preference patterns. For example, in the 'characteristics' model of consumer behaviour pioneered by Gorman (1956, 1980), Stone (1956) and Lancaster (1966), and recently estimated by Pudney (1981a), it is a transformation of the goods which generates utility, and it may be quite plausible to assume that preferences are separable or even additive in the transformed characteristics (food, shelter, mate, etc.) rather than in the market goods which have no direct role in satisfying wants.
26. Frisch (1959) and Houthakkar (1960) have demonstrated that direct additivity have important implications for the complete set of demand functions.
27. See Houthakkar (1960, pp.248)
28. See Frisch (1959, pp.186-87)
29. See Theil (1967)
30. See Thomas (1987, pp.58-60)
31. For a lucid exposition of various approaches to the aggregation problem, see Deaton and Muellbauer (1980, pp. 148-58) and also Thomas (1987, pp. 66-70).
32. Klein (1975, pp. 359-61) has shown that the macro savings function derived by aggregating micro savings functions will include an inequality parameter apart from the aggregate income. Specifying the individual saving function as $(s^k/y^k) = a_0 + a_1 \log y^k$ and assuming that log normal distribution for y^k, Klein obtains the macro savings function as $(\overline{s}/\overline{y}) = a_0 + a_1[(\sigma^2/2) + \log \overline{y}]$ where δ is the standard deviation of log (y).

4

DIFFERENT SPECIFICATIONS OF COMPLETE DEMAND SYSTEM

INTRODUCTION

Throughout the Eighteenth and Nineteenth centuries the empirical approach to consumer behaviour had made little progress in the measurement of demand functions despite its early and promising beginning. Ernst Engel who formulated the famous empirical law of food consumption in 1857 made an outstanding contribution. Since then numerous empirical studies have been undertaken to test various theoretical postulates of consumer behaviour and to quantify the extent of response of the consumers to changes in economic factors such as income, prices, stock of wealth and so on, and also to changes in other socio-demographic factors such as household size and composition, occupation of household, social and regional affiliation of the household etc.

By 1939, most of the strengths and weaknesses of what we may call the classical demand analysis had been proved and most of the techniques still in use had been discovered. The classical approach was the application of variations in least-squares single-equation fittings to both time-series and cross-section data of the market models based as far as possible on the theoretical results of Slutsky (1915) and Allen and Hicks (1934). Much of this work, together with a great deal of empirical analysis was done by Schultz (1938). Since then there have been a number of important developments on both the theoretical and empirical analysis of demand. Wold (1952) and Stone (1953) have consolidated the theoretical and empirical work on static demand analysis in the first half of twentieth century. Samuelson (1938) introduced the theory of revealed preference. Houthakker (1950) and Samuelson (1950) worked on the derivation of conditions under which demand functions may lead back to preference mapping, i.e., the consistency or integrability problem. On the empirical side, the work of Stone (1953) on the treatment of the special problems associated with durables and the application of the more sophisticated computational and econometric techniques, the work of Prais and Houthakker (1955) on the analysis of family budgets, and the work of Houthakker and Taylor (1966) on dealing with a wider range of commodities and upgrading of the Stone's methodology were noteworthy.

Since 1960s, there has been a growing body of literature on Complete Demand System (CDS), which involves the simultaneous estimation of a set of demand equation for all consumer items purchased by consumers. Interest in complete demand system arises out of both theoretical and practical reasons. Stone (1954b), Houthakker (1960) and Theil (1965) have laid the foundation for this approach. With the increasing availability of extensive data for a number of commodities of consumer expenditure for many years as well as increasing access to better computing facilities, many researchers now engaged in the estimation of complete demand system (CDS). By now, a variety of complete demand systems have been proposed for econometric use. All of them pay strong allegiance to neoclassical demand theory and most of them introduce theoretical restrictions as well as some from of separability in order to simplify the model and reduce the number of parameter. In this chapter, an attempt has been made to provide the specifications and features of some the most popular demand systems widely used in the empirical analysis of the theory of consumer behaviour.

The plan of exposition of the present chapter is as follows: Section 1 is the introduction. Section 2 provides a comparative analysis of single demand equations versus system of demand equations to know the advantage of later over the former. Section 3 examines the specifications and features of some the important utility based demand systems widely used in empirical analysis. The characteristics of some of the non-utility based demand system are presented in Section 4. Section 5 deals with a class of non-additive flexible models which claims dual purpose of providing better description of observed behaviour and allows empirical verification of the postulates of consumer theory. Section 6 provides the specifications of dynamic linear and quadratic demand systems basically meant for durable goods. We end on the concluding note of this chapter in Section 7.

SINGLE DEMAND EQUATIONS VERSUS SYSTEM OF DEMAND EQUATIONS

There are two distinct approaches to the estimation of demand equations. The first and original approach concentrates on the demand for a particular commodity or commodity groups. The second approach developed almost entirely since the 1960s, involves the simultaneous estimation of complete demand systems containing demand equation for every commodity or commodity group purchased by consumers.

The neoclassical static theory of consumer behavior tells us that the utility maximizing consumer's demand for any community is dependent on the prices of all commodities and his total expenditure (a proxy variable for income) on these commodities, that is

$$q_i = q_i\,(p_1, p_2, \ldots, p_n, y) \qquad (i = 1,2,3\ldots,n) \qquad (4.2.1)$$

where q_i is the quantity demanded, p_i is its price and 'y' is the total expenditure.

Time-series data on movements of quantity purchased in response to variation in prices and income provide the information suitable for estimating the commodity demand functions (Allen and Bowley, 1935; Schultz, 1938; Wold and

Jureen, 1953; Stone, 1954 and Houthakker, 1965). Consumer theory unfortunately tells us nothing about the precise functional form of equation (4.2.1). But it will depend on consumer's preferences, which is little known a priori. Another difficulty is that all the prices appear in the demand equation are not very useful from empirical point of view. Since the sample size (or the data set) is always limited and the degrees of freedom problem often preclude the use of many explanatory variables. So it is not possible to include all prices in the demand equation as specified in (4.2.1).

Therefore, the functional forms for the demand equation which usually simplify the estimation process are selected and the explanatory price variables are limited to own-price, price of close substitutes and complements and/or the general price level. Changes in taste are then allowed for the inclusion of a time trend as an additional variable. The popular specification of single demand equations for commodity '*i*' assuming an additive stochastic disturbance term for the linear form[1] and a multiplicative disturbance term for the double-logarithmic form[2] can be written as

$$q_i = \alpha_0 + \alpha_1 p_i + \alpha_2 p_j + \alpha_3 P + \alpha_4 y + \alpha_5 t + u_i \tag{4.2.2}$$

$$q_i = \alpha_0 \, p_i^{\alpha_1} \, p_j^{\varepsilon_2} \, P^{\alpha_3} \, y^{\alpha_4} \, e^{\alpha_5 t + u_i} \tag{4.2.3}$$

and another specification of demand function is the following semi-logarithmic demand function (Prais and Houthakker, 1955)[3] which is not so popular in empirical analysis is

$$q_i = \alpha_0 + \alpha_1 \ln(p_i) + \alpha_2 \ln(p_j) + \alpha_3 P + \alpha_4 \ln(y) + u_i \tag{4.2.4}$$

where p_j is the price of the substitutes or complements, '*P*' is the index of general price level and '*t*' is the time. Equation (4.2.2) has the obvious advantage being linear while equation (4.2.3) has the additional advantage that its parameters are the elasticities of quantity demanded with respect to the prices and income[4].

There is also a difficulty over interpretation of the variables, '*y*' which has been so far referred to as total expenditure. Many studies using time series consider consumer's disposable income (instead of total expenditure) as the explanatory variable so that the two variables viz. disposable income and total expenditure are identical in the sense that saving is zero. If a considerable proportion of the current income is not devoted to current expenditure but is saved, then this leads to consider the consumer as an inter-temporal utility maximizer. If this is the case, current demand for any commodity is theoretically dependent on all current and future prices and on some 'total resource' type variable.

In so far as consumer theory provides restrictions in the form of individual demand equations such as (4.2.2) and (4.2.3), the researcher faces the choice of either (i) accepting the restrictions and imposing them prior to estimation or (ii) estimating the equations in their absence and then testing for their validity. In the single demand equation context, homogeneity is the strongest restriction. Imposing homogeneity (before estimation) implies that the demand is a function of relative prices and real total expenditure. Hence, replacing equation such as (4.2.2) and (4.2.3) by

$$q_i = \alpha_0 + \alpha_1\left(\frac{p_i}{P}\right) + \alpha_2\left(\frac{p_j}{P}\right) + \alpha_3\left(\frac{y}{P}\right) + \alpha_3 t + u_i \qquad (4.2.5)$$

$$\text{and } q_i = \alpha_0\left(\frac{p_i}{P}\right)^{\alpha_1}\left(\frac{p_j}{P}\right)^{\alpha_2}\left(\frac{y}{P}\right)^{\alpha_4} e^{\alpha_5 t + u_i} \qquad (4.2.6)$$

Now that for the logarithmic formulation (4.2.3), imposing homogeneity is implied imposing the restriction $\alpha_1 + \alpha_2 + \alpha_3 + \alpha_4 = 0$. Alternatively if (4.2.2) and (4.2.3) are estimated in unrestricted form, then homogeneity can be easily tested using (4.2.3). Since given homogeneity, the sum of the elasticities in this equation equal to zero. If this sum is significantly different from zero, then homogeneity is rejected. The most popular procedure is to work in terms of relative prices and income. This has the advantage of increasing the degrees of freedom by reducing the number of price variables and also eliminates the problem of multicollinearity. But the standard procedure of excluding all prices except those of substitutes and complements is theoretically unacceptable since the cross substitution effects of changes in the prices of unrelated goods may justifiably be assumed to be very small but their income effect is not small.

Finally, attention is hardly ever paid to the restriction that demand equation should be such that $p_i q_i < y$. For example, the logarithmic formulation (4.2.3) can normally hold over a restricted range of 'y'. This is because for luxury goods equation (4.2.3) implies that there is always some sufficiently high value of 'y' for which $p_i q_i > y$. Similarly, for necessities, there is always being some sufficiently low value of 'y' which makes $p_i q_i < y$. But either the linear formulation (4.2.2) or the logarithmic formulation (4.2.3) when used for all commodities in a demand system can satisfy all the restrictions implied by consumer theory.

The second approach to the estimation of system of demand equations[5] covering all current expenditure made by the consumer has drawn the attention of the researchers in early 1970s. This approach enables us to use various single equation and cross equation restrictions as implied by the theory of consumer behaviour in the formulation as well as estimation of demand systems because most of the theoretical restrictions on the demand equations are cross equation restrictions. An econometric study of the system of demand equations would estimate the complete system for a single household or group of households. A stochastic term is introduced in each equation and the budget constraint is added to the system. So the system consists of the $(n+1)$ equations,

$$q_i = q_i\left(p_1, p_2, \ldots, y, u_i\right) \qquad (i = 1, 2, \ldots, n) \tag{4.2.7}$$

where $\Sigma p_i q_i = y$, the quantities of each of the commodities $\left(q_1, q_2, \ldots, q_n\right)$ are treated as endogenous variables, while their prices $\left(p_1, p_2, \ldots, p_n\right)$ and income of the consumer 'y' are treated as exogenous variables. The estimation of complete demand system is important in identifying the interdependence among the goods, specifically the effects of changes in prices of certain goods on the demand for other goods.

The complete demand systems[6] that have been proposed so far may be broadly grouped into three categories: (a) models based on additivity or 'want independence' assumption, (b) a priori models or non-utility based models and (c) 'non-additive' or 'flexible' models. The chronological development of different complete demand systems also followed roughly the above order of classification. Stone's Linear Expenditure System and its variants and Houthakker's Addilog systems belong to the first category. These models are primarily meant as improvements of Engel curves and partial demand relations. They are also forerunners of using preference theory for describing consumer behaviour.

The class of a priori models, pioneered by Barten, Byron and Theil, emerged soon after as competing models under the banner of 'non-utility based models' and aimed at testing the neo-classical postulates of consumer theory. In reaction to the criticisms of additive models, the class of 'non-additive' models has come into existence. This class of flexible models claims dual purpose provides better description of observed behaviour vis-a-vis restrictive or additive models and allows empirical verification of consumer theory. The classification of complete demand systems is as follows:[7](i) *Additive Models*-Linear Expenditure System (Stone, 1954) and its variants; Hierarchic Linear Expenditure System (Stone, 1954 and Deaton, 1975); Addilog Demand System (Houthakker,1960); Double-log Demand System (Theil,1965); and Dynamic Linear Expenditure System (Pollack, 1970 and Philps, 1973) (ii) *Non-utility based models (a priori models)*:-Rotterdam Demand Systems (Theil, 1965 and Barten, 1968); Linear Demand System (Biron, 1967 & 1968) and Quadratic Expenditure Models (Howe, 1975 and Pollack and Wales, 1978) (iii) *Non-additive flexible models*:-Nasse Expenditure System (Stone, 1954 and, Nasse, 1970); Translog Demand System (Christen et. al., 1975) and Almost Ideal Demand System (Deaton and Muelbauer, 1980).

ADDITIVE DEMAND SYSTEMS

Even though the introduction of theoretical restrictions reduce the number of parameters of a system of demand equations, severe limitations still stem from the large number of parameters contained in these demand systems. The assumptions of additivity (Pigou, 1910; Houthakker, 1960) provide a means of alleviating these limitations. The additive utility function, in spite of its restrictive consequences, has been very popular, particularly for broad commodity groups, because of its simplicity of specification and estimations as well as less demanding data requirements. Further restrictions on the additive utility functions with Frisch's want independence assumption enables the estimation of a complete set of direct and cross-price elasticities from income elasticities, expenditure weights, and money flexibility (Frisch, 1959). The money flexibility coefficient can be computed if the direct price elasticity for a want-independent commodity or group of commodities is reliably known.

LINEAR EXPENDITURE SYSTEM (LES)

Stone (1954) has developed a popular demand system known as the linear expenditure system (LES), which has wide range of applications in applied demand analysis. He has derived a set of linear demand equations maximizing the Stone-Geary utility function (first proposed by Klein and Rubin, 1947-48) subject to the budget constraint. He derived the linear demand equations by imposing the general restrictions and the particular restriction of additivity. The LES in its well known form is written as:[8]

$$\hat{p}q = \hat{p}\gamma + \beta\left(y - p'\gamma\right) \qquad (4.3.1a)$$

Alternatively (4.3.1a) implies

$$p_i q_i = p_i \gamma_i + \beta_i \left(y - \sum_{j=1}^{n} p_j \gamma_j \right) \quad (i = 1, 2, 3 \ldots n) \qquad (4.3.1b)$$

and $$q_i(y,p) = \gamma_i + (\beta_i / p_i)\left(y - \sum_{j=1}^{n} p_j\gamma_j\right) \quad (i = 1, 2, 3 \ldots n)$$

(4.3.1c)

where $0 < \beta_i < 1; \Sigma\, \beta_i = 1$ and $(y - p'\gamma) > 0$; and $\hat{p}$ is the diagonal matrix of prices; q is the vector of quantities demanded; γ is the vector of 'necessity' or 'committed quantities'[9] which the consumer buys first, and his residual money income, $(y - p'\gamma)$ otherwise known as 'supernumerary' or 'uncommitted' income is then spent in fixed proportions 'β_i' on *i*th good. This interpretation, though often useful, can be over-restrictive. There is no reason to expect the elements of 'γ' always to be positive and in some cases 'γ' is a function of price. The parameter 'β ' is the vector marginal budget shares (MBS).

This system satisfies the aggregation, symmetry and homogeneity restrictions. It can be seen that equations (4.3.1c) satisfies the homogeneity restriction and the adding-up restriction, if $\Sigma\beta_i = 1$. The substitution matrix would be negative semi-definite, if ($0 < \beta_i < 1$) for all '*i*', and, $\left(y - \sum_{j=1}^{n} p_j\gamma_j\right) > 0$ which in turn rules out the existence of inferior and complementary commodities. The system yields linear Engel curves. The model is also consistent with respect to aggregation over individuals provided we assume an identical 'β' vector for all consumers. The vector, however, can vary across consumer. The consistency with respect to aggregation over commodities requires the use of item specific 'γ' vector as weight for computing group price indices.

The direct utility function underlying the linear expenditure system is the Stone-Geary utility function which assumes that utilities are additive and specified as:

$$u(q) = \prod_{i=1}^{n} (q_i - \gamma_i)^{\beta_i} = \sum \beta_i \log(q_i - \gamma_i) \quad (4.3.2)$$

Maximization of (4.3.2) subject to budget constraint, y = $\Sigma p_i q_i$, yields the Marshallian demand functions i.e. the quantity equation (4.3.1c) in which q_i is a function of prices and income. Substituting the quantity equation of (4.3.1c) into (4.3.2) and simplifying it, generates the indirect utility function for LES as

$$u^*(y, p) = \left(y - \sum_j p_j \gamma_j\right) \Big/ \left(\beta_0 \prod_k p_k^{\beta_k}\right) \qquad (4.3.3)$$

where $\beta_0 = \prod_k \beta_k^{\beta_k}$. The indirect utility function in (4.3.3) in line with the ordinary demand function is also homogenous of degree zero in prices and income. Using the Roy's identity, the same set of demand functions (4.3.1b) can be derived from this indirect utility function. The utility function (4.3.2) is non-additive. However, if for all '*i*', the utility function (4.3.2) belongs to the class of homothetic (Bergson family) functions, then (4.3.3) reduces to an additive form

$$u^*(y, p) = \prod_k (y/p_k)^{\beta_k/\beta_0} \qquad (4.3.4)$$

It is noted that both direct and indirect utility functions will be additive only in the case of homothetic utility function. As per the duality approach, the indirect utility function (4.3.3) can also be alternatively represented by an interrelated function known as the cost (or expenditure) function which is

$$c(u, p) = \sum_j p_j \gamma_j + u\, \beta_0 \prod_k p_k^{\beta_k} \qquad (4.3.5)$$

The Hicksian compensatory demand functions can be derived from (4.3.5) using Shephrd's lemma. Substitution of the indirect utility function into the compensatory demand functions generates the same demand equations as in (4.3.1c)[10].

In case of LES for any commodity '*i*', the income elasticity (η_{i0}) and uncompensated price elasticity with respect to *j*th price (η_{ij}) are given by:

$$\eta_{io} = \beta_i\, y/(p_i q_i) \qquad (4.3.6)$$

$$\eta_{ij} = -\delta_{ij} + (\delta_{ij} - \beta_i) p_j \gamma_j / (p_i q_i) \tag{4.3.7}$$

where $\delta_{ij} = 1$ for $i = j$ and $\delta_{ij} = 0$ for $i \neq j$.

The income and price elasticities are not constant and vary with the level of income and consumption as well as prices. If $0 < \beta_i < 1$ and $\gamma_i > 0$ for all '*i*', then it follows that all commodities are normal, price inelastic and pair-wise gross-substitutes. For necessities ($\eta_{i0} < 1$), the income elasticity increases to unity with income but it decreases to unity for luxury goods ($\eta_{i0} > 1$). This is not in conformity with the empirical evidence in the behaviour of income elasticity particularly for food items. This property stems from linear Engel curves and viewed as the theoretical limitation of LES. If $\gamma_i = 0$ for all '*i*', it reduces to linear Engel curves passing through the origin, $p_i q_i = \beta_i y$ (a property of homothetic functions) with unitary price and income elasticity.

There are some complications in the estimation of LES because even though the system is linear in variables, it is non-linear in parameter involving the product of γ_i and β_i. There are several approaches to the estimation of this system. The first approach is an iterative process and known as 'system least squares' method proposed by Stone (1954).[11] Parks (1968) modified this procedure in such a way that the resulting estimators coincided with the corresponding maximum likelihood estimators and also provide asymptotic variance and covariance of the estimators. Similarly, maximum likelihood estimators have also been derived for some of the variants of LES (Barten, 1969; Pollack and Wales, 1969).

The LES in spite of its limitations, viz., linearity of the Engel curves, inelastic price-quantity demand curves, and incapability of incorporating complementary and inferior commodities, has found extensive empirical application. This demand system has been estimated in a number of studies for various countries such as Stone (1954) and later Stone, Brown and Rowe (1965) for Britain; Pallinck (1964) for Belgium; Leoni (1967) for Italy; Parks (1969) for Sweden; Pollack and Wales (1969) for USA; Yoshihara (1969) for Japan; Van Broekhoven (1971) for Belgium; Solari (1971) for Denmark France, Italy,

Norway, United Kingdom and Switzerland, Sanz-Ferror (1972) for Belgium; Sanz-Ferror (1973) for Spain and Deaton (1975) for Britain; Paul and Rudra (1964); Bhattacharya (1967); Joseph(1968); Radhakrishna and Murty (1980) and Murty (2005) for India. This is due to its relative simplicity from the point of view of its estimation and interpretation. This model has also been used in a number of studies for international comparison of demand structures (Parks, 1969; Baschet and Debreu, 1971; Goldberger and Gamaletsos, 1970; Theil, 1971; Solari, 1971 and Barten, 1973).

VARIANTS OF LINEAR EXPENDITURE SYSTEM

The linear expenditure system can be made flexible by allowing its parameters to vary with the change in demographic profile, dynamic behaviour related to past consumption, change in consumers taste etc.[12] In all these cases the vectors 'β' and 'γ' can in fact be made into matrices of parameters. The columns of 'β' should always add up to zero except the first column that adds up to unity because of the budget constraint.

LES with Demographic Profile

Demographic variables such as family size and age composition have traditionally played a major role in the analysis of household budget data. Family size and composition, race, religion, age, and education have all been used as demographic variables in demand studies, although only recently in the context of complete demand system (Pollak and Wales, 1980, 2002).

There are two ways to include for demographic variables in the demand system. First, given enough data, it is always possible to estimate separately the demand systems for sub-samples of households with identical demographic profiles. This approach allows all the parameters of the demand system to depend on the demographic profile and does not require specifying the form of the relationship between the parameters and the demographic variables. Under this approach the only data relevant to the analysis of households with a particular demographic profile are observations on households with that profile.

The second approach introduces specifications that relate the behaviour of household with different demographic profiles. Here, we describe only one specification i.e. 'demographic translating'[13], which introduce in the context of a single demographic variable - for definiteness, household size, which is denoted by 'm'. It is assumed that each household's demand equations are given by LES in which β's are independent of the demographic variables and γ's depend linearly on the number of persons in the household as follows:

$$\gamma_i = \gamma_i^* + \delta_i m \tag{4.3.8a}$$

The implied demand system is given by

$$p_i q_i = p_i \left(\gamma^* + \delta_i m\right) + \beta_i \left(y - \sum p_j \gamma_j^* - \sum p_j \delta_j m\right) \tag{4.3.8b}$$

The effect of the increase in the family size on the consumption of a particular good must, thus, viewed in the context of allocating expenditure among all goods. The direction of the effect of increase in the household size on the consumption of the *i*th good cannot be inferred from the direction of the effect of such a change on the parameter 'γ_i'. Indeed, there is no presumption that in the increase in the household size will increase rather than decrease, γ_i since changes in γ_i regardless of the direction, implies a reallocation of the expenditure among the goods but leave total expenditure unchanged. Further, introducing the detailed household characteristics with the parameter γ_i such that γ_i depends linearly on those household characteristics (m_k) using the translation method as

$$\gamma_i = \gamma_i^* + \sum_k \delta_k m_k \tag{4.3.8c}$$

where m_k (k=1, 2, 3,.....,r) denotes the household's demographic characteristics. The implied demand system is given by

$$p_i q_i = p_i \left(\gamma_i^* + \sum_k \delta_{ik} m_k\right) + \beta_i \left(y - \sum_j p_j \gamma_j^* - \sum_j \sum_k p_j \delta_{ik} m_k\right) \tag{4.3.8d}$$

The indirect utility function from which the demand system (4.3.8d) can be derived using Roy's identity is given by

$$u^*(y, p) = y - \sum_j p_j\gamma_j^* - \sum_j\sum_k p_j\delta_{ik}m_k \Big/ \beta_0\prod_k p_k^{\beta_k} \quad (4.3.9a)$$

where $\beta_0 = \Sigma_k \beta_k^{\beta_k}$. Its equivalent expenditure/cost function is given by

$$c(u, p) = \sum_j p_j\gamma_j^* - \sum_j\sum_k p_j\delta_{ik}m_k + u^*\beta_0\prod_k p_k^{\beta_k} \quad (4.3.9b)$$

The Hicksian compensatory demand functions can be derived form (4.3.9b) using Shephard's lemma. Substitution of the indirect utility function into the compensatory demand functions generates the same demand equations (4.3.8d).The advantage of this approach relates the behaviour of households with demographic profile is that it enables to draw inferences about the behaviour of households with one demographic profile from observations with different profiles.

LES with habit formation hypothesis

The LES model can also be extended by introducing habit formation aspects[14] by replacing the vector 'γ' by some lagged values of consumption (Pollak and Wales, 1969); Deaton and Wigley, (1971); Dahiman and Kievmarken, (1971). In the dynamic variant of the LES model otherwise known as habit formation or lagged/partial/stock adjustment model, the 'committed quantity parameter for each commodity in postulated to depend on the quantity of consumption of the previous period.

The parameter 'γ_i' in the LES can sometimes be interpreted as necessary quantities but, there is no presumption that it is physiologically rather than psychologically necessary. Indeed, it seems plausible that the 'necessary quantity' of a good should depend, at least in part, on past consumption of the good. The simplest assumption is that the necessary quantity of each good is proportional to consumption of that good in that previous period which can be stated as

$$\gamma_{it} = \gamma_i^* + \delta_i q_{it-1} \quad (4.3.10)$$

where q_{it-1} is the demand of the ith commodity in the previous period, is the habit formation coefficient. Here γ_i^* can be interpreted as 'physiologically necessary' component of γ_{it} and $\delta_i q_{it-1}$ as 'psychologically necessary' component of it.

If all good are subject to habit formation of the type described in (4.3.10) than the utility function becomes

$$u(q_t, q_{t-1}) = \sum \beta_i \log\left(q_i - \gamma_i^* - \delta_i q_{it-1}\right) \quad (4.3.11)$$

Maximizing (4.3.11) subject to the budget constraint results the following demand system.

$$p_{it} q_{it} = p_{it}\left(\gamma_i^* + \delta_i q_{it-1}\right) + \beta_i \left(y_t - \sum_j p_{jt}\left(\gamma_j^* + \delta_j^* q_{it-1}\right)\right) \quad (4.3.12)$$

The adding-up and the second order conditions require that

$$0 < \beta_i < 1; \quad \sum \beta_i = 1 \text{ and } \sum_j p_{jt}\left(\gamma_i^* + \delta_i q_{it-1}\right) < y_t \quad (4.3.13)$$

In the above model, the change in taste is said to be quantity diminishing when $\gamma_j^* > 0$; while it is quantity augmenting if $\gamma_j^* < 0$ for the *i*th commodity. It can be seen that any change in either prices or income or both would have sustained impacts on future consumption over a number of periods. The dynamic process will be stable if $\left|\gamma_i^*\right| < 1$ for all '*i*'. The dynamic generalisation of the static Stone-Geary utility function under the habit formation hypothesis will be obtained by replacing γ_i with $\gamma_{it} = \gamma_i^* + \delta_i q_{it-1}$ in (4.3.2).

One important advantage of the dynamic models is that we can distinguish between short-run and long-run elasticities. The short-run elasticities ignore the presence of the lagged dependent variable and are therefore computed just as in static model, i.e., with $\gamma_i^* = 0$ for all '*i*', where as long-run elasticities assume equilibrium levels for the lagged dependent variables and are obtained from the long-run demand functions. These long-run demand functions underlying the model (4.3.12) are

$$p_i q_i = p_i \gamma_i + \beta_i^{**}\left(y - \sum_{j=1}^{n} p_j \gamma_j^{**}\right) \quad (i = 1, 2, 3, \ldots, n) \tag{4.3.14a}$$

where

$$\beta_i^{**} = \left(\beta_i/(1-\gamma_i^*)\right) \Big/ \sum_j \left(\beta_j/(1-\gamma_j^*)\right) \text{ and } \gamma_i^{**} = \gamma_i^*/\left(1-\gamma_i^*\right) \tag{4.3.14b}$$

Thus, long-run demand functions (4.3.14a) are quite similar in structure to their static counterparts (4.3.1b), albeit with new parameters β^{**} and γ^{**} as defined above. The β^{**} and γ^{**} parameters may be interpreted as long-run equilibrium 'marginal budget shares' and 'committed quantities' respectively. The long-run income and price elasticities will, therefore, have similar expression as in (4.3.6) and (4.3.7) with β and γ^* replaced by β^{**} and γ^{**} respectively.

The dynamic version of LES was estimated by Pollak and Wales (1969); Wales (1970) Deaton and Wigley (1971) and Dahlman and Klermarken (1971).

LES with changes in taste\preferences

The LES can also be made flexible to allow for changes in the consumer's tastes by allowing its parameters to vary with time. Stone (1954) has suggested that the LES parameters be expressed as:

$$\beta_{it} = \beta_i + \beta_i^* t \text{ and } \gamma_{it} = \gamma_i + \gamma_i^* t \tag{4.3.15}$$

However, β_i are considered to capture changes in consumer's taste which is generally considered by time trends in parameters, hence $\gamma_i^* = 0$. Incorporating this into the demand system, LES model can be rewritten as

$$p_{it}\, q_{it} = p_{it}\gamma_i + \left(\beta_i + \beta_i^* t\right)\left(y_t - \sum_{j=1}^{n} p_{jt}\gamma_j\right) \qquad (i=1,2,3,\ldots,n)$$

(4.3.16)

The budget constraint along with second order conditions would require, $0 < \beta_i < 1; \sum_i \beta_i^* = 1; \sum_i \beta_i^* = 0$ and $\sum_{j=1}^{n} p_j\gamma_j < y_t$.

It is easy to identify the direct / indirect utility functions and also the cost function underlying the above model.

It is easy to identify the direct, indirect and cost function underlying the above model. They are the simple generalizations of equations (4.3.2), (4.3.3) and (4.3.5) in which we replace β_i with. $(\beta_i + \beta_i^* t)$. Likewise the income and price elasticities can be generalized from (4.3.6) and (4.3.7).

Extended Linear Expenditure System (ELES)

The Extended Linear Expenditure System (ELES) was first developed by Lluch (1973) and later estimated by Lluch, Powell Williams (1977).[15] It is an important variant of LES which brings saving within the framework of LES. This is done either by an inter-temporal or an atemporal utility maximization framework. Following Howe (1975), the ELES can be obtained from an atemporal utility maximization of the familiar Stone-Geary utility function subject to an inter-temporal budget constraint by treating 'saving' as a commodity with zero 'subsistence quantity'. Define a demand system for $(n+1)$ goods, where the $(n+1)$th good is saving. Let the atemporal utility function be the Stone-Geary form which is

$$u(q) = \sum_{j=1}^{n+1} \beta_j^* \log\left(q_j - \gamma_j\right) \qquad (4.3.17)$$

where $\beta_j^* > 0$; $\left(q_j - \gamma_j\right) > 0$ and $\sum_{j=1}^{n+1} \beta_j^* = 1$.

Maximization of this utility function (4.3.17) subject to a budget constraint $\sum_{j=1}^{n+1} p_j q_j = z$, where $z = \rho w + y + L(y)$ is considered a priori concept of permanent income, ρ is the rate of reproduction of non-human wealth (capital), '*w*' is the non-human wealth, '*y*' is the exogenous flow of labour income and *L(y)* is the rate of flow of labour income. The above maximization yields the familiar Klein-Rubin (1947-48) demand functions,

$$q_i = \gamma_i - \frac{\beta_i^*}{p_i} \sum_{j=1}^{n+1} p_j \gamma_j + \frac{\beta_i^*}{p_i} z \qquad (i = 1, 2, \ldots, n+1) \qquad (4.3.18)$$

Since, the (*n*+1)th good is saving and the subsistence quantity' of saving is assumed to be equal to zero.[16]

$$p_{n+1}\, q_{n+1} = s \text{ and } \gamma_{n+1} = 0. \qquad (4.3.19)$$

Substitute the assumptions (4.3.19) and rewrite the demand function (4.3.18) in expenditure form,

$$p_i q_i = p_i \gamma_i + \beta_i^* \left(z - \sum_{j=1}^{n} p_j \gamma_j \right) \qquad (4.3.20a)$$

and
$$s = \beta_{n+1}^* \left(z - \sum_{j=1}^{n} p_j \gamma_j \right) \qquad (4.3.20b)$$

From (4.3.20a), it is clear that β^*_{n+1} is the marginal propensity to save. Define the marginal propensity to consume as $\mu \equiv 1 - \beta_{n+1}^*$ and the marginal budget share as $\beta_i = \frac{\beta_i^*}{\mu}$. Note that $\sum_{j=1}^{n} \beta_j = 1$. Rewriting (4.3.20a) in vector notation and using $\beta_i^* = \mu\, \beta_i$ obtain the expenditure equation of the ELES as developed by Lluch (1973).

$$\hat{p}q = \hat{p}\gamma + \mu\,\beta\left(z - p'\gamma\right) \tag{4.3.21}$$

The consumption function associated with the ELES is obtained either directly by summing expenditure equations (4.3.21) over the *'n'* consumption items or by subtracting saving (4.3.20b) from permanent income,

$$v = \mu\, z + \left(1 - \mu\right) p'\gamma\ . \tag{4.3.22}$$

In Lluch's formulation, marginal propensity to consume (MPC) is equal to the ratio of the subjective rate of discount 'δ ' to the rate of reproduction of capital 'ρ'. In Howe's formulation, *m* depends on the utility function parameter β^*_{n+1}. To get the same MPC as obtained by Lluch, the requirement is β^*_{n+1} to be defined a priori as $(1\text{-}\delta/p)$ since δ/p $(=\mu) \equiv (1-\beta^*_{n+1})$. To retain the MPC between 0 and 1, the required condition is that unconventional assumption of a subjective rate of discount (δ) should be smaller than the rate of reproduction of capital (ρ). This assumption implies the imposition of original restrictions, $\beta_i^* > 0$ and $\Sigma\beta^*_j = 1$ on the utility function.

The alternative development of ELES is the use current income (y^*) instead of permanent income (z) in the budget constraint. Then, the following equations obtained from utility maximization are

$$\hat{p}q = \hat{p}\gamma + \mu\,\beta\left(y^* - p'\gamma\right) \tag{4.3.23}$$

$$v = \mu\, y^* + \left(1 - \mu\right) p'\gamma \tag{4.3.24}$$

which represent the expenditure and consumption functions respectively. In this case, saving is out of current income and 'μ' is the marginal propensity to consume for a given current income. Thus, an alternative ELES based on current income is legitimate in its own right rather than a mere proxy concept when permanent income is not available. Any other concept of income could be incorporated a priori in the budget constraint and the resultant propensity to consume of the equations (4.3.21) and (4.3.22) would be defined accordingly.

The ELES was first estimated by Belandria using the household budget data of Venezuelan cities. The theoretical aspects of this model were systemized by Powell (1973). Further contributions have been made by Betancourt (1973) using Chile data; Howe (1974) using Colombia data; Musgrove (1977) using Latin America data; Lluch and Williams (1977) using Korea and Mexico data and Williams (1977) using Yugoslavia data and in (1980) using Australia data. Some of the recent empirical studies using ELES are Ali (1985), Burney and Akmal (1991) and Martin (1991).

HIERARCHIC LINEAR EXPENDITURE SYSTEM (HLES)

This demand system was first proposed by Stone (1954) and then further developed by Deaton (1975). The concept of 'multi-stage' (or tree) budgeting deals with allocation of the consumer expenditure first on commodity groups then on commodity sub-groups within a group in a step-wise or hierarchical fashion. In this formulation, it is assumed that in the first stage a consumer allocates his expenditure to broad group of commodities taking into account group prices and expenditure. In the second stage and subsequent stages, group expenditure is allocated to within the sub-group of commodities taking into account sub-group (within the group) prices and the group expenditure allocated in the first stage.[17]

The above process of sequential allocation is assumed to proceed along various branches in the entire budgeting has a tree like structure. Only in certain demand models, LES, being one among them, are consistent with above multistage budgeting. Strotz (1957, 1959) and Gorman (1959) have analysed the conditions under which multi-stage budgeting is consistent. It should be noted that additivity assumption of the LES is more stringent than the strong separability that is needed for consistency. Let us examine the above approach using the LES model specified earlier as in (4.3.3b)

$$p_i q_i = p_i \gamma_i + \beta_i \left(y - \sum_{j=1}^{n} p_j \gamma_j \right). \qquad (4.3.25)$$

Let us denote the group price indices with capital subscripts and small letter subscripts to individual items. Also let us assume that the 'n' items are partitioned into 'N' groups. By summing the equations (4.3.25) over $i \in R$ and denoting the group expenditure by V_R, the typical group expenditure system can be obtained as

$$V_R = \sum_{i \in R} p_i \gamma_i + \sum_{i \in R} \beta_i \left(y - \sum_{j=1} p_j \gamma_j \right) \quad (R=1,2,3\ldots,N) \qquad (4.3.26)$$

The equations (4.3.26) can be rewritten in an identical form like (4.3.25) by defining group price index p_R and the quantity index q_R as,

$$p_R = \sum_{i \in R} p_i \gamma_i \Big/ \sum_{i \in R} \gamma_i \quad \text{and} \quad q_R = V_R / p_R \qquad (4.3.27)$$

Substituting the above expressions of (4.3.27) in (4.3.26), we get the group equivalent of (4.3.25) as

$$p_R q_R = p_R \gamma_R + \beta_n \left(y - \sum_S p_S \gamma_S \right) \quad (R=1,2,3\ldots,N) \qquad (4.3.28)$$

where $\beta_R = \sum_{i \in R} \beta_i$ and $\gamma_R = \sum_{i \in R} \gamma_i$. The equations for the item belonging to *Rth* group can be rewritten as

$$p_i q_i = p_i \gamma_i + \frac{\beta_i}{\beta_R} \left(V_R - \sum_{j \in R}^{n} p_j \gamma_j \right) \text{ for } i \in R \qquad (4.3.29)$$

It can be seen that the parameters of the first stage model equations (4.3.28) and the sub-group models equations (4.3.29) together give the estimates of the complete model (4.3.25). Since individual prices are mostly collinear, these indices are likely to give close approximation to the group price indices as required in equations (4.3.29) for consistent aggregation (Deaton, 1975).

ADDILOG DEMAND SYSTEMS (ADS)

Houthakker (1960) has introduced both the Direct and Indirect Addilog Demand Systems based on specific forms of additive utility functions. Of the two addilog systems-direct and indirect, the later has been widely used in empirical analysis.[18] In many empirical studies, this model (IAS) has been compared with the LES.[19]

Direct Addilog System (DAS)

The direct utility function underlying direct addilog demand system is specified as

$$u(q) = \sum_{i=1}^{n} (\alpha_i / \beta_i) q_i^{\beta_i} \tag{4.3.30}$$

Since, the utility function is a sum of the logarithmic function of '*n*' commodities, it is abbreviated to addilog (or additive logarithmic) utility function. Maximization of (4.3.30) subject to the budget constant yields the Direct Addilog System (DAS) in budget share form as:

$$w_i = \alpha_i q_i^{\beta_i} \Big/ \sum_{j=1}^{n} \alpha_j q_j^{\beta_j} \qquad (i = 1, 2, .3, ..., n) \tag{4.3.31}$$

The general restrictions of consumer theory other than second order conditions as well as the particular restriction of additivity are built into the model. The second order conditions require that $\beta_i > -1$ for all '*i*'.

By inspection it can be seen that (4.3.31) is homogeneous of degree zero in α_i parameters and hence one of the α_i's can be fixed arbitrarily as a utility scaling factor. We may use the normalization condition $\alpha_n = 1$ or $\Sigma\alpha_i = 1$. It can be seen that the demand system in (4.3.31) is highly non-linear in parameters and not very much appealing for econometric analysis. The direct estimation of the model is less tractable. Houthakker (1960) has suggested an estimation procedure in which the logarithm of ratio of expenditure on pairs of commodities is considered for eliminating the complex denominator in (4.3.31).

Assuming the *nth* commodity as the reference good, a simple manipulation would modify (4.3.31) as

$$\ln(p_i / p_n) = (\alpha_i / \alpha_n) + (\beta_i - 1)\ln q_i - (\beta_n - 1)\ln q_n \left[i = 1, 2, 3, ..., n-1 \right] \tag{4.3.32}$$

The inverse demand system[20] in (4.3.32) can be estimated by imposing equality constraint for β_n coefficient across equations.

The expressions for income and price elasticities are less tractable. Perhaps it is possible to use an analogous procedure used in direct translog model.

Indirect Addilog System (IAS)

Houthakker (1960) has specified the indirect additive utility function with its underlying indirect addilog demand systems[21] as,

$$u^*(y,p) = \sum_i (\alpha_i / \beta_i)(y / p_i)^{\beta_i} \tag{4.3.33}$$

The demand system underlying (4.3.33) can be shown as

$$w_i = \frac{\alpha_i (y / p_i)^{\beta_i}}{\sum_{j=1}^{n} \alpha_j (y / p_j)^{\beta_j}} \qquad (i = 1,2,.....n) \tag{4.3.34}$$

The above demand functions are homogeneous of degree zero in prices and income and satisfy the adding-up and symmetry conditions. Satisfaction of the second order conditions requires that $\beta_i > 1$ for all '*i*'. These conditions are not imposed in the estimation process but rather used as a check for their fulfillment. Like DAS, one of the parameters of IAS is required to be fixed arbitrarily as a scaling factor. The IAS can be estimated using the non-linear method of estimation. The IAS model permits non-linear Engel curves and also includes both substitute and complementary goods.

In the IAS, for commodity '*i*', the income elasticity (η_{i0}), and the direct and cross-price elasticities (η_{ij}) are given by

$$\eta_{i0} = 1 + \beta_i - \sum_j \beta_j w_j \tag{4.3.35}$$

$$\eta_{ij} = \beta_j (w_j - \delta_{ij}) \tag{4.3.36}$$

where $\delta_{ij} = 1$ for $i = j$ and $\delta_{ij} = 1$ for $i \neq j$.

However, it can be seen from the above expressions that the model is as restrictive as any other additive model, and further, in this model, the cross-price elasticities with respect to the price of a commodity are identical for all commodities[22] but depend upon the price change.

The indirect addilog model has been estimated by Parks (1969) for Sweden; Yoshihara (1969) for Japan; Somermeyer et al. (1962) for Holland; and Radhkrishna et al. (1979), Radhakrishna and Murty (1981), Murty (1982) for India. In many of its applications, the performance of the indirect addilog model has been compared with the LES and the results of such comparisons did not however lead to the same conclusions. For instance, the results of Parks, Yoshihara, and Theil suggest that the LES performs much better than both the direct and indirect addilog demand systems; while Radhakrishna and Murty (1981) suggest that the indirect addilog model gives better fit to cross-section data.

DOUBLE-LOG DEMAND SYSTEM (DLDS)

The demand system very often used in empirical research is the double-log demand system which is specified as,

$$q_i = \alpha_i\, y^{\beta_i} \prod_{j=1}^{n} p_j^{\gamma_{ij}} \quad (i = 1,2,3,\ldots,n) \tag{4.3.37a}$$

The logarithm form of equation (4.3.37a) becomes

$$\log q_i = \log\alpha_i + \beta_i \log y + \sum_j \gamma_{ij} \log p_j \quad (i = 1,2,3,\ldots\ldots,n) \tag{4.3.37b}$$

where β_i is the expenditure elasticity. The additivity condition requires that income elasticity of each commodity must be equal to unity. If the variables p_i/q_i and y are restricted to positive values, the budget share form of (4.3.37a) is

$$w_i = \left(\frac{p_i q_i}{y}\right) = \left(\alpha_i \prod_{j=i}^{n} p_j^{\gamma_{ij}}\, p_i\right) y^{\beta_i - 1} \tag{4.3.38}$$

Suppose $\beta_i > 0$ for some good '*i*', then $w_i \to \infty$ as $y \to \infty$. Therefore, the budget share, $w_i > 1$ for $y > y_0$, where y_0 is the level of total expenditure at which $\Sigma p_i q_i = y$. Since, w_i in a monotonically increasing function of 'y', y_0 is a unique point. Thus, if $\beta_i > 1$ for a single commodity, the budget constraint is violated. If the parameter, $\beta_i \leq 1$ for all 'i' then $p_i q_i > 0$, so β_i cannot be less than unity because of the restriction $\Sigma p_i q_i (1-\beta_i) = 0$. Thus, $\beta_i = 1$ for all goods 'i'. Generally, with given prices, the expenditure pattern of the consumer will change when his income increases. So the expenditure elasticities not equal to unity is violated by this demand function.[23]

Theil (1965) derived a simplified version of the above double-log demand system from the following differential specification of a system of demand equations[24]:

$$w_i\, d(\log q_i) = \beta_i \left(d(\log y) - \sum_{k=i}^{n} w_k d(\log p_k) \right) + \sum_{j=i}^{n} \gamma_{ij} \left(d(\log p_i - \sum_{k=1}^{n} \beta_k d(\log p_k) \right) \tag{4.3.39}$$

where $w_i = p_i q_i / y$ and β_i and γ_{ij} are constants satisfying

$$\text{(i) } \gamma_{ij} = \gamma_{ji} \quad \text{(ii) } \Sigma\beta_i = 1 \text{ and (iii) } \sum_{j=1}^{n} \gamma_{ij} = \phi\, \beta_i \tag{4.3.40}$$

($\phi = \dfrac{\partial \log y}{\partial \log \lambda}$, where λ is the Lagrange multiplier)

Using condition (iii) of (4.3.40), the demand system (4.3.39) reduces to a system of partial deferential equation[25] of the form as

$$\frac{\partial q_i}{\partial y} = \frac{\beta_i}{p_i} \qquad (i = 1, 2, 3, \ldots, n) \tag{4.3.41}$$

$$\frac{\partial q_i}{\partial p_j} = \frac{\beta_i q_j}{p_i} + \left(\gamma_{ij} - \phi\, \beta_i \beta_j\right) \frac{y}{p_j} \qquad (i, j = 1, 2, 3, \ldots, n) \tag{4.3.42}$$

The solution of the equations in (4.3.41) provides demand system as

$$q_i = \frac{\beta_i y_i}{p_i} + \beta_i (p_1, p_2, \ldots\ldots, p_n) \tag{4.3.43}$$

If the differential specification holds for all positive prices and income, β_i must be zero since the quantity demanded approaches to zero. Then, the resulting demand system is

$$q_i = \beta_i (y_i / p_i). \quad (4.3.44)$$

The demand system (4.3.44) is in double log form and such demand function can be derived from the maximization of direct logarithmic utility function, u = $\Sigma\beta_i$ (logq_i) where $\beta_i > 0$ and $\Sigma\beta_i = 1$. The demand system (4.3.44) is a special case of the double-log demand system (4.3.37b) as discussed above. It is also popularly known as Cobb-Douglas demand system (CDDS). The CDDS is a leading example of the demand systems exhibiting expenditures proportionately. A major shortcoming of the double-log utility functions is that it allows homothetic preferences which imply unitary income elasticities so that Engel curves are straight lines through the origin. The budget shares are always constant with CDDS.

This model was estimated subject to the usual restrictions in a number of studies by Byron in1968 using Australian data and in 1970 using Dutch data; Lluch, 1971 using Spanish data; Court, 1967 using New Zealand data. The result of these studies with constant elasticity system more or less tends to support those of the Rotterdam system.

NON-UTILITY BASED DEMAND SYSTEMS

The class of 'a priori' models, pioneered by Barten, Byron and Theil, emerged soon after as competing models under the banner of 'non-utility based models' and aimed at testing the neo-classical postulates of consumer theory. In this approach, demand functions are specified without any reference to the existence of the utility function and theoretical restrictions (adding-up, homogeneity, and symmetry) are generally imposed as restrictions on parameters in the estimation procedure. The most familiar models of this type are the Rotterdam Demand System, Constant Elasticity Demand System and Quadratic Demand System etc. This approach is also consistent with the theory of consumer behaviour since the fulfillment of theoretical restrictions implies that the demand equations have been generated from a utility function.

ROTTERDAM DEMAND SYSTEM (RDS)

This demand model was introduced by Theil (1965) and Barten (1966) and later explored by Theil (1967,1975 & 1980). It maintains some of the spirit of the traditional double logarithm specifications, but it avoids most of the problems that arises in the double-log model, $\log q_i = \beta_i \log y + \Sigma\gamma_{ij} \log p_j$, and is quite flexible with regards to the possibility of imposing parameter restrictions. Unlike the other models considered here, the Rotterdam model is formulated in terms of differential (or discrete differences for the purpose of application) of the above double-log model.[26] It has three versions viz. absolute price version, relative price version and preference independent version.

The demand functions arising from utility maximization subject to the budget constraint can be written in terms of prices and a measure of real income $(\tilde{y} = y/P)$. The logarithmic differential of the demand function (or the differential of the double-log as given above) can be written as

$$d(\log q_i) = \eta_{i0} d\{\log(y/P)\} + \sum_{j=1}^{n} \eta_{ij} d\log(p_j) \qquad (4.4.1)$$

where η_{i0} is the income /expenditure elasticity of the *ith* good and η_{ij} is the compensated price elasticity of good '*i*' with respect to *jth* price. Weighting each demand equation of the above differential demand system by the expenditure share, w_i one can obtain the re-parameterization of equation (4.4.1) as

$$w_i\, d(\log q_i) = (w_i)\eta_{i0}\, d\{\log(y/P)\} + \sum_{j=1}^{n} (w_i)(\eta_{ij})\, d\log(p_j) \qquad (4.4.2a)$$

$$w_i\, d(\log q_i) = \mu_i\, d\{\log(y/P)\} + \sum_{j=1}^{n} \theta_{ij}\, d(\log p_j) \qquad (4.4.2b)$$

Equation (4.4.2b) is the absolute price version of Rotterdam model where $\eta_{i0} = \left(\frac{\mu_i}{w_i}\right)$ and $w_i\eta_{ij} = \theta_{ij}$. The parameter μ_i is the marginal budget share and it is the income elasticity η_{i0} weighted by the expenditure share or equivalently (it is the derivatives of the expenditure on the *ith* commodity with respect to income). The parameter θ_{ij} is the compensated cross-price elasticity, η_{ij} weighted by the expenditure share. In the above model (4.4.2b), '*P*' is the Divisia Price index and is defines as $\left(P = \sum_i w_i d(\log p_i)\right)$. Homogeneity requires $\sum_{j=i}^{n} \theta_{ij} = 0$ for all '*i*'; the Slutsky symmetry condition implies the symmetry of the matrix 'θ' with $\theta_{ij} = \theta_{ji}$; adding-up condition implies that $\Sigma\mu_i = 1$; and finally the classical second order condition requires that the matrix 'θ' to be negative semi-definite. The first three sets of restrictions can be imposed on the estimation procedure in a straight forward manner. The inequality constraint implied by the last condition is more difficult to impose but the restriction can be used to check on the validity of the numerical results. The income elasticity (η_{i0}) and the compensated price elasticity (η_{ij})are given by:

$$\eta_{i0} = \mu_i / w_i \quad \text{and} \quad \eta_{ij} = \theta_{ij} / w_i \tag{4.4.3}$$

Using the homogeneity condition $\left(\sum_{j=i}^{n} \theta_{ij} = 0\right)$, we can easily arrive at an alternate formulation of the Rotterdam model, called the relative price version. In this model price changes are measured relative to a marginal price index, *P** which is known as the Frisch Price index and is defined as $\left(P^* = \sum_i \mu_i\, d(\log p_i)\right)$. This version of Rotterdam model is specified as

$$w_i\, d(\log q_i) = \mu_i d\{\log(y/P)\} + \sum_{j=1}^{n} \nu_{ij}\, d(\log p_j / P^*) \qquad (4.4.4)$$

where $\theta_{ij} = \nu_{ij} - \left(\sum_j \nu_{ij}\right)\mu_j$. The matrix '$v$' should be symmetric and negative definite with $\sum_i \nu_{ij} = \sum_j \nu_{ji} = -\sigma\mu_i$ where $\sigma = \sum_i \sum_j \nu_{ij}$. Therefore, the relative price version is a meaningful specification in case of restrictions on 'v_{ij}'. If we choose an additive utility function, then we have to impose the restrictions $v_{ij} = 0$ for $i \neq j$ so that $v_{ij} = -\sigma\mu_i$.

Under preference independence, the relative price version of the model becomes very simple. Substituting $v_{ij} = 0$ in equation (4.4.4), we can obtain the preference independent version of Rotterdam model as

$$w_i\, d(\log q_i) = \mu_i\, d\{\log(y/P)\} + \nu_{ii}\, d(\log p_j / P^*) \qquad (4.4.5)$$

For the purpose of estimation of the Rotterdam differential logarithm model (4.4.2b), it must be modified in several respects.[27] The estimation of the model (4.4.2b) is generally based on the discrete analog of this equation and is given by

$$w^* Dq_{it} = \sum_{j=1}^{n} \theta_{ij} D\, p_{jt} + b_i\, Dq_{it} + u_{it}$$

$$(i = 1, 2, \ldots\ldots, n)\, and\, (t = 1, 2, \ldots\ldots\ldots, T) \qquad (4.4.6)$$

where the operator 'D' represents the log differences: Dq_{it} = log q_{it} – log $q_{it\text{-}1}$. The weight $w_{it}^* = 1/2(w_{it} + w_{it+1})$ is the average budget share in successive periods. Thus, the variable, $Dq_t = \sum w_{it}^* Dq_t$ is a value weighted average of the logarithms differences of the quantities demanded. It is, thus, a volume index (i.e. Divisia volume index) of the change in total consumption and can be interpreted as a measure of the change in real income $[d\log(\tilde{y})]$ of equation (4.4.2b).

This model has been estimated by a number of researchers in different countries. It has been estimated and tested by Barten (1968) using Dutch data; Theil (1970, 1971) extensively applied the model to Dutch and British data; Deaton (1974) has considered six variants of this system under the assumption of homogeneity, symmetry and additivity using national accounts data of U.K. for the period 1900-70. Attempts were also made to compare the performance of this model with other models. Parks (1969) compared the performance RDS with LES and IAS.

The model, however, suffers from the limitation that it can not be derived from any well-behaved utility function unlike LES and addilog systems. Further, the model does not generally satisfy the integrability condition, a requirement very crucial and vital for a model in the first difference form as indicated earlier.

LINEAR DEMAND SYSTEM (LDS)

In the literature, one comes across the constant elasticity model (Byron (1967, 1968, 1969)] as the simplest a priori model. But, it is well known that this model does not allow imposition of neoclassical restrictions, including the budget constraint at each sample observation. One needs to impose these restrictions approximately at sample mean values. For this reason, we prefer to present a close substitute with fewer problems i.e. the linear demand system. This demand system may be classified under the category of a priori models, which do not underlie any specific utility function, direct or indirect. However, this model can also be made theoretically consistent by imposing neoclassical properties of consumer theory as parametric restrictions in the estimation procedure. Further, the model allows us to test the empirical validity of these postulates. We may write the LDS as

$$p_i q_i = \alpha_i + \beta_i y + \sum_j \gamma_{ij} p_j \qquad (i = 1, 2, 3 \ldots\ldots, n) \qquad (4.4.7)$$

The budget constraint requires that

$$\sum_i \alpha_i = 0; \sum_i \beta_i = 1; \sum_i \gamma_{ij} = 0 \ (j = 1, 2, ..., n).$$

The homogeneity property is expressed as $\alpha_i = 0$. Unlike the other models, the substitution matrix involves variable prices, quantities and income. Therefore, the symmetric condition can be imposed only at the sample mean values of the variables and does not necessarily imply, $\gamma_{ij} = \gamma_{ji}$ for $i \neq j \ (i, j = 1, 2, ..., n)$ all. The negativity conditions imply the negative semi-definiteness of the Slutsky substitution matrix, which can be only verified after estimation.

QUADRATIC EXPENDITURE SYSTEM (QES)

The linearity of the underlying Engel curves and the consequent behaviour of income elasticities of demand at different income levels in the LES have lead to intensive search for alternative non-linear specifications. One such model is a simple quadratic generalisation of the LES with minimum possible increase in the number of parameters. The added advantage with the model is that LES can be obtained from it as a special case.

Following Howe, Pollak, and Wales[28] (1979), any demand system quadratic in total expenditure can be written in the following form

$$q_i(y, p) = A_i(p)y^2 + B_i(p)y + C_i(p) \quad (i = 1, 2, 3 ...., n) \qquad (4.4.8)$$

where A_i, B_i, *and* C_i are functions of prices only. They have shown that (4.4.8) would be a theoretically consistent demand system if and only if $q_i(y, p)$ is of the form

$$q_i(y, p) = \frac{1}{g^2}(h_i h \frac{g_i}{g})(y - f)^2 + \frac{g_i}{g}(y - f) + f_i \qquad (4.4.9)$$

where *f*, *g* and *h* are homogeneous functions in prices with degree one; and f_i, g_i, and h_i are partial derivatives of *f*, *g* and *h* with respect to p_i respectively. Further, the demand system in (4.4.9) can be derived from the following class of indirect utility functions:

$$u^*(y,p) = -\frac{g(p)}{y - f(p)} - \frac{h(p)}{g(p)} \qquad (4.4.10)$$

A particular member of this class which provides a direct generalisation of the LES can be obtained when

$$f(p) = \sum_j p_k \gamma_k;\; g(p) = \prod_k p_k^{\beta_k} \; and \; h(p) = \sum_j \alpha_j p_j \qquad (4.4.11)$$

subject to $0 < \beta_i < 1$ for all 'i' and $\sum_j \beta_j = 1$.

Obtain the appropriate indirect utility function substituting (4.4.11) in (4.4.10). Then, using Roy's identity, the following form of QES can be obtained

$$p_i q_i = p_i \gamma_i + \beta_i (y - \sum_{j=1}^{n} p_j \gamma_j) + (\alpha_i p_i - \beta_i \sum_{j=1}^{n} \alpha_j p_j)(y - \sum_{j=1}^{n} p_j \gamma_j)^2 \prod_k p_k^{2\beta_k}$$

$$(i = 1, 2, 3, \ldots\ldots\ldots, n) \qquad (4.4.12)$$

The relationship between the QES and the LES is obvious. The parameter vector $(\alpha_1, \alpha_2 \ldots\ldots\ldots \alpha_n)$ differentiates the QES from the LES.[29] It can be verified that (4.4.12) is a complete demand system. By duality theory, there exists a class of direct utility functions corresponding to the class of indirect utility functions in (4.4.10). Though, it would be interesting to identify the particular form the direct utility function underlying the QES but it is difficult to specify its functional form. Since, the direct utility function underlying the QES (4.4.12) is non-additive except under special cases, it allows wider substitution possibilities (see Pollak, 1971). Further, the quadratic Engel curves underlying the QES make it more flexible than the LES.

The income elasticity (η_{i0}) and price elasticities (η_{ij}) of demand for the ith commodity can be derived as

$$\eta_{i0} = \left(\frac{y}{p_i q_i}\right)\beta_i + \frac{2y}{p_i q_i}(\alpha_i p_i - \beta_i \sum_{j=1}^{n} \alpha_j p_j)(y - \sum_{j=1}^{n} p_j \gamma_j) \prod_k p_k^{-2\beta_k}$$

$$(4.4.13)$$

$$\eta_{ij} = -\delta_{ij} + \frac{(\delta_{ij} - \beta_i)p_j\gamma_j}{p_i q_i} + \frac{1}{p_i q_i}$$

$$\left((\delta_{ij} - \beta_i)p_j\alpha_j - 2\left\{\beta_j + [p_j\gamma_j/(y - \sum p_j\gamma_j)]\right\}(\alpha_i p_i - \beta_i \sum_{j-1}^{n} \alpha_j p_j)\right)$$

$$\left(y - \sum_{j=1}^{n} p_j\gamma_j\right)^2 \prod_k p_k^{2\beta_k} \qquad (4.4.14)$$

where $\delta_{ij} = 1$ for all $i = j$ and $\delta_{ij} = 0$ for $i \neq j$. The above elasticity formula of QES (4.4.13) and (4.4.14) will reduces to their LES counterparts as in (4.3.6) and (4.3.7) when for all 'i'. Differentiating the income elasticity in (4.4.13) with respect to 'y' we have

$$\frac{\partial \eta_{i0}}{\partial y} = \frac{k_i y}{p_i q_i} + \frac{1 - \eta_{i0}}{p_i q_i}\left(\beta_i + k_i(y - \sum_{j=1}^{n} p_j\gamma_j)\right) \qquad 4.4.15a)$$

where $$k_i = 2(\alpha_i p_i - \beta_i \sum_j \alpha_j p_j)\prod_k p_k^{2\beta_k} \qquad (4.4.15b)$$

Thus, the behaviour of η_{i0} with respect to y also depends on k_i. The sign of and hence, that of $\partial\eta_{i0}/\partial y$ cannot be determined a priori. But when $k_i = 0$ for all 'i' (as in LES) is an unattractive property mentioned earlier. The expression, k_i in QES makes it more flexible than the LES. Moreover, changes in taste and preferences can be incorporated by introducing time trends in 'β ' parameters. Likewise habit formation hypothesis can also be incorporated through the 'γ ' vector (see Pollak and Wales, 1978).

NON-ADDITIVE DEMAND SYSTEMS

In reaction to the criticisms of additive models, the class of 'non-additive' models has come into existence. This class of non-additive flexible models claims dual purpose provides better description of observed behaviour and allows empirical verification of the postulates of consumer theory. The most familiar models of this type are Nasse Expenditure System (NSE), Translog Demand System (TDS) and Almost Ideal Demand System (AIDS) and their variants.

NASSE EXPENDITURE SYSTEM (NES)

Another non-additive variant of LES is the Nasse model[30], which allows inferior commodities and also specific substitution between commodity groups. In this model following the suggestion of Stone (1954), the 'committed quantity' parameter for each commodity is assumed to depend on all price ratios in a specific way. This results in a matrix of 'committed quantity' parameters. One advantage of this generalisation is that the LES model is obtained as a special case when we restrict all off-diagonal elements of the matrix of 'committed quantity' parameters to zero values. Some forms of separability like group-wise independence (or block diagonality) can also be introduced by suitable parametric restrictions. The Nasse (1970) model has the following form:

$$p_i q_i = p_i \gamma_i(p) + \beta_i \left(y - \sum_{j=1}^{n} p_j \gamma_j(p) \right) \qquad (i = 1, 2, 3, \ldots, n) \qquad (4.5.1a)$$

where,
$$\gamma_i(p) = \sum_{j=1}^{n} p_j \gamma_{ij} \left(p_j / p_i \right)^{1/2} \qquad (4.5.1b)$$

The budget constraint along with the second order condition requires that $0 < \beta_i < 1$ for all 'i' and $\sum \beta_i = 1$. The homogeneity property is built into the model specification. The symmetry conditions require $\gamma_{ij} = \gamma_{ji}$ for $i \neq j$ ($i, j = 1, 2, \ldots, n$). Since the 'committed quantity' for any commodity is no longer a constant, but depends on all prices, we cannot generalize the Stone-Geary direct utility function for the derivation of this model. However, we can generalize the indirect utility function of the LES. By virtue of duality result, the direct utility function will exist. The indirect utility function underlying the Nasse model can be shown as

$$u^{*}(y,p)=\left(y-\sum_{i}\sum_{j}\gamma_{ij}(p_i p_j)^{1/2}\right)\Big/\left(\beta_0\prod p_k^{\beta_k}\right) \tag{4.5.2}$$

where, $\beta_0=\prod_k \beta_k^{\beta_k}$. Clearly equation (4.5.2) is non-additive except when $\gamma_{ij}=0$ for all (i,j =1,2,3..,n) i.e when $u^{*}(y,p)$ belongs to Bergson family. Using Roy's identity, it can be verified that equation (4.5.2) gives rise to the demand system as in (4.5.1). Like LES, the changes in consumer taste can be incorporated by specifying the 'β ' parameters as linear functions of time. There is, however, no obvious way of obtaining the habit formation version for the Nasse model.

The expenditure elasticity (η_{i0}) and price elasticities (η_{ij}) are given by

$$\eta_{i0}=\beta_i/w_i\ ,\ \text{where } w_i=\sum_i p_i q_i \tag{4.5.3}$$

$$\eta_{ij}=-\delta_{ij}+\left(\{(\delta_{ij}-\beta_i)p_j\gamma_j(p)\}/p_i q_i\right)+$$

$$\left(\{(\gamma_{ij}(p_i\,p_j)^{1/2}-\delta_{ij}\gamma_i(p)p_j\}/2p_i q_i\right) \tag{4.5.4}$$

Clearly these elasticities depend on the income and price structure in a complex way. The uncompensatory price elasticities in (4.5.4) reduces to its LES counterparts (4.3.7) when $\gamma_{ij}=0$ for all $i\neq j$ and (i,j = 1, 2, 3,........,n).

TRANSLOG DEMAND SYSTEM (TDS)

The demand systems discussed so far underlie a number of general restrictions like adding-up, homogeneity, symmetry derived from consumer theory, as well as particular restriction like additivity imposed 'a priori' on the structure of preferences. These restrictions are treated as part of maintained hypothesis eith in the specification of the demand system (e.g., LES and IAS models) or in an ad hoc manner (e.g., RDS and LDS models). The need for testing the empirical validity of these restrictions in a behavioral framework has prompted the search for more flexible functional forms[31] like the transcendental logarithmic utility function (or Translog utility function). These functional forms are claimed to be local second order approximation to any general utility function. The Translog demand system have been first introduced in production theory and later extended to utility analysis by Christensen, Jorgenson and Lau (1975). Corresponding to the direct and indirect translog utility functions there are direct and indirect Translog demand systems.

Direct Translog (DTL) Demand System

Following Christensen et. al., (1975) the direct translog utility function can be written as

$$-\log u(q) = \alpha_0 + \sum_i \alpha_i \log q_i + \frac{1}{2}\sum_i \sum_j \beta_{ij} \log q_i \log q_j \qquad (4.5.5)$$

where the negative sign of the left hand side is meant for preserving the symmetry between direct and indirect translog forms. It is clear that the utility function in (4.5.5) is quadratic in logarithms of quantities consumed and reduces to additive form when $\beta_{ij} = 0$ for all $i \neq j$ and the linear logarithmic form when $\beta_{ij} = 0$ for all $(i,j = 1,2,3..,n)$. Maximizing (4.5.5) subject to budget constraint would give the Direct Translog (DTL) demand system as

$$w_i(y,p) = \frac{p_i q_i}{y} = \frac{\alpha_i + \sum_{j=1}^{n} \beta_{ij} \log q_j}{\alpha_m + \sum_{j=1}^{n} \beta_{mj} \log q_j} \quad (i = 1,2,3...,n) \qquad (4.5.6)$$

where $a_m = \Sigma\alpha_i$ and $\beta_{mj} = \Sigma\beta_{ij}$. Unlike the other demand systems, the DTL in budget share form is homogeneous of degree zero in income and prices as well as in parameters, α and β. Consequently, a normalisation of the type $\alpha_m = 1$ is needed for its estimation. It can be shown that the estimated value shares as well as β_{ij}s are invariant to rescaling of 'q' variables. However, α_{ij}s are not invariant. Regarding the econometric specification, the DTL has similar feature as that of DAS model and, therefore, shares the problems of estimation. Since the

DTL is nonlinear, methods like maximum likelihood or direct non-linear procedures are appropriate for its estimation.

Indirect Translog (ITL) Demand System

The widespread use of the consumer's cost and indirect utility function as a representation of preferences in empirical analysis has produced a number of attractive specifications. The first is the translog indirect utility function of Christensen et al., (1975) which is one of the classes of flexible functional forms discussed by Diewert (1974). The five translog forms viz., HTL, LTL, Log-TL, BTL and GTL containing a double sum over the log prices which correspond to preferences ordering represented by indirect utility functions are analysed below. The homothetic translog (HTL), the simplest member of the translog family, is the best starting point. The HTL indirect utility function is given by:

$$u^*(y,p) = \log y - \sum_i \alpha_i \log p_i - 1/2 \sum_i \sum_j \beta_{ij} \log p_i \log p_j \quad (4.5.7a)$$

where, $\beta_{ij} = \beta_{ji}$ for all i, j;

$$\sum_j \beta_{ij} = 0 \text{ for all } i \text{ and } \sum_i \alpha_i = 1 \quad (4.5.7b)$$

For symmetry, adding-up and homogeneity requires that $\beta_{ij}=\beta_{ji}$ for all i, j and $\sum_i \alpha_i = 1$ are to be imposed in the estimation procedure. Similarly, the requirement such as $\sum_j \beta_{ij} = 0$ for all '*i*' should also hold. When working with translog demand system, it is convenient to use Roy's identity to derive the demand system in share form

$$w_i(y,p) = \alpha_i + \sum_j \beta_{ij} \log p_j \quad (4.5.8)$$

As its name indicates, the HTL corresponds to homothetic preferences and hence, the corresponding demand systems exhibits expenditures proportionately.[32] Although, this property makes the HTL uninteresting for empirical demand analysis, we discuss it here for three reasons. First, because the HTL is the simplest translog, it provides a good introduction to the entire translog family. Second, the HTL is a useful building block for formulating interesting demand systems; it is common translog form that unites the translog family. Third, the HTL plays an important role in the analysis of consumer/producer behaviour. The HTL indirect utility function (4.5.7) can be solved explicitly for the log of cost / expenditure function (or in the terminology of production theory, the log of cost function)

$$\log y = \log q + \sum_i \alpha_i \log p_i + 1/2 \sum_i \sum_j \beta_{ij} \log p_i \log p_j \qquad (4.5.9)$$

where 'q' is the quantity demanded and 'y' is the total expenditure (or cost). (This translog cost function, suitably generalized to allow nonconstant returns to scale and technical progress, is the most popular specification in the empirical analysis of cost functions and factor demand systems).

The HTL, like all members of the translog family is a generalisation of the Cobb-Douglas and reduces to it when all of the β's are 0. The α's of the HTL have a straightforward behavioral interpretation such as when all prices are unity, the α's are equal to the expenditure shares. As we show below, thes also has straight forward behavioral interpretation.

The Linear Translog (LTL) indirect utility function is given by

$$u^*(y, p) = \log(y - \sum_i \beta_i p_i) - \sum_i \alpha_i \log p_i - 1/2 \sum_i \sum_j \beta_{ij} \log p_i \log p_j \qquad (4.5.10a)$$

where,

$$\beta_{ij} = \beta_{ji.} \quad \sum \beta_{ij} = 0 \ \text{ for all}'i' \ \text{ and } \sum \alpha_i = 1 \qquad (4.5.10b)$$

The LTL is obtained by translating the origin of the HTL, a process that might loosely be described as introducing 'committed quantities' into the homothetic system. The LTL share equations are given by

$$w_i(y,p) = \left(\beta_i p_i / y\right) + \left(\alpha_i + \sum_j \beta_{ij} \log p_j\right)\left(1 - \sum \beta_j p_j / y\right)$$

(4.5.11)

which corresponds to a demand systems linear in expenditure. Both the LES and HTL are special case of LTL. The LTL, the first translog form in the literature, was first proposed by Lau and Mitchell (1971) and estimated by Manser (1976).

The Log-Translog (Log-TL) indirect utility function is given by:

$$u^*(y,p) = -\sum_i \alpha_i \log(p_i / y) - 1/2 \sum_i \sum_j \beta_{ij} \log(p_i / y) \log(p_j / y)$$

(4.5.12a)

where, $\beta_{ij} = \beta_{ji}$; $\sum_i \sum_j \beta_{ij} = 0$ and $\sum_i \alpha_i = 1$ (4.5.12b)

and the corresponding share equation is given by

$$w_i(y,p) = \frac{\alpha_i + \sum_j \beta_{ij} \log p_j - \log y \sum_j \beta_{ij}}{\sum \alpha_i + \sum_i \sum_j \beta_{ij} \log p_j} = \frac{\alpha_i + \sum_j \beta_{ij} \log p_j - \log y \sum_j \beta_{ij}}{1 + \sum_i \sum_j \beta_{ij} \log p_j}$$

(4.5.13)

As the Log-TL shares equations are linear in the log of total expenditure. The Log-TL belongs to the PIGLOG class.[33] The Log-TL has played a major role in demand system estimation. Both the Log-TL and the Basic Translog (BTL) are often referred to as the 'translog'.[34] The indirect utility function of Basic Traslog (BTL) introduced by Christensen, Jorgenson, and Lau (1975) is given by

$$u^*(y,p) = -\sum_i \alpha_i \log(p_i / y) - 1/2 \sum_i \sum_j \beta_{ij} \log(p_i / y) \log(p_j / y)$$

(4.5.14a)

where, $\beta_{ij} = \beta_{ji}$ and $\sum \alpha_i = 1$ (4.5.14b)

It is straight foreword to show that the BTL share equations are given by

$$w_i(y,p)=\frac{\alpha_i+\sum_j \beta_{ij}\log(p_j/y)}{1+\sum_i\sum_j \beta_{ij}\log(p_j/y)} \tag{4.5.15a}$$

or equivalently $$w_i(y,p)=\frac{\alpha_i+\sum \beta_{ij}\log p_j-\log y\sum_j \beta_{ij}}{1+\sum\sum \beta_{ij}\log p_j-B\log y} \tag{4.5.15b}$$

where, $B=\sum_i\sum_j \beta_{ij}$. For symmetry, adding-up and homogeneity requires that $\beta_{ij}=\beta_{ji}$ for all i, j and $\sum_i \alpha_i=1$ are to be imposed in the estimation procedure. (The normalisation rule $\sum_i \alpha_i+\sum_i\sum_j \beta_{ij}=1$ is sometimes more convenient than $\sum_i \alpha_i=1$; but when $\sum_i\sum_j \beta_{ij}=0$, the two normalisation rules are equivalent.)

The Log-TL is a special case of the BTL obtained by imposing the constraint,

$$B=\sum\sum \beta_{ij}=0 \tag{4.5.16}$$

so that the expenditure drops out of the denominator of the share equation (4.5.15b). The HTL is obtained from the BTL by imposing 'n' parameter restrictions such as

$$\sum_j \beta_{ij}=0 \qquad (i=1,2,3,\ldots\ldots\ldots,n) \tag{4.5.17}$$

with these 'n' restrictions, the expenditure term and the price terms drop out in the denominator, and the expenditure term drops out the numerator of the share equations (4.5.15b).

The income elasticity (η_{i0}) and price elasticities (η_{ij}) of BTL, one of the most popular demand systems of the translog family, can be shown as

$$\eta_{i0} = 1 + \left(w_i \sum_j \beta_{mj} - \sum_j \beta_{ij} \right) \Big/ w_i k \tag{4.5.18}$$

$$\eta_{ij} = -\delta_{ij} + \left(\beta_{ij} w_i \beta_{mj} \right) \Big/ w_i k \quad (i, j = 1, 2, \ldots, n) \tag{4.5.19}$$

where $k = \sum_i \alpha_i + \sum_j \beta_{mj} \log(p_j / y$; $\beta_{mj} = \sum_i \beta_{ij}$; δ_{ij}=1 for $i = j$ and δ_{ij}=0 for $i \neq j$.

Like DTL, the income and price elasticities are invariant under rescaling of prices and income (homogeneous of degree zero) in case of BTL.

The generalized translog (GTL) is obtained by translating the BTL, in the same way that the LTL was obtained by translating the HTL. The indirect utility function is given by

$$u^*(y, p) = \sum_i \alpha_i \log\left(p_i \Big/ (y - \sum_k \beta_k p_k) \right) - 1/2$$

$$\sum_i \sum_j \beta_{ij} \log\left(p_i \Big/ (y - \sum_k \beta_k p_k) \right) \log\left(p_j \Big/ (y - \sum_k \beta_k p_k) \right) \tag{4.5.20}$$

where $\beta_{ij} = \beta_{ji}$ and $\sum \alpha_i = 1$.

The corresponding the share system is given by

$$w_i(y, p) = \frac{\beta_i p_i}{y} + \left(1 - \left(\sum \beta_k p_k / y\right)\right) \frac{\alpha_i + \sum_j \beta_{ij} \log\left(p_j / \left(y - \sum \beta_k p_k\right)\right)}{1 + \sum \sum \beta_{jk} \log\left(p_j / \left(y - \sum \beta_k p_k\right)\right)} \tag{4.5.21}$$

The GTL includes as a special case both the BTL (when all of the β_k are zero for all '*i*') and the LTL when ($\sum_j \beta_{ij} = 0$ for all 'i')

ALMOST IDEAL DEMAND SYSTEM (AIDS)

Efforts in applied demand analysis have centered on specifying demand equations that allows non-linear Engel curves and non-separable preferences. Almost Ideal Demand System (AIDS) is one of such functional form proposed by Deaton-Muellbauer (1980). This model has overcome most of the limitations of demand systems mentioned above and hence, the adjective is 'almost ideal'. The AIDS model is the first order approximation in any demand system and it perfectly aggregates over consumers without forcing linearity on the Engel curves.

The AIDS model is a times-series generalisation of PIGLOG (Price Independent Generalized LOGarithms) Engel function, $w_i = \alpha_i + \beta_i \log y$, where w_i is the budget share of the *i*th item and *y* is the total expenditure of the household. The time-series generalisation would require the inclusion of price explicitly in the above PIGLOG Engel function. This can be achieved by making the parameter '*a*' and '*b*' as functions of prices in a number of ways. The AIDS model is one such attempt.

Alternatively, the demand system can also be derived using an appropriate cost/expenditure function. A general PIGLOG cost function may be specified as

$$\log c(u,p) = (1-u)\log a(p) + u \log b(p) \qquad (4.5.22a)$$

or

$$\log c(u,p) = \log a(p) + u\left[\log b(p) - \log a(p)\right] \qquad (4.5.22b)$$

where '*u*' is the specified level of utility, and *a (p)* and *b (p)* are positive linear homogenous functions of prices. The functions *a (p)* and *b (p)* are interpreted as the cost of subsistence and cost of bliss respectively.[35] The Deaton and Muellbauer (1980) have chosen the following functional forms for *a (p)* and *b (p)*:

$$\log a(p) = a_0 + \sum_{i=1}^{n} a_i \log p_i + (1/2)\sum_{i=1}^{n}\sum_{j=1}^{n} \gamma_{ij}^{*} \log p_i \log p_j \qquad (4.5.23)$$

$$\log b(p) = \log a(p) + \beta_0 \prod_{j=1}^{n} p_j^{\beta_j} \qquad (4.5.24a)$$

$$\log b(p) - \log a(p) = \beta_0 \prod_{j=1}^{n} p_j^{\beta_j} \qquad (4.5.24b)$$

Now substituting (4.5.23) and (4.5.24b) into (4.5.22b), the AIDS cost function becomes

$$\log c(u,p) = \alpha_0 + \sum_{i=1}^{n} \alpha_i \log p_i + (1/2)\sum_{i=1}^{n}\sum_{j=1}^{n} \gamma_{ij}^{*} \log p_i \log p_j + u\,\beta_0 \prod_{j=1}^{n} p_j^{\beta_j} \tag{4.5.25}$$

where α, β *and* γ are parameters of the cost function. The Hicksian demand function can be derived directly from equation (4.5.25) using Shephard's lemma[36] as

$$w_i(y,p) = \alpha_i + \sum_{j=1}^{n} \gamma_{ij} \log p_j + \beta_i u \beta_0 \prod_{j=1}^{n} p_j^{\beta_j} \tag{4.5.26a}$$

where $\gamma_{ij} = 1/2(\gamma_{ij}^{*} + \gamma_{ji}^{*})$. (4.5.26b)

For utility maximizing consumer, total expenditure is equal to the cost and using this relation u can be eliminated from (4.5.26a). Then it will reduce to an AIDS model as[37]

$$w_i(y,p) = \alpha_i + \sum_{j=1}^{n} \gamma_{ij} \log p_j + \beta_i \log(y/P) \quad (i = 1, 2, 3.....,n) \tag{4.5.27a}$$

where $\log P = \alpha_0 + \sum_{i=1}^{n} \alpha_i \log p_i + (1/2)\sum_{i-1}^{n}\sum_{j=1}^{n} \gamma_{ij} \log p_i \log p_j$

(4.5.27b)

Equation (4.5.27a) can be thought of as a first order approximation to any unknown functional relationship on budget share with income and prices. The theoretical restrictions on the cost function (4.5.25) along with the condition (4.5.26b) translate themselves into restriction on the parameter of (4.5.27a). These restrictions are,

Adding–up: $\sum_{i=1}^{n} \alpha_i = 1; \quad \sum_{i=1}^{n} \beta_i = 0 \;\; and \;\; \sum_{i=1}^{n} \gamma_{ij} = 0$ (4.5.28)

Homogeneity: $\sum_{j=1}^{n} \gamma_{ij} = 0$ (4.5.29)

Symmetry: $\gamma_{ij} = \gamma_{ji}$ for all $i \neq j$ (4.5.30)

It is well known that the adding-up restrictions (4.5.28) are part of maintained hypothesis of any demand system because of the data construction itself. For the same reason, this hypothesis cannot be tested. Thus, with the help of AIDS one can test only the restrictions implied by homogeneity (4.5.29) and symmetry (4.5.30) and any other a priori restrictions like implicit or explicit additivity, homotheticity etc.

Like in other functional form, negativity conditions cannot be tested through any restriction on the parameters. The negativity conditions are satisfied for the AIDS model if the matrix 'C' with its elements as

$$c_{ij} = \gamma_{ij} + \beta_i \beta_j \log(y/P) - w_i \delta_{ij} + w_i w_j$$

is negative semi-definite.

For the AIDS model, it can be shown that the expenditure elasticities (η_{i0}) and uncompensatory price elasticities (η_{ij}) are given by

$$\eta_{i0} = 1 + \beta_i / w_i \tag{4.5.31}$$

and $$\eta_{ij} = -\delta_{ij} + \gamma_{ij} - \beta_i \left(\alpha_j + \sum_{i=1}^{n} \gamma_{ij} \log p_i \right) \Big/ w_i \tag{4.5.32}$$

where $\delta_{ij} = 0$ for all $i = j$ and $\delta_{ij} = 0$ for all $i \neq j$

The most interesting feature of (4.5.27a) from econometric viewpoint is that it is very close to being linear. Apart from the expression P in (4.5.27a), the parameters can be estimated equation-by-equation using the OLS. With regard to P, the restrictions on α and γ ensure that (4.5.27b) defines P as a linear homogeneous function of the individual prices. In many practical situations, where prices are nearly collinear, P may be approximately by an exogenous price index, for example the index used by Stone, $\log P^* = \Sigma w_j \log p_j$. The model using this approximation is called the Linearly Approximated Almost Ideal Demand System (LA-AIDS)[38]. In case, we do not want to use the approximation for P, then the AIDS model in

(4.5.27a) will be non-linear in parameters and will therefore require non-linear estimation methods.

DIFFERENT VARIANTS OF AIDS

In consumer demand analysis variables, other than prices and income is often included in demand equation. For instance, in study using cross-section data, demographic variables might be included, and in studies using time series data, trends and seasonal variables might be included. One must be careful to incorporate these demand shift variables in a manner that maintains the theoretical properties of model. The general methods for incorporating demand shifters in demand system include scaling, translating etc.

Like the linear expenditure system, the AIDS model can be made more flexible and analytically more reliable by allowing the intercept term, α_i of the share equations expressed as a linear function of the other explanatory variables like the demographic characteristics, dynamic behaviour related to past consumption, change in consumers taste etc. as suggested by Deaton (1980). A quadratic extension of this model has also been proposed by Blundell, Pashardes and Weber (1993) and further refined by Meenakshi and Ray (1999). There are several other versions of AIDS model like Quadratic AIDS, Generalised AIDS (Bollino, 1987); inverse AIDS (Eales and Unnevehr, 1994), Dynamic AIDS (Blanciforte and Green, 1983)

AIDS with demographic profile

The model proposed by Deaton and Muellbauer (1980) is a flexible functional form which derives the budget share equation starting from the specification of a cost function belonging to PIGLOG family. It can be extended by introducing household characteristics with the translating method.[39] The budget share form of the AIDS model incorporating demographic characteristics is as follows:

$$w_i = \alpha_i + \sum_r \delta_{ir} m_r + \beta_i \log(y / P) + \sum_j \gamma_{ij} \log p_j \tag{4.5.33}$$

The indirect utility function incorporating the demographic characteristics is given by:

$$u^*(p,y) = \left(\log y - \alpha_0 - \sum_i \alpha_i \log p_i - \sum_r \delta_{ir} m_r \log p_i - 1/2 \sum_i \sum_j \log p_i \log p_j\right) \Big/ \prod p_j^{\beta_j}$$

(4.5.34a)

Because of the additivity restriction given by $\sum_{i=1}^{n} w_i = 1$,

parameters are constrained as follows:

$$\alpha_k = 1 - \sum_{i=1}^{n-1} \alpha_i ; \; \delta_{kr} = -\sum_{i=1}^{n-1} \delta_{ir} ; \; \beta_k = -\sum_{i=1}^{n-1} \beta_i \text{ and } \gamma_{kj} = -\sum_{i=1}^{n-1} \gamma_{ij}$$

(4.5.34b)

The equivalent expenditure function for this model is:

$$\log c(u,p) = (1-u)\log a(p) + u \log b(p) \tag{4.5.35}$$

where $b(p) = \prod (p_j)^{\beta_j}$ defines price aggregator.

The Inverse Almost Ideal Demand System (IAIDS)

Although, the AIDS model has been employed successfully in a number of applications, there exist some (perishable) commodities for which the assumption of predetermined (fixed) prices at the market level may be untenable for a given interval of observations. The assumption is that quantity is predetermined by production at the market level, and since it is not storable, price must adjust so the available quantity is consumed. In such situations, it is appropriate to use an inverse form of the AIDS model (IAIDS). The key to the development of such a model is to begin with an alternative representation of preferences, dual to the cost function. This representation is known as the distance function.[40]This model was first proposed by Eales and Unnevehr (1994) and later developed into an inverse Rotterdam system and applied it to the demand for fish. Huang (1990) used the theoretical development of Anderson (1980) and the distance function to generate a system of inverse demands, which were applied to composite food and nonfood commodities.

To derive an Inverse AIDS model, it is necessary to specifying an appropriate distance function. It possesses the same properties as the cost function; i.e. it is linear homogeneous, concave, and non-decreasing in quantities (as opposed to prices); and it is decreasing in utility, rather than increasing (Diewert, 1982). It also has a derivative property similar to the cost function (Deaton, 1979, p. 394). That is, at the optimum, differentiation with respect to the quantity of a particular good yields the compensated inverse demand for that good. Thus, in a manner similar to Deaton and Muellbauer's derivation of the AIDS model (1980) a logarithmic distance function may be specified as

$$\ln D(u,q) = (1-u)\ln a(q) + u \ln b(q) \tag{4.5.36}$$

Because the distance function has the same requirements as the cost function to be consistent with theory (with quantities substituted for prices), log *a(q)* and log *b(q)* may be specified in a manner analogous to that of applied in AIDS:[41]

$$\log a(q) = \alpha_0 + \sum_i \alpha_i \ln q_i + 1/2 \sum_i \sum_j \gamma_{ij}^* \ln q_i \ln q_j \tag{4.5.37a}$$

$$\ln b(q) = \beta_0 \prod_j q_j^{-\beta_j} + \ln a(q) \tag{4.5.37b}$$

This parameterization of equation (4.5.36) yields[42]

$$\ln D(u,q) = \alpha_0 + \sum_i \alpha_i \ln q_i + 1/2 \sum_i \sum_j \gamma_{ij}^* \ln q_i \ln q_j + u\beta_0 \prod_j q_j^{-\beta_j} \tag{4.5.38}$$

Differentiation of (4.5.38) w.r.t. q_i yields a set of compensated inverse demands which relates the budget share of good *'i'* (w_i) to quantities of all goods in the system, *q*s and utility level, *'u'*.[43]

$$\partial \ln D / \partial \ln q_i \,(= w_i) = \alpha_i + \sum_j \gamma_{ij} \ln q_j - \beta_i u \beta_0 \prod_j q_j^{\beta_j} \tag{4.5.39a}$$

where $\gamma_{ij} = 1/2(\gamma_{ij}^* + \gamma_{ji}^*)$ (4.5.39b)

Inversion of the distance function at the optimum yields the direct utility function which may be used to uncompensate the inverse demands:[44]

$$u(q) = -\frac{\ln a(q)}{\left(\ln b(q) - \ln a(q)\right)} \tag{4.5.40}$$

This yields a system of inverse demand functions which will be called the Inverse Almost Ideal Demand System (IAIDS):[45]

$$w_i = \alpha_i + \sum_j \gamma_{ij} \ln q_j + \beta_i \ln Q \tag{4.5.41a}$$

with ln(Q) given by

$$\ln Q = \alpha_0 + \sum_i \alpha_i \ln q_i + 1/2 \sum_i \sum_j \gamma_{ij} \ln q_i \ln q_j \tag{4.5.41b}$$

Like the AIDS model, homogeneity, and symmetry involve only with the fixed unknown coefficients and so may be easily tested or imposed. These restrictions are:

$$\text{Adding up} : \sum_i \alpha_i = 1,\ \sum_i \gamma_{ij} = 0,\ \sum_i \beta_i = 0 \tag{4.5.42a}$$

$$\text{Homogeneity:}\ \sum_i \gamma_{ij} = 0 \tag{4.5.42b}$$

$$\text{Symmetry:}\ \gamma_{ij} = \gamma_{ji} \tag{4.5.42c}$$

Expenditure elasticity (η_{i0}), uncompensated price elasticities (η_{ij}) and compensated price elasticities (η^*_{ij}) are given below:

Expenditure elasticity:

$$\eta_{0j} = -\left(1 - \beta_i / w_i\right) \tag{4.5.43}$$

Uncompensated price elasticity:

$$\eta_{ij} = -\delta_{ij} + \left(\gamma_{ij} + \beta_i (w_j - \beta_j \ln Q)\right) / w_i \tag{4.5.44}$$

Compensated price elasticity:

$$\eta^*_{ij} = \eta_{ij} + w_j (1 - \beta_i / w_i) \tag{4.5.45}$$

As it stands, equation (4.5.41a) requires nonlinear estimation. It would be convenient if one could substitute an approximation to the quantity index equation (4.5.41b) which did not depend on unknown parameters, such as Stone's quantity index. Obviously, the justification employed by Deaton and Muellbauer (1980) for the AIDS model, that prices in time-series data are collinear, is not appropriate for the IAIDS model. Quantities do not move together. Thus, the adequacy of the approximation is an empirical question and no generalization can be made for the LA/IAIDS model[46].

Quadratic Almost Ideal Demand System (QAIDS)

An extension of the AIDS model is the Quadratic Almost Ideal Demand System (QAIDS) proposed recently by Blundell, Pashardes and Weber (1993). It is more general than the AIDS model because it allows non-monotonic behaviour between the budget share of an item and the logarithmic of total expenditure.

Let us assume that household preferences belong to the following quadratic logarithmic family of cost function:

$$\log c(u,p) = \log a(p) + \frac{u\,b(p)}{1-\lambda b(p)u} \qquad (4.5.46)$$

where 'u' is utility , 'p' denotes the vector of prices and *a (p)* and *b (p)* are functions that are homogenous of degree 1 and 0 respectively in prices. On choice of the following functional forms for *a (p)* and *b (p)* in equation (4.5.46) yields the Quadratic Almost Ideal[47] demand system that has been very popular recently. The functional forms of a(p) and b(p) are specified as

$$\log a(p) = \alpha_0 + \sum_i \alpha_i \log p_i + 1/2 \sum_i \sum_j \gamma_{ij} \log p_i \log p_j \, ; \sum_i \alpha_i = 1 \qquad (4.5.47a)$$

$$b(p) = \beta_0 \prod_j p_j^{\beta_j} \; ; \; \sum_j \beta_j = 0 \qquad (4.5.47b)$$

The QAIDS model, which is a quadratic extension of Deaton and Muellbauer's AIDS model, reduces to the later when $\lambda = 0$. In budget share terms, the QAID demand system is given as follows:

$$w_i = \alpha_i + \sum_{j-1}^{n} \gamma_{ij} \log p_j + \beta_i \log y^* + \lambda \beta_i (\log y^*)^2 \quad (4.5.48)$$

where, $y^* = y/a(p)$ is real expenditure and y is total money expenditure. The following restrictions on the demand parameters will be imposed on the demand system as part of the maintained hypothesis.

.Adding Up: $\sum \alpha_i = 1, \quad \sum \beta_i = 0, \quad \sum \gamma_{ij} = 0$ for all 'i' (4.5.49a)

Homogeneity: $\sum_j \gamma_{ij} = 0$ (4.5.49b)

Symmetry: $\gamma_{ij} = \gamma_{ji}$ (4.5.49c)

The parameters of this demand system (4.5.48) afford easy economic interpretation. The parameter α_i is the share of an item in the budget share of a subsistence household at base year prices. The QAIDS allows for the possibility of a non-monotonic relation between budget shares and total expenditure. Thus, unlike the AIDS, the QAIDS model allows the possibility of an inferior item becoming normal or vice versa, as one move across the expenditure spectrum. The expression for expenditure elasticities (η_{i0}) and price elasticities (η_{ij}) of the QAID demand system are given by:

$$\eta_{i0} = 1 + \beta_i / w_i (1 + 2\lambda \log y) \quad (4.5.50a)$$

$$\eta_{ij} = -\delta_{ij} + 1/w_i \left(\gamma_{ij} - \alpha_j \beta_i (1 + 2\lambda \log y)\right) \quad (4.5.50b)$$

We can also extend the QAIDS by incorporating the following functional form for *a(p)*, while *b(p)* takes the same form as in (4.5.47a).

$$\log a(p) = \alpha_0 + \log\left(\sum_i \alpha_i p_i^{\sigma}\right)^{1/\sigma} + 1/2 \sum_i \sum_j \gamma_{ij} \log p_i \log p_j \quad (4.5.51)$$

The extended QAIDS to be referred as EQAIDS, is thus, given by

$$w_i = a_i(p) + \sum_{j-1}^{n} \gamma_{ij} \log p_j + \beta_i \log y^* + \lambda\, \beta_i (\log y^*)^2 \qquad (4.5.52a)$$

where $a_i(p) = \alpha_i p_i^\sigma \Big/ \sum_j \alpha_j p_j^\sigma$ and $y^* = y/a(p)$. (4.5.52b)

Note that EQAIDS[48] extends QAIDS through $\sigma \neq 0$, to allow the 'subsistence budget share' of the '*i*' item to vary with prices. The EQAIDS is thus, a two parameter generalisation of the widely used AIDS and reduces to the later when $\lambda = \sigma = 0$.

The QAIDS (rank-2) can be further extended to a rank-3 demand system called as Generalised Quadratic Almost ideal demand system (GQAIDS) introduced by Banks, Blundell and Lewbel (1992) to allow non-additive among the price terms via $\sigma \neq 0$. In budget share form, GQAIDS is given by[49]

$$w_i = a_i(p) + \sum_{j-1}^{n} \gamma_{ij} \log p_j + \beta_i \log y^* + \lambda_i (\log y^*)^2 \qquad (4.5.53a)$$

where $a_i(p) = \alpha_i p_i^\sigma \Big/ \sum_j \alpha_j p_j^\sigma$ and $y^* = y/a(p)$ (4.5.53b)

The nested version of GQAIDS reduces to rank-2 models like EQAIDS (4.5.52*a*) when $\lambda_i = \lambda\beta_i$; to QAIDS (4.5.48) when $\lambda_i = \lambda\beta_i$ and $\sigma = 0$; finally to AIDS $\lambda_i = 0$ and $\sigma = 0$.

Generalized Almost Ideal Demand System (GAIDS)

Among the theoretical alternatives we like to identify particular alternatives that will preserve the desirable features of the AIDS will allow demand shifter to be incorporated parsimoniously and flexibly. One such alternative approach to adopt a generalized version of AIDS is the Generalized Almost Ideal Demand System (GAIDS).[50] The Generalized almost ideal demand system (GAIDS), first developed by Bollino (1987). The expenditure function used to characterize the GAIDS model allows for a portion of total expenditure to be allocated to 'committed' quantities which are unobservable and must be estimated along with the other parameters in the demand system. The GAIDS cost/expenditure function can be expressed as

$$c(u,p) = p'\gamma + c^{*}(u,p) \qquad (4.4.54)$$

where 'γ' denotes the vector of 'committed quantities' and $c^{*}(u, p)$ is the cost/expenditure function for 'supernumerary expenditure'(its functional form is identical as defined in the almost ideal demand system). In the GAIDS model, the share equation for the budget shares of good 'i'

$$w_i = \frac{p_i\gamma_i}{y} + \frac{y^{*}}{y}\left(\alpha_i + \sum_{j=1}^{n}\gamma_{ij}\ln p_j + \beta_i \ln(y^{*}/P)\right) \qquad (4.4.55a)$$

where $y^{*} = y - p'\gamma$ and

$$\log P = \alpha_0 + \sum_{i=1}^{n}\alpha_i \log p_i + (1/2)\sum_{i-1}^{n}\sum_{j=1}^{n}\gamma_{ij}\log p_i \log p_j \qquad (4.4.55b)$$

The GAIDS model can also be viewed as a generalisation of the Linear Expenditure System (LES), in which the marginal budget shares are no longer constant, but are of the AIDS form. The 'committed' quantities are independent of prices and expenditure, suggesting that augmenting the γ vector by making each 'committed' quantities as a linear function of 'z' to take in to account demographic and other shifting variables/ factors.

The same approach can be applied in the GAIDS model to incorporate any type of demand shifter, producing estimates that are invariant to change in quantity units. To see this replace each committed quantity with linear function z:

$$\gamma_i = \gamma_i^{*} + \delta_i z \qquad (4.5.56)$$

Then the share equation will take the form

$$w_i = \frac{p_i\left(\gamma_i^{*} + \delta_i z\right)}{y} + \frac{y^{*}}{y}\left(\alpha_i + \sum_{j=1}^{n}\gamma_{ij}\ln p_j + \beta_i \ln(y^{*}/P)\right) \qquad (4.5.57)$$

Thus, augmenting, the 'committed' quantities in this fashion do not appear to imply any restriction on how '*z*' affects the demand for any particular good '*i*'.

Dynamic AIDS (DAIDS)

More recent attempts to introduce dynamic elements into demand model include those Blanciforte and Green (1983) who made AIDS model dynamic by incorporating habit effects; the homogeneity and symmetry restrictions which were rejected by Deaton and Muellbauer are tested with more dynamic generalizations. In most of the literature, habit effects are incorporated through introduction of a lagged dependent variable. Habit effects were first introduced into Linear Expenditure System (LES) by Pollak and Wales (1969) by assuming that 'the necessary quantity of each good is proportional to consumption of that commodity in the previous period'. The essence of his habit formation analysis is that: (i) past consumption influences current preferences and hence current demand, and (ii) that a higher level of past consumption of a good implies a higher level of present consumption. Moreover, high autocorrelation found in the AIDS model can be corrected by rightly specifying the model by incorporating habits. AIDS model can be made Dynamic by extending the original model with the specification that α_i as a linear function of previous consumption levels as[51]

$$\alpha_{it} = \alpha_i^* + \delta_i \, q_{it-1} \qquad (4.5.58)$$

This linear habit scheme follows the approach of Pollack and Wales (1969). The parameter δ_i is the habit formation coefficient. The linear function of habit formation can be divided into two parts: α^*_i can be interpreted as a 'physiologically necessary' component whereas $\delta_i \, q_{it-1}$ is the 'psychologically necessary' component. Here, $\delta_i > 0$ implies past consumption influences current consumption of a good, and higher levels of past consumption implies higher levels of present consumption.

By substituting the above equation (4.5.58) in AIDS equation (4.5.27a) we get the 'Dynamic' Version of AIDS.

$$w_i = \alpha_i^* + \delta_i w_{it-1} + \sum \gamma_{ij} \log p_j + \beta_i \log(y/P) \quad (4.5.59a)$$

where $\gamma_{ij} = 1/2(\gamma_{ij}^* + \gamma_{ji}^*)$ (4.5.59b)

and $\log(P) = \alpha_0 + \sum_i \alpha_i \log p_i + \frac{1}{2}\sum_i \sum_j \gamma_{ij} \log p_i \log p_j$ (4.5.59c)

The habit forming effects incorporated in AIDS play an important role in determining future consumption level. Hence such effects should be incorporated while estimating demand systems.

DYNAMIC DEMAND SYSTEMS

The demand models discussed so far are essentially static in nature and attempts to make the parameters depend on time, past consumption (Pollak & Wales, 1969) or even explicit inclusion of time as an explanatory variable. In reality, current purchase of durable goods depend not only on current income and prices, but also on income profile, level of stocks held, habit formation, income expectations and so on. These factors introduce elements of dynamism into the consumer's decision making process. Since in practice, it is not possible to incorporate all these factors and some of which are not directly observable, attempts have, therefore, been made to evolve dynamic analytical models that are simple and can be conveniently estimated.

There are two approaches to the analysis of dynamic demand models. In the first approach, variables such as stock, current purchases of durables etc. are included in the utility function to be maximized subject to a budget constraint and depreciation rules. The studies of Tintner (1938); Boulding (1950); Cramer (1957), Fisher and Shell (1969); Houthakker & Taylor (1970), Mattei (1971); Phlips (1973) etc. belongs to this category. The second approach is to postulate the demand model itself in terms of stock, state variables etc. The models of Stone & Rowe (1957), Houthakker & Taylor (1970) etc. are some of the models belongs to the second category.

DYNAMIC LINEAR EXPENDITURE SYSTEM

Fisher and Shell (1969); Pollak and Wales (1969); Pollak (1970) and Phlips (1972) have dynamised the Stone and Geary utility function by expressing γ in equation (4.3.2) as a linear function lagged quantities (i.e. q_{it-1}, q_{it-2} in discrete time) or to stock (of durables) s_i. To stay within the framework of linear expenditure system, the relation should be linear, i.e.,

$$\gamma_i = \gamma_i^{\circ} + \alpha_i s_i \tag{4.6.1}$$

Leading to $u(q) = \sum_i \beta_i \log\left(q_i - \gamma_i^{\circ} - \alpha_i s_i\right)$ (4.6.2)

When $\alpha_i > 0$, the taste change is quality diminishing and when $\alpha_i < 0$, the taste change is quality augmenting. It is important to realize that different decisions in the past lead to different preference ordering in the present according to (4.6.2). A specification γ_{it} as linear function of q_{it-1} was suggested by Pollak and Wales (1969).

The dynamic utility function (4.6.2) is the short-run utility function. In the dynamic context, the short-run is indeed defined as a framework of analysis in which the variables under study have no time to adjust fully so as to attain a steady state. The long-run is then; by definition is such that the variables will reach a position of rest or at an equilibrium point. The steady state or long-run equilibrium will be characterised by the fact that, $q_{it} = q_{it-1}$ (for all t) or $q_{it} - q_{it-1}$ for discrete time and $q_i = 0$ for continuous time. The same is true for s_i for which $s_1 = q_i - \delta_i s_i = 0$ which implies for continuous time.

Now maximizing (4.6.2) subject to the budget constraint leads to a system of demand functions (expenditure functions) as

$$q = \left(\gamma^{\circ} + \hat{\alpha}\, s\right) + \hat{p}^{-1}\beta\left(y - p'\left(\gamma^{\circ} + \hat{\alpha}\, s\right)\right) \tag{4.6.3a}$$

$$\hat{p}q = \hat{p}\left(\gamma^{\circ} + \hat{\alpha}\, s\right) + \beta\left(y - \hat{p}\left(\gamma^{\circ} + \hat{\alpha}\, s\right)\right) \tag{4.6.3b}$$

Algebraically,

$$p_i q_i = (\gamma_i^\circ + \alpha_i s_i) p_i + \beta_i \left(y - \sum_j p_j (\gamma_j^\circ + \alpha_j s_j) \right) \quad (4.6.3c)$$

where $\beta_i > 0; (q_i - \gamma_i^\circ - \alpha_i) > 0; \sum \beta_i = 0$; '$q$' is the vector of current purchases; γ is the vector of constants; 's' is the vector of stock; $\hat{\alpha}$ and $\hat{p}$ are the diagonal matrices of constants and prices, respectively. Equation (4.6.3b) or (4.6.3c) is the linear expenditure system (short-run) in which the state variable 's_i' is included. But the long-run expenditure system is of the same form as the static linear demand system.

$$\hat{p}q = \hat{p}\gamma^* + \beta^* (y - p'\gamma^*) \quad (4.6.4a)$$

or

$$p_i q_i = \gamma_i^* p_i + \beta_i^* \left[y - \sum_j p_j \gamma_j^* \right] \quad (4.6.4b)$$

where

$$\gamma_i^* = \frac{\delta_i \gamma_i^\circ}{\delta_j - \alpha_j} \text{ and } \beta_i^* = \left(\frac{\delta_i \beta_i}{\delta_i - \alpha_i} \right) \Big/ \left(\sum_j \frac{\delta_j \beta_j}{\delta_j - \alpha_j} \right) \quad (4.6.4c)$$

In the long-run equilibrium, $s_i = 0$ (and denote $\delta s_i / \delta_t = s_i^*$) implies quantities purchased are equal to consumption or depreciation ($\delta_i s_i$). Replacing s_i by y/δ_i in the first order condition and taking into account the budget constraint equation (4.6.2) will lead to the system of long-run expenditure equations (4.6.4a) and the corresponding long-run utility function is given by

$$u(q) = \sum_i \beta_i^* \log(q_i - \gamma_i^*) \quad (4.6.5)$$

It is noticed that $\gamma_i^* = \dfrac{\delta_i \gamma_i^\circ}{\delta_i - \alpha_i}$ is larger than γ_i° when, $\alpha_i > 0$, i.e., for habit forming commodities and r_i^* is smaller than γ_i° when i.e., for durable. The long-run income and price elasticities obey the static formula with β_i and γ_i and replaced by β^*_i and γ^*_i respectively. The short-term demand functions can be incorporated as a partial adjustment process to long-run demand functions. The difference of the estimates, where k_{ii} (where $k_{ii} = \delta_i - a_i$) provides an estimate of the adjustment coefficients. It implies that greater is the rate of depreciation for a given α_i the faster the habits wear off and the faster the habits can adjust to the equilibrium level, s^*. The same is true for the stock of durable goods. The greater is the influence of (α_i) on habits for a given δ_i, the smaller is the reaction coefficient and conversely for the durables, i.e., when α_i is negative.

Clements, Evan and Ironmonger (1978) developed a new dynamic version of the LES. The dynamics is derived from the utility function specifications, which includes an adjustment cost term. Andrikopoulos, Brox and Gamaletsos (1984) applied Dynamic Generalised Linear Expenditure System (DGLES) for demand forecasting of different commodities using Canadian data. The recent empirical studies on dynamic linear expenditure system are Lamm(1982), Ray (1986), Chambers (1992) and finally the study of Taube and Mcdonald (1991) using the Dynamic Almost Ideal Demand System which incorporate consumer expectations are noteworthy.

DYNAMIC QUADRATIC EXPENDITURE SYSTEM

A more straightforward procedure has been adopted by Houthakker and Taylor (1970); Weiserbs (1972, 1974) and Phlips (1972) who maximise a quadratic utility function dependent upon stocks, state variables and current purchases subject to a budget constraint. They choose to work with a quadratic utility function, probably because its first order partial derivatives are linear, so that equilibrium conditions are linear in the variables. The quadratic utility function is

$$u(q,s) = q'a - s'b + \frac{1}{2}q'\hat{A}\,q + q'\hat{B}\,s + \frac{1}{2}s'\hat{C}\,s \qquad (4.6.6)$$

where 'q' and 's' are vectors of current purchases and stocks, respectively; a and b constant vectors; $\hat{A}$, $\hat{B}$ and $\hat{C}$ are (constant) nonsingular diagonal matrices. The vectors 'q' and 's' are functions of time, which are treated as continuous. The element of dynamism is introduced through accumulation function $\dot{s} = q - \hat{D}s$, where $\hat{D} = \hat{\delta}$ is a diagonal and nonsingular matrix with δ_i, on the main diagonal (Houthakker and Taylor, 1970). The last equation of the model is the budget constrains, $p'q = y$. The finite approximation to the first order condition gives the estimating equation.

$$q_t = k_0 + k_1 q_{t-1} + k_2 \lambda_t p_t + k_3 \lambda_{t-1} p_{t-1} \tag{4.6.7}$$

where $k_0 = -\left[I + \frac{1}{2}\left(\hat{A}^{-1}\hat{B} + \hat{D}\right)\right]^{-1} \hat{A}^{-1}\hat{D}a$

$$k_1 = \left[I + \frac{1}{2}\left(\hat{A}^{-1}\hat{B} + \hat{D}\right)\right]^{-1} \left[I - \frac{1}{2}\left(\hat{A}^{-1}\hat{B} + \hat{D}\right)\right]$$

$$k_2 = \left[I + \frac{1}{2}\left(\hat{A}^{-1}\hat{B} + \hat{D}\right)\right]^{-1} \hat{A}^{-1}\left(I + \frac{1}{2}\hat{D}\right)$$

$$k_3 = -\left[I + \frac{1}{2}\left(\hat{A}^{-1}\hat{B} + \hat{D}\right)\right]^{-1} \hat{A}^{-1}\left(I - \frac{1}{2}\hat{D}\right)$$

The diagonal elements of $\hat{B}$, b_{ii} play the same role as α_i in the dynamic linear expenditure system.

The quadratic model[52] is inferior in terms of forecasting performance (Taylor and Weiserbs, 1972). The empirical results based on these models indicate that the associated short-term and long-term elasticities do differ appreciably.

CONCLUSION

A variety complete demand systems have been proposed for econometric use. All pay strong allegiance to the neo-classical demand theory. Most of the demand systems introduce restrictions in order to simplify the model and to reduce the number of parameters to be estimated. The models based on well behaved utility functions satisfy the theoretical restrictions such as adding-up, homogeneity and the Slutsky symmetry conditions but the later two restrictions must be imposed while estimation of non-utility based demand systems. The large number of parameters in demand systems offers more descriptive flexibility but this advantage must be weighed against the advantages of simplicity offered by other models.

On theoretical grounds, however, none of the models dominates its competitors. The choice of specification for empirical work must then be made on an empirical basis as the models differ in their computational problems and in empirical performance. Comparisons of the model's predictive abilities on non- sample data would be desirable. The models can also be compared on the basis of goodness of fit to the sample data for each commodity separately; the concept of average information accuracy is generally applied to evaluate the overall fit of the model to the data. The elasticity estimates at mean level expenditure shares are also contrasted for such comparison.

NOTES

1. See Schultz (1938). He estimated linear demand equations without the independent variable, income. The time trend was used as a proxy for the effects of increasing income among other variables. Also see Allen and Bowley (1935).
2. See Stone (1954). A similar specification was used by Wold and Jureen (1953) and Houthakker, 1965.
3. Prais and Houthakker (1955) estimated the semi-logarithmic demand function using the budget data of 1938 for British middle-class families.
4. The classic example of the single-equation approach to demand analysis probably the massive study by Stone (1954) consumer's expenditure on non-durable goods during 1920-38 for U.K. Stone's work is notable for his attempt to employ theory to refine the estimating procedure of demand equations.
5. One is interested in complete system demand functions rather than each demand function taken individually because the system as a whole provides important information on the degree and nature of interrelationship of the demand functions. More specifically, the demand systems identifies the effects of change in price of certain goods on the demand for other goods (for details refer Lau, 1976 and Thomas, 1987)

6. See Powell, (1974); Barten (1977); Deaton and Muellbauer (1980); Deaton (1986); Theil and Clements (1987) and Pollak and Wales (1992) and Deaton (1997); and Radhakrishna and Murty (1999).
7. See Radhakrishna and Murty (1999)
8. See Stone (1954, 19720; Barten (1997); Deaton and Muellbauer (1980); Phlips (1983) and Deaton (1986).
9. This interpretation of γ_i is only suggestive and not always possible to do so, particularly when $\gamma_i < 0$. A negative γ_i is, however, not inconsistent with theory. Further, $\gamma_i < 0$ allows own-price elasticity to exceed unity in magnitude. When every $\gamma_i > 0$, LES admit only price inelastic goods.
10. This approach is explored in more detail in AIDS model.
11. Stones search procedure though has a good record of convergence but it is typically slow.
12. Linear Expenditure System (LES) has number of variants, generalisation and several other modifications and extensions. In this chapter, few such variants are presented.
13. For details of LES with 'demographic translation' and 'demographic scaling' refer Pollak and Wales, 1992.
14. For details of LES with habit formation hypothesis refer Pollak and Wales, 1992.
15. Cross-sectional estimation of the LES and ELES was first undertaken by Belendria (1971) and subsequently reformulated by Powell (1974) and Howe (1974).
16. For details of ELES with saving as commodity with zero 'subsistence quantity' refer Howe (1975)
17. See Strotz (1959) and Gorman (1959) for the conditions under which multi-stage budgeting is consistent. The additivity condition of LES is needed for consistency of multi-stage budgeting in HLES.
18. The direct addilog system is perhaps less universally familiar because it has proved analytically intractable and its inconvenient form has made it difficult either to use and to compare with other model. Deaton (1974) has found that it can be expressed in the Rotterdam framework by an appropriate selection of parameters so that its empirical and theoretical properties can be compared directly with other models which are also expressible in Rotterdam format.
19. As far as the analytical aspects of the two models viz., LES and IAS are concerned, the assumption of direct additivity implicit in LES appears to be less restrictive than the assumption of indirect additivity implicit in the later model. LES is also easier to estimate and offer fewer complications than the IAS model (see Brown and Deaton, 1972 for the details).
20. See Anderson (1980) and Waymark (1980) for the theoretical discussions on price-dependent inverse demand systems.
21. This system was first proposed by Leser (1941-42) and has been extensively used by Somermeyer et al. (1972, 1973)
22. Houthakker (1960) has shown that an indirect utility function is additive if and only if the cross-price elasticities with respect any price are identical for all commodity groups.

23. To satisfy condition (iii), we need further restrictions on the parameters.
24. For details refer Theil (1965): The information approach to demand analysis.
25. See McFadden's "Note on Professor Theil's Demand System", University of California (mimeo).
26. Several demand systems like the Rotterdam, the AIDS, the CBS model can also be seen as special cases of a general differential equation for the budget share i.e. $dw_i = w_iDq_i + w_iDp_i - w_iDy$ where the operator symbol 'D' stands for total differential of log of the variable.
27. Different demand equations can be obtained by applying different parameterization of the differential budget share equations, $Dw_i = w_iDq_i + w_iDp_i - w_i\, Dy$. The term parameterization refers to the assumptions made concerning the constancy of certain parameters of the model. Since all the parameters are, in general, a function of total expenditure and prices, the assumptions of constancy over the period of observations is in fact an assumption as important as the choice of the model.
28. The studies by Diwert (1974), Muellbauer (1975) and Carlevaro (1976) examined some demand systems quadratic in total expenditure. Pollak and Wales (1978) have also proposed a quadratic expenditure system almost similar to the one presented here. The essential difference between the two is that $\alpha(p)$ is a geometric rather than an arithmetic price index.
29. It may be noted that (4.4.10) reduces itself to the indirect utility function of the LES if $\alpha_i = 0$ for all 'i'. This particular form (4.4.10) is a monotonic transformation of (4.3.3).
30. The NASSE Expenditure System is generally used as the second stage model. It is non-additive model and allows inferior goods. It is used to estimate the parameter of the broad item like vegetables, fruits, nuts in the 'other food' group.
31. A demand system is said to be a 'flexible functional form' if it is capable of providing a second order approximation to the behaviour of any theoretically plausible demand system at a point in the price-expenditure space.
32. Expenditure proportionality plays crucial role in the theory of aggregation over good. Expenditure proportionality implies that the budget shares of every good is independent of household total expenditure, thus, contradicts the Engel's Law. Most of the standard closed-form globally defined demand systems exhibit expenditure proportionality. For details refer Blackorby, Primont and Russell (1978).
33. The AIDS model like the log-TL is a member of both the translog family and the PIGLOG class.
34. The log-TL has recently played a major role in the demand system estimation (Jorgenson, 1990). In the literature, we rarely find the log-TL as a separate demand system as both log-TL and basic- translog system are referred to as translog demand system. Pollak and Wales (1992) distinguishes log-TL and basic- translog as two different demand systems to avoid confusion.

35. If utility is scaled such that $0 \leq u \leq 1$, then a(p) determines the quantities to reach the level of subsistence ($u = 0$) and b(p) determines the quantities to achieve bliss ($u = 1$).
36. As per Shephard's lemma, the price derivatives of the cost function are the quantities demanded i.e. $\delta c\ (u,p)/\delta p_i = q_i$; multiply both sides of this equation by $p_i / c\ (u,p)$ will provide $\delta\ log c\ (u,p)/\delta\ log p_i = p_i q_i / c\ (u,p) = p_i q_i / y = w_i$.
37. In a series of articles, Lewbel (1987, 1991, and 1995) has extended the Gorman's concept of 'rank' of an Engel curve to any demand system. He has introduced the idea of a fractional demand systems expressed in budget share form. According to this approach, the rank of any demand system is defined as the minimum number of function in income (including the constant term) required such that all of the Engel curves can be expressed as linear combination of these income functions. The rank of a demand function is also equal to the minimum number of functions in prices required to express the cost or indirect utility function. Based on these definitions, the LES and its variants and AIDS have rank two and the quadratic extensions of the LES and AIDS have rank three. A rank three demand systems are supposed to extract all the information available in budget data.
38. Deaton and Muellbauer (1980) with British data have found that the parameter estimates did not very much between the non-linear estimation and the linear version of AIDS (i.e LA\AIDS). Pashardes (1993) argued that Stone's approximation of the price index leads to bias in parameter estimates of AIDS. The bias will be more serious for micro-level data than the aggregate time series data like ours.
39. See Pollak and Wales (1992) for detail analysis on 'demographic translation' and 'demographic scaling'.
40. The distance function characterizes the amount by which all quantities consumed must be changed proportionately to attain a particular level of utility. That is, it gives the proportional 'distance' along any ray through the origin that quantities must be reduce or inflated to reach a particular indifference surface. The distance function is defined implicitly by $u(q/D\ (u,q))$.
41. Interpretation of $a(q)$ and $b(q)$ are analogous to those of $a(p)$ and $b(p)$ for the AIDS model. If utility is scaled such that, $0 \leq u \leq 1$ then $a(q)$ gives the value by which q must be divided to reach subsistence ($u = 0$) and $b(q)$ is the value by which q must be divided to achieve bliss ($u = 1$).
42. The following logarithmic distance function is not the dual of the AIDS logarithmic cost function. To our knowledge, no closed-form solution for the dual of the AIDS log-cost function exists.
43. The derivative property of the distance function is $\delta\ D(u,q)/\delta\ q_i = \pi_i$, where the π_is are prices normalized by expenditure on all goods in the system, that is, p_i / y . The derivative of the distance function with respect to the quantity of any good in the system yields compensated inverse demands [Deaton (1979, p.394)]. This may be manipulated by multiplying both sides by and remembering that if 'q' is the bundle for which $u(q) = u$

then $D(u, q) = 1$. This results in compensated inverse demand in share form:

$$\left(\partial D(u,q)/\partial q_i\right)\left(q_i/D(u,q)\right) = \partial \ln D(u,q)/\partial \ln q_i = p_i q_i / y = w_i .$$

44. If q^* is the consumption bundle proportional to 'q' which lies on indifference surface u, then $D(u, q^*) = 1$. If equation (4.5.36) is evaluated at q^*, then In $D(u,q^*) = 0 = (1-u)$In a(q^*) + u In b (q^*) = In a (q*) + u {In b (q*) –In a (q^*)} and, therefore, . See Deaton (1979, p.393).
45. Barten and Bettendorf (1989) derived a linearised version of equation (4.5.41a) in first difference form and observed its similarity to an inverse form of the AIDS model. However, their form was derived from an inverse Rotterdam model. See also Moschini and Vissa (1991).
46. This is, also, true for the AIDS model as well. That is the adequacy of the approximation is always an empirical question. However, often those who employ LA/AIDS do not check its validity for their particular application. Theoretically, the accuracy of the approximation is of little importance. However, from the practical perspective, the availability of a linear approximation is of some interest. This is especially true if the IAIDS model is to be embedded within a market model, where issues of concern include not only ease of estimation, but model solutions as well.
47. For QAIDS refer Blundell, Pashardes and Weber (1993); Dickens, Fry and Pashardes (1993); Meenakshi and Ray (1999); and Alston, Chalfant and Piggott (2001)
48. See Banks, Blundell and Lewbel (1992); Ray (1996); and Meenakshi and Ray (1999) for EQAIDS.
49. See Banks, Blundell and Lewbel (1992); Ray (1996); and Meenakshi and Ray (1999) for GQAIDS.
50. See Bollino (1987); Bollino and Violi (1990). Pollak and Wales (1992) for GAIDS.
51. See Pollak (1970); Blanciforte and Green (1983); Alessi and Kapteyn (1991) and Heien and Durham (1991) for DAID.
52. A slightly different discrete dynamic quadratic model was estimated by Mattei (1971) using Swiss data.

5

SPECIFICATION AND ESTIMATION OF LINEAR EXPENDITURE SYSTEM AND ITS VARIANTS

INTRODUCTION

To bridge the gap between theory and empirics in demand analysis, restrictive hypothesis on the structures of individual consumer preferences are often made. The well-known and analytically simple working hypothesis is the additivity of the utility function. Houthakker (1960) being the first to introduce this additivity assumption both direct and indirect has received the attention of many researchers[1] those who have studied its empirical implication in applied demand analysis during 1970s. The analytical implication of such hypothesis is tremendous. The well known and popular demand systems obeying this additivity assumption are the Linear Expenditure System, the Direct and Indirect Addilog Systems etc. The LES being the widely experimented demand system was originally developed by Richard Stone as early as 1954. Later, it has been shown by Stone and Geary that this demand system can be derived from the Klein-Robin utility index of cost of living.

The important assumptions underlying the LES model are the linearity of all the Engel curves, constancy of committed quantities and marginal budget shares. Stone himself pointed out the inability of this model to capture price responses. Attempts are being made to overcome these as well as other structural limitations like the range of own price elasticity which lies between -1 to 0 $(-1 < \eta_{ii} < 0)$. The violation of the Engel's law and the exclusion of complimentary goods, which is a consequence of the additivity hypothesis form the analysis. Stone (1964) and Nasse (1970) have suggested to assume the 'committed quantities' (γ_i) parameter as a function of prices. Pollak and Wales (1969) enhanced its applicability by making γ_i to depend on time using their habit formation concept. Brown and Heien (1972) had further, generalized LES to include complementary goods and relaxed the ranges of own price elasticities to vary between $-\infty$ to 0 $(-\infty < \eta_{ii} < 0)$.

This chapter is structured into ten sections. Section 1 is the introduction. The LES along with its theoretical restrictions are explained in Section 2. Section 3 deals with the direct and indirect utility functions along with the cost function associated with LES. Section 4 analyses the implication of additivity restriction of LES. The estimable model of LES and its variants in budget share form along with its theoretical restrictions, and the measures of goodness of fit are presented in Section 5. Section 6 provides the method of estimation of LES and its variants. A brief note of the data base and the consumer price index used for the estimation of LES and its variants are presented in Section 7 and Section 8 respectively. Section 9 narrates the magnitude and nature of inter-sectoral and inter-temporal variations in consumption patterns in Orissa and all India. Section 10 deals with the empirical analysis of LES and its variants. Finally, Section 11 is the concluding remarks of this chapter.

LINEAR EXPENDITURE SYSTEM (LES)

We now turn to consider the model of consumer demand which results when the utility functions is of the Stone Geary form

$$u = \sum_{i=1}^{n} \beta_i \log(q_i - \gamma_i)$$

in which β's and γ's are parameters with

$$0 < \beta_i < 1, \quad \gamma_i \geq 0, \qquad (i = 1,2,......,n)$$

$$\sum_{i=1}^{n} \beta_i = 1$$

and the function being defined only for

$$(q_i - \gamma_i) > 0 \qquad (i = 1,2,......,n)$$

This function was shown by Geary (1949) to justify a true cost of living index which had been proposed by Klein and Rubin (1947). The demand functions which it generates have been developed and applied extensively by Stone (1954, 1962, 1964, 1965 & 1966) and Stone, Brown, and Rowe (1964).

Defining the parameter vectors as

$$\beta = \{\beta_1,...,\beta_n\}' \quad and \quad \gamma = (\gamma_1,...,\gamma_n)'$$

we may express the Stone-Geary utility function in matrix form as

$$u = \beta' \log(q - \gamma), \tag{5.2.1}$$

$$0 < \beta < \iota, \qquad \gamma \geq 0, \quad \iota'\beta = 1 \quad and \quad (q - \gamma) > 0^2$$

Differentiating u with respect to 'q' gives the vector of marginal utilities of the goods

$$u_q = \frac{\partial u}{\partial q} = (\hat{q} - \hat{\gamma})^{-1} \beta .$$

Alternatively, we have

$$u_i = \frac{\partial u}{\partial q_i} = \beta_i (q_i - \gamma_i)^{-1} \qquad (i = 1,2,......,n),$$

with $\beta > 0$ and $(q - \gamma) > 0$, clearly $u_q > 0$. The second order derivative matrix is

$$U = \frac{\partial u_q}{\partial q'} = -(\hat{q} - \hat{\gamma})^{-1} \hat{\beta} (\hat{q} - \hat{\gamma})^{-1}$$

Alternatively, we have

$$u_{ij} = \frac{\partial^2 u}{\partial q_i \, \partial q_j} = \begin{cases} -\beta_i (q_i - \gamma_i)^{-2} & \text{if } i = j \\ 0 & \text{if } i \neq j \end{cases} \qquad (i, j = 1, 2, \ldots\ldots, n).$$

The Stone-Geary utility function is, thus, directly additive. With $\beta_i > 0$ and $(q_i - \gamma_i) > 0$ for all 'i', diminishing marginal utility operates for each good. The matrix U is diagonal and has all its diagonal elements negative, thus, it is negative definite. Its inverse,

$$U^{-1} = -(\hat{q} - \hat{\gamma})\hat{\beta}^{-1}(\hat{q} - \hat{\gamma})$$

is also negative definite.

The complete set of demand functions can be obtained on maximizing 'u' subject to $p'q = y$, with y and p given. Setting the first derivatives of the Lagrangian function as $u_q = \lambda \, p$ gives

$$(\hat{q} - \hat{\gamma})^{-1} \, \beta = \lambda \, p,$$

that is

$$\beta = \lambda(\hat{q} - \hat{\gamma}) \, p = \lambda \, \hat{p}(q - \gamma) \qquad (5.2.2)$$

Pre-multiplying by ι' and using $\iota'\beta = 1$ and $p'q = y$ yields

$$\iota'\beta = \lambda \, \iota' \hat{p}(q - \gamma) = \lambda \, p'(q - \gamma) = \lambda(p'q - p'\gamma) = \lambda(y - p'\gamma) = 1.$$

Hence, we have

$$\lambda = (y - p'\gamma)^{-1} \qquad (5.2.3)$$

Alternatively, we have

$$\lambda = \left(y - \sum_i p_i \, \gamma_i \right)^{-1}$$

Substituting (5.2.3) into (5.2.2) gives

$$\beta = (y - p'\gamma)^{-1} \, \hat{p} \, (q - \gamma)$$

So, we have, $\hat{p}(q-\gamma)=(y-p'\gamma)\beta$

or $$\hat{p}q=\hat{p}\gamma+(y-p'\gamma)\beta \tag{5.2.4a}$$

Finally, we have

$$q=\gamma+(y-p'\gamma)\,\hat{p}^{-1}\beta\,. \tag{5.2.5a}$$

Alternatively, the last two equations can be written as

$$p_iq_i=p_i\gamma_i+\beta_i\left(y-\sum_j p_j\gamma_j\right) \quad (i=1,2,....,n) \tag{5.2.4b}$$

$$q_i=\gamma_i+\beta_ip_i^{-1}\left(y-\sum_j p_j\gamma_j\right) \quad (i=1,2,.......,n) \tag{5.2.5b}$$

Equation (5.2.4a) may be written as

$$\begin{aligned}\hat{p}q &= y\beta+\hat{p}\gamma-p'\gamma\ \beta\\ &= y\ \beta+\hat{\gamma}\ p-\beta\ \gamma'\ p\\ &= y\ \beta+(I-\beta\ \iota')\hat{\gamma}\ p\end{aligned} \tag{5.2.6a}$$

Alternatively, we have

$$p_iq_i=\beta_i\ y+\sum_{j=1}^{n}(\delta_{ij}-\beta_i)\gamma_jp_j \quad (i=1,2.....,n) \tag{5.2.6b}$$

where $$\delta_{ij}=\begin{cases}1\ if\ i=j\\ 0\ if\ i\neq j\end{cases}$$

and 'δ_{ij}' is the Kronecker delta. Thus in (5.2.6a), the specific expenditure on each good is a linear homogeneous function of income and prices. For this reason the model is referred to as the *linear expenditure system,* or more precisely as Stone's linear expenditure system.

A useful interpretation of the parameters of this system is that given income y and prices $p_1,....,p_n$; the consumer first purchases 'minimum required quantities' of each good γ_1 of good-1; γ_2 of good-2 and so γ_n of good-n at the given prices, these costs $\sum_j p_j \gamma_j$, which may be termed 'subsistence income'.

He is left with $\left(y - \sum_j p_j q_j \right)$, which may be termed as 'supernumerary income'. He then distributes the 'supernumerary income' among the goods in the proportions $\beta_1, \ldots\ldots, \beta_n$ (The β 's are thus identified with the μ 's, the marginal budget shares of the previous chapter). Recall that the utility function is defined only for $(q_i - \gamma_i) > 0 \quad (i = 1, 2, \ldots\ldots, n)$; it makes no prediction about the behaviour of a consumer for whom $y - \sum_j p_j (q_j - \gamma_j) < 0$ since he cannot afford to acquire $\gamma_1, \gamma_2 \ldots, \gamma_n$ at the going prices. There is of course no need to interpret the $\gamma's$ as physical minima.[3]

Now consider the demand functions themselves. The income slope vector is readily found from (5.2.5a):

$$q_y = \frac{\partial q}{\partial y} = \hat{p}^{-1} \beta . \tag{5.2.7a}$$

Alternatively, we have

$$\left(\frac{\partial q_i}{\partial y} \right) = \beta_i p_i^{-1} \quad (i = 1, 2, \ldots. n). \tag{5.2.7b}$$

The Engel curves which relate quantities to income, with all prices given, are linear which can be specified as

$$q_i = \left(\gamma_i - \beta_i p_i^{-1} \sum_j p_j \gamma_j \right) + \left(\beta_i p_i^{-1} \right) y \quad (i = 1, 2, \ldots\ldots, n). \tag{5.2.8}$$

The linearity is being already apparent from the fact that $\left(\frac{\partial q_i}{\partial y}\right)$ does not vary with 'y'. The price slope matrix is also to be as

$$Q_p = \frac{\partial q}{\partial p'} = -(y - p'\gamma)\,\hat{p}^{-1}\,\hat{\beta}\,\hat{p}^{-1} - \hat{p}^{-1}\beta\,\gamma' \qquad (5.2.9a)$$

Alternatively, we have

$$\left(\frac{\partial q_i}{\partial p_j}\right) = \begin{cases} -(y - p'\gamma)\beta_i\,p_i^{-2} - \beta_i\gamma_i\,p_i^{-1} & \textit{if } i = j \\ -\beta_i\,\gamma_j p_i^{-1} & \textit{if } i \neq j \end{cases} \qquad (5.2.9b)$$

The demand curves which relate quantities to own-prices, income and all other prices being given, are hyperbolic and given by

$$q_i = \left[(1 - \beta_i)\gamma_i\right] + \left[\beta_i\left(y - \sum_{j \neq i} p_j\,\gamma_j\right)\right]p_i^{-1} \qquad (5.2.10)$$

The hyperbolicity being already apparent from the form of $\left(\frac{\partial q_i}{\partial p_i}\right)$.[4]

It is observed that q_y and Q_p satisfies the following restrictions (5.2.11) to (5.2.14), since the linear expenditure system has been obtained by classical utility maximization. Thus,
First, Engel aggregation is given by,

$$p'q_y = p'\hat{p}^{-1}\beta = \iota'\beta = 1 \qquad (5.2.11)$$

Second, Cournot aggregation is given by,

$$Q_p'\,p = -(y - p'\gamma)\,\hat{p}^{-1}\,\hat{\beta}\,\hat{p}^{-1}\,p - \gamma\,\beta'\hat{p}^{-1}p$$

$$= -(y - p'\gamma)\hat{p}^{-1}\hat{\beta}\,\iota - \gamma\,\beta'\iota = -\left[(y - p'\gamma)\hat{p}^{-1}\beta + \gamma\right] = -q$$

(5.2.12)

Third, the symmetry condition is shown by,

$$\left(Q_p + q_y q'\right)' = -\left[\left(y - p'\gamma\right)\hat{p}^{-1}\hat{\beta} + \gamma\,\beta'\right]\hat{p}^{-1} + \left[\gamma + \left(y - p'\gamma\right)\hat{p}^{-1}\beta\right]\beta'\hat{p}$$

$$= -\left(y - p'y\right)\hat{p}^{-1}\left(\hat{\beta} - \beta\,\beta'\right)\hat{p}^{-1} = \left(Q_p + q_y\,q'\right) \quad (5.2.13)$$

Fourth, the homogeneity condition is shown by,

$$Q_p\,p = -\left(y - p'\gamma\right)\hat{p}^{-1}\beta\;\hat{p}^{-1}p - \hat{p}^{-1}\,\beta\,\gamma'\,p$$

$$= -\left(y - p'\gamma\right)\hat{p}^{-1}\beta - \hat{p}^{-1}\beta\,\gamma'\,p = -y\,\hat{p}^{-1}\,\beta = -q_y\,y \quad (5.2.14)$$

Finally, the budget constraint is satisfied which is apparent from

$$p'q = p'\gamma + \left(y - p'\gamma\right)p'\hat{p}^{-1}\,\beta = p'\gamma + \left(y - p'\gamma\right) = y \quad (5.2.15a)$$

since, $\quad p'\,\hat{p}^{-1}\,\beta = \iota'\beta = 1.$

We have seen that Stone's linear expenditure system is derivable from maximization of a particular utility function. In fact, it is the only linear expenditure system which can be derived from a classical utility function.

We now focus on the behaviour of the average budget shares as income varies, prices being given. Multiplying (5.2.4) by y^{-1}, we obtain the average budget share vector

$$w = y^{-1}\hat{p}q = y^{-1}\,\hat{p}\gamma + y^{-1}\left(y - p'\gamma\right)\beta$$

$$= \left(y^{-1}\,p'\gamma\right)\left[\left(p'\,\gamma\right)^{-1}\hat{p}\,\gamma\right] + y^{-1}\left(y - p'\gamma\right)\beta = \alpha\,w^{*} + \left(1 - \alpha\right)\beta \quad (5.2.15b)$$

Alternatively, we have

$$w_i = \alpha\,w_i^{*} + \left(1 - \alpha\right)\beta_i \qquad \left(i = 1,.2,........, n\right) \quad (5.2.15c)$$

where $\alpha = p'\gamma / y$. α is the ratio of subsistence income to total income and $(1-\alpha) = (y-p'\gamma)/y$ is its complement i.e. the ratio of supernumerary income to income. The ratio, $w_i^{*} = p_i\gamma_i / p'\gamma$ are the 'subsistence budget shares' which give the composition of expenditures by a consumer whose income is at the subsistence level $p'\gamma$, and $w^* = (w_1^*, w_2^*, \ldots, w_n^*)'$ is the 'subsistence budget share vector'. From (5.2.15a), we see that at any income level 'y', the average budget share, w_i^* is the weighted average of the subsistence budget share, w_i^* and the marginal budget share, β_i where the weights being the ratios of subsistence income to total income and supernumerary income to total income, respectively. At substance income $y = p'\gamma, \alpha = 1$ and $1 - \alpha = 0$, so that all the weight is on w_i^* and the average budget shares are just the subsistence budget shares.[5] As income rises, α falls and 1–α will also rise and the weights shift to the marginal budget shares. As income rises indefinitely, the average budget shares approach the (constant) marginal budget shares. The linear expenditure system with linear Engel curves, thus, makes a clear distinction between the composition of expenditure at low and high income levels.

Now, consider the income elasticities, $\eta_{i0} = \beta_i / w_i$. As income rises from subsistence level, w_i moves from towards β_i so that η_{i0} moves from β_i / w^*_i towards 1. The path of the income elasticity is rising, constant, or falling according as β_i is less than, equal to, or greater than w^*_i. The classification of goods into luxuries, neutrals, and necessities remains unchanged over the income range (although it may depend on prices). Again these are consequences of the linearity of Engel curve.

UTILITY ASPECTS OF THE DEMAND FUNCTIONS

Inserting $q = q(y, p)$ from (5.2.5a) into the $u(q)$ of (5.2.1) we find the indirect utility function[6] of the linear expenditure function model:

$$u = u^*(y, p) = \beta' \log\left[(y - p'\gamma)\, \hat{p}^{-1}\, \beta\right]$$

$$= \beta' \log \beta + \log(y - p'\gamma) - \beta' \log p \qquad (5.3.1a)$$

Alternatively, we have

$$u^*(y,p) = \sum_i \beta_i \log \beta_i + \log\left(y - \sum_i p_i \gamma_i\right) - \sum_i \beta_i \log p_i \tag{5.3.1b}$$

Thus, the marginal utility of income is given by

$$\lambda = u_y^* = \partial u^* / \partial y = (y - p'\gamma)^{-1} \tag{5.3.2}$$

as shown at (5.2.3). The vector of marginal utilities of prices is given by

$$u_p^* = \partial u^* / \partial p = -\left[(y - p'\gamma)^{-1} \gamma + \hat{p}^{-1} \beta\right] \tag{5.3.3}$$

which incidentally equals to $-\lambda q$ in accordance with (3.3.1c) in chapter-3.

With the marginal utility of income function, $\lambda = \lambda\,(y, p) = (y - p'y)$, its income and price slopes are given by

$$\lambda_y = -(y - p'\gamma)^{-2} \qquad \lambda_p = (y - p'\gamma)^{-2}\,\gamma \tag{5.3.4}$$

The income elasticity of λ (marginal utility of income) is given by

$$\eta_{\lambda y} = \lambda_y\, \lambda^{-1}\, y = y(y - p'\gamma)^{-1} \tag{5.3.5}$$

This parameter has an intuitive interpretation in the present model, which is a better interpretation in terms of its reciprocal, the income flexibility

$$\phi = -(y - p'\gamma)/y \tag{5.3.6a}$$

or rather in terms of the absolute value of as,

$$|\phi| = (y - p'\gamma)/y \tag{5.3.6b}$$

and $|\phi|$ is the ratio of supernumerary income to income, which is equal to (1 -α). The decomposition (5.2.15b) may, thus, be written as

$$w_i = (1 - |\phi|)\, w^* + |\phi|\, \beta_i \tag{5.3.7}$$

The 'supernumerary ratio', $(y - p'\gamma)/y$, would seem to be a natural welfare indicator in the present model-it rises from 0 to 1 as y rises from $p'\gamma$ to ∞ with prices given. As $\eta_{\lambda y}$ is the negative of the reciprocal of $(y-p'\gamma)/y$, it rises with the rise in income level. Thus, it is used as a welfare indicator.

In the present model, the first order conditions could be solved for $q = q(y, p)$ and $\lambda = \lambda(y, p)$ explicitly. Thus, the fundamental matrix expressions for differentials of q and λ, which are exploited in the general theory of chapter-3. Nevertheless, it is instructive to illustrate the general theory with the present model. To facilitate this, we first use (5.2.5a) to rewrite the second derivative matrix in Stone's demand system as

$$U=-(\hat{q}-\hat{\gamma})^{-1}\hat{\beta}(\hat{q}-\hat{\gamma})^{-1}=-\left[(y-p'\gamma)\,\hat{p}^{-1}\hat{\beta}\right]^{-1}\hat{\beta}\left[(y-p'\gamma)\hat{p}^{-1}\hat{\beta}\right]^{-1} \tag{5.3.8}$$

the inverse of which is

$$U^{-1}=-(y-p'\gamma)^{2}\,\hat{p}^{-1}\,\hat{\beta}\,\hat{p}^{-1} \tag{5.3.9}$$

Now the general results of income and price slopes of the demand functions (i.e. q_y *and* Q_p) and marginal utility of income function (i.e. λ_y and λ_p) may be derived as follows. Pre-and post-multiply (5.3.9) by p' and p respectively:

$$p'\,U^{-1}\,p=-(y-p'\gamma)^{-2}\,\iota'\hat{\beta}\,\iota=-(y-p'\gamma)^{2}$$

since, $p'\,\hat{p}^{-1}=\iota'$ *and* $\iota'\,\hat{\beta}\,\iota=\iota\,\beta=1$.

Therefore, $\left(p'\,U^{-1}\,p\right)^{-1}=-(y-p'\gamma)^{-2}=\lambda_y$ (5.3.10)

in view of (5.3.4). Let us derive,

$$\lambda\,q_y+\lambda_y\,q=(y-p'\gamma)\,\hat{p}^{-1}\beta-(y-p'\gamma)^{-2}\left[\gamma+(y-p'\gamma)\,\hat{p}^{-1}\,\beta\right] \tag{5.3.11}$$

using (5.2.3), (5.2.5a), (5.2.7a) and (5.3.4). Next we can derive

$$\lambda_y\,U^{-1}p=-(y-p'\gamma)^{-2}\left[-(y-p'\gamma)^{2}\,\hat{p}^{-1}\,\hat{\beta}\,\hat{p}^{-1}\right]p=\hat{p}^{-1}\,\beta=q_y \tag{5.3.12}$$

using (5.2.7a), (5.3.4) and (5.3.9). Finally we can derive

$$\lambda U^{-1} - \lambda \lambda_y^{-1} q_y q_y' - q_y q' = (y - p'\gamma)^{-1} \left[-(y - p'\gamma)^2 \hat{p}^{-1} \hat{\beta} \hat{p}^{-1} \right]$$

$$-(y - p'\gamma)^{-1} \left[-(y - p'\gamma)^2 \right] \hat{p}^{-1} \beta \beta' \hat{p}^{-1}$$

$$-\hat{p}^{-1} \beta \left[\gamma + (y - p'\gamma) \hat{p}^{-1} \beta \right]'$$

$$= -(y - p'\gamma) \hat{p}^{-1} \hat{\beta} \hat{p}^{-1} - \hat{p}^{-1} \beta \gamma' = Q_p \qquad (5.3.13)$$

using (5.2.3), (5.2.5a), (5.2.7a), (5.2.9a) and (5.3.4).

We derive the income elasticity and marginal budget share vectors; price coefficients will be taken up in Section 3.3.

Since, $q_y = \hat{p}^{-1} \beta$, the marginal budget share vector is given by

$$\mu = \hat{p}\, q_y = \beta ;$$

Alternatively, we have

$$\mu_i = \beta_i \qquad (i = 1, 2, \ldots\ldots\ldots, n).$$

Hence, the average budget share vector is

$$w = y^{-1} \hat{p}\, q = (1 + \phi)\, w^* - \phi \beta , \qquad (5.3.14)$$

The income elasticity vector is

$$\eta_0 = \hat{w}^{-1} \mu = \left[(1 + \phi) \hat{w}^* - \phi \hat{\beta} \right]^{-1} \beta ; \qquad (5.3.15)$$

Alternatively, we have

$$\eta_{io} = \beta_i \left(w_i^* - \phi (\beta_i - w_i^*) \right) \quad (i = 1, 2, \ldots\ldots, n) \qquad (5.3.16)$$

Note that inferior goods are ruled out by these demand functions as q_y, ϕ and η_0 are all positive and also directly derived from an additive utility function.

ADDITIVE UTILITY

The Stone-Geary utility function is directly additive, so that one may rely on the theory of Section 3.4 to derive, for the linear expenditure system, all the price coefficient matrices in terms of the income coefficient vectors and the income flexibility, ϕ. Alternatively, the price coefficient matrices could be derived directly by manipulating q_y and Q_p; in that event the results would serve to illustrate the additivity theory. We start with

$$q_y = \hat{p}^{-1}\beta \,;\; \mu = \beta \text{ and } \phi = -(y - p'\gamma)\, y^{-1}$$

and then proceed to utilize the theorems of Section 3.4. For the uncompensated price slope matrix we find

$$Q_p = \phi\, y \hat{q}_y\, \hat{p}^{-1} - q_y \left(q + \phi\, y\, q_y\right)'$$

$$= \phi\, y\, \hat{p}^{-1}\hat{\beta}\, \hat{p}^{-1} - \hat{p}^{-1}\beta\left(\gamma - \phi\, y\, \hat{p}^{-1}\beta + \phi y\, \hat{p}^{-1}\beta\right)$$

$$= \phi\, y\, \hat{p}^{-1}\, \hat{\beta}\, \hat{p}^{-1} - \hat{p}^{-1}\, \beta\gamma' \tag{5.4.1}$$

as indeed we have at (5.2.9a). For the utility-compensated price slope matrix, we find

$$Q_p^* = \phi y\, \hat{q}_y \left(\hat{p}^{-1} - \iota q_y'\right) = \phi\, y\, \hat{p}^{-1}\, \hat{\beta}\left(\hat{p}^{-1} - \iota\beta'\hat{p}^{-1}\right)$$

$$= \phi\, y\, \hat{p}^{-1}\left(\hat{\beta} - \beta\beta'\right)\hat{p}^{-1} : \tag{5.4.2a}$$

Alternatively, we have

$$\left(\frac{\partial q_i}{\partial p_j}\right)^* = \begin{cases} \phi\, y\, p_i^{-2}\, \beta_i (1 - \beta_i) & \text{if } i = j \\ -\phi\, y\, p_i^{-1}\, p_j^{-1}\, \beta_i\, \beta_j & \text{if } i \neq j. \end{cases} \tag{5.4.2b}$$

Note that in the present system, as in any directly additive[7] ones, all goods are Hicks-Allen substitutes with $\phi < 0$, $\beta_i > 0$,

$\beta_j > 0$ and $\left(\frac{\partial q_i}{\partial p}\right)^* > 0$ for all $i \neq j$.

For the marginal utility of income compensated price slope matrix,

$$Q_p^{**} = \phi\, y\, \hat{p}^{-1}\, \hat{q}_y = \phi\, y\, \hat{p}^{-1}\, \hat{\beta}\, \hat{p}^{-1} ; \tag{5.4.3a}$$

Alternatively we have

$$\left(\frac{\partial q_i}{\partial p_j}\right)^{**} = \begin{cases} \phi\, y\, p_i^{-2}\, \beta_i & \text{if } i = j \\ 0 & \text{if } i \neq j. \end{cases} \tag{5.4.3b}$$

Note that in the present system, as in any directly additive ones, all specific substitution effects are zero: $\left(\frac{\partial q_i}{\partial p_j}\right)^{**} = 0$ for all $i \neq j$.

For the uncompensated price elasticity matrix, we have

$$H = \phi\hat{\eta} - \eta w'(I + \phi\hat{\eta}) = \phi\hat{\eta} - \eta(w' + \phi w'\hat{\eta}) = \phi\hat{\eta} - \eta(w + \phi\beta)'$$

$$= \phi\hat{\eta} - \eta\left(y^{-1}\,\hat{p}\gamma\right)'; \tag{5.4.4a}$$

Alternatively, we have

$$\eta_{ij} = \begin{cases} \eta_i\left(\phi - y^{-1}\, p_i\, \gamma_i\right) & \text{if } i = j \\ -\eta_i\, y^{-1}\, p_j\, \gamma_i & \text{if } i \neq j \end{cases} \tag{5.4.4b}$$

In the present model, each of the uncompensated own-price elasticity must lie between -1 and 0, so that demand is price-inelastic in the usual sense (Stone 1965, p.285). This may be shown as follows:

$$\eta_{ii} = \eta_i\left(\phi - y^{-1}\, p_i\, \gamma_i\right) = -\eta_i\, y^{-1}\left[(y - p'\gamma) + p_i\, \gamma_i\right]$$

$$= -\eta_i\, y^{-1}\left[\beta_i^{-1}\, p_i(q_i - \gamma_i) + p_i\, \gamma_i\right]$$

$$= -\eta_i\, y^{-1}\left[\beta_i^{-1}\, p_i q_i + \left(1 - \beta_i^{-1}\right) p_i\, \gamma_i\right]$$

$$= -\beta_i\, p_i^{-1}\, q_i^{-1}\, y\, y^{-1}\left[\beta_i^{-1}\, p_i q_i + \left(1 - \beta_i^{-1}\right) p_i\, \gamma_i\right]$$

$$= -1 + (1 - \beta_i)\, q_i^{-1}\, \gamma_i \tag{5.4.4c}$$

with $0 < \beta_i < 1$ and $0 \le \gamma_i < q_i$, it must be the case that $-1 \le \eta_{ii} \le 0$.

For the utility-compensated price elasticity matrix,

$$H^* = \phi\hat{\eta} - \phi\eta\, w'\hat{\eta} = \phi\,\hat{\eta}\left(I - \iota\beta'\right); \tag{5.4.5a}$$

Alternatively, we have

$$\eta_{ij}^* = \begin{cases} \phi\eta_i\left(1-\beta_i\right) & if\ i = j \\ \\ -\phi\eta_i\,\beta_j & if\ i \ne j \end{cases} \tag{5.4.5b}$$

Each of the utility-compensated own-price elasticity must lie between 0 and 1:

$$\eta_{ii}^* = \phi\,\eta_i\left(1-\beta_i\right) = -\left(y - p'\gamma\right)y^{-1}\,\beta_i\,p_i^{-1}\,q_i^{-1}\,y\left(1-\beta_i\right)$$

$$= -p_i\left(q_i - \gamma_i\right)p_i^{-1}\,q_i^{-1}\left(1-\beta_i\right) = -\left(1-\beta_i\right)\left(1-q_i^{-1}\gamma_i\right) \tag{5.4.5c}$$

with $0 < \beta_i < 1$ and $0 \le \gamma_i < q_i$, clearly $-1 < \eta_{ii}^* \le 0$.

For the marginal-utility-of-income-compensated price elasticity matrix we find

$$H^{**} = \phi\hat{\eta}; \tag{5.4.6a}$$

Alternatively,

$$\eta_{ij}^{**} = \begin{cases} \phi\,\eta_i & if\ i = j \\ \\ 0 & if\ i \ne j \end{cases} \tag{5.4.6b}$$

Each of the marginal-utility-of-income-compensated own-price elasticity must lie between 0 and 1:

$$\eta_{ii}^{**} = \phi\eta_i = -\left(y - p'\gamma\right)y^{-1}\,\beta_i\,p_i^{-1}\,q_i^{-1}y$$

$$= -\,p_i\left(q_i - \gamma_i\right)p_i^{-1}\,q_i^{-1} = -\,(1 - q_i^{-1}\gamma_i) \tag{5.4.6c}$$

since, $0 \le \gamma_i < q_i$, clearly $-1 \le \eta_{ii}^* < 0$.

The economy of parameterization which is associated with directly additive utility[8] is apparent in Stone's linear expenditure system, which after all uses only (2n–1) independent parameters. These are (n-1) independent elements of β (since, $\iota'\beta = 1$) and the 'n' elements of 'γ'

SPECIFICATION OF ESTIMABLE LES MODELS AND MEASURES OF GOODNESS-OF-FIT

The purpose of this section is to carry out the analysis of LES a little further by incorporating household size and time trend where the later is used as a proxy for examining the shift in the consumers taste and preferences for various commodity groups over time while the former as a proxy for examining the operation of economics and diseconomies of scale in household consumption.[9] The four models estimated for analysis are the simple Linear Expenditure System named as LES-1; a flexible form of LES by incorporating household size in its budget share parameter and it is named as LES-2; and another flexible[10] form of LES obtained by replacing its budget share parameter by linear time trend which has been abbreviated as LES-3. The fourth model is the non-additive variant of LES popularly known the Nasse Expenditure System (NES), which allows specific substitution between commodity groups[11].

ESTIMABLE LES MODELS

We have estimated the additive stochastic models of LES and its three different variants in budget share form separately for rural and urban households using time-series data. The additive stochastic specifications of the estimable models of LES and its variants from which the parameters are estimated for the present analysis are:

(i) the simple Linear Expenditure System (LES-1) in budget share form whose additive stochastic specification is:

$$\text{LES-1: } w_{it} = v_{it}\gamma_i + \beta_i\left(1 - \sum_{j=1}^{n} v_{jt}\gamma_j\right) + u_{it} \quad i = 1, 2, \ldots, n \ \& \ t = 1, 2, \ldots, T \tag{5.5.1}$$

(ii) the budget share form of the Linear Expenditure System replacing the marginal budget share parameter by a linear function of average household size (LES-2), the additive stochastic specification of which is:

$$\text{LES-2: } w_{it} = v_{it}\gamma_i + (\beta_i + \theta_i m_i)\left(1 - \sum_{j=1}^{n} v_{jt}\gamma_{jt}\right) + u_{it} \quad i = 1, 2, \ldots, n \ \& t = 1, 2, \ldots, T \tag{5.5.2}$$

(iii) the budget share form of the Linear Expenditure System replacing the budget share by a linear time trend (LES-3), the additive stochastic specification of which is:

$$\text{LES-3: } w_{it} = v_{it}\gamma_i + \left(\beta_i + \theta_i^{*} t\right)\left(1 - \sum_{j=1}^{n} v_{jt}\gamma_j\right) + u_{it} \quad i = 1, 2, \ldots n \ \& t = 1, 2, \ldots, T \tag{5.5.3}$$

(iv) the additive stochastic specification of the Nasse Expenditure System (NES) in budget share form is:

$$\text{NES: } w_{it} = v_{it}\gamma_i(v) + \beta_i\left[1 - \sum_{j=1}^{n} v_{jt}\gamma_j(v)\right] + u_{it} \quad i = 1, 2, \ldots n \ \& \ t = 1, 2, \ldots, T \tag{5.5.4}$$

with $\gamma_i(v) = \sum_{j=1}^{n} \gamma_{ij}\left(v_{jt}/v_{it}\right)^{1/2}$.

The disturbance terms, $u_{it}s$ in the above models are assumed to have,

$$E(u_{it}) = 0 \ \text{for all i and t} \quad \text{and} \quad E(u_{it}\,u_{js}) = \begin{cases} \sigma_{ij} & \text{for } t = s \\ 0 & \text{for } t \neq s \end{cases} \tag{5.5.5}$$

In the above models, w_i is the budget share of ith commodity group; m_i is the average household size; t is the time trend; 'v_i' is the normalized price index of ith commodity group; $\beta_i s$ and $\gamma_i s$ are the parameters of the system. The parameter β_i is the marginal budget share and γ_i is interpreted as committed quantities. This interpretation is only suggestive and it is not always possible to do so particularly when γ_i is negative. A negative γ_i is not inconsistent with theory.[12] The additional parameter θ_i in LES-2 is the household size coefficient and θ^*_i in LES-3 is the marginal preference coefficient of *ith* commodity.

As regards to the estimation of LES, the most straight forward procedure is to minimise the sum of squared residuals over all expenditure budget share equations and time periods. This procedure is appealing for its simplicity and is a straightforward generalisation of single equation ordinary least squares, but it is devoid of any a priori specification of the error structure and hence, does not indicate the sampling properties of estimators. Parks (1969) modified this procedure in such a way that the resulting estimators coincided with the corresponding maximum likelihood estimators and also provided asymptotic variance-covariance of the estimators.[13]

THEORETICAL RESTRICTIONS

The fulfillment of the second order condition of equilibrium requires β_i=0 which restricts the inclusion of inferior goods. Since the underlying utility function of LES is additive, it becomes an unrealistic specification when we deal with finer level of commodity aggregation. The additivity, besides not allowing inferior goods, imposes too strong a specification on price effects. Nevertheless, this may not pose a problem for broad group of consumption items.

The satisfaction of the budget constraints along with the second order conditions would require,

$$0 < \beta_i < 1, \sum \beta_i = 1 \text{ and } \left(1 - v_j \gamma_j\right) = 0 \text{ for } i, j = 1, 2, \ldots\ldots, n. \tag{5.5.6}$$

The homogeneity conditions for LES and its variants would require,

$$\sum_{j=1}^{n}\gamma_{ij}=0\ , \qquad \text{for } i=1, 2,\ldots\ldots, n. \qquad (5.5.7)$$

The symmetry condition would require,

$$\gamma_{ij}=\gamma_{ji}, \qquad \text{for } i=j\ \ (i,j=1,2,\ldots,n). \qquad (5.5.8)$$

In addition to the above restrictions, for additivity LES-2 and LES-3 would require,

$$\sum_{i=1}^{n}\theta_i=0 \text{ and } \sum_{i=1}^{n}\theta_i^*=0 \qquad (5.5.9)$$

For the satisfaction of the budget constraints and second order condition, the Nasse Expenditure System (NES) would require,

$$0<\beta_i<1 \ \textit{and}\ \sum\beta_i=1 \ \text{ for } i=1, 2,\ldots\ldots, n. \qquad (5.5.10)$$

but the 'committed quantity' for any commodity is no longer a constant but depends on all prices. The NES allows specific substitution between commodity groups. While estimating NES, the lower off-diagonal coefficients of the γ matrix are restricted to zero to achieve the additive separability between the commodity groups. The zero restrictions are necessary to get negative own price elasticities.[14]

ELASTICITIES

For the ith commodity group, the expenditure elasticity (η_{i0}), the uncompensatory price elasticity with respect price to jth price (η_{ij}) and household size elasticity (η_{is}) for the LES models are given by[15]

$$\eta_{i0}=\beta_i/w_i \qquad (5.5.11)$$

$$\eta_{ij}=-\delta_{ij}+\left(\delta_{ij}-\beta_i\right)v_j\gamma_j/w_i \qquad (5.5.12)$$

where $\delta_{ij} = 0$ for all $i = j$ *and* 0 otherwise

$$\eta_{is} = \frac{\eta\theta_i}{w_i}\left(1 - \sum v_j\gamma_j\right) \tag{5.5.13}$$

Note that expenditure and price elasticities are not constant but vary with the level of income, consumption level and prices. If $0 < \beta_i < 1$ and $\gamma_{ij} > 0$ for all *'i'*, then it follows that all commodities must be 'normal', price inelastic and pair-wise net substitutes. For any demand system linear in income, it can be shown that income elasticity increases (decreases) towards unity with income for necessary (luxury) goods. This is not in conformity with empirical evidence on the behaviour of expenditure elasticity w.r.t. changes in total expenditure, particularly for staple food items like cereals. Therefore, this property, which stems from linear Engel curves, is viewed as a theoretical limitation of the LES. Using the partial differentiation of the Nasse Expenditure System (NES) mentioned above and then simplifying the elasticity formula, the expenditure and price elasticity of the Nasse model can be shown as

$$\eta_{i0} = \beta_i / w_i \tag{5.5.14}$$

$$\eta_{ij} = \left(-\delta_{ij} + \left[\left(\delta_{ij} - \beta_i\right)v_j\gamma_j(v)\right] + \left[\gamma_{ij}(v_iv_j)^{1/2} - \delta_{ij}v_i\gamma_i(v)\right]/2\right)\Big/w_i \tag{5.5.15}$$

Clearly, these elasticities depend on total expenditure and price structure in a complex way. One may have to compute these elasticities at mean levels or for some specific year. The above expression of elasticity for NES reduces to LES-1 when for .

GOODNESS OF FIT

In order to examine the goodness of fit, we have applied adjusted R² $\left(\overline{R}^2\right)$ and F-statistic. In addition to this, we have also computed the square of the correlation coefficients (R^2_w) between the observed and predicted budget shares for the sample period to confirm the goodness of fit of the models. The above goodness of fit measures is supplemented by Theil's measure of information accuracy[16] separately for each items of consumption. If w_{it} and $\hat{w}_{it}$ are observed and predicted budget shares of ith commodity for period 't' then Theil's measure information inaccuracy (TMII) is defined as

$$\pi_i = \frac{1}{m}\sum_t \hat{w}_{it} \log\left(\frac{\hat{w}_{it}}{w_{it}}\right) + (1 - w_{it})\log\left(\frac{1-\hat{w}_{it}}{1-w_{it}}\right) \qquad i = 1,2,......,n$$

(5.5.16)

If the estimates are exact than $w_{it} = \hat{w}_{it}$ and π_i will be zero. The only overall (or across all equations) measure of goodness of fit is the Theil's measure of average information inaccuracy (TMAII) which can be computed by lumping together the budget shares of all commodities. The Theil's measure of average information inaccuracy is defined as

$$\pi = \frac{1}{m}\left(\sum_i \sum_t w_{it} \log\left(\frac{\hat{w}_{it}}{w_{it}}\right)\right) \qquad i = 1,2,....,n \text{ and } t = 1,2,....,m$$

(5.5.17)

where are budget share and estimated budget shares respectively for *ith* item in t[th] period.

METHOD OF ESTIMATION OF LES AND ITS VARIANTS

The two methods discussed in the previous section are fairly general and applicable to any of the complete demand systems. However, not all models use the above methods. Some of them have their specified methods of estimation. In what follows, we shall discuss, briefly, the methods of estimation used for some of the models of chapter 3. In particular, we shall stress on the estimation of Linear Expenditure System and its variants.

Stone (1954) has suggested a two-stage iterative procedure for estimating the parameters in LES. Since the system in (3.1.1) is quadratic in parameters, it becomes linear if one set of parameters is assumed to be known. The second set of parameters can be estimated by ordinary least squares. Using this estimated second set as given, the first set can be estimated by ordinary least squares. The new set of parameters is used as the initial set and procedure is repeated until two successive iterations give approximately identical estimates for the parameters. This procedure, in practice, is very slow and may take a large number of iterations. Also, attention has not been paid to singularity problem or the properties and standard errors of the parameter estimates. In view of these difficulties, alternative methods have been developed. Parks (1969) maximum likelihood method and Slater's (1972) linearization procedure[17] are two among them.

Parks' method is essentially a two stage iterative procedure to maximize the concentrated log likelihood function w.r.t. the two sets of parameters in LES. He deleted the last equation to avoid singularity of Ω.

Recalling the model in (5.2.4b) and adding a stochastic disturbance term 'u_{it}', we have,

$$p_{it}q_{it} = p_{it}\,\gamma_i + \beta_i\,(y_t - p_{jt}\,\gamma_j) + u_{it}\ (\text{i} = 1, 2, \ldots \text{n}, \text{t} = 1,2,\ldots, \text{T}) \tag{5.6.1}$$

The disturbance terms, $u_{it}s$ in the above models are assumed to have,

$$E(u_{it}) = 0 \ \text{for all i and t} \quad \text{and} \quad E(u_{it}\,u_{js}) = \begin{cases} \Omega & \text{for } t = s \\ 0 & \text{for } t \neq s \end{cases} \tag{5.6.2}$$

Assuming that 'u' follows a multivariate normal distribution with mean zero and variance-covariance matrix, Ω. In (5.6.1), Ω is singular because of the adding-up property which implies $\iota'\Omega = 0$ that. We can formulate the likelihood function for (5.6.1) by deleting one equation for each 't'. Without loss of generality, we can delete the last equation[18]. Denoting the truncated random error as u^*_t and truncated Ω as Ω*, the concentrated log-likelihood function can thus be written as,

$$\ln(L) = -T/2(n-1)\ln(2\pi) - T/2\ln\left|\Omega^{*}\right| - 1/2\sum_{t=1}^{T} u_t^{*'}\Omega^{*-1}u_t^{*} \quad (5.6.3a)$$

$$\text{or } \ln(L) = T/2\log n - (T(n-2)/2)(1+\log 2\pi) - T/2\ln\left|A\right| \quad (5.6.3b)$$

where A = $1/T\sum_t u_t u_t' + \iota\iota'$ is the MLE of Ω. A typical element of A in this case is

$$a_{ij} = \begin{bmatrix} \frac{1}{T}(v_i - x_i\gamma)' \;\; (v_j - x_j\gamma) \\ \frac{1}{T}(w_i - z\beta_i)' \;\; (w_j - z\beta_j) \end{bmatrix} \quad (5.6.4)$$

where $\gamma' = (\gamma_1, \gamma_2, ...\gamma_n)$ and $\beta' = (\beta_1, \beta_2, ..., \beta_n)$ are the parameter vectors and dropping the time suffix 't', the 'T 'component vectors are

$$v_i = p_i q_i - \beta_i y_i; \quad w_i = p_i q_i - p_i\gamma_i; z_i = y_i - \sum_{j=1}^{n} p_j\gamma_j \text{ and}$$

$$x_i = (-\beta_i p_1, -\beta_i p_2, \ldots, (1-\beta_i)p_i, \ldots, -\beta_i p_n), \quad (5.6.5)$$

Then, (5.6.5) can be rewritten in any one of the following two forms.

$$v_i = x_i\gamma_i + u_i \text{ and } w_i = z_i\beta_i + u_i \quad (i = 1, 2, \ldots n) \quad (5.6.6a)$$

or equivalently in vector form as,

$$v = x\gamma + u \text{ and } w = z\beta + u \quad (5.6.6b)$$

where

$$v = \begin{bmatrix} v_1 \\ v_2 \\ \vdots \\ v_n \end{bmatrix}, \; x = \begin{bmatrix} x_1 \\ x_2 \\ \vdots \\ x_n \end{bmatrix}, \; w = \begin{bmatrix} w_1 \\ w_2 \\ \vdots \\ w_n \end{bmatrix} \text{ and } u = \begin{bmatrix} u_1 \\ u_2 \\ \vdots \\ u_n \end{bmatrix}.$$

Now, the first order conditions for maximizing (5.6.2) w.r.t. β and γ are:

$$\frac{\partial \log L^*}{\partial \beta_k} = \sum_{i=1}^{n} a^{ik} z'(w_i - z\beta_i) = 0 \quad (k = 1, 2, \ldots\ldots, n) \tag{5.6.7a}$$

$$\frac{\partial \log L^*}{\partial \gamma} = \sum_{i=1}^{n}\sum_{j=1}^{n} a^{ij} (z_i' v_j - x_i' x_j c) = 0 \tag{5.6.7b}$$

where a^{ij} is the (i, j) th element of A^{-1}.

Since, the first order conditions of the maximum likelihood function gives rise to non-linear equations in parameters, the maximum likelihood estimates can only be obtained by iterative procedure. The iterative procedure is to start with, $A = I$ and $\gamma = 0$. Then estimate β by least square using (5.6.7a). Using this estimated β then estimate γ by least square using (5.6.7b). Now, a new estimate for 'A' is obtained by using (5.6.4). With this newly estimated 'A' as the starting point, the above procedure is repeated until β and γ converge to a desirable accuracy. The standard errors of the parameter estimates can be obtained by inverting the information matrix, M, where

$$M = \begin{bmatrix} \dfrac{\partial^2 \log L^*}{\partial \beta\, \partial \beta'} & \dfrac{\partial^2 \log L^*}{\partial \beta\, \partial \gamma'} \\[2ex] \dfrac{\partial^2 \log L^*}{\partial \gamma\, \partial \beta'} & \dfrac{\partial^2 \log L^*}{\partial \gamma\, \partial \gamma'} \end{bmatrix} \tag{5.6.8}$$

The contemporaneous covariance matrix of the disturbance $\Omega = (\sigma_{ij})$ is singular because of the adding-up criterion. Under the assumption of multivariate normality of the *u's* the log-likelihood function can be maximized by standard non-linear full information maximum likelihood method, with the provision of handling singularity of Ω and imposing $\sum \beta_i = 1$. The estimation procedure followed in some studies is a modified version of the Guass-Newton method suggested by

Marquardt (1963). Alternatively, a number of numerical methods to estimate the parameters in (5.6.1) like linearization, steepest descent, Marquardt's method are available in the literature. The linearization procedure is computationally simple. The quickness of convergence of this procedure depends on the initial guess solution and the degree of non-linearity of the demand system. We have used the linearised iterative procedure for the estimation of LES and its variants in this study.

THE DATA

The consumer expenditure data used for estimating LES and its variants consists of Orissa and all-India average monthly per capita consumer expenditure (MPCE) on nine broad commodity groups and the corresponding monthly per capita total consumer expenditure (MPCTE) separately for rural urban households. The expenditure data has been taken from the published NSS reports of different rounds form 42nd round (July,1986-June,1987) to 61st round (July,2004-June,2005) on consumer expenditure excluding the 49th and 60th rounds for. which the consumer price indices are not compatible. The period covered is, therefore, from July 1986 to June 2005. For each round of the NSS survey, we have estimated the average monthly per capita expenditure of all the expenditure classes for each item of consumption to generate item-wise time-series data. Form the 61st round grouped data, we have estimated the average monthly per capita expenditure for three population groups based on ranking by the level of monthly per capita total expenditure MPCTE viz., the bottom 30 per cent (low income group), the middle 40 per cent (middle income group) and the top 30 percent (high income group), separately for the rural and urban sector of the state of Orissa as well as for all India. The nine broad specific items considered here are cereals and substitutes; pulses and its products; milk and its products; edible oil and fats; meat, fish and egg; other food items, clothing (which including clothing and beddings); fuel and light; other non-food items. The above data has been computerized and broad checks for consistency has been carried out. The database so obtained would be treated either as a pooled time-series of cross-section data, expenditure classes being cross-section units and NSS rounds as time points or time-series data if the expenditure figures of all expenditure classes taken into account. In this chapter, we have used both cross-section data of 61st round and the time-series data as mentioned above.

CONSUMER PRICE INDEX

Prices of different commodities are the important determinants in a demand system. The retail price data used for estimating LES and its variants is the time-series of consumer price indices for industrial workers and agriculture labour[19] compiled and released by the Labour Bureau, Ministry of Labour (GoI). The Labour Bureau compiled state-wise and all India consumer price indices for these two categories of worker for different financial years as well as calendar years. We have used both calendar year and financial year consumer price indices as the proxy variables for retail prices of different commodities. The calendar year consumer price indices are used if the period of the NSS round is a calendar year (from January to December) and financial year consumer price indices are used as an approximation for agricultural-year price indices if the period of the NSS round coincides with the agricultural-year (form July to June) as agricultural-year price indices for all items are not available. Further, the consumer price indices for industrial worker are used for estimating demand systems in urban areas and for agriculture labourer are used for estimating the demand systems rural areas for the state as well as all India. To maintain consistency between time-series of consumer price indices and the period of NSS round, we have not considered the consumer expenditure data for 49th and 60th rounds and the price indices of 1995-96 so data the consumer price indices consistent with NSS rounds and commodity classification can be obtained. The consumer price indices so obtained have been used for estimating LES and its variants in this chapter.

MAGNITUDE AND NATURE OF INTER-SECTORAL AND TEMPORAL VARIATIONS IN CONSUMPTION PATTERNS

In most of the cross-sectional studies based on NSS data, consumption pattern of rural and urban sectors of the country has been separately examined. These studies revealed marked differences in the consumption pattern in the two sectors of the country.[20] These studies also revealed that several items appear to be luxuries in the rural sector happens to be the necessity items in the urban sector. The factors responsible for such differences seem to be numerous. The principal ones being the difference in the standard of living between the two sectors, the difference in the relative prices and in the extent of monetization prevailing in the two sectors, variation in the occupational pattern and so on. Apart from the broad inter-sectoral variations, considerable inter-temporal variations in consumption pattern also exist within each sector.[21] This section deals with the inter-sectoral as well as inter-temporal variation in consumption pattern in the state of Orissa in particular and in India in general.

INTER-SECTORAL AND INTER-INCOME-GROUP VARIATIONS IN CONSUMPTION PATTERNS

Before discussing the results of estimated models, it would be useful to look at the pattern of consumption expenditure in the rural and urban areas of Orissa as well as all-India. The monthly per capita consumption expenditure (MPCE in Rs.) and the budget share (in percentage) of each commodity group for three income (or population) groups viz., bottom 30 per cent (low income group); middle 40 per cent (middle income group) and top 30 per cent (high income group) separately for rural and urban areas during 2004-05 are presented in *Tables-1* and 2. The figures in the tables reveal some well known patterns of consumption expenditure in the rural and urban areas of the State and the country.

The average share of consumption expenditure on all food items put together has a large share of 55.05 per cent and all non-food items commands 44.95 per cent of the total budget in rural India during 2004-05. Under food items, cereals and its substitutes constitute a major chunk of about 18.21 per cent followed by other non-food items (17.36 per cent) of the total budget in the rural areas of the country. When we compare the expenditure patterns of different income groups, the share of food expenditure is the highest (66.43 per cent) for the low income group and the lowest (44.49 per cent) for the high income group but the share of non-food expenditure is the highest (55.51 per cent) for the high income group and the lowest (33.57 per cent) for the low income group during 2004-05. The share of expenditure on cereals and substitutes; pulses and its products; edible oil and other food items is also the highest for low income group and the lowest for high income group. But the share of expenditure on milk and its product and meat fish and egg follows the reverse pattern among these two income groups in the rural areas of the country. The percentage of expenditure on pan, tobacco and intoxicants and fuel and light is relatively higher for the low income group and relatively lower for the high income group. The reverse is the case for clothing and other non-food items between these two income groups (*Table-1*).

In rural Orissa, the average consumption expenditure on all food items has a larger share of 61.57 per cent and all non-food items have a smaller share of 38.43 per cent during 2004-05. The share of food expenditure is much higher and non-food expenditure is much lower in rural Orissa compared to the rural India figures. Under all food items, cereals and substitutes constitute a major share of 28.27 per cent followed by other food items expenditure of 19.62 per cent of the total budget during 2004-05. The percentage of expenditure on cereals and substitutes; pulses and its products; and edible oil is the highest for low income group and the lowest for high income group but the share of expenditure on milk and its products is the highest for high income group. For meat, fish and egg, it is the highest for middle income group. The share of expenditure on these two items is the lowest for low income group. Further, the share of expenditure on pan, tobacco and intoxicants, fuel and light is the highest for low income group

Table 1

Item-wise Monthly Per Capita Consumption Expenditure (in Rs.) and Budget Share (in Percentage) for Different Income/Population Groups in India (2004-05)

	Rural				*Urban*			
Commodity Groups	*Bottom* 30%	*Middle* 40%	*Top* 30%	*All*	*Bottom* 30%	*Middle* 40%	*Top* 30%	*All*
Cereals and substitutes	82.27	101.56	121.62	101.77	86.96	107.35	128.16	107.44
	(30.12)	(22.02)	(11.15)	(18.21)	(21.44)	(13.30)	(5.56)	(10.21)
Pluses and its products	11.13	16.65	24.57	17.18	14.95	22.26	30.51	22.51
	(4.08)	(3.61)	(2.25)	(3.07)	(3.68)	(2.76)	(1.32)	(2.14)
Milk and its products	11.92	39.77	99.91	47.31	29.20	73.49	159.21	83.30
	(4.36)	(8.62)	(9.16)	(8.47)	(7.19)	(9.10)	(6.91)	(7.92)
Edible oil and fats	16.40	24.83	37.36	25.72	22.21	35.69	49.53	36.37
	(6.01)	(5.38)	(3.43)	(4.60)	(5.47)	(4.42)	(2.15)	(3.46)
Meat ,fish and egg	7.81	16.05	35.08	18.60	14.52	25.78	47.74	28.47
	(2.86)	(3.48)	(3.22)	(3.33)	(3.57)	(3.19)	(2.07)	(2.71)
Other food items	51.89	86.96	166.67	97.02	78.22	142.42	324.35	169.32
	(19.00)	(18.86)	(15.28)	(17.36)	(19.28)	(17.64)	(14.08)	(16.09)
Total food items	181.41	285.82	485.20	307.60	246.05	406.98	739.50	447.41
	(66.43)	(61.98)	(44.49)	(55.05)	(60.66)	(50.42)	(32.11)	(42.51)
Pan, tobacco and intoxicants	7.97	14.21	24.27	15.03	10.39	16.13	26.92	17.04
	(2.92)	(3.08)	(2.23)	(2.69)	(2.56)	(2.00)	(1.16)	(1.62)
Fuel and light	35.38	53.00	87.07	56.84	54.16	93.76	180.72	104.62
	(12.96)	(11.49)	(7.98)	(10.17)	(13.35)	(11.62)	(7.84)	(9.94)
Clothing	4.97	15.90	68.36	25.33	8.62	27.06	111.46	42.09
	(1.82)	(3.45)	(6.27)	(4.53)	(2.12)	(3.35)	(4.83)	(4.00)

Contd.

Commodity Groups	Rural Bottom 30%	Rural Middle 40%	Rural Top 30%	Rural All	Urban Bottom 30%	Urban Middle 40%	Urban Top 30%	Urban All
Other non-food items	43.35	92.22	425.60	153.99	86.37	263.20	1244.81	441.20
	(15.87)	(20.00)	(39.03)	(27.56)	(21.29)	(32.61)	(54.04)	(41.92)
Total non-food items	91.68	175.33	605.28	251.19	159.53	400.15	1563.91	604.95
	(33.57)	(38.02)	(55.51)	(44.95)	(39.34)	(49.58)	(67.89)	(57.49)
Total Expenditure	273.09	461.15	1090.48	558.78	405.59	807.13	2303.41	1052.36
	(100)	(100)	(100)	(100)	(100)	(100)	(100)	(100)

Note: Computed from NSS Report No. 508, National Sample Survey Organisation, Ministry of Statistics and Programme Implementation, Government of India.

and the lowest for high income group. But the share of expenditure on clothing, other non-food items and all non-food items is the highest for high income group and lowest for low income group (*Table-2*). This is a major deviation in the consumption pattern of non-food items in the rural areas of the state from the all-India pattern. The above analysis reveals not only the overall inter-income-group variation in the pattern of consumption expenditure in rural sector of Orissa and all-India but also overall variation in the pattern of consumption expenditure between rural Orissa and rural India. Further, it is a clear indication that the standard of living of rural consumers in the state is relatively lower than their counterparts in the country.

The pattern of consumption expenditure of urban households in India is quite different from their rural counterparts. In urban India, the share of food items expenditure is 42.51 per cent which is much lower than the all non-food expenditure of 57.49 per cent of the total budget during 2004-05. The same pattern expenditure on all food and non-food items is observed for the high income group. But a reverse pattern of expenditure is observed for the low and middle income groups for these two broad items. For the low income group, the share of food expenditure of 60.66 per cent is much higher than the non-food expenditure of 39.34 per cent. For the middle income group, the share of food expenditure of 50.42 per cent is marginally higher than non-food expenditure of 49.58 per cent of the total budget in urban India during 2004-05. This clearly indicates that the low and middle income groups have a reverse overall expenditure pattern but the high income group enjoys the same overall pattern of consumption expenditure in urban India. It also reveals that the overall urban consumption pattern is influenced by the high income group of the country (*Table-1*).

On the other hand, in urban Orissa the overall share of all food and non-food items expenditure are almost the same (around 50 per cent). The share of food expenditure (49.93 per cent) is marginally lower than the share of non-food expenditure (50.07 per cent) in urban Orissa during 2004-05.

Cereals and substitutes and other food items constitute 10.22 and 16.05 per cent respectively of the total budget under food items, and other non-food items constitute a major share 41.92 per cent under all non-food items in urban Orissa. Further, the share of expenditure of most of the food items except milk and its products is the highest for the low income group and the lowest for high income group in urban India. Under non-food items, the share of expenditure on clothing and other non-food items is the highest for high income group and the lowest for the low income group and reverse is the case for pan, tobacco and intoxicants and fuel and light for these two income groups in urban Orissa. Almost the same pattern of urban India consumption expenditure is noticed in urban Orissa except pan, tobacco, and intoxicants (*Table-2*).

The above analysis reveals distinct rural-urban and income (population) group variations in the consumption pattern in the state as well as in the country. When we compare the rural-urban consumption pattern in India, non-food expenditure is much higher than food expenditure in urban sector where as food expenditure is much higher than non-food expenditure in rural sector. Almost the same pattern rural-urban variation in the consumption of food and non-food expenditure is observed in Orissa with marginally higher share of expenditure on all non-food items than all food items in the urban areas of the state. The lower and middle income group in rural areas spend a higher proportion of their budget on food items especially on cereals and substitutes; pulses and its products; edible oil; and meat, fish and egg and other non-food items. The budget shares decline as we move up the income ladder except for milk and milk products and all non-food items.

TEMPORAL VARIATION IN CONSUMPTION PATTERNS

The monthly per capita consumer expenditure in rural areas during 55th round of NSS was 373.27 as against the all India average of is 486.16. The MPCE in the rural Orissa on food items was higher being 64.12 per cent of the total expenditure as against 59.40 at all India level. The expenditure on non-food items is 35.88 per cent of the total expenditure as against the

Table 2

Item-wise Monthly Per Capita Consumption Expenditure (in Rs.) and Budget Share (in Percentage) for Different Income/Population Groups in Orissa (2004-05)

	Rural				Urban			
Commodity Groups	*Bottom 30%*	*Middle 40%*	*Top 30%*	*All*	*Bottom 30%*	*Middle 40%*	*Top 30%*	*All*
Cereals and substitutes	102.36	126.75	140.55	112.75	114.68	135.22	147.03	127.51
	(37.80)	(27.52)	(13.63)	(28.27)	(28.79)	(17.32)	(8.93)	(16.84)
Pluses and its products	7.90	14.12	24.53	11.47	12.64	26.19	33.50	18.96
	(2.92)	(3.06)	(2.38)	(2.88)	(3.17)	(3.35)	(2.04)	(2.50)
Milk and its products	3.02	13.00	43.16	10.18	11.96	38.95	93.32	35.91
	(1.11)	(2.82)	(4.19)	(2.55)	(3.00)	(4.99)	(5.67)	(4.74)
Edible oil and fats	12.04	19.36	31.53	16.17	17.52	27.65	40.24	24.57
	(4.45)	(4.20)	(3.06)	(4.05)	(4.40)	(3.84)	(2.44)	(3.24)
Meat ,fish and egg	10.13	21.36	43.36	16.74	20.06	40.36	67.87	33.79
	(3.74)	(4.64)	(4.21)	(4.20)	(5.04)	(5.17)	(4.12)	(4.46)
Other food items	52.17	93.64	191.34	78.27	76.84	143.57	367.76	137.39
	(19.27)	(20.33)	(18.56)	(19.62)	(19.29)	(18.39)	(22.34)	(18.14)
Total food items	187.61	288.22	474.46	245.58	253.69	411.93	749.71	378.13
	(69.29)	(62.57)	(46.03)	(61.57)	(63.68)	(52.76)	(45.55)	(49.93)
Pan, tobacco and intoxicants	7.62	12.30	20.95	13.52	11.24	38.16	24.29	13.28
	(2.81)	(2.67)	(2.03)	(3.53)	(2.82)	(4.89)	(1.48)	(1.75)
Fuel and light	35.87	56.54	87.59	47.13	53.30	67.97	149.02	78.72
	(13.25)	(12.27)	(8.50)	(11.82)	(13.38)	(8.71)	(9.05)	(10.39)
Clothing	5.76	19.12	54.29	14.50	10.40	23.32	128.48	27.95
	(2.13)	(4.15)	(5.27)	(3.64)	(2.61)	(2.99)	(7.81)	(3.69)

Contd.

Commodity Groups	Rural				Urban			
	Bottom 30%	*Middle* 40%	*Top* 30%	*All*	*Bottom* 30%	*Middle* 40%	*Top* 30%	*All*
Other non-food items	33.90	84.46	393.52	78.16	69.73	239.39	594.51	(259.23)
	(12.52)	(18.34)	(38.18)	(19.59)	(17.50)	(30.66)	(36.12)	(34.23)
Total non-food items	83.15	172.41	556.34	153.31	144.67	368.84	896.30	379.18
	(30.71)	(37.43)	(53.97)	(38.43)	(36.32)	(47.24)	(54.45)	(50.07)
Total Expenditure	270.76	460.64	1030.80	398.89	398.35	780.76	1646.01	757.31
	(100)	(100)	(100)	(1000	(100)	(100)	(100)	(100)

Note: Computed from NSS Report No. 508, National Sample Survey Organisation, Ministry of Statistics and Programme Implementation, Government of India.

all India average of 40.60 per cent. This indicates that the average living standard in rural Orissa as reflected by consumer expenditure is much below the living standard in rural India. In the Urban Orissa, the MPCE was 618.48 as against the all India average of Rs.854.92. In urban Orissa, the percentage of expenditure under food items was 56.95 as compared to the corresponding all India figures of 48.66 per cent. The expenditure on non-food items to total expenditure in urban Orissa was 43.05 as against the all India level of 51.94 per cent. This shows that the living standard of the people in urban Orissa is also lagging behind of their counterparts in the country. The percentage of expenditure on food and non-food items to total expenditure are 56.95 and 43.05 in urban Orissa against 64.12 and 35.88 in the rural areas of the state. This indicates that the quality of life in urban areas is much better than rural areas. Although the expenditure on food items has always been higher than the expenditure on non-food items, the percentage expenditure on food items in the total budget in Orissa has gradually declined over the years. The expenditure on food items to total expenditure was 75.1 per cent in the rural areas and 72 per cent in urban areas during 42nd round (1986-87) and these percentages have declined to 64 per cent in the rural areas to 56 per cent in urban areas in the year 1999- 2000 (55th round of NSS). This is indicative of a gradual improvement in the living standards of the people in rural and urban Orissa. The percentage distribution of monthly per capita consumption expenditure (MPCE) on different food and non food items separately for the rural and urban sector of Orissa and all India from 42nd round (1986-87) to 61st round (2004-05) is presented in *Tables-3 to 6* to examine the temporal variation in consumption pattern in the state as well as in the country.

It is observed from *Table-3* that the cereal consumption has drastically declined from 27.17 per cent to 18.21 per cent during the period from 1986-87 to 2004-05 with constant rate of 0.503 per cent per annum in rural India. During this period, there is also a drastic fall of all food items from 65.67 per cent to 55.05 per cent. But the food items like pulses and its products; milk and its products; edible oil; meat, fish and egg has also marginally declined at a constant rate of 0.062, 0.043, 0.064 and 0.010 per cent per annum respectively. But the consumption of other food items (which include vegetables, salt, spices, sugar, gur etc.) has marginally increased at a constant rate of 0.017 per cent per annum. The clearly indicates that the sharp fall in the consumption expenditure on food is due to sharp fall in the consumption of expenditure in cereals and its substitutes since the average share of cereals and its substitutes is about 23 per cent of the total budget. We can compare the fluctuations in the consumption expenditure of different food items on the basis of co-efficient of variation. The co-efficient of variation is the highest both for cereals and its substitutes and edible oil (14.1 per cent) and it is the lowest (3.8 per cent) for other food items. The coefficient of variation is 6.9 per cent for all food items which is a major constituent of the total budget with the average share of 60.4 per cent. The trend is just the reverse for most of the non-food items in rural India. The percentage share of other non-food item and all non-food items have drastically increased. The other non-food items have increased with constant rate of 0.594 per cent per annum. The percentage share of expenditure of clothing and fuel & light has marginally increased at a constant rate of 0.119 and 0.009 per cent per annum whereas the share of expenditure of pan, tobacco and intoxicants has declined at a constant rate of 0.057 per cent per annum.

The above analysis reveals that the percentage share of expenditure of different food items except other food items has declined and the share of expenditure of different non-food items except pan, tobacco and intoxicants has increased during the period from 1986-87 to 2004-05. This is an important indication in the improvement in the standard of living of the rural populations of the country. Another important feature of the consumption pattern in rural India is that the percentage share of food expenditure (60.4 per cent) is much higher than the percentage share of non-food expenditure (39.6 per cent). Among different non-food items, the coefficient of variation is the highest for other non-food items (16.4 per cent) followed

Table 3
Percentage Distribution of Monthly Per Capita Consumption Expenditure (MPCE) of Broad Commodity Groups of different NSS Rounds for Rural India

Comm. Groups/ Rounds	*Cereal & its Substitutes*	*Pluses & its Products*	*Milk & its Products*	*Edible Oil & Fats*	*Meat, Fish & Egg*	*Other Food*	*Total Food*	*Pan, Tobacco & Intox.*	*Fuel and Light*	*Clothing*	*Other Non-food*	*Total Non-food*	*Total Expendi-ture*
42nd	27.17	3.92	9.57	4.89	3.73	16.40	65.67	3.46	7.61	7.53	15.73	34.33	100.00
43rd	26.51	3.97	8.62	5.62	3.23	15.82	63.77	3.18	7.44	6.65	18.95	36.23	100.00
44th	26.38	4.08	8.94	4.33	3.50	16.62	63.85	3.40	7.26	7.50	18.00	36.15	100.00
45th	24.29	4.39	9.69	4.80	3.61	17.50	64.28	3.53	7.62	6.41	18.16	35.72	100.00
46th	24.88	4.35	9.42	5.98	3.50	17.83	65.97	3.63	7.73	4.84	17.83	34.03	100.00
47th	24.23	4.19	8.99	5.45	3.37	16.84	63.08	4.49	7.04	5.03	20.36	36.92	100.00
48th	26.66	3.92	9.39	4.98	3.44	16.59	64.97	3.32	7.04	5.62	19.05	35.03	100.00
49th	27.61	3.93	7.19	4.44	3.09	17.64	63.90	3.48	8.01	5.46	19.14	36.10	100.00
50th	24.50	3.81	9.50	4.42	3.33	17.62	63.17	3.19	7.35	5.37	20.92	36.83	100.00
51st	24.56	3.66	8.87	4.60	3.18	16.17	61.04	2.95	7.00	7.04	21.96	38.96	100.00
52nd	23.54	3.74	9.41	4.58	3.18	15.91	60.34	2.74	7.13	7.73	22.05	39.66	100.00
53rd	22.17	3.75	9.95	4.05	2.98	15.83	58.73	2.95	7.16	6.99	24.16	41.27	100.00
54th	23.11	3.65	9.56	4.33	3.31	16.87	60.83	2.87	7.86	5.85	22.60	39.17	100.00
55th	22.37	3.81	8.75	3.74	3.32	17.42	59.40	2.87	7.52	6.85	23.36	40.60	100.00
56th	20.22	3.43	8.68	3.42	3.59	16.94	56.29	3.02	8.36	7.26	25.07	43.71	100.00
57th	19.35	3.38	8.41	3.68	3.36	17.29	55.46	2.98	8.80	7.09	25.66	44.54	100.00
58th	18.39	3.26	8.53	3.99	3.44	17.40	55.02	2.81	8.98	7.09	26.10	44.98	100.00
59th	18.04	3.12	8.08	4.44	3.24	16.97	53.88	2.58	9.24	6.97	27.34	46.12	100.00
60th	18.28	2.98	8.43	4.60	3.29	16.35	53.94	2.51	9.59	7.05	26.91	46.06	100.00
61st	18.21	3.07	8.47	4.60	3.33	17.36	55.05	2.69	10.17	4.53	27.56	44.95	100.00

Note: Computed from different NSS Reports, National Sample Survey Organisation, Ministry of Statistics and Programme Implementation, Government of India.

by clothing (15.2 per cent) and it is the lowest for fuel and light (11.87 per cent). The coefficient of variation for all non-food items is still lower which stood at 10.6 per cent. The average percentage share of pan, tobacco and intoxicants is the lowest (3.1 per cent) and other non-food items is the highest (22.07 per cent) in the rural sector of the country.

Table-4 reveals the inter-temporal variations in the consumption expenditure patterns of different food and non-food items in urban India. The pattern of food and nonfood expenditure in urban India is quite different from that of rural India. In rural India, food expenditure is much higher than non-food expenditure over the period 1986-87 to 1995-96. During the period 1997-98, the non-food expenditure was marginally higher than food expenditure thereafter non-food expenditure was much higher than food expenditure till 2004-05. The expenditure on different food items like cereals and its substitutes; pulses and its products; milk and its products; edible oil; meat, fish and egg; other food items and all food items had a downward trend and different non-food items except clothing have a upward trend during the period from 1986-87 to 2004-05. Food expenditure declined at a constant rate 0.984 per cent per annum. The sharp decline in food expenditure was mainly due to the decline in the expenditure on cereals and substitutes and other food items. Expenditure on cereals and substitutes and other food item have declined at a constant rate of 0.324 and 0.234 per cent per annum respectively. The sharp rise in food expenditure especially after 1998 is due to the sharp rise in expenditure on other non-food items. Among food items the percentage of variation is the highest (22.35 per cent) for edible oil and the lowest (8.64 per cent) for other food items. On the other hand, the percentage variation among non-food items is the highest (20.52 per cent) for pan, tobacco and intoxicants and the lowest (13.39 per cent) for clothing. But the overall variation in the percentage distribution of food and non-food expenditure is almost the same with 12 per cent.

The percentage distribution of MPCE on food and non-food expenditure for rural Orissa presented in *Table-5* reveals

Table 4
Percentage Distribution of Monthly Per Capita Consumption Expenditure (MPCE) of Broad Commodity Groups of Different NSS Rounds for Urban India

Comm. Groups/ Rounds	*Cereal & its Substitutes*	*Pluses & its Products*	*Milk & its Products*	*Edible Oil & Fats*	*Meat, Fish & Egg*	*Other Food*	*Total Food*	*Pan, Tobacco & Intox.*	*Fuel and Light*	*Clothing*	*Other Non-food*	*Total Non-food*	*Total Expendi-ture*
42nd	15.37	3.19	10.47	5.35	4.13	19.43	57.93	2.74	6.83	6.60	25.90	42.07	100.00
43rd	15.02	3.38	9.53	5.29	3.54	19.15	55.92	2.61	6.69	6.00	28.78	44.08	100.00
44th	15.75	3.48	10.02	4.73	3.97	19.20	57.14	2.65	6.59	6.22	27.39	42.86	100.00
45th	14.48	3.37	9.91	4.90	3.83	19.03	55.52	2.54	6.46	6.66	28.81	44.48	100.00
46th	14.21	3.50	9.91	5.94	3.76	19.53	56.85	2.75	6.60	4.77	29.03	43.15	100.00
47th	14.17	3.42	10.05	5.76	3.64	19.06	56.10	2.58	6.38	5.82	29.11	43.90	100.00
48th	15.14	3.16	10.43	5.14	3.61	18.57	56.04	2.33	6.32	5.44	29.87	43.96	100.00
49th	17.08	3.43	8.97	4.78	3.49	19.89	57.65	2.91	8.37	4.57	26.50	42.35	100.00
50th	14.28	3.04	9.80	4.39	3.39	19.76	54.65	2.34	6.58	4.68	31.74	45.35	100.00
51st	14.65	3.04	9.72	4.51	3.41	18.10	53.44	2.04	6.68	5.53	32.30	46.56	100.00
52nd	13.28	3.06	9.42	4.14	3.19	16.97	50.06	1.86	6.39	7.12	34.57	49.94	100.00
53rd	13.52	2.82	9.72	3.66	3.03	16.86	49.62	1.84	7.08	5.83	35.64	50.38	100.00
54th	13.27	2.85	9.44	3.73	3.21	17.14	49.64	1.92	7.29	5.51	35.64	50.36	100.00
55th	12.50	2.84	8.68	3.14	3.13	17.77	48.06	1.90	7.75	6.05	36.24	51.94	100.00
56th	11.16	2.42	8.30	2.72	3.03	16.17	43.80	1.87	8.39	6.36	39.58	56.20	100.00
57th	10.62	2.39	8.13	2.88	2.77	16.34	43.13	1.78	8.94	6.20	39.96	56.87	100.00
58th	10.10	2.26	7.73	3.89	2.67	15.83	42.47	1.70	9.01	6.01	40.81	57.53	100.00
59th	10.13	2.22	7.82	3.42	2.67	15.72	41.98	1.57	9.17	5.88	41.39	58.02	100.00
60th	10.11	2.10	7.83	3.54	2.63	15.44	41.64	1.55	9.02	5.96	41.83	58.36	100.00
61st	10.21	2.14	7.92	3.46	2.71	16.09	42.51	1.62	9.94	4.00	41.92	57.49	100.00

Note: Computed from different NSS Reports, National Sample Survey Organisation, Ministry of Statistics and Programme Implementation, Government of India.

that the average percentage of monthly per capita expenditure on cereal and its substitutes is 36.20 in rural Orissa as against 23.0 per cent for rural India. But the average percentage of MPCE on different food items like pulses and its products; milk and its products; edible oil and other food items are much lower in the rural sector of the state as compared to its counterparts in the country. This clearly reveals the variation in the consumption pattern in rural Orissa from rural India. Like urban India, the share of food expenditure exhibits an overall downward trend while the share of non-food expenditure exhibits an overall upward trend in rural Orissa. The share of food expenditure has declined at a constant rate of 0.509 per cent per annum but the share of non-food expenditure has increased at a constant rate of 0.513 per cent per annum. The trend of different food items indicates that the decline in food expenditure is mainly due to the decline in the share of cereals and its substitutes (0.746 per cent per annum); pulses and its products (0.360 per cent per annum); edible oil (0.034 per cent per annum); and meat, fish and egg (0.034 per cent per annum). But other food items and different non-food items show an upward trend. The co-efficient of variation calculated for different food items indicate that the variation in the consumption expenditure is the highest (15.24 per cent) for edible oil and the lowest (5.90 per cent) for all food items. Among non-food items, the variation is the highest for clothing with 20.32 per cent and the lowest for all non-food items with 11.02 per cent.

The percentage distribution of MPCE on food and non-food expenditure for urban Orissa presented in *Table-6* reveals that the consumption expenditure in urban Orissa is quite different from its rural counterpart. The share of food expenditure was much higher than the share of non-food expenditure till 55th round (1999-2000) thereafter the trend was reversed. Like urban India, the share of food expenditure exhibits an overall down-ward trend while the share of non-food expenditure exhibits an overall upward trend in urban Orissa. The share of food expenditure has declined at a constant rate of 0.803 per cent per annum but the share of non-food

Table 5
Percentage Distribution of Monthly Per Capita Consumption Expenditure (MPCE) of Broad Commodity Groups of Different NSS Rounds for Rural Orissa

Comm. Groups/ Rounds	Cereal & its Substitutes	Pluses & its Products	Milk & its Products	Edible Oil & Fats	Meat, Fish & Egg	Other Food	Total Food	Pan, Tobacco & Intox.	Fuel and Light	Clothing	Other Non-food	Total Non-food	Total Expendi-ture
42nd	40.77	2.94	2.36	3.73	4.76	14.79	69.35	3.42	8.98	7.26	10.99	30.65	100.00
43rd	41.48	2.67	2.27	3.80	4.04	14.62	68.88	2.78	9.07	5.98	13.29	31.12	100.00
44th	43.08	3.40	2.01	4.64	4.45	11.37	68.95	2.69	8.71	5.84	13.81	31.05	100.00
45th	39.37	4.15	2.38	3.65	4.16	16.97	70.68	3.06	7.53	5.33	13.4	29.32	100.00
46th	36.00	3.30	2.31	4.44	4.41	15.99	66.44	2.84	7.50	5.24	17.98	33.56	100.00
47th	40.41	3.22	2.14	4.14	4.59	15.32	69.82	3.16	7.73	5.16	14.13	30.18	100.00
48th	37.78	3.04	2.41	3.97	4.60	14.78	66.59	3.48	7.82	7.91	14.2	33.41	100.00
49th	39.23	3.08	2.06	3.20	4.12	14.57	66.28	2.77	8.76	5.08	17.11	33.72	100.00
50th	39.07	2.66	2.40	3.14	4.12	16.66	68.05	2.94	9.23	4.87	14.91	31.95	100.00
51st	41.70	2.64	2.31	3.14	3.77	13.99	67.55	2.70	8.02	5.67	16.06	32.45	100.00
52nd	36.95	2.71	2.08	3.10	3.93	15.13	63.90	2.47	7.73	8.07	17.83	36.1	100.00
53rd	38.97	2.64	2.26	2.83	3.36	14.47	64.53	2.35	8.72	8.17	16.23	35.47	100.00
54th	37.08	2.67	2.63	3.20	3.25	15.91	64.74	1.93	8.46	6.00	18.87	35.26	100.00
55th	36.08	2.82	2.09	2.90	3.64	16.57	64.11	2.67	8.01	6.56	18.65	35.89	100.00
56th	33.36	2.63	2.45	2.79	3.70	17.91	62.85	2.34	8.83	6.97	19.01	37.15	100.00
57th	33.02	2.88	1.83	3.28	4.24	17.78	63.04	3.39	8.20	7.74	17.63	36.96	100.00
58th	27.44	2.72	2.26	3.19	4.34	18.77	58.71	2.46	9.99	7.63	21.21	41.29	100.00
59th	27.58	2.46	2.11	3.65	4.44	17.80	58.04	2.54	10.99	7.48	20.95	41.96	100.00
60th	27.16	2.67	2.98	3.94	4.13	17.56	58.44	2.64	10.57	7.65	20.7	41.56	100.00
61st	28.29	2.88	2.55	4.05	4.20	19.60	61.57	2.61	11.82	3.64	20.36	38.43	100.00

Note: Computed from different NSS Reports, National Sample Survey Organisation, Ministry of Statistics and Programme Implementation, Government of India.

expenditure has increased at a constant rate of 0.808 per cent per annum. The trend of different food items indicates that the decline in food expenditure is mainly due to the decline in the share of cereals and substitutes; milk and its products; edible oil and other food items. The average share of milk and its products is much less, and the average share of meat, fish and egg and other food items is much more than the corresponding all India figures. As regards to non-food items, the share of pan, tobacco and intoxicants is much more than and the share other non-foods is much less than the corresponding urban India figures. The co-efficient of variation for different food items shows that it is the highest (23.0 per cent) for milk and its products and the lowest (6.5 per cent) for other food items. Among the non-food items, the variation in expenditure is the highest (21.5 per cent) for clothing and the lowest (18.2 per cent) for fuel and light in urban Orissa.

EMPIRICAL ANALYSIS

Among the complete demand systems, the Linear Expenditure System (LES) has received more attention, since the additive utility function from which it is derived, has very rigid specification and ensures the fulfillment of almost all the theoretical restrictions. Some researchers have estimated this demand system from time-series data (Bhattacharya, 1967) while others from time-series of cross-section data (Radhakrishna and Murty, 1973). They do examine whether the theoretical properties do or do not hold in practice. They explore whether the demand system (LES) provides a satisfactory description of consumer behavior at a reasonable level of commodity aggregation. The LES also gives rise to linear Engel curves. The severity of this restriction can be moderated to some extent in time-series models designed mainly for providing predictions at the mean level without change in income distribution, either by introducing time trends into the parameters (Stone, 1955 and Murty, 2005) or by resorting to habit formation hypothesis (Pollack and Wales, 1969). Even these modifications also may fail to forge a link between consumption pattern and income distribution.

Table 6
Percentage Distribution of Monthly Per Capita Consumption Expenditure (MPCE) of Broad Commodity Groups of Different NSS Rounds for Urban Orissa

Comm. Groups/ Rounds	*Cereal & its Substitutes*	*Pluses & its Products*	*Milk & its Products*	*Edible Oil & Fats*	*Meat, Fish & Egg*	*Other Food*	*Total Food*	*Pan, Tobacco & Intox.*	*Fuel and Light*	*Clothing*	*Other Non-food*	*Total Non-food*	*Total Expendi-ture*
42nd	20.51	3.00	10.03	4.52	5.00	19.41	62.47	2.84	7.01	9.46	18.22	37.53	100.00
43rd	22.10	3.25	5.76	4.92	4.88	19.80	60.73	2.72	7.13	6.89	22.53	39.27	100.00
44th	22.27	3.45	5.65	4.03	4.45	20.22	60.07	2.89	6.87	6.21	23.96	39.93	100.00
45th	20.69	3.47	5.54	4.11	4.13	21.55	59.48	2.87	6.79	5.47	25.39	40.52	100.00
46th	18.63	3.52	5.17	4.48	5.16	19.64	56.60	2.69	6.31	6.53	27.87	43.4	100.00
47th	22.25	3.74	4.56	5.02	5.87	20.31	61.76	2.78	6.12	6.45	22.89	38.24	100.00
48th	15.85	2.86	4.67	4.15	5.96	19.66	53.15	2.71	5.38	6.19	32.57	46.85	100.00
49th	24.26	3.47	5.14	3.79	5.19	17.69	59.53	3.32	9.58	3.15	24.42	40.47	100.00
50th	19.96	2.89	4.93	3.47	5.01	21.52	57.78	2.76	7.43	5.25	26.78	42.22	100.00
51st	18.51	3.08	5.51	3.99	5.18	19.78	56.04	2.59	6.93	5.21	29.23	43.96	100.00
52nd	17.12	3.21	4.34	3.23	3.99	17.99	49.88	1.76	6.18	7.25	34.93	50.12	100.00
53rd	19.51	2.71	5.21	3.11	4.10	19.91	54.55	2.22	7.10	6.41	29.72	45.45	100.00
54th	18.68	3.02	5.56	3.63	4.04	20.29	55.23	3.09	8.21	7.64	25.83	44.77	100.00
55th	22.75	3.15	4.73	2.99	4.65	18.68	56.95	1.95	8.35	6.20	26.55	43.05	100.00
56th	16.07	2.64	5.26	2.57	4.32	17.37	48.23	2.12	8.47	6.72	34.46	51.77	100.00
57th	16.36	2.62	5.07	2.93	4.38	17.47	48.83	1.93	9.29	6.56	33.39	51.17	100.00
58th	13.08	2.20	4.97	2.53	2.84	18.75	44.37	1.70	9.32	7.36	37.25	55.63	100.00
59th	14.48	2.33	4.35	3.16	4.71	18.14	47.16	2.24	9.08	6.30	35.22	52.84	100.00
60th	15.42	2.25	4.18	3.25	4.18	18.37	47.65	2.99	9.59	5.99	33.78	52.35	100.00
61st	16.84	2.50	4.74	3.24	4.46	18.14	49.93	1.75	10.39	3.69	34.24	50.07	100.00

Note: Computed from different NSS Reports, National Sample Survey Organisation, Ministry of Statistics and Programme Implementation, Government of India.

The Linear Expenditure system in spite of its limitations viz., linearity of the Engel curves, and inelasticity of the price-quantity demand curves, incapability of incorporating complementary and inferior commodities has found extensive empirical applications.[22] This is essentially due to its relative simplicity from the point of view of estimation and interpretation. In some applications, the LES model can be made flexible by allowing its parameters to change with the change in the level of income, demographic features, and dynamic behavior related to past consumption, shift in the consumer's taste and preference etc. LES has been extended by making the vector of 'γ ' parameters to depend on prices (stone, 1964; Nasse, 1970, Radhakrishna and Ravi,1992); by introducing habit formation aspects by replacing the vector of 'γ ' parameters by some function of lagged values of consumption[23] and also by incorporating household size either in the vector of β parameters or in the vector of parameters.[24]

It is seen from the foregoing discussion that no single demand system can adequately represent the consumption patterns over a wide range of total expenditure and one has to resort to different variants of LES. The choice is now among these variants. If one takes into consideration the fulfillment of theoretical properties as desirable features, the simple LES has a distinct edge over its variants as well as NES since simple LES fulfills all the desirable theoretical properties.

The empirical implication of the relationship between income and own- price elasticity of commodities is somewhat disturbing. Especially in the time-series data, the item expenditure and total expenditure are highly correlated.[25] The responses of total expenditure and hence the expenditure elasticities are more or less not accurately estimated and the type of relationship between income and own-price elasticity mentioned above induces a structure on the estimates of the latter vis-a-vis the former. The resulting estimates of own price elasticity, thus, would be different from what might be obtained on the basis of less restrictive functional forms. It is, thus, important to see the extent to which the estimates of own price elasticity based on the LES or similar systems differ from those based on flexible system of demand equations.

We have estimated the additive stochastic models of LES and its three different variants in budget share form separately for rural and urban households using time-series estimates of per capita specific consumption expenditure and the corresponding total expenditure on nine broad commodity groups collected and compiled from different published reports of the NSS from 1986-87 (42nd round) to 2004-05 (61st round) excluding 49th and 60th rounds to avoid the overlapping of consumer price indices. The analysis thus covered the period from 1986-87 to 2004-05. The four models estimated for analysis are the simple Linear Expenditure System named as LES-1; a flexible form of LES by incorporating household size in its budget share parameter named as LES-2 and another flexible form of LES obtained by replacing its budget share parameter by linear time trend which has been abbreviated as LES-3. The fourth model is the non-additive variant of LES popularly known the Nasse Expenditure System (NES), which allows specific substitution between commodity groups. We have estimated LES-2 and LES-3 by incorporating the household size and time trend separately in the vectors of β and γ parameters and found that the results are better with appropriate signs when the above two variables (household size and time trends) are incorporated in the budget share parameters of LES. We have also estimated all the four models using both expenditure equations and budget share equations of these models and found better results when the parameters are estimated from the budget share equations. To make the analysis simpler, we have not presented and analysed the estimates obtained from the expenditure equations of LES and its variants and also the estimates obtained from the LES-2 and LES-3 incorporating household size and time trend in the committed quantity parameters of LES.

PARAMETER ESTIMATES

We now proceed with the evaluation of the reliability of the parameter estimates to see how far these estimates are theoretically meaningful and statistically satisfactory. The parameter estimates along with t-ratios, adjusted, R^2 ($\overline{R}^2$)

F-values and Theil's measures of information inaccuracy (π_i) of four models viz., LES-1, LES-2, LES-3 and NES separately for the rural and urban sectors of Orissa and all India are presented in *Tables-7 to 22*. The frequency of the magnitude of t-ratios of marginal budget shares, committed quantities, size and preference coefficients, and the range of variation of ($\bar{R}^2$) values for different specifications of LES model is also given in *Table-23*. The t-ratios of most of the estimates of marginal budget share parameters (β_i) and the committed quantity parameters (γ_{ij}) in LES-1 and NES; the estimates of the parameters β_i and γ_{ij} along with the estimate of the parameter (θ_i) of the household size variable in LES-2 and the estimates of the parameters β_i and γ_{ij} along with the estimates of the parameter (θ^*_i) of the time trend variable in LES-3 are found to be significant exceeding the value of 2 in magnitude in all the above models.

The parameter estimates along with the values of t-ratios (in the parentheses below each of the estimates in the tables), $\bar{R}^2$, F-statistic and Theil's measures of information inaccuracy (π_i) of LES-1 separately for the rural and urban sectors of Orissa and all India are presented in *Tables-7 to 10*. For LES-1, out of 36 marginal budget share coefficients (MBS), 30 (83 per cent) coefficients are found to be highly significant with very high values of t-ratios. The t-ratios of the rest of 6 (17 per cent) marginal budget share coefficients are not significant which vary from 1 to 2. But out of the 324 estimates of committed quantity parameters (γ_{ij}), 216 (67 per cent) estimates are found to be significant with t-ratios exceeding the value of 2. The t-ratios of 88 (27 per cent) parameter estimates of committed quantity vary from 1 to 2. For the rest of 20 (6 per cent) estimates, the t-ratios are less than unity. The F-values which show the joint significance as well as goodness fit of the demand equations are found to be highly significant in all the 36 estimated equation of LES-1 with values exceeding 10. The $\bar{R}^2$ values which reflect the goodness of fit as well as the explanatory power of the estimated equations are also found to be high in most of the cases. Out of 36 equations estimated under LES-1, 16 (44 per cent) equations have $\overline{R}^2$ values greater than 0.9; 19 (54 per cent) equations have $\overline{R}^2$ values vary from 0.8 to 0.9. To supplement the above measure of goodness of fit, we have estimated the Theil's measures of information inaccuracy (π_i). It is observed that the π_i values are closer to zero; the best value in most the demand equations. We have also estimated another measure of goodness fit, the squared correlation between the observed and estimated budget shares (R^2_w) are found to vary over a wide range from 0.552 to 0.945. The only overall or across all equations measure of goodness of fit used is the Theil's measure of average information inaccuracy (π) which is also found to be closer to zero (*Table-24*). Looking at the closeness of the observed and estimated budget shares of LES-1, one finds that the simple LES is a strong contender of choice in spite of its limitations that it includes linear Engel curves and its inability to capture the non-linearity/curvature of budget data.

The parameter estimates obtained from the Linear Expenditure System with demographic specification (LES-2) presented in *Tables-11 to 14* separately for the rural and urban sectors of Orissa and all India. The t-ratios are found to be significant for most of the estimates of this demand system. Out of 36 estimates of the marginal budget share estimates, 26 (72 per cent) estimates are found to be significant with t-ratios exceeding the value of 2. Similarly, the household size coefficients (θ_i) is also found significant in most of the equations of this demand system. Out of 36 size coefficients (θ_i), 24 (67 per cent) coefficients are found to be significant with t-ratios exceeding 2. But out of the 324 estimates of committed quantity parameters (γ_{ij}), 238 (73 per cent) estimates are found to be significant with t-ratios exceeding by 2. The t-ratios of 67 (21 per cent) estimates lying in between 1 to 2 and the rest of 19 (6 per cent) estimates are less than unity. The F-values of all the 36 equations estimated under LES-2 are found to be highly significant with values much more than 10. The goodness of fit as well as the explanatory power of the equation judged on the basis of the value of $\overline{R}^2$ reveals that out of 36 demand equations, 22 (61 per cent) demand equations have $\overline{R}^2$ values more than 0.9; the $\overline{R}^2$ value of the rest of 14 (39 per cent) equations various between 0.8 to 0.9. From the squared correlation between the observed and estimated budget shares R_w^2, it is noticed that the value of most of the R_w^2 are found to be more than 0.8 and also greater than the corresponding estimates of R_w^2 obtain from LES-1. To supplement the above two measures of goodness of fit, we have also estimated the Theil's measure of information accuracy (π_i) and found that π_i values are close to zero indicating the best fit of these demand equations to the sample budget share data. Further, the overall goodness of fit of all the equations measured by Theil's measure of average information inaccuracy (π) is also found to be closer to zero, the best value (*Table-24*). When we compare the overall performance of LES-1 with LES-2 on the basis of the above estimates, it is observed that the performance of LES-2 with demographic specification is better than the simple LES (without demographic specification). This may be due to the significant effect of the household size on the expenditure pattern of the households in both rural and urban sectors of Orissa and all India.

The parameter estimates of Linear Expenditure System obtained by replacing the marginal budget shares by a time trend variable named as LES-3 separately for the rural and urban sector of Orissa and all India are presented in *Tables-15 to 18*. It is noticed that most of the estimates are found to be significant. Out of the 36 marginal budget share coefficients (β_i), 25 (69 per cent) coefficients are found to be significant with t-ratios exceeding 2. Out of the rest of the insignificant marginal budget share coefficients, for 8 (22 per cent) coefficients, t-ratios vary from 1 to 2. The preference coefficients (θ_i^*) are also found to be significant in most of the cases. Out of 36 preference coefficients, 22 (61 per cent) coefficients are found to be significant with t-ratios exceeding 2. Of the remaining 14 coefficients, the t-ratios of 8 (22 per cent) coefficients vary from

Table 7
Parameter Estimates of Linear Expenditure System (LES-1): Rural India

Commodity Group	Marginal Budget Share (MBS) β_i	Cereals & its substitutes γ_{i1}	Pulses & its products γ_{i2}	Milk & its products γ_{i3}	Edible Oil & Fats γ_{i4}	Meat, Fish & Egg γ_{i5}	Other Food γ_{i6}	Fuel & Light γ_{i7}	Clothing γ_{i8}	Other Non-food γ_{i9}	$\bar{R}^2$	F-value	TMII
		Committed Quantities (or coefficients) of											
Cereals &	0.135	-0.288	-0.451	-0.857	-0.883	-1.513	2.526	2.619	0.148	-1.302	0.945	155.09	0.00007
its substitutes	(15.099)	(-1.283)	(-2.187)	(-1.843)	(-1.998)	(-2.413)	(3.401)	(4.365)	(0.195)	(-2.726)			
Pulses &	0.028	-1.881	-0.098	-0.517	0.598	0.529	0.435	0.460	0.539	-0.065	0.919	102.74	0.00001
its Products	(1.711)	(-2.617)	(-0.107)	(-2.174)	(3.715)	(2.003)	(1.255)	(2.601)	(3.752)	(-0.091)			
Milk & its	0.113	0.055	1.514	-0.033	0.155	-0.884	-1.564	0.919	-0.408	0.248	0.852	51.63	0.00004
Products	(14.559)	(1.040)	(3.563)	(-0.644)	(2.157)	(-1.683)	(-4.777)	(2.208)	(-2.559)	(1.294)			
Edible oil & Fats	0.043	-2.296	-2.107	-0.553	-0.055	3.390	3.205	-1.718	-1.288	1.421	0.812	38.77	0.00013
	(1.918)	(-3.720)	(-2.979)	(-3.458)	(-1.507)	(4.129)	(2.009)	(-4.297)	(-3.711)	(2.728)			
Meat, Fish & Egg	0.044	1.818	-0.732	-0.638	-0.144	-0.057	-2.137	0.068	1.881	-0.058	0.819	40.59	0.00002
	(24.208)	(3.325)	(-2.273)	(-1.830)	(-1.146)	(-0.766)	(-4.063)	(1.931)	(2.224)	(-1.205)			
Other Food Items	0.189	-0.188	-0.623	-0.075	0.544	-0.250	-1.253	0.183	0.104	1.559	0.852	51.70	0.00004
	(17.113)	(-2.184)	(-2.310)	(-1.194)	(3.738)	(-2.259)	(-3.767)	(2.271)	(1.747)	(4.890)			
Fuel & Light	0.054	2.664	-3.866	0.067	1.139	0.262	-2.381	-0.105	0.392	1.616	0.908	88.81	0.00004
	(14.661)	(3.919)	(-5.422)	(1.128)	(4.142)	(2.200)	(-3.170)	(-1.363)	(2.130)	(2.902)			
Clothing	0.091	2.532	2.866	0.503	-1.796	-1.798	-0.058	1.154	-1.065	-2.338	0.830	43.81	0.00054
	(21.721)	(3.494)	(4.286)	(2.260)	(-3.488)	(-3.580)	(-1.008)	(3.731)	(-2.298)	(-4.787)			
Other Non-	0.304	-1.850	0.784	1.078	0.639	3.656	-0.754	-1.994	-0.346	-1.214	0.950	169.54	0.00006
food Items	(28.064)	(-3.588)	(2.344)	(1.448)	(2.763)	(3.332)	(-2.441)	(-3.910)	(-1.557)	(-2.898)			

Note: Computed from the time-series consumption expenditure data of 42nd to 61st NSS rounds.

Table 8
Parameter Estimates of Linear Expenditure System (LES-1): Urban India

	Marginal Budget Share (MBS)	*Committed Quantities (or coefficients) of* Cereals & its substitutes	Pulses & its products	Milk & its products	Edible Oil & Fats	Meat, Fish & Egg	Other Food	Fuel & Light	Clothing	Other Non-food			
Commodity Group	β_i	γ_{i1}	γ_{i2}	γ_{i3}	γ_{i4}	γ_{i5}	γ_{i6}	γ_{i7}	γ_{i8}	γ_{i9}	$\bar{R}^2$	*F-value*	*TMII*
Cereals &	0..059	-0.334	2.704	0.864	-0.844	0.866	-1.958	-0.754	-1.567	1.022	0.957	200.37	0.00005
its substitutes	(28.505)	(-1.247)	(3.318)	(2.812)	(-2.679)	(2.997)	(-3.271)	(-1.356)	(-2.156)	(2.279)			
Pulses & its	0.018	-0.957	-1.051	-0.902	-0.224	1.143	-2.165	3.407	-1.914	2.664	0.956	197.47	0.00001
Products	(1.215)	(-2.250)	(-2.369)	(-2.032)	(-1.022)	(3.858)	(-3.190)	(4.481)	(-3.797)	(3.166)			
Milk & its	0.104	1.697	1.938	-0.208	-0.527	-1.065	-2.611	1.267	-2.964	2.473	0.946	157.43	0.00002
Products	(58.445)	(3.630)	(2.199)	(-1.061)	(-1.727)	(-2.133)	(-2.034)	(2.781)	(-2.868)	(2.827)			
Edible oil	0.035	1.253	3.484	-3.302	-0.542	1.675	-1.253	-0.997	-1.357	1.039	0.891	73.60	0.00011
& Fats	(38.445)	(3.142)	(2.204)	(-3.773)	(-1.330)	(2.543)	(-2.867)	(-1.187)	(-2.244)	(2.591)			
Meat, Fish	0.035	-0.191	1.820	-0.364	0.866	-0.023	-2.481	-0.679	-2.031	3.084	0.873	62.05	0.00003
& Egg	(36.860)	(-1.559)	(3.974)	(-1.132)	(2.062)	(-0.342)	(-4.912)	(-1.197)	(-4.566)	(5.036)			
Other Food	0.174	1.937	2.321	-1.856	-0.212	1.106	-0.132	3.323	-2.680	-3.807	0.909	90.28	0.00004
Items	(47.658)	(2.691)	(2.531)	(-2.372)	(-1.280)	(3.131)	(-0.455)	(2.077)	(-2.521)	(-4.321)			
Fuel & Light	0.063	-0.344	-1.162	0.606	1.311	0.496	1.192	-0.317	-1.053	-0.728	0.959	211.02	0.00003
	(22.431)	(-1.090)	(-3.926)	(1.327)	(4.269)	(1.370)	(3.652)	(-1.780)	(3.263)	(-2.185)			
Clothing	0.113	-1.351	-0.860	0.612	1.334	-0.535	0.682	-1.089	-0.114	1.321	0.846	49.58	0.00016
	(33.156)	(-3.829)	(-2.440)	(1.610)	(3.396)	(-1.496)	(1.161)	(-3.765)	(-1.330)	(3.241)			
Other Non-	0.401	0.404	-0.712	0.655	0.135	-0.788	2.235	-1.706	0.916	-1.139	0.949	168.09	0.00009
food Items	(46.476)	(1.114)	(-2.338)	(2.383)	(1.141)	(-2.637)	(4.323)	(-3.799)	(2.829)	(-4.549)			

Note: Computed from the time-series consumption expenditure data of 42nd to 61st NSS rounds.

Table 9

Parameter Estimates of Linear Expenditure System (LES-1): Rural Orissa

	Marginal Budget Share (MBS)	Committed Quantities (or coefficients) of											
		Cereals & its substitutes	Pulses & its products	Milk & its products	Edible Oil & Fats	Meat, Fish & Egg	Other Food	Fuel & Light	Clothing	Other Non-food			
Commodity Group	β_i	γ_{i1}	γ_{i2}	γ_{i3}	γ_{i4}	γ_{i5}	γ_{i6}	γ_{i7}	γ_{i8}	γ_{i9}	$\overline{R}^2$	*F-value*	*TMII*
Cereals &	0.252	-0.388	0.501	1.563	-1.515	1.568	-1.233	-0.299	-0.516	0.319	0.902	81.19	0.00026
its substitutes	(10.385)	(-1.231)	(1.223)	(3.070)	(-3.411)	(3.685)	(-3.889)	(-1.211)	(-2.378)	(1.045)			
Pulses & its	0.023	-2.431	-1.119	2.153	0.594	-0.572	-0.563	1.092	-1.144	1.989	0.855	53.20	0.00009
Products	(1.255)	(-3.585)	(-2.260)	(3.303)	(1.540)	(-1.143)	(-1.427)	(4.494)	(-3.127)	(3.785)			
Milk & its	0.031	0.893	0.174	-0.185	-0.870	-0.302	1.183	1.101	-0.819	-1.176	0.861	55.87	0.00006
Products	(18.023)	(2.078)	(0.137)	(-0.248)	(-2.154)	(-1.596)	(3.662)	(3.332)	(-2.483)	(-2.520)			
Edible oil	0.036	-1.287	-1.673	2.436	-0.178	-1.284	-1.297	2.076	3.769	-2.561	0.789	33.75	0.00013
& Fats	(1.414)	(-3.490)	(-3.065)	(4.311)	(-0.693)	(-3.745)	(-3.256)	(5.851)	(7.797)	(-0.917)			
Meat, Fish	0.056	-0.421	-2.772	0.852	0.834	-0.260	1.087	1.002	0.320	-0.643	0.874	60.48	0.00003
& Egg	(17.825)	(-1.803)	(-2.023)	(2.615)	(2.529)	(-0.215)	(3.504)	(3.966)	(1.719)	(-0.541)			
Other Food	0.184	-0.644	0.728	-0.677	1.919	-0.901	-1.569	0.712	1.248	-0.815	0.862	56.11	0.00022
Items	(26.871)	(-1.367)	(1.329)	(-1.929)	(2.212)	(-2.794)	(-4.898)	(1.455)	(3.184)	(-2.455)			
Fuel & Light	0.0674	0.413	-1.865	-0.625	0.560	-0.051	1.321	-0.155	2.505	-2.103	0.824	41.14	0.00018
	(11.686)	(1.618)	(-2.991)	(-2.655)	(1.823)	(-0.738)	(2.712)	(-0.883)	(4.591)	(-4.003)			
Clothing	0.068	-1.236	2.271	2.058	-2.022	-1.133	0.923	-1.248	-1.314	1.701	0.918	84.81	0.00097
	(26.443)	(-2.861)	(3.350)	(2.847)	(-3.154)	(-1.837)	(1.097)	(-2.272)	(-3.052)	(2.323)			
Other Non-	0.284	-0.833	-0.183	1.742	-0.515	0.832	-0.446	0.554	-0.826	-0.326	0.805	37.25	0.00038
food Items	(15.089)	(-1.715)	(-0.673)	(5.501)	(-1.468)	(2.992)	(-1.919)	(1.651)	(-2.515)	(-1.633)			

Note: Computed from the time-series consumption expenditure data of 42nd to 61st NSS rounds.

Table 10

Parameter Estimates of Linear Expenditure System (LES-1): Urban Orissa

		Committed Quantities (or coefficients) of											
	Marginal Budget Share (MBS)	*Cereals & its substitutes*	*Pulses & its products*	*Milk & its products*	*Edible Oil & Fats*	*Meat, Fish & Egg*	*Other Food*	*Fuel & Light*	*Clothing*	*Other Non-food*			
Commodity Group	β_i	γ_{i1}	γ_{i2}	γ_{i3}	γ_{i4}	γ_{i5}	γ_{i6}	γ_{i7}	γ_{i8}	γ_{i9}	$\bar{R}^2$	*F-value*	*TMII*
Cereals & its substitutes	0.093 (36.673)	-0.931 (-3.636)	2.099 (3.641)	-0.302 (-1.250)	0.663 (1.112)	-1.120 (-4.668)	-1.377 (-2.227)	0.232 (1.943)	1.021 (3.482)	-0.285 (-1.146)	0.925	92.43	0.00020
Pulses & its Products	0.023 (17.884)	-0.304 (-2.946)	-0.266 (-1.906)	0.196 (0.117)	0.228 (1.667)	-0.384 (-1.856)	-0.970 (-2.255)	1.698 (3.573)	0.633 (1.925)	-0.832 (-3.306)	0.807	37.59	0.00008
Milk & its Products	0.079 (26.744)	1.454 (3.871)	1.664 (4.364)	-0.352 (-1.035)	-1.969 (-2.455)	-1.311 (-2.399)	-1.592 (-3.667)	1.783 (2.237)	1.726 (3.065)	-1.402 (-3.451)	0.835	45.67	0.00022
Edible oil & Fats	0.033 (1.877)	-0.846 (-2.680)	-0.134 (-1.442)	-0.910 (-2.556)	-0.067 (-0.419)	-0.473 (-2.262)	1.974 (4.577)	-0.691 (-2.459)	0.761 (2.815)	0.387 (1.114)	0.832	44.46	0.00016
Meat, Fish & Egg	0.066 (48.042)	-0.684 (-2.086)	0.764 (2.333)	-0.779 (-2.266)	-0.494 (-1.257)	-1.099 (-4.262)	2.425 (3.518)	0.777 (2.151)	0.217 (0.044)	-1.127 (-2.238)	0.925	89.46	0.00042
Other Food Items	0.239 (32.386)	-1.092 (-3.326)	0.638 (2.853)	-0.212 (-1.246)	1.073 (3.042)	-0.748 (-2.323)	-1.567 (-4.654)	0.386 (1.254)	0.518 (2.355)	1.005 (4.721)	0.903	84.02	0.00014
Fuel & Light	0.063 (52.962)	0.986 (2.954)	0.255 (1.973)	0.860 (2.743)	0.360 (1.462)	-0.724 (-1.841)	-1.840 (-2.823)	-0.099 (-1.584)	0.314 (1.560)	-0.113 (-1.821)	0.899	80.38	0.00010
Clothing	0.042 (28.354)	1.155 (3.545)	-0.442 (-1.073)	-0.657 (-2.587)	-1.017 (-4.074)	0.752 (2.260)	0.848 (3.075)	0.385 (1.077)	-0.507 (-1.856)	-0.517 (-2.551)	0.875	62.73	0.00058
Other Non-food Items	0.364 (63.324)	0.778 (2.738)	-0.994 (-2.914)	1.765 (3.267)	-0.050 (-0.018)	0.797 (3.690)	0.367 (1.589)	-0.508 (-1.931)	-1.108 (-3.259)	-1.055 (3.054)	0.911	87.74	0.00037

Note: Computed from the time-series consumption expenditure data of 42nd to 61st NSS rounds.

Table 11

Parameter Estimates of Linear Expenditure System with Demographic Specification ((LES-2): Rural India

	Marginal Budget Share	H. Size Coefficients	Committed Quantities (or coefficients) of											
			Cereals & its subst.	Pulses & its products	Milk & its products	Edible Oil & Fats	Meat, Fish & Egg	Other Food	Fuel & Light	Clothing	Other Non-food			
Commodity Group	β_i	θ_i	γ_{i1}	γ_{i2}	γ_{i3}	γ_{i4}	γ_{i5}	γ_{i6}	γ_{i7}	γ_{i8}	γ_{i9}	$\bar{R}^2$	F-value	TMII
Cereals & its substitutes	0.129	0.042	-0.203	2.148	-0.670	-1.215	-2.238	1.467	1.360	0.504	-1.153	0.918	100.72	0.0064
	(2.170)	(2.816)	(-1.874)	(3.036)	(-1.387)	(-2.315)	(-4.879)	(2.688)	(2.356)	(1.115)	(-2.586)			
Pulses & its Products	0.029	0.003	-1.715	-0.475	-0.530	1.038	-2.025	0.100	0.258	0.806	2.544	0.912	91.30	0.0004
	(1.920)	(1.668)	(-3.523)	(-1.950)	(-2.207)	(3.345)	(-4.867)	(0.091)	(1.350)	(2.094)	(4.615)			
Milk & its Products	0.114	0.001	0.017	1.349	-0.033	0.170	-0.885	-1.699	1.091	-0.344	0.335	0.843	48.41	0.0052
	(3.339)	(0.754)	(0.379)	(2.691)	(-0.952)	(1.986)	(1.294)	(-3.004)	(2.207)	(-2.526)	(2.318)			
Edible oil & Fats	0.042	-0.023	0.834	-1.479	-0.959	-0.014	1.905	2.881	-2.763	-1.713	1.309	0.913	93.99	0.0028
	(0.427)	(-6.043)	(2.428)	(-2.992)	(-1.248)	(-2.529)	(1.767)	(4.435)	(-2.093)	(-1.589)	(1.191)			
Meat, Fish & Egg	0.045	-0.001	0.909	0.468	-0.466	-0.857	-0.316	0.923	0.480	0.738	-1.879	0.857	58.43	0.0018
	(1.362)	(-0.519)	(5.124)	(1.137)	(1.951)	(-3.723)	(-2.055)	(7.698)	(3.385)	(3.210)	(-3.154)			
Other Food Items	0.190	0.010	-0.191	0.556	-0.067	-0.505	-0.196	-1.402	0.088	0.872	0.843	0.867	57.79	0.0004
	(3.358)	(1.861)	(-2.183)	(1.859)	(-2.384)	(-1.727)	(-0.920)	(-2.446)	(2.251)	(1.869)	(3.863)			
Fuel & Light	0.059	-0.027	3.055	-5.288	0.047	0.497	0.372	-0.476	-0.108	0.600	1.301	0.934	127.97	0.0095
	(3.587)	(-5.376)	(3.184)	(-2.952)	(0.130)	(1.441)	(0.464)	(-0.449)	(-4.050)	(2.854)	(2.390)			
Clothing	0.095	0.031	0.828	0.412	0.606	-0.966	-0.969	0.246	1.218	-0.533	-0.841	0.836	45.94	0.0011
	(2.760)	(4.715)	(3.347)	(7.504)	(1.148)	(-2.476)	(-2.464)	(1.433)	(2.052)	(-4.090)	(-2.361)			
Other Non-food Items	0.298	-0.037	-1.776	0.399	1.036	0.452	2.312	1.045	-0.793	-1.416	-1.261	0.933	125.88	0.0015
	(5.973)	(-2.609)	(-3.452)	(1.458)	(2.259)	(1.190)	(3.225)	(2.579)	(-3.560)	(-1.878)	(-2.346)			

Note: Computed from the time-series consumption expenditure data of 42nd to 61st NSS rounds.

Table 12

Parameter Estimates of Linear Expenditure System with Demographic Specification ((LES-2): Urban India

			Committed Quantities (or coefficients) of											
	Marginal Budget Share	*H. Size Coefficients*	*Cereals & its subst.*	*Pulses & its products*	*Milk & its products*	*Edible Oil & Fats*	*Meat, Fish & Egg*	*Other Food*	*Fuel & Light*	*Clothing*	*Other Non-food*			
Commodity Group	β_i	θ_i	γ_{i1}	γ_{i2}	γ_{i3}	γ_{i4}	γ_{i5}	γ_{i6}	γ_{i7}	γ_{i8}	γ_{i9}	$\overline{R}^2$	*F-value*	*TMII*
Cereals & its	0.058	0.035	-0.525	0.314	1.327	-0.636	0.625	-2.233	0.683	-0.557	1.002	0.968	275.52	0.0056
substitutes	(2.854)	(4.367)	(-3.820)	(4.313)	(1.456)	(-1.983)	(2.846)	(-3.694)	(3.012)	(-2.882)	(2.501)			
Pulses & its	0.017	0.002	-0.406	-0.064	-0.822	0.052	1.145	-0.705	1.822	-0.882	-0.140	0.958	205.86	0.0023
Products	(1.710)	(1.319)	(-2.536)	(-1.988)	(-1.132)	(2.051)	(2.899)	(-1.092)	(2.857)	(-2.161)	(-2.042)			
Milk & its	0.107	0.012	1.549	2.628	-0.023	-0.225	-1.311	-2.722	1.948	-3.460	1.616	0.961	219.71	0.0692
Products	(3.290)	(4.594)	(3.048)	(4.540)	(-0.301)	(-1.428)	(-2.876)	(-3.812)	(3.999)	(-5.694)	(2.957)			
Edible oil	0.036	0.011	0.590	-0.755	-0.654	-1.127	1.648	-1.007	0.948	-2.725	3.081	0.875	62.81	0.0052
& Fats	(1.171)	(3.148)	(1.522)	(-1.778)	(-1.051)	(-2.486)	(3.105)	(-2.873)	(2.911)	(-4.861)	(5.425)			
Meat, Fish	0.035	0.006	-4.368	3.248	-0.051	-0.065	-0.023	-0.499	0.236	0.844	0.679	0.908	81.74	0.0180
& Egg	(2.151)	(2.925)	(-3.046)	(2.247)	(-1.032)	(-0.041)	(-1.567)	(-2.222)	(2.115)	(-2.126)	(3.503)			
Other Food	0.172	-0.001	0.049	1.848	-1.290	-0.360	1.049	-0.832	2.154	-1.386	-1.232	0.905	81.23	0.0013
Items	(6.962)	(-0.647)	(1.023)	(2.172)	(-2.983)	(-2.433)	(3.019)	(-2.093)	(1.983)	(-3.033)	(-2.808)			
Fuel & Light	0.062	0.021	-0.869	-1.019	0.865	0.206	0.185	0.754	-0.347	-0.501	0.726	0.977	378.47	0.0011
	(2.272)	(2.219)	(-2.465)	(-3.161)	(2.761)	(1.448)	(1.698)	(2.462)	(-3.389)	(2.157)	(2.982)			
Clothing	0.112	0.001	-0.494	-1.081	0.711	0.936	-0.354	-0.560	0.117	-1.365	2.091	0.824	42.17	0.0039
	(4.665)	(0.566)	(-2.174)	(-3.403)	(2.768)	(3.487)	(-2.409)	(-2.112)	(1.491)	(-2.378)	(5.692)			
Other Non-	0.401	-0.086	0.667	-1.208	0.522	-0.015	-0.850	1.247	-0.777	1.157	-0.744	0.948	162.77	0.0046
food Items	(5.244)	(-2.093)	(2.360)	(-3.238)	(2.453)	(-0.619)	(-2.746)	(3.525)	(-2.712)	(3.030)	(-2.891)			

Note: Computed from the time-series consumption expenditure data of 42nd to 61st NSS rounds.

Table 13

Parameter Estimates of Linear Expenditure System with Demographic Specification ((LES-2): Rural Orissa

			Committed Quantities (or coefficients) of											
	Marginal Budget Share	H. Size Co-efficients	Cereals & its subst.	Pulses & its products	Milk & its products	Edible Oil & Fats	Meat, Fish & Egg	Other Food	Fuel & Light	Clothing	Other Non-food			
Commodity Group	β_i	θ_i	γ_{i1}	γ_{i2}	γ_{i3}	γ_{i4}	γ_{i5}	γ_{i6}	γ_{i7}	γ_{i8}	γ_{i9}	$\bar{R}^2$	F-value	TMII
Cereals & its substitutes	0.252 (7.354)	0.034 (3.351)	-1.039 (-3.918)	1.654 (2.107)	1.139 (2.576)	-0.202 (-1.086)	1.276 (3.459)	-0.695 (-2.949)	-0.057 (-0.995)	-1.093 (-2.913)	-0.982 (-2.591)	0.825	42.52	0.0023
Pulses & its Products	0.024 (1.838)	-0.011 (-1.634)	-2.283 (-3.066)	-0.102 (-0.299)	2.685 (6.880)	1.555 (6.181)	-1.558 (-3.932)	-1.546 (-2.652)	0.708 (1.327)	-1.966 (-3.121)	2.508 (4.179)	0.896	72.64	0.0026
Milk & its Products	0.032 (2.996)	-0.022 (-2.701)	0.709 (2.637)	0.198 (1.711)	-0.216 (-1.032)	0.803 (2.037)	-1.951 (-3.157)	0.746 (2.744)	3.260 (4.799)	-1.204 (-3.757)	-2.344 (-3.139)	0.879	65.41	0.0063
Edible oil & Fats	0.036 (1.011)	0.018 (1.350)	0.388 (1.081)	-1.245 (-3.468)	1.178 (3.562)	-0.651 (-1.131)	-1.121 (-3.806)	-0.731 (-1.142)	1.236 (2.452)	1.996 (3.086)	-1.051 (-2.675)	0.887	70.83	0.0034
Meat, Fish & Egg	0.056 (4.577)	0.041 (4.534)	0.259 (1.196)	1.670 (3.626)	0.754 (2.778)	-0.402 (-1.094)	-0.101 (-0.757)	-0.253 (-1.968)	-0.775 (-2.257)	-1.665 (-2.093)	0.513 (1.221)	0.975	71.20	0.0004
Other Food Items	0.184 (8.637)	-0.022 (-1.140)	-0.452 (-2.382)	-0.128 (-1.861)	-0.280 (-1.659)	1.101 (3.066)	-1.294 (-4.417)	-0.386 (-2.070)	0.354 (2.322)	0.499 (2.702)	0.586 (2.415)	0.908	89.34	0.0014
Fuel & Light	0.069 (7.840)	-0.041 (-2.501)	-0.857 (-2.487)	-0.740 (-3.053)	-0.416 (-2.650)	0.380 (1.966)	-0.338 (-2.804)	0.050 (0.714)	-0.143 (-1.541)	0.115 (1.632)	1.949 (4.884)	0.920	103.33	0.0029
Clothing	0.068 (1.886)	-0.020 (-2.087)	-1.504 (-3.903)	2.226 (4.338)	0.913 (3.067)	-0.610 (-1.124)	-1.252 (-3.151)	0.835 (2.887)	-1.283 (-3.279)	-0.013 (-0.448)	0.687 (2.362)	0.836	45.84	0.0016
Other Non-food Items	0.280 (8.660)	0.024 (3.042)	-0.942 (-2.847)	0.757 (-2.571)	-0.823 (-2.042)	1.405 (3.122)	-0.463 (-1.432)	1.047 (3.445)	-0.628 (-2.630)	0.021 (0.616)	-0.375 (-1.877)	0.913	90.83	0.0027

Note: Computed from the time-series consumption expenditure data of 42nd to 61st NSS rounds.

Table 14
Parameter Estimates of Linear Expenditure System with Demographic Specification ((LES-2): Urban Orissa

	Marginal Budget Share	H. Size Co-efficients	Committed Quantities (or coefficients) of											
			Cereals & its subst.	Pulses & its products	Milk & its products	Edible Oil & Fats	Meat, Fish & Egg	Other Food	Fuel & Light	Clothing	Other Non-food			
Commodity Group	β_i	θ_i	γ_{i1}	γ_{i2}	γ_{i3}	γ_{i4}	γ_{i5}	γ_{i6}	γ_{i7}	γ_{i8}	γ_{i9}	$\overline{R}^2$	F-value	TMII
Cereals & its substitutes	0.097 (2.211)	0.040 (2.890)	-0.529 (-2.408)	1.138 (2.887)	-1.397 (-3.352)	1.365 (3.940)	-1.335 (-3.079)	-1.241 (-2.660)	0.192 (1.408)	0.916 (2.843)	0.892 (2.098)	0.908	88.767	0.0013
Pulses & its Products	0.023 (1.099)	0.004 (2.389)	-0.406 (-2.661)	-0.080 (-1.905)	-0.251 (-2.153)	0.282 (2.571)	-0.023 (-0.883)	0.272 (2.034)	-0.042 (-0.955)	0.257 (2.085)	-0.010 (-0.704)	0.929	113.832	0.0002
Milk & its Products	0.076 (2.810)	0.001 (0.634)	0.852 (2.896)	0.142 (1.306)	-0.653 (-3.069)	-0.527 (-2.402)	-0.465 (-2.382)	-0.612 (-2.655)	0.916 (3.236)	0.831 (3.068)	-0.483 (-2.439)	0.837	46.116	0.0080
Edible oil & Fats	0.034 (1.242)	0.009 (2.971)	-0.671 (-2.441)	1.210 (3.133)	-0.862 (-3.078)	-0.479 (-2.088)	-0.450 (-2.293)	0.889 (2.897)	-0.207 (-2.077)	-0.109 (-1.041)	0.678 (2.759)	0.845	49.192	0.0052
Meat, Fish & Egg	0.069 (2.838)	0.004 (3.509)	0.505 (2.221)	1.180 (3.472)	-0.858 (-2.488)	-0.024 (-1.429)	-0.473 (-4.051)	-0.525 (-2.320)	0.730 (2.243)	0.347 (2.642)	-0.854 (-2.904)	0.926	113.438	0.0009
Other Food Items	0.242 (3.552)	0.003 (1.244)	-0.273 (-2.365)	-0.293 (-2.421)	-0.192 (-1.228)	0.169 (1.042)	-0.571 (-2.237)	-0.522 (-2.666)	0.317 (2.416)	0.381 (2.244)	0.984 (2.680)	0.903	88.394	0.0001
Fuel & Light	0.062 (4.608)	-0.007 (-2.284)	0.916 (3.899)	0.799 (2.641)	1.083 (3.025)	0.812 (2.811)	-2.917 (-1.612)	-1.245 (-2.848)	-0.221 (-2.974)	0.548 (2.284)	0.226 (1.951)	0.913	94.792	0.0025
Clothing	0.062 (5.821)	-0.018 (-3.225)	1.466 (3.676)	-1.198 (-3.778)	-0.545 (-2.094)	0.066 (0.114)	-0.503 (-2.432)	1.680 (3.073)	0.044 (1.544)	0.082 (2.740)	-1.091 (-3.297)	0.862	56.387	0.0022
Other Non-food Items	0.336 (12.816)	-0.036 (-3.694)	0.219 (1.759)	0.099 (3.772)	0.787 (2.969)	0.492 (2.469)	0.585 (2.665)	0.653 (2.126)	-1.471 (-3.796)	-1.091 (-3.527)	-0.274 (-2.448)	0.907	88.629	0.0014

Note: Computed from the time-series consumption expenditure data of 42nd to 61st NSS rounds.

1 to 2 and 6 (17 per cent) coefficients are less than unity. On the other hand, the estimates of the committed quantity parameters (γ_{ij}) are found to be significant in most of the cases. Out of the 324 estimates of γ_{ij}, 217 (67 per cent) estimates are found to be significant with t-ratios exceeding 2 in magnitude and 87 (27 per cent) estimates are found to be insignificant with t-ratios varies from 1 to 2. The rest of 20 estimates (6 per cent) of γ_{ij} are found to highly insignificant with t-ratios less than 1. As regards to the goodness of fit as well as the explanatory power of the demand equations judged on the basis of $\bar{R}^2$, it is found that out of 36 demand equations under LES-3, 12 (33 per cent) demand equations have $\bar{R}^2$ values greater than 0.9 and for the rest of 24 (67 per cent) equations $\bar{R}^2$ values varies between 0.8 to 0.9. The F-values are found to be highly significant in most of the demand equations. The squared correlation coefficients between observed and estimated budget shares R^2_w are found to vary from 0.6 to 0.9 and marginally higher for some equation and lower for some other equations in LES-3 as compared to LES-1 and LES-2. The Theil's measures of information inaccuracy (π_i) values are found to be close to zero for most of the equations indicating the closeness between observed and estimated budget shares. The Theils' measure of average information inaccuracy (π) used for judging the overall fitness of all the equations of the demand systems are also found to be close to zero in both rural and urban sectors of Orissa and all India (*Table-24*).

It is observed from the above analysis that the performance of LES-3 is better than the performance of LES-1. This clearly indicates that preference of the consumer for different commodities changes over time in both rural and urban sectors of all India as well as all Orissa. But when we compare the performance of LES-3 with LES-1 and LES-2, the performance of LES-2 is relatively better than the performance of both LES-1 and LES-3 with a large number of significant estimates of and also relatively better fit of demand equations which is evident from $\bar{R}^2$ and F-values.

Table 15
Parameter Estimates of Linear Expenditure System with Linear Time Trend (LES-3): Rural India

	Marginal Budget Share	Preference Co-efficients	Committed Quantities (or coefficients) of Cereals & its subst.	Pulses & its products	Milk & its products	Edible Oil & Fats	Meat, Fish & Egg	Other Food	Fuel & Light	Clothing	Other Non-food			
Commodity Group	β_i	θ_i^*	γ_{i1}	γ_{i2}	γ_{i3}	γ_{i4}	γ_{i5}	γ_{i6}	γ_{i7}	γ_{i8}	γ_{i9}	$\bar{R}^2$	F-value	TMII
Cereals & its	0.138	-0.005	-0.590	-0.100	0.086	-0.547	0.661	0.778	0.981	-0.567	-0.702	0.893	75.376	0.0010
substitutes	(8.918)	(-2.902)	(-2.398)	(-1.455)	(1.255)	(-1.726)	(2.656)	(3.042)	(3.326)	(-2.056)	(-3.537)			
Pulses & its	0.028	-0.002	-0.512	-0.337	0.212	1.192	0.736	-0.743	-0.446	0.171	-0.274	0.903	83.403	0.0001
Products	(1.323)	(-1.635)	(-2.236)	(-1.556)	(1.355)	(3.419)	(2.436)	(-2.365)	(-2.846)	(1.429)	(-1.122)			
3.Milk & its	0.112	-0.003	0.001	1.487	-0.814	0.277	-0.187	-1.172	0.762	-0.558	0.204	0.825	42.335	0.0068
Products	(6.678)	(-3.539)	(0.501)	(3.564)	(-1.249)	(2.286)	(-1.138)	(-4.036)	(2.838)	(-2.673)	(2.045)			
Edible oil	0.044	-0.001	-0.846	-0.507	-0.766	-0.218	1.303	1.397	-0.457	-0.933	1.027	0.846	49.332	0.0011
& Fats	(0.751)	(-0.956)	(-2.833)	(-2.372)	(2.797)	(-1.524)	(2.867)	(2.849)	(-1.191)	(-2.582)	(2.716)			
Meat, Fish	0.045	0.001	0.733	0.726	-0.358	-0.415	-0.457	-0.812	0.554	0.841	-0.813	0.907	88.147	0.0032
& Egg	(1.678)	(1.096)	(2.537)	(2.301)	(-1.299)	(-1.330)	(-1.057)	(-2.714)	(2.722)	(2.838)	(-2.543)			
Other Food	0.192	0.002	-0.226	-0.656	-0.063	-0.172	-0.217	-0.526	0.164	1.143	0.554	0.830	44.059	0.0008
Items	(11.005)	(2.050)	(-1.820)	(-2.325)	(-0.165)	(-1.733)	(-2.233)	(-3.737)	(1.250)	(4.740)	(2.878)			
Fuel & Light	0.063	0.001	0.599	-0.403	-0.395	-0.390	0.413	-0.532	-0.381	0.643	0.447	0.905	85.464	0.0001
	(13.628)	(1.847)	(3.430)	(-2.628)	(-1.886)	(-1.731)	(-2.350)	(-2.401)	(-1.069)	(2.899)	(2.642)			
Clothing	0.091	-0.020	0.789	1.121	0.462	-0.315	-0.883	-0.566	0.404	-0.425	-0.587	0.850	51.005	0.0038
	(12.719)	(-5.474)	(2.565)	(3.039)	(2.267)	(-1.353)	(-3.093)	(-2.606)	(0.819)	(-1.123)	(-0.848)			
Other Non-	0.288	0.027	-0.303	0.844	-0.129	0.232	-0.624	1.645	-0.782	-0.260	-0.623	0.877	63.878	0.0023
food Items	(10.449)	(5.916)	(-1.067)	(2.600)	(-1.252)	(1.050)	(-2.559)	(3.969)	(-2.497)	(-1.411)	(-2.124)			

Note: Computed from the time-series consumption expenditure data of 42nd to 61st NSS rounds.

Table 16

Parameter Estimates of Linear Expenditure System with Linear Time Trend (LES-3): Urban India

	Marginal Budget Share	Preference Co-efficients	*Committed Quantities (or coefficients) of*											
			Cereals & its subst.	Pulses & its products	Milk & its products	Edible Oil & Fats	Meat, Fish & Egg	Other Food	Fuel & Light	Clothing	Other Non-food			
Commodity Group	β_i	θ_i^*	γ_{i1}	γ_{i2}	γ_{i3}	γ_{i4}	γ_{i5}	γ_{i6}	γ_{i7}	γ_{i8}	γ_{i9}	$\bar{R}^2$	*F-value*	*TMII*
Cereals & its	0.066	-0.003	-0.548	0.804	0.664	-0.152	0.376	-0.791	-0.361	-0.887	0.938	0.917	99.596	0.0000
substitutes	(4.344)	(-9.292)	(-2.490)	(2.627)	(2.298)	(-1.208)	(2.328)	(-2.457)	(-1.317)	(-2.936)	(3.088)			
Pulses & its	0.018	-0.001	-0.755	-0.031	-0.359	-0.110	0.478	-0.404	0.487	0.747	-0.055	0.956	199.691	0.0001
Products	(1.027)	(-3.077)	(-2.515)	(-0.799)	(-2.236)	(-1.266)	(2.447)	(-2.565)	(2.234)	(2.573)	(-0.834)			
Milk & its	0.111	-0.001	1.050	0.693	-0.606	0.996	-0.729	-0.834	0.772	-0.611	-0.733	0.901	87.750	0.0001
Products	(6.370)	(-3.352)	(3.568)	(2.557)	(-1.749)	(2.543)	(-2.754)	(-2.742)	(2.967)	(-1.659)	(-2.302)			
Edible oil	0.035	-0.002	0.800	0.865	-0.699	-0.419	0.768	-1.227	-0.814	0.560	0.167	0.852	51.248	0.0000
& Fats	(1.506)	(-4.967)	(2.322)	(2.966)	(-2.788)	(-1.753)	(2.276)	(-3.626)	(-2.181)	(1.158)	(1.238)			
Meat, Fish	0.036	-0.001	-0.408	-0.829	0.774	-0.330	-0.256	0.434	-0.747	0.779	0.583	0.825	42.390	0.0004
& Egg	(6.503)	(-1.991)	(-1.212)	(-2.552)	(2.264)	(-1.782)	(-1.044)	(2.032)	(-2.913)	(2.680)	(2.543)			
Other Food	0.175	-0.002	0.595	0.561	-0.734	-0.709	0.542	-0.781	0.392	0.746	-0.612	0.887	70.309	0.0001
Items	(8.574)	(-4.675)	(2.225)	(2.544)	(-2.899)	(-2.949)	(1.617)	(-2.907)	(1.072)	(2.179)	(-2.810)			
Fuel & Light	0.064	0.003	-0.707	-0.477	0.851	-0.637	-0.317	0.558	-0.271	0.617	0.383	0.965	251.849	0.0003
	(5.005)	(4.640)	(-2.509)	(-2.227)	(2.644)	(-2.763)	(-1.021)	(2.856)	(-1.084)	(2.897))	(1.236)			
Clothing	0.113	0.001	0.66	-0.149	0.412	0.551	-0.339	-0.544	-0.776	-0.482	0.660	0.868	59.332	0.0001
	(6.450)	(1.267)	7(2.378)	(-1.272)	(2.229)	(2.861)	(-1.172)	(-2.493)	(-2.651)	(-1.425)	(2.790)			
Other Non-	0.382	0.007	0.609	-0.121	-0.244	0.296	0.209	0.723	-0.235	-0.560	-0.677	0.887	70.857	0.0000
food Items	(7.180)	(5.471)	(2.505)	(-1.343)	(-1.805)	(2.142)	(2.237)	(2.662)	(-2.102)	(-2.514)	(-3.184)			

Note: Computed from the time-series consumption expenditure data of 42nd to 61st NSS rounds.

Table 17
Parameter Estimates of Linear Expenditure System with Linear Time Trend (LES-3): Rural Orissa

	Marginal Budget Share	Preference Co-efficients	Committed Quantities (or coefficients) of											
			Cereals & its subst.	Pulses & its products	Milk & its products	Edible Oil & Fats	Meat, Fish & Egg	Other Food	Fuel & Light	Clothing	Other Non-food			
Commodity Group	β_i	θ_i^*	γ_{i1}	γ_{i2}	γ_{i3}	γ_{i4}	γ_{i5}	γ_{i6}	γ_{i7}	γ_{i8}	γ_{i9}	$\overline{R}^2$	F-value	TMII
Cereals & its	0.256	0.024	-1.039	0.654	1.139	0.800	0.776	-0.695	-0.557	-0.495	-0.582	0.825	42.522	0.0019
substitutes	(7.354)	(3.351)	(-2.918)	(2.785)	(3.576)	(2.286)	(2.459)	(-1.149)	(-1.316)	(-1.913)	(-2.391)			
Pulses & its	0.026	-0.001	-0.283	-0.102	0.685	0.555	-1.588	-0.546	0.708	-0.605	1.176	0.896	77.798	0.0004
Products	(1.838)	(-1.634)	(-1.066)	(-1.299)	(2.790)	(2.546)	(-3.396)	(-2.652)	(2.327)	(-2.521)	(3.179)			
Milk & its	0.032	-0.001	0.709	0.198	-0.216	-0.803	-0.346	0.746	0.260	-0.204	-0.344	0.879	65.409	0.0063
Products	(1.996)	(-0.701)	(2.637)	(0.549)	(-1.032)	(-2.637)	(-2.183)	(2.744)	(1.799)	(-1.757)	(-1.139)			
Edible oil	0.036	0.008	0.388	-0.245	1.178	-0.251	-0.920	-0.731	0.705	0.996	-1.121	0.838	46.510	0.0034
& Fats	(0.961)	(1.850)	(1.095)	(-0.936)	(3.562)	(-1.131)	(-2.295)	(-0.142)	(0.912)	(2.915)	(-2.675)			
Meat, Fish	0.056	-0.001	0.459	1.674	0.754	-0.204	-0.301	-1.253	-0.977	-1.364	1.212	0.975	351.200	0.0004
& Egg	(7.840)	(-0.726)	(2.896)	(2.626)	(2.778)	(-1.094)	(-1.257)	(-3.968)	(-2.257)	(-3.093)	(3.221)			
Other Food	0.179	-0.010	-0.452	1.136	-1.280	0.838	-0.993	-0.686	0.354	0.499	0.586	0.908	89.340	0.0011
Items	(9.637)	(-3.140)	(-1.382)	(3.061)	(-1.059)	(3.066)	(-3.417)	(-3.070)	(1.322)	(1.402)	(2.615)			
Fuel & Light	0.066	-0.001	0.857	-0.740	-0.816	0.780	-0.787	1.650	-0.743	0.564	-0.766	0.820	40.967	0.0008
	(7.840)	(-0.501)	(1.487)	(-2.453)	(-2.650)	(2.966)	(-2.804)	(3.714)	(-2.841)	(1.632)	(-2.884)			
Clothing	0.065	0.005	-0.504	0.826	1.313	-0.810	-1.252	0.835	-1.283	-0.813	1.687	0.836	45.840	0.0016
	(1.886)	(-2.087)	(-1.303)	(2.838)	(3.467)	(-1.724)	(-3.151)	(2.687)	(-3.279)	(-2.848)	(3.362)			
Other Non-	0.285	-0.022	-0.742	-0.757	-0.823	1.405	-0.463	1.201	-0.368	0.721	-0.575	0.802	35.965	0.0022
food Items	(8.660)	(-3.042)	(-2.847)	(-2.571)	(-2.942)	(3.122)	(-1.232)	(3.745)	(-1.330)	(2.516)	(-2.077)			

Note: Computed from the time-series consumption expenditure data of 42nd to 61st NSS rounds.

Table 18
Parameter Estimates of Linear Expenditure System with Linear Time Trend (LES-3): Urban Orissa

			Committed Quantities (or coefficients) of												
	Marginal Budget Share	*Preference Co-efficients*	*Cereals & its subst.*	*Pulses & its products*	*Milk & its products*	*Edible Oil & Fats*	*Meat, Fish & Egg*	*Other Food*	*Fuel & Light*	*Clothing*	*Other Non-food*				
Commodity Group	β_i	θ_i^*	γ_{i1}	γ_{i2}	γ_{i3}	γ_{i4}	γ_{i5}	γ_{i6}	γ_{i7}	γ_{i8}	γ_{i9}	$\bar{R}^2$	*F-value*	*TMII*
Cereals & its	0.101	-0.004	-0.392	0.599	-0.864	0.639	0.683	-1.365	0.775	0.236	-0.311	0.924	88.763	0.024
substitutes	(9.288)	(-4.646)	(-1.015	(2.525)	(-2.835)	(2.334)	(2.482)	(-3.799)	(2.843)	(1.823)	(-1.163)			
Pulses & its	0.024	-0.001	0.461	-0.771	-0.843	0.662	-0.872	0.610	0.416	-0.376	0.713	0.825	42.552	0.002
Products	(1.477)	(-1.697)	(1.194)	(-2.725)	(-2.938)	(2.498)	(-2.953)	(2.617)	(2.249)	(-1.395)	(2.539)			
Milk & its	0.078	-0.003	0.839	0.462	-0.677	-0.504	0.248	-0.938	0.810	0.468	-0.708	0.964	238.155	0.015
Products	(7.309)	(-4.193)	(2.467)	(1.167)	(-2.369)	(-2.044)	(1.117)	(-2.903)	(2.848)	(1.101)	(-2.482)			
Edible oil	0.033	-0.001	0.517	-0.873	-0.811	-0.858	0.805	1.035	0.489	-1.080	0.774	0.833	45.052	0.003
& Fats	(0.532)	(-0.724)	(1.404)	(-2.879)	(-2.707)	(-2.955)	(2.445)	(3.079)	(1.282)	(-3.388)	(2.528)			
Meat, Fish	0.069	-0.010	-0.778	0.705	0.956	-1.033	-0.436	-0.599	-0.890	1.058	1.016	0.975	357.815	0.002
& Egg	(6.876)	(-3.604)	(-2.421)	(2.693)	(3.019)	(-3.467)	(-1.186)	(-1.396)	(-2.658)	(3.750)	(3.421)			
Other Food	0.243	0.008	-1.031	0.724	-0.859	0.121	-0.311	-0.640	0.530	0.464	1.002	0.871	60.538	0.007
Items	(5.933)	(3.497)	(-3.275)	(2.410)	(-2.564)	(0.871)	(-1.171)	(-2.507)	(2.382)	(1.197)	(3.706)			
Fuel & Light	0.061	0.002	-0.544	0.560	0.437	0.444	-1.143	-1.353	-0.465	1.305	0.759	0.829	41.232	0.001
	(4.651)	(2.757)	(-1.390)	(2.464)	(-1.002)	(1.179)	(-2.188)	(-2.590)	(-2.324)	(2.856)	(2.786)			
Clothing	0.045	0.002	-0.713	0.661	-0.468	-0.374	0.617	0.533	0.950	-0.401	-0.805	0.844	48.623	0.003
	(5.703)	(0.956)	(-2.657)	(2.404)	(-1.370)	(-1.898)	(2.528)	(2.267)	(2.861)	(-1.328)	(-2.652)			
Other Non-	0.347	0.007	0.720	-0.869	0.741	-0.782	0.588	1.098	-0.389	-0.616	-0.491	0.850	50.855	0.005
food Items	(6.569)	(5.430)	(2.554)	(-2.862)	(2.407)	(-2.794)	(2.131)	(3.752)	(-1.464)	(-2.482)	(-1.338)			

Note: Computed from the time-series consumption expenditure data of 42nd to 61st NSS rounds.

One of the non-additive alternative specification of LES is the Nasse-Expenditure System (NES) in which the committed quantity parameters (γ_{ij}) are made function of prices. The parameter estimates of the fourth model (NES) separately for the rural and urban sectors of the country as well as the state are presented in *Tables-19 to 22*. Like LES-1, most of the estimates of marginal budget shares of this model are found to be significant with t-ratios exceeding 2. Out of the 36 budget share coefficients (β_i), 31 (86 per cent) coefficients are found to be significant with t-ratios exceeding 2. For the rest of the 5 (14 per cent) coefficients, the t-ratios vary from1 to 2. But relatively a smaller proportion of the estimates of the committed quantity parameters (γ_{ij})of this model are found to be significant. Out of 324 parameters estimated, γ_{ij} 198 (61 per cent) estimates are found to significant and the rest 126 (39 per cent) estimates are found to be not significant. The t-ratio of 82 (25 per cent) estimates of γ_{ij} lie between 1 and 2 and 44 (14 per cent) estimates are less than unity. The explanatory power and goodness of fit of the equations of the model judged on the basis of $\bar{R}^2$ values, it is found that out of the 36 equations; only 15 (42 per cent) equations have values greater than 0.9 and 17 (47 per cent) equations have values lying in between 0.8 to 0.9. The goodness of fit as well as the joint significance of parameters as indicated by the F-values are found to be significant for all equations of the model with values more than 10. The squared correlation coefficients between the actual and estimated budget shares (R^2_w) are relatively low and vary from 0.5 to 0.8. Most of the R^2_w values also found to be less than their corresponding values in LES-1, LES-2 and LES-3. The Theil's measures of information inaccuracy (π_i) values are found to be close to zero for most of the equations indicating the closeness between observed and estimated budget shares. The Theil's measure of average information inaccuracy (π) used for judging the overall fitness of all the equations of the demand system are found to be not very close to zero (*Table-24*). So the overall performance of NES is relatively poor as compared to LES-1, LES-2 and LES-3 even though it is a non-additive variant of LES.

Table 19
Parameter Estimates of Nasse Expenditure System (NES): Rural India

		Committed Quantities (or coefficients) of											
	Marginal Budget Share	*Cereals & its subst.*	*Pulses & its products*	*Milk & its products*	*Edible Oil & Fats*	*Meat, Fish & Egg*	*Other Food*	*Fuel & Light*	*Clothing*	*Other Non-food*			
Commodity Group	β_i	γ_{i1}	γ_{i2}	γ_{i3}	γ_{i4}	γ_{i5}	γ_{i6}	γ_{i7}	γ_{i8}	γ_{i9}	$\bar{R}^2$	*F-value*	*TMII*
Cereals & its	0.129	-0.237	-0.249	-0.240	-0.319	-0.986	1.034	0.917	0.575	-0.493	0.952	177.82	0.00007
substitutes	(15.556)	(-2.556)	(-0.282)	(-1.444)	(-1.035)	(-2.321)	(3.576)	(2.086)	(1.335)	(-1.705)			
Pulses & its	0.038	0.201	-0.276	0.063	-0.083	0.224	-0.052	-0.053	-0.067	0.041	0.923	107.71	0.00001
Products	(1.610)	(1.554)	(-3.069)	(1.295)	(-0.830)	(2.051)	(-0.276)	(-0.555)	(-0.807)	(0.014)			
Milk & its	0.090	-0.559	-0.776	-0.200	-0.518	1.731	0.684	-0.544	-0.142	0.324	0.752	27.35	0.00004
Products	(13.242)	(-3.380)	(-2.906)	(-2.135)	(-0.384)	(1.705)	(1.383)	(-2.285)	(-0.154)	(3.308)			
Edible oil	0.045	0.286	0.993	0.082	-0.145	-0.513	-1.001	0.409	0.135	-0.245	0.828	42.52	0.00013
& Fats	(1.935)	(2.602)	(4.995)	(1.468)	(-2.406)	(-2.087)	(-5.821)	(3.194)	(1.446)	(-2.744)			
Meat, Fish	0.035	-0.168	0.063	0.061	0.011	-0.168	0.204	-0.178	0.158	0.017	0.829	43.72	0.00002
& Egg	(16.995)	(-1.296)	(0.241)	(1.294)	(0.107)	(-2.261)	(1.070)	(-1.905)	(-2.155)	(0.198)			
Other Food	0.189	0.019	0.136	-0.068	0.390	-0.161	-1.525	0.102	0.687	0.421	0.868	59.41	0.00004
Items	(17.354)	(1.033)	(2.117)	(-1.315)	(3.848)	(-2.321)	(-4.806)	(2.246)	(4.840)	(3.045)			
Fuel & Light	0.079	-0.938	0.680	0.733	-0.462	0.378	1.247	-0.308	-0.874	-0.455	0.943	148.32	0.00004
	(16.945)	(-2.189)	(0.722)	(0.481)	(-1.575)	(0.900)	(1.795)	(-2.989)	(-3.148)	(-1.493)			
Clothing	0.088	-0.959	-0.931	-0.273	0.808	0.956	0.939	-0.978	-0.432	0.869	0.924	108.12	0.00054
	(14.636)	(-3.543)	(-3.268)	(-3.385)	(3.560)	(4.503)	(4.009)	(-5.764)	(-3.385)	(0.785)			
Other Non-	0.308	-0.742	0.292	0.437	0.318	1.664	-0.340	-0.788	-0.471	-0.368	0.955	189.27	0.00006
food Items	(18.503)	(-1.548)	(2.287)	(2.424)	(0.839)	(3.318)	(-0.480)	(-3.368)	(-1.533)	(-1.115)			

Note: Computed from the time-series consumption expenditure data of 42nd to 61st NSS rounds.

EFFECT OF CHANGE IN TASTE AND PREFERENCES ON DEMAND PATTERN

The effect of change in consumer's taste and preference on demand pattern in general and on MBS in particular can be quantified by comparing simple LES (LES-1) with its variant LES-3. The differences in the MBS between LES-3 and LES-1 are attributable to household's change in taste for different commodities over time. The effect of preference coefficients reflecting the change in consumer's taste for different commodities over time (expressed per annum) along with preference elasticities separately for the rural and urban sectors of Orissa and all India are presented in *Table-29*. As noted earlier, use of time trend is only a crude way of measuring taste changes. The changes in MBS in LES-3 are to be interpreted as annual changes because of the way in which the time trend variable is incorporated in marginal budget share coefficient of LES.

The taste and preference coefficients have significant effect on cereals and its substitutes; milk and its products, other food items, clothing and other non-food items in both sectors of Orissa and all-India. The marginal effect of taste changes are negative for most of the food items except meat, fish and egg and other food items in rural India but positive for most of the non-food items except clothing in both the sector of India. On the other hand, the pattern of taste changes are little different for Orissa. The marginal effect of taste changes are also negative for most of the food and non-food item except cereals and its substitutes, edible oil and clothing in rural Orissa but positive for all non-food items in urban Orissa. Almost similar rural-urban variation in demand pattern due to change in taste over time is also noticed from the estimated preference elasticities. This implies that at the margin, taste and preferences seem to reduce the money income allocated to most of the food groups thereby increasing its allocation to different non-food items both in the rural and urban sectors of the state as well as the country.

Table 29
Estimates of Preference Coefficients and Elasticities from LES-3 for Nine Commodity Groups: Orissa and All-India

	Preference Coefficients				*Preference Elasticity*			
	India		*Orissa*		*India*		*Orissa*	
Commodity Group	*Rural*	*Urban*	*Rural*	*Urban*	*Rural*	*Urban*	*Rural*	*Rural*
Cereals & its substitutes	-0.0054	-0.0034	0.0242	-0.0043	-0.2499	-0.1252	0.7202	0.1367
Pulses & its products	-0.0016	-0.0008	-0.0012	-0.0006	-0.2103	-0.2013	-0.4765	0.0682
Milk & its products	-0.0026	-0.0015	-0.0010	-0.0031	-0.1550	-0.1127	0.7016	-0.4826
Edible oil & fats	-0.0011	-0.0016	0.0077	-0.0013	0.1762	-0.1539	0.3921	0.1254
Meat, fish & egg	0.0008	-0.0006	-0.0013	-0.0097	0.0563	-0.2189	0.4867	-0.2062
Other food items	0.0021	-0.0024	-0.0102	0.0081	-0.2006	-0.1403	-0.5965	-0.2117
Fuel & light	0.0013	0.0034	-0.0013	0.0017	0.2179	0.1691	-0.1207	0.2641
Clothing	-0.0204	-0.0004	0.0049	0.0024	-0.1534	-0.1132	-0.0519	-0.0708
Other non-food items	0.0268	0.0072	-0.0218	0.0070	0.2992	0.2115	-1.0353	0.1547

Note: Computed from the time-series consumption expenditure data of 42nd to 61st NSS rounds.

CONCLUSION

The LES and its variants have been estimated using time series data complied from different NSS rounds at nine commodity level of classification separately for rural and urban sectors of Orissa and all India. The retail price data used for estimating LES and its variants is the compiled consumer price indices of agricultural labour for the rural sector and industrial workers for the urban sector released by the labour bureau from time to time separately for Orissa and all India. The empirical analysis led to the following broad conclusion.

The above analysis reveals distinct rural-urban and income (population) group variation in the consumption pattern in the state well as in the country. When we compare the rural-urban consumption pattern in India, food expenditure is much higher than non-food expenditure in rural sector where as non-food expenditure is much higher than food expenditure in urban sector. Almost the similar pattern rural-urban variation in food and non-food expenditure is observed in Orissa with the share of non-food expenditure marginally higher than food expenditure in the urban Orissa. The low and middle income groups in rural areas spend a higher proportion of their budget on food items especially on cereals and substitutes; pulses and its products; edible oil; and meat, fish and egg and other non-food items. The budget shares decline as we move up the income ladder except for milk and milk products.

It is observed from the analysis of temporal variation in consumption pattern that the percentage share of expenditure of different food items except other food items has declined and the share of expenditure of non-food items except pan, tobacco and intoxicants has increased during the period from 1986-87 to 2004-05. This is an important indication in the improvement of the living standards of the people of the state as well as the country. Another important feature of the consumption pattern of the country is that the percentage share of food expenditure is much higher than the percentage share of non-food expenditure. The trend of different food items indicate that the decline in food expenditure is mainly due to the decline in the share of cereals and substitutes; milk and its products; edible oil and other food items. The average share of milk and its products is much less and the average share of meat, fish and egg and other food item is much more in Orissa than the corresponding all India figures. As regards to non-food items, the share of pan, tobacco and intoxicants expenditure is much more and the share of other non-food expenditure is much less in Orissa than the corresponding all India figures.

It is evident that although NES is a non-additive variant LES, its performance is relatively poor than the other three variants. On the basis of the statistical criteria, it is found that the performance of LES-2 is relatively better than LES-1, LES-3 and NES. However, to judge the most suitable functional form of the model, we have applied the economic a priori criteria in which we have compared the sign and magnitude of the estimates of β_i, γ_i θ_i and θ_i^* along with the different elasticities estimated from these models. Further, the simple LES (LES-1) model seems to overestimate the own-price effects for some items and underestimate for some other items of consumption as compared to other flexible models like LES-2, LES-3 and NES. But the estimates obtained from LES-2 for most of the food and non-food groups are found to be plausible compared to other variants judged on the basis of their sign and magnitude. Further, the estimates of marginal budget shares obtained from LES-2 for most of the food and non-food groups follow certain definite patterns in Orissa and all India. Hence, the performance of LES-2 is better than LES and its other variants.

It is also observed that the MBS are somewhat 'robust' across model specifications. However, minor differences do exist between model specifications. The NES underestimates most of the food and non-food items where as LES-1 and LES-3 overestimates few staple food items like cereal and its substitutes and pulses and its products and other non-food items in both rural and urban sectors of Orissa and all India. It is also noticed that the estimates of marginal budget shares obtained from LES-2 for most of the nutritious food items like milk and its products, meat, fish and egg and other food items as well as the staple food items like cereals and pulses seems to be the plausible values compared to its variants.

The above empirical analysis reveals a distinct rural-urban variation in demand pattern of different food and non-food items. For most of the food items, rural expenditure elasticities are higher than urban expenditure elasticities and it is reversed for most of the non-food items. This is a clear indication of higher standard of living of the urban households than their rural counterparts in Orissa and all India. Further, the expenditure elasticities in the state for most of the food groups are higher and most of the non-food groups are lower as compared to the all-India level. It also indicates that the standard of living of the people in the state is relatively lower than the all India level.

It is also noticed that the urban households are less responsive to price changes for most of the food items and more responsive to price changes for most of the non-food items than their rural counterparts both in the rural and urban sectors of the state as well as the country. When we compare the own-price elasticities of Orissa and India, it is noticed that these elasticities in Orissa are higher for most of the food and non-food groups except meat, fish and egg compared to all India indicating that most of the food and non-food items are relatively inelastic in the state than that of the country.

Generally, increase in household size, ceteris paribus, seems to decrease the money income allocated to cereals and its substitutes and pulses and products at the margin, implying economies of scale. The opposite, namely diseconomies of scale seems to happen in different non-food items. Among food items, cereals and its substitutes; pulses & its products and edible oil seem to exhibit economies of scale where as other food items exhibit diseconomies in both the sectors but milk and its products and meat, fish and egg seem to exhibit diseconomies of scale only in the rural sector of the state and the country. On the other hand, other non-food items and fuel and light seem to exhibit diseconomies of scale in both the sectors where as clothing exhibits economies of scale in the country and diseconomies of scale in the state. This shows a marked hierarchy in the consumer basket. Milk and its products, meat, fish and egg and other food item are probably given lesser priority in rural household compared to cereals and its substitutes and pulses and its products in the event of increase in household size. But other non-food items and fuel and light exhibit diseconomies of scale but clothing exhibits economies of scale in both rural and urban sector of the state as well as of the country.

It is also revealed that the use of time trend is only a crude way of measuring taste changes. The changes in MBS in LES-3 are to be interpreted as annual changes because of the way in which the time trend variable is incorporated in MBS of LES-3. The taste and preference coefficients have significant effect on cereals and its substitutes; milk and its products, other food items, clothing and other non-food items in both sectors of Orissa and all-India. The marginal effect of taste changes are negative for most of the food items except meat, fish and egg and other food items in rural India but positive for most of the non-food items except clothing in both the sector of India. On the other hand, the pattern of taste changes are little different for Orissa. The marginal effect of taste changes are also negative for most of the food and non-food item except cereals and its substitutes, edible oil and clothing in rural Orissa but positive for all non-food items in urban Orissa. Almost similar rural-urban variation in demand pattern due to change in taste over time is also noticed from the estimated preference elasticities. This implies that at the margin, taste and preferences seem to reduce the money income allocated to most of the food groups thereby increasing its allocation to different non-food items both in the rural and urban sectors of the state as well as the country.

The results also show that flexible models that are theoretically superior provide unacceptable positive price responses for some commodities and have violated the second order conditions of utility maximization. Imposition of ad-hoc separability restrictions would result negative own-price responses which in turn would not ensure the fulfillment of second order conditions in these models. The tests of nested hypotheses also confirm the need for inclusion of household size, consumer taste, income group and rural urban dummies along with their interaction variables in the demand system[28].

NOTES

1. This Linear Expenditure System has been estimated in a number of studies for various countries such as Stone (1954) and later Stone, Brown and Rowe (1965) for Britain; Pallinck (1964) for Belgium; Leoni (1967) for Italy; Parks (1969) for Sweden; Pollack and Wales (1969) for USA; Yoshihara (1969) for Japan; Van Broekhoven (1971) for Belgium; Solari (1971) for Denmark France, Italy, Norway, United Kingdom and Switzerland, Sanz-Ferror (1972) for Belgium; Sanz-Ferror (1973) for Spain and Deaton (1975) for Britain; Paul and Rudra (1964); Bhattacharya (1967); Joseph(1968); Radhakrishna and Murty (1980) and Murty (2005) for India. This is due to its relative simplicity of its estimation and interpretation. This model has also been used in a number of studies for international comparison of demand patterns such as Parks (1969); Baschet and Debreu (1971); Goldberger and Gamaletsos (1970); Theil (1971); Solari (1971) and Barten (1973).
2. We are using the conventions that for two $n \times 1$

$$a = \left(a_1, \ldots, a_n\right)' \qquad c = (c_1, \ldots, c_n)',$$

$$\left.\begin{matrix} a < c \\ c > a \end{matrix}\right\} \text{ means } a_i < c_i \qquad (i = 1, \ldots, c_n),$$

$$\left.\begin{matrix} a \leq c \\ c \geq a \end{matrix}\right\} \text{ means } a_j \leq c_i \qquad (i = 1, \ldots, c_n).$$

3. This interpretation its parameters suggests that the Stone-Geary functional form may be useful in contexts other than the allocation of consumer expenditures. In an empirical study of the work on disincentives of the negative income tax, Leuthol (1968) had used the utility function

$$u = b \log\left(L - \bar{L}\right) + (1 - b) \log\left(Y - \bar{Y}\right)$$

Where L = hours of leisure, Y = disposable income, b is a parameter (measuring relative marginal valuation of L and Y) as are $\bar{L}$ = minimum required leisure and $\bar{Y}$ = = minimum required disposable income. In the no-tax-no-unearned-income situation, this function is maximized subject to the time-budget constraint

$$K = L + w^{-1} Y$$

Where K = total hours available and w = hourly wage rate. For less special situations, the constraint is appropriately modified. Constrained maximization yields a supply curve of labor (analogous to our demand functions), which is then estimated. Those estimates can be translated into estimates of b, $\bar{L}$ and $\bar{Y}$ where upon the response of work effort to a radically different tax-transfer law may be projected. Some of the analysis in Christensen's (1967) study of savings and the rate of interest is based upon an inter-temporal utility function which generalizes the CES functional form in the same manner as the Stone-Geary function generalizes the Cobb-Douglass functional form namely by introducing 'minimum required quantities'.

4. It may be surprising to find for all . It states that all goods are gross complements. In the Hicks-Allen definition, they will all be substitutes in the present model, since the utility function is directly additive.
5. For details of LES with saving as commodity with zero 'subsistence quantity' refer Howe (1975).
6. The duality relationship linking direct and indirect utility functions are mentioned by Houthakker (1960) and explored in detail by Samuelson (1966).
7. Houthakker (1960) has shown that the indirect utility function can be written in the additive form if and only if the cross-price elasticities with respect to any price are identical for all commodity groups.
8. If the utility function is additive, then the income elasticity of marginal utility of income does not vary with income. It also reduces the number parameter to be estimated.
9. For details see Deaton (1997) and Murty (1999).
10. A demand system is said to be a 'flexible functional form' if it is capable of providing a second order approximation to the behaviour of any theoretically plausible demand system at a point in the price-expenditure space.
11. The NASSE Expenditure System is generally used as the second stage model. It is non-additive model and allows inferior goods. It is used to estimate the parameter of the broad item like vegetables, fruits, nuts in the 'other food' group.
12. The interpretation for γ_i is only suggestive and it is not always possible to do so, particularly when γ_i is negative. A negative γ_i, however, not inconsistent with theory. Further, a negative γ_i allows own-price elasticity to exceed unity. When every γ_i is positive, LES admits only price inelastic goods.
13. The maximum likelihood estimators have also been derived for other variants of LES (Pollack & Wales, 1969). For the estimation LES and its variants we have used the linearised iterative procedure which yields the maximum likelihood estimates (Solari, 1971; Slater, 1972). In the above model the error sums to zero and the covariance between u_{it} and total expenditure is also zero. LES has been estimated assuming that the variance and covariance matrix $\Omega = \delta^2 I$, so that no equation is to be deleted while estimating the LES model.

14. See Nasse (1970), Deaton (1976) and Murty (1999).
15. For different elasticity formulae, see Pollack and Wales (1992), Chung (1994) and Murty (1999).
16. For Theil's Measure of Information Inaccuracy, see Theil (1975).
17. A comprehensive treatment of estimation procedures is given in Deaton (1974).
18. See Barten (1967).The maximum likelihood estimates are invariant to the choice of the equation. In case we assume $\Omega = \sigma^2 I$, there is no need of deleting any equation.
19. For details refer Sharma (2005): Wholesale and consumer price index, Central Statistical Organisation, New Delhi and Minhas, Jain, Kansal and Saluja (1987).
20. Refer the studies of Rudra and Roy (1966); Sinha (1966); Gupta (1968, 1973); Mahajan (1971) and Panda (1996, 2005).
21. See Panda (1996, 2005).
22. Refer the studies of Stone (1954, 1964); Paelinck (1964); Leoni (1967); Parks (1969); Pollak and Wales (1969); Yosihara (1969); and Dahlman and Klermarken (1971).
23. Refer the studies of Stone, Pollack and Wales (1969); Deaton and Weighly (1971); and Dahlman and Klermarken (1972).
24. See Meenakshi and Ray (1999) and Murty (2005).
25. Due to this restrictive property of LES, a number of alternative models like NES and SNAM were developed to overcome this problem.
26. Additivity the own price elasticity of a commodity becomes approximately proportional to the corresponding expenditure elasticity; indirect additivity imposes a linear relationship between these two elasticities. (Deaton, 1974)
27. Deaton (1997) has remarked that economies of scale in the food items is not credible, despite empirical evidence from a number of developing and developed countries to that effect (pp. 267).
28. See Murty (2005) for the details.

Appendix Table 1

Uncompensatory Own-price, Cross-price and Expenditure Elasticities Estimated from Simple LES (LES-1): All-India

	Uncompensatory Own and Cross-price Elasticities With Respect to Price of									
Commodity Groups	*Cereals & its Substitutes*	*Pulses & its Products*	*Milk & its Products*	*Edible Oil & Fats*	*Meat, Fish & Egg*	*Other Food*	*Fuel & Light*	*Clothing*	*Other Non-food*	*Expenditure Elasticity*
					Rural India					
Cereals & its substitutes	-0.564	0.156	0.295	0.325	1.000	-0.875	-1.044	-0.049	0.509	0.586
Pulses & its products	0.616	-0.720	0.178	-0.220	0.786	-0.151	-0.183	-0.180	0.025	0.739
Milk & its Products	-0.018	-0.521	-0.985	-0.057	0.316	0.541	-0.434	0.158	-0.097	1.247
Edible oil & Fats	0.748	2.097	0.189	-0.795	-1.207	-3.237	1.078	0.465	-0.554	0.943
Meat, Fish & Egg	-0.596	0.253	0.220	0.053	-0.951	0.741	-0.695	-0.630	0.068	1.274
Other Food Items	0.060	-0.211	0.025	-0.196	0.088	-0.868	-0.071	-0.362	-0.214	1.123
Fuel & Light	-0.870	1.330	-0.023	-0.418	-0.093	0.823	-0.666	-0.608	-0.631	0.691
Clothing	-0.835	-0.997	-0.175	0.666	1.008	0.020	-0.989	-0.872	0.974	1.115
Other Nonfood Items	0.606	-0.271	-0.371	-0.235	-1.309	0.261	1.194	0.374	-0.921	1.414
					Urban India					
Cereals & its substitutes	-0.358	-0.595	-0.187	0.155	-0.194	0.475	-0.641	1.021	-0.226	0.443
Pulses & its products	0.213	-0.497	0.412	0.041	-0.257	0.478	-0.770	0.405	-0.144	0.614
Milk & its Products	-0.378	-0.427	-0.923	0.097	0.239	0.576	-0.287	0.670	-0.507	1.119
Edible oil & Fats	-0.279	-0.768	0.715	-0.669	-0.376	0.806	0.225	0.287	-1.190	0.816
Meat, Fish & Egg	0.709	-0.401	0.079	-0.018	-0.853	0.547	0.153	0.430	-1.345	1.044
Other Food Items	-0.431	-0.512	0.402	0.039	-0.248	-0.766	-0.793	0.567	0.842	0.976
Fuel & Light	0.074	0.248	-0.127	-0.233	-0.108	-0.255	-0.709	-0.624	0.156	0.849
Clothing	1.637	0.538	-0.566	-0.612	0.345	-0.151	0.926	-0.940	-2.508	1.221
Other Nonfood Items	-0.091	0.603	-0.143	-0.025	0.178	-0.497	0.389	-0.870	-0.984	1.635

Note: Computed from the grouped time-series consumption expenditure data of 42nd to 61st NSS rounds.

Appendix Table 2

Uncompensatory Own-price, Cross-price and Expenditure Elasticities Estimated from Simple LES (LES-1): All-Orissa

	Uncompensatory Own and Cross-price Elasticities With Respect to Price of									
Commodity Groups	*Cereals & its Substitutes*	*Pulses & its Products*	*Milk & its Products*	*Edible Oil & Fats*	*Meat, Fish & Egg*	*Other Food*	*Fuel & Light*	*Clothing*	*Other Non-food*	*Expenditure Elasticity*
					Rural Orissa					
Cereals & its substitutes	-0.648	-0.203	-1.679	1.602	-4.355	2.645	0.141	0.200	-0.038	0.687
Pulses & its products	2.946	-0.763	-0.955	-2.809	0.236	2.788	-0.515	0.832	-0.921	0.800
Milk & its Products	-1.791	-1.289	-0.885	0.371	1.776	-2.203	-1.241	0.318	0.544	1.361
Edible oil & Fats	1.005	1.492	-1.081	-0.955	1.356	0.551	-0.980	-1.464	1.186	1.008
Meat, Fish & Egg	1.576	1.207	-1.711	-1.636	-0.852	-0.463	-0.474	-1.291	0.298	1.348
Other Food Items	0.483	-0.296	2.076	-1.230	3.263	-0.973	-0.336	-0.096	0.378	1.127
Fuel & Light	-2.493	1.042	6.940	-2079	3.741	-4.391	-0.723	-0.974	0.975	0.769
Clothing	3.337	-0.925	-3.076	0.864	0.469	-0.393	0.591	-0.910	-0.790	1.051
Other Nonfood Items	-0.568	0.339	5.416	-2.429	2.695	-2.058	0.684	0.562	-0.956	1.181
					Urban Orissa					
Cereals & its substitutes	-0.424	-1.651	0.070	-0.658	3.637	2.645	-0.597	-0.679	0.075	0.487
Pulses & its products	0.960	-0.639	-0.046	-0.558	2.045	0.428	-0.461	-0.599	0.221	0.738
Milk & its Products	-2.343	-3.694	-0.965	1.502	3.260	3.455	-3.212	-0.851	0.403	1.489
Edible oil & Fats	0.844	1.186	0.268	-0.751	0.353	-3.239	0.451	-0.170	-0.101	0.889
Meat, Fish & Egg	0.152	1.270	0.182	0.374	-0.843	-1.514	-0.211	-0.049	0.300	1.428
Other Food Items	0.679	-0.944	0.049	-0.018	0.179	-0.856	-0.103	-0.116	-0.263	1.225
Fuel & Light	-0.664	-1.463	-0.200	-0.839	1.390	3.250	-0.698	-1.136	-0.656	0.813
Clothing	-0.938	0.271	0.392	1.525	-0.486	-3.064	-0.106	-0.952	0.677	1.254
Other Nonfood Items	-0.622	1.947	-0.414	0.013	-1.377	-2.216	0.956	0.677	-0.985	1.498

Note: Computed from the grouped time-series consumption expenditure data of 42nd to 61st NSS rounds.

Appendix Table 3
Uncompensatory Own-price, Cross-price, Expenditure and Size Elasticities Estimated from LES with Demographic Specification (LES-2): All-India

	Uncompensatory Own and Cross-price Elasticities With Respect to Price of										
	Cereals & its Substitutes	*Pulses & its Products*	*Milk & its Products*	*Edible Oil & Fats*	*Meat, Fish & Egg*	*Other Food*	*Fuel & Light*	*Clothing*	*Other Non-food*	*Expenditure Elasticity*	*Size Elasticity*
Commodity Groups						*Rural India*					
Cereals & its substitutes	-0.506	-0.064	0.020	0.038	0.069	-0.044	-0.081	-0.003	0.045	0.561	0.649
Pulses & its products	0.359	-0.678	0.116	-0.244	0.463	0.067	-0.066	-0.172	-0.099	0.767	0.615
Milk & its Products	-0.005	-0.518	-0.944	-0.058	0.294	0.546	-0.403	0.138	-0.097	1.256	-0.672
Edible oil & Fats	-0.957	5.090	1.157	-0.766	-3.014	-6.854	3.962	2.009	-1.758	0.922	0.225
Meat, Fish & Egg	-0.116	-0.423	0.057	0.177	-1.035	1.339	-0.444	-0.324	0.260	1.327	-0.645
Other Food Items	0.042	-0.130	0.016	-0.126	0.047	-0.886	-0.044	-0.242	-0.144	1.128	-0.324
Fuel & Light	-2.692	4.912	-0.044	-0.987	-0.358	0.444	-0.566	-1.245	-1.396	0.746	-0.460
Clothing	0.383	3.617	0.295	-0.502	-1.430	-3.060	1.250	-0.829	-0.780	1.114	0.830
Other Nonfood Items	1.050	-0.249	-0.644	-0.101	-2.366	-0.654	1.955	0.856	-0.948	1.471	-0.706
						Urban India					
Cereals & its substitutes	-0.356	0.178	0.070	-0.028	0.045	-0.131	0.167	-0.240	0.054	0.442	0.564
Pulses & its products	0.223	-0.467	0.282	-0.007	-0.184	0.330	-0.617	0.285	0.022	0.584	0.428
Milk & its Products	-0.144	-0.243	-0.878	0.017	0.123	0.256	-0.191	0.307	-0.146	1.150	0.540
Edible oil & Fats	0.101	0.169	-0.139	-0.659	0.065	-0.155	0.038	-0.103	0.117	0.837	0.533
Meat, Fish & Egg	0.043	-0.032	0.000	0.001	-0.844	0.034	-0.002	0.027	-0.073	1.066	0.801
Other Food Items	-0.011	-0.417	0.286	0.068	-0.241	-0.748	-0.498	0.300	0.479	0.966	-0.221
Fuel & Light	-0.056	-0.065	0.054	0.064	0.053	0.048	-0.684	0.182	0.002	0.838	-0.273
Clothing	0.245	0.214	-0.139	-0.650	0.274	0.111	-0.024	-0.959	-1.162	1.188	0.729
Other Nonfood Items	-0.251	1.198	-0.191	0.005	0.323	-0.924	0.869	-1.530	-1.184	1.609	-0.469

Note: Computed from the time-series consumption expenditure data of 42nd to 61st NSS rounds.

Appendix Table 4
Uncompensatory Own-price, Cross-price, Expenditure and Size Elasticities Estimated from LES with Demographic Specification (LES-2):All-Orissa

	Uncompensatory Own and Cross-price Elasticities With Respect to Price of										
Commodity Groups	*Cereals & its Substitutes*	*Pulses & its Products*	*Milk & its Products*	*Edible Oil & Fats*	*Meat, Fish & Egg*	*Other Food*	*Fuel & Light*	*Clothing*	*Other Non-food*	*Expenditure Elasticity*	*Size Elasticity*
					Rural Orissa						
Cereals & its substitutes	-0.625	-0.461	-3.395	5.621	-3.481	1.663	0.019	0.292	0.312	0.687	0.720
Pulses & its products	4.574	-0.733	-1.430	-4.890	0.772	3.850	-0.401	0.917	-1.749	0.820	0.477
Milk & its Products	-3.766	-2.081	-0.846	2.499	1.563	-3.500	-1.879	0.571	1.570	1.388	-0.702
Edible oil & Fats	0.001	-0.011	0.015	-0.993	-0.004	-0.003	0.009	0.013	-0.016	1.005	0.392
Meat, Fish & Egg	0.223	0.304	0.404	-0.324	-0.842	-0.469	-0.069	-0.603	0.857	1.368	-0.487
Other Food Items	2.060	0.067	2.463	-7.651	4.977	-0.997	-0.217	-0.251	-0.352	1.132	-0.597
Fuel & Light	-2.389	1.190	7.315	-4.731	4.122	-4.567	-0.728	-1.065	0.874	0.785	-0.221
Clothing	3.627	-0.950	-3.223	0.721	0.543	-0.373	0.636	-0.974	-0.907	1.059	-0.852
Other Nonfood Items	0.672	2.367	8.139	-12.832	5.421	-3.364	0.738	-0.013	-0.943	1.127	-0.745
					Urban Orissa						
Cereals & its substitutes	-0.417	-0.347	0.022	-0.056	0.258	0.192	-0.058	-0.047	0.003	0.511	0.357
Pulses & its products	0.251	-0.628	0.028	-0.223	0.459	-0.464	0.005	-0.027	0.001	0.750	0.561
Milk & its Products	-2.298	-3.374	-0.982	1.403	3.116	3.269	-3.069	-0.827	0.375	1.433	0.485
Edible oil & Fats	-0.112	0.025	-0.039	-0.746	-0.025	0.234	-0.053	-0.002	0.016	0.897	0.516
Meat, Fish & Egg	1.017	2.974	-0.842	-1.536	-0.834	-2.059	4.712	1.617	-3.385	1.496	0.509
Other Food Items	0.675	-0.933	0.041	0.018	0.129	-0.886	-0.080	-0.080	-0.237	1.239	-0.424
Fuel & Light	-0.894	-1.225	-0.348	-1.381	1.647	3.785	-0.726	-1.421	-1.150	0.806	-0.185
Clothing	-5.770	6.990	1.343	-0.037	2.477	-5.147	-1.251	-1.089	0.751	1.189	-0.767
Other Nonfood Items	-1.946	9.581	-0.586	-0.875	-4.091	-3.522	1.321	0.348	-1.269	1.476	-0.696

Note: Computed from the grouped consumer expenditure data collected from 42nd to 61st round NSSO Reports.

Appendix Table 5
Uncompensatory Own-price, Cross-price, Expenditure and Preference Elasticities Estimated from LES with Linear Time Trend (LES-3): All-India

	Uncompensatory Own and Cross-price Elasticities With Respect to Price of										
Commodity Groups	*Cereals & its Substitutes*	*Pulses & its Products*	*Milk & its Products*	*Edible Oil & Fats*	*Meat, Fish & Egg*	*Other Food*	*Fuel & Light*	*Clothing*	*Other Non-food*	*Expenditure Elasticity*	*Preference Elasticity*
						Rural Orissa					
Cereals & its substitutes	-0.499	0.042	-0.036	0.246	-0.289	-0.329	-0.477	0.232	0.733	0.599	-0.250
Pulses & its products	0.583	-0.610	-0.085	-0.508	-0.305	0.298	0.437	-0.009	-0.033	0.743	-0.210
Milk & its Products	0.000	-0.542	-0.946	-0.108	0.071	0.732	-0.321	0.204	-0.084	1.238	-0.155
Edible oil & Fats	1.619	0.846	0.322	-0.726	-1.007	-5.033	0.222	0.969	-0.013	0.975	0.176
Meat, Fish & Egg	-0.231	-0.287	0.162	0.122	-1.096	0.962	-0.577	-0.387	0.180	1.311	0.056
Other Food Items	0.072	-0.219	0.021	-0.193	0.075	-0.921	-0.063	-0.353	-0.209	1.140	-0.201
Fuel & Light	-0.997	0.877	0.290	-0.159	1.092	0.449	-0.628	-0.748	-0.479	0.797	0.218
Clothing	-0.978	-1.228	-0.170	0.518	1.104	0.581	-1.069	-0.833	1.102	1.061	-0.153
Other Nonfood Items	0.306	-0.227	0.035	-0.009	0.174	-0.444	0.305	0.068	-1.098	1.407	0.298
						Urban India					
Cereals & its substitutes	-0.375	-0.220	-0.447	0.331	-0.105	0.217	-0.423	0.386	-0.263	0.498	-0.125
Pulses & its products	0.493	-0.451	0.098	0.257	-0.136	0.113	-0.425	-0.722	0.033	0.624	-0.201
Milk & its Products	-1.036	-0.176	-0.853	0.106	0.446	0.262	-0.440	0.395	0.186	1.199	-0.113
Edible oil & Fats	-0.839	-0.698	0.871	-0.624	-0.232	0.739	0.248	-0.160	-0.646	0.849	-0.154
Meat, Fish & Egg	0.849	0.552	-0.145	0.211	-0.819	-0.274	0.646	-0.876	-0.648	1.079	-0.219
Other Food Items	-0.526	-0.140	0.253	0.147	-0.137	-0.740	-0.610	-0.083	1.188	0.980	-0.140
Fuel & Light	0.098	0.116	-0.081	-0.051	0.031	-0.083	-0.669	-0.335	-0.037	0.868	0.169
Clothing	2.384	1.054	-0.881	-0.421	0.561	-0.508	1.467	-0.963	-2.992	1.148	-0.113
Other Nonfood Items	-0.103	0.020	0.040	-0.128	-0.036	-0.012	0.040	0.123	-1.142	1.641	0.212

Note: Computed from the time-series consumption expenditure data of 42nd to 61st NSS rounds.

Appendix Table 6
Uncompensatory Own-price, Cross-price, Expenditure and Preference Elasticities Estimated from LES with Linear Time Trend (LES-3): All-Orissa

	Uncompensatory Own and Cross-price Elasticities With Respect to Price of										
Commodity Groups	*Cereals & its Substitutes*	*Pulses & its Products*	*Milk & its Products*	*Edible Oil & Fats*	*Meat, Fish & Egg*	*Other Food*	*Fuel & Light*	*Clothing*	*Other Non-food*	*Expendi-ture Elasticity*	*Preference Elas-ticity*
					Rural Orissa						
Cereals & its substitutes	-0.642	-0.461	-3.395	5.621	-3.481	1.663	0.019	0.292	0.312	0.698	0.720
Pulses & its products	4.574	-0.757	-1.430	-4.890	0.772	3.850	-0.401	0.917	-1.749	0.899	-0.477
Milk & its Products	-3.766	-2.081	-0.862	2.499	1.563	-3.500	-1.879	0.571	1.570	1.405	0.702
Edible oil & Fats	0.001	-0.011	0.015	-0.922	-0.004	-0.003	0.009	0.013	-0.016	1.002	0.392
Meat, Fish & Egg	-0.223	0.304	1.404	-0.324	-0.887	-0.469	-0.069	-0.603	-0.857	1.351	0.487
Other Food Items	2.060	0.067	2.463	-7.651	4.977	-1.016	-0.217	-0.251	-0.352	1.102	-0.597
Fuel & Light	-2.389	1.190	7.315	-4.731	4.122	-4.567	-0.681	-1.065	0.874	0.754	-0.121
Clothing	3.627	-0.950	-3.223	0.721	0.543	-0.373	0.636	-1.052	-0.907	1.106	-0.052
Other Nonfood Items	0.672	2.367	8.139	-12.832	5.421	-3.364	0.738	-0.013	-0.925	1.128	-1.035
					Urban Orissa						
Cereals & its substitutes	-0.457	-7.080	0.245	-0.619	5.050	2.674	-1.077	-0.891	0.100	0.524	0.137
Pulses & its products	-0.118	-0.668	0.092	-1.056	2.193	-1.412	-0.442	-0.530	-0.218	0.789	0.068
Milk & its Products	-2.507	-3.050	-1.043	1.889	-0.514	5.724	-0.938	-1.130	0.346	1.475	-0.483
Edible oil & Fats	1.597	0.266	0.428	-0.755	0.888	-5.072	-0.501	0.319	0.354	0.871	0.125
Meat, Fish & Egg	3.639	-4.859	-1.186	1.372	-0.820	-1.500	1.671	-1.275	-2.437	1.503	-0.206
Other Food Items	0.683	-0.930	0.038	-0.031	0.126	-0.821	-0.091	-0.106	-0.269	1.246	-0.212
Fuel & Light	-0.606	-1.211	0.126	-0.481	2.136	1.733	-0.664	-0.948	-0.577	0.798	0.264
Clothing	-0.726	0.352	0.247	1.481	-1.018	-3.133	0.229	-1.121	0.607	1.171	-0.071
Other Nonfood Items	-0.474	3.391	-0.126	0.197	-2.020	-1.840	0.215	0.433	-1.195	1.502	0.155

Note: Computed from the time-series consumption expenditure data of 42nd to 61st NSS rounds.

Appendix Table 7
Uncompensatory Own-price, Cross-price and Expenditure Elasticities Estimated from NES: All-India

	Uncompensatory Own and Cross-price Elasticities With Respect to Price of									
	Cereals & its Substitutes	*Pulses & its Products*	*Milk & its Products*	*Edible Oil & Fats*	*Meat, Fish & Egg*	*Other Food*	*Fuel & Light*	*Clothing*	*Other Non-food*	*Expenditure Elasticity*
Commodity Groups					*Rural Orissa*					
Cereals & its substitutes	-0.474	-0.023	-0.026	-0.034	-0.106	0.074	0.086	0.008	0.008	0.589
Pulses & its products	0.114	-0.630	0.036	-0.045	0.148	-0.019	-0.025	-0.031	-0.032	0.746
Milk & its Products	-0.155	-0.645	-0.859	-0.139	1.014	0.503	-0.606	-0.033	-0.033	1.237
Edible oil & Fats	0.154	0.445	0.044	-0.526	-0.268	-0.451	0.188	0.062	0.062	0.958
Meat, Fish & Egg	-0.123	0.039	0.045	0.008	-0.880	0.098	-0.111	-0.110	-0.110	1.320
Other Food Items	0.002	0.011	-0.007	0.037	-0.018	-1.097	0.009	0.057	0.057	1.136
Fuel & Light	-0.258	0.157	0.023	-0.122	0.102	0.224	-0.590	-0.202	-0.203	0.732
Clothing	-0.316	-0.256	-0.089	0.257	0.307	0.005	-0.275	-0.981	0.120	1.056
Other Nonfood Items	-0.050	0.017	0.030	0.021	0.111	-0.015	-0.088	-0.027	-1.327	1.445
					Urban India					
Cereals & its substitutes	-0.322	0.621	-0.090	-0.180	0.073	-0.377	0.521	-1.032	-1.031	0.455
Pulses & its products	0.027	-0.481	0.093	-0.003	-0.047	0.111	-0.129	0.104	0.104	0.612
Milk & its Products	-0.128	-0.280	-0.741	0.261	0.138	0.933	-0.191	0.693	0.689	1.137
Edible oil & Fats	0.115	-0.242	0.142	-0.481	-0.026	0.274	0.124	-0.004	-0.005	0.791
Meat, Fish & Egg	0.092	-0.062	0.037	-0.009	-0.733	0.091	0.012	0.074	0.074	1.099
Other Food Items	0.113	0.127	-0.145	-0.010	0.048	-0.922	0.156	-0.140	-0.140	0.998
Fuel & Light	0.041	0.046	-0.128	-0.100	-0.070	0.052	-0.526	-0.121	-0.122	0.860
Clothing	0.409	0.131	-0.167	-0.273	0.098	-0.023	0.161	-1.293	0.208	1.181
Other Nonfood Items	0.006	-0.028	0.005	0.002	-0.006	0.027	-0.017	0.045	-1.415	1.636

Note: Computed from the time-series consumption expenditure data of 42nd to 61st NSS rounds.

Appendix Table 8

Uncompensatory Own-price, Cross-price and Expenditure Elasticities Estimated from NES: All-Orissa

	Uncompensatory Own and Cross-price Elasticities With Respect to Price of									
	Cereals & its Substitutes	*Pulses & its Products*	*Milk & its Products*	*Edible Oil & Fats*	*Meat, Fish & Egg*	*Other Food*	*Fuel & Light*	*Clothing*	*Other Non-food*	*Expenditure Elasticity*
Commodity Groups					*Rural Orissa*					
Cereals & its substitutes	-0.689	0.009	0.183	-0.258	0.175	-0.104	-0.008	-0.007	-0.008	0.676
Pulses & its products	0.349	-0.665	-0.108	-0.325	0.024	0.309	-0.077	0.104	0.104	0.895
Milk & its Products	-0.191	-0.131	-0.638	0.048	0.181	-0.232	-0.160	0.035	0.035	1.399
Edible oil & Fats	0.143	0.182	-0.122	-0.688	0.173	0.073	-0.146	-0.189	-0.189	1.007
Meat, Fish & Egg	0.239	0.177	-0.232	-0.276	-1.132	-0.056	-0.072	-0.199	-0.199	1.372
Other Food Items	-0.076	0.035	-0.348	0.702	-0.544	-1.086	0.092	0.013	0.013	1.101
Fuel & Light	-0.850	0.386	2.419	-1.363	1.211	-1.553	-0.706	-0.415	-0.415	0.773
Clothing	0.871	-0.255	-0.692	0.384	0.252	-0.398	0.075	-1.158	-0.058	1.125
Other Nonfood Items	0.059	-0.009	-0.780	1.012	-0.485	0.264	-0.197	-0.101	-1.281	1.143
					Urban Orissa					
Cereals & its substitutes	-0.487	1.176	0.008	0.141	-0.817	-0.518	0.088	0.168	0.168	0.497
Pulses & its products	0.199	-0.588	-0.001	-0.131	0.462	0.078	-0.088	-0.120	-0.120	0.797
Milk & its Products	-0.703	-1.198	-0.546	0.470	1.077	0.896	-0.907	-0.247	-0.247	1.503
Edible oil & Fats	0.223	0.283	0.062	-0.601	0.068	-0.599	0.096	-0.058	-0.058	0.894
Meat, Fish & Egg	0.128	0.283	0.023	0.195	-1.051	-0.420	-0.040	0.048	0.048	1.497
Other Food Items	-0.111	0.145	-0.011	0.010	-0.048	-1.007	0.024	0.023	0.023	1.259
Fuel & Light	-0.146	-0.834	-0.064	-0.279	0.670	0.986	-0.644	-0.372	-0.373	0.826
Clothing	-0.398	0.111	0.143	0.616	-0.223	-0.944	-0.021	-1.317	0.585	1.195
Other Nonfood Items	0.065	-0.371	0.027	0.003	0.276	0.145	-0.066	-0.043	-1.543	1.547

Note: Computed from the time-series consumption expenditure data of 42nd to 61st NSS rounds.

6

SPECIFICATION AND ESTIMATION OF THE VARIANTS OF ALMOST IDEAL DEMAND SYSTEM

INTRODUCTION

Since Richard Stone (1954) first estimated a system of demand equations derived explicitly from consumer theory, there has been a continuing search for alternative specifications and functional forms of demand systems. Many demand systems have been proposed but some important early demand systems, apart from the Linear Expenditures System (Stone,1954) are the Linear Demand System (Byron, 1967), Double-log Demand System (Wold & Jureen,1953), Rotterdam Demand System (Theil, 1965 & Barten, 1966), Addilog Demand System (Houthakker,1960). Some of the recent and widely used demand systems are the Translog Demand system (Christensen, Jorgensen and Lau, 1975) and the Almost Ideal Demand System (Deaton and Muellbaueer, 1980). The linear, double-log and Rotterdam demand systems can be dubbed as a priori or statistical models. These models are neither theoretically consistent nor can be integrated with larger economic tools like general equilibrium. The other category of models such as LES and Addilog systems are theoretically consistent but highly restrictive because of additive preferences. The additive preferences do not allow inferior goods into the analysis. In LES, commodities can only be gross substitutes but not complements. Hence, the additive models are unrealistic for empirical use and also need non-linear estimation. Due to these limitations of the early demand models, recent effort in applied demand analysis have centered around specifying demand systems that allow non-linear Engel curves and non-separable preferences. It aggregates perfectively over consumers without forcing linearity on the Engel curves. The Almost Ideal Demand System proposed by Deaton and Muellbauer (1980) is one such functional form. This model overcomes most of the limitations of additive models and hence, the adjective 'almost ideal'. This model has been extensively estimated and also is used to test neoclassical restrictions-homogeneity and symmetry and 'a priori' restriction called explicit additivity.

We have used the Almost Ideal Demand System (AIDS) which has enjoyed great popularity in applied demand analysis for a number of reasons. First, it is derived from a specified PIGLOG cost functions and, thus, corresponds to a well defined preference structure, which is convenient for welfare analysis. These so called PIGLOG[1] preferences; also have the property of consistent aggregation from the micro to the macro (market) level while allowing non-linear Engel curves. Secondly, the functional form of the preferences is flexible[2] in the sense that it can be thought of as a local second order approximation to an unknown preference structure. Thirdly, homogeneity and symmetry restrictions depend only on estimated parameters and so are easily imposed and/or tested. Fourthly, Deaton and Muellbauear (1980) suggested a linear approximation of the AIDS model, which performs well if prices are collinear. This advantage of the AIDS model has been quite important, as the linear approximation of AIDS model (LA\AIDS) is frequently estimated in practice by a number of researchers.[3] Fifthly, the LA\AIDS (and AIDS) models can be expanded to include other explanatory variables in a way exactly similarly to the LES.[4] It can be, further, generalized to quadratic[5] and other higher rank demand systems[6] and it can also be made dynamic by including the past behavior and habit formation effect of the consumer[7] like LES. So the performance of the AIDS model can be compared with the LES model.

Blanciforte and Green (1983) have made Almost Ideal Demand System dynamic by incorporating habit effects. The homogeneity and symmetry restrictions rejected by Deaton and Muellbauer (1980) are tested with dynamic generalizations. They accepted the hypothesis of habit effects in consumption. Moreover, the presence of high autocorrelation in AIDS model can be corrected by rightly specifying the model incorporating habits. Alessi and Kapteyn (1991) incorporated both habit formation and interdependent preferences in AIDS. They have estimated the Dynamics AIDS model using mean perceived budget shares representing interdependent preferences as dependent variable and a lagged mean perceived budget share along with income and prices as explanatory variables.

In this chapter, we have estimated different variants of Almost Ideal Demand System such as AIDS including family size as an additional explanatory variable and AIDS imposing neoclassical restrictions like homogeneity, homogeneity and symmetry simultaneously and a priori restriction called explicit additivity. We have also tested some hypothesis like no price effect, no economies of household size effect, and no money illusion using time-series of household budget data on nine broad commodity groups.

This chapter is designed into seven sections. Section 1 is the introduction. Section 2 deals with derivation of Almost Ideal Demand System and its demographic extension incorporating household size as an additional explanatory variable. It also provides other variants of AIDS imposing the theoretical restrictions like homogeneity, symmetry, both homogeneity and symmetry and a priori restriction such as explicit additivity. Section 3 provides a brief account of estimable models of AIDS with its variants and generalisations. The method of estimation is explained in Section 4. The database used for estimating AIDS with its variants and generalisations is given in Section 5. The empirical analysis of AIDS with its variants and generalisations is analysed in

Section 6. Finally, Section 7 is the concluding remarks of the chapter.

THE ALMOST IDEAL DEMAND SYSTEM WITH ITS EXTENSIONS AND GENERALISATIONS

The Almost Ideal Demand System (AIDS) proposed by Deaton and Muellbauer (1980) is the time-series generalisation of PIGLOG Engel function (Leser, 1963). The time-series generalisation would require the inclusion of prices explicitly into the Engel function. This can be achieved by making the parameters,α and β in (6.2.1) as functions of prices in a number of ways. The AIDS model is one such attempt. It has also approximated to any locally-nonsatiated utility function arbitrarily well up to second order. The starting point of this model is the semi-log form of Engel curve suggested by Working (1943) and later used by Leser (1963) by expressing the budget share (w_i) as a linear function of the logarithm of total expenditure (y) as

$$w_i = \alpha_i + \beta_i \ln(y) \qquad (6.2.1)$$

The parameters α and β are, generally, function of prices. Since, the budget shares are the logarithmic derivatives of the cost function α and β and are functions of prices, equation (6.2.1) corresponds to differential equations of the form

$$\partial \ln c(u,p)/\partial \ln p_i = \alpha_i(p) + \beta_i(p) \ln c(u,p) \qquad (6.2.2)$$

The general solution of differential equations (6.2.2) is the translog (or PIGLOG) cost function given by

$$\ln(y) = \ln c(u,p) = (1-u)\ln\{a(p)\} + u\ln\{b(p)\} \qquad (6.2.3)$$

where $\ln\{a(p)\} = \ln(P) = \alpha_0 + \alpha' \hat{p} + (1/2)\,\hat{p}'\Gamma\,\hat{p}$ (6.2.4a)

and $\ln\{b(p)\} = \ln\{a(p)\} + \beta_0 \beta' \hat{p}$ (6.2.4b)

In sum notation we have,

$$\ln a(p) = \ln(P) = \alpha_0 + \sum \alpha_i \ln p_i + 1/2 \sum_i \sum_j \gamma^*_{ij} \ln p_i \ln p_j \qquad (6.2.4c)$$

and $$\ln b(p) = \ln a(p) + \beta_0 \prod p_j^{\beta_j} \tag{6.2.4d}$$

The above cost function (6.2.3) is a utility-weighted geometric mean of the linear homogeneous functions, *a(p)* and *b(p)* where *a(p)* representing subsistence consumption [or the cost functions of the very poor ($u = 0$)] and *b(p)* is regarded as additional 'bliss' consumption [or the cost functions of the very rich ($u = 1$)].[8] Such preferences are called the PIGLOG class by Muellbauer (1976). A full system of demand equations within the Working-Leser class can be generated by suitable choice of the liner homogeneous functions *a(p)* and *b(p)*. The translog cost/expenditure function can be derived (in simplified matrix form) by substituting (6.2.4a) and (6.2.4b) into (6.2.3) as,

$$c(u,p) = \alpha_0 + \alpha'\hat{p} + (1/2)\hat{p}'\Gamma\hat{p} + u\beta_0\beta'\hat{p} \tag{6.2.5a}$$

In sum notation we have,

$$c(u,p) = \alpha_0 + \sum_i \alpha_i \ln p_i + 1/2 \sum_i \sum_j \gamma_{ij}^* \ln p_i \ln p_j + u\beta_0 \prod p_j^{\beta_j} \tag{6.2.5b}$$

Using Shephard's lemma[9], the matrix formulation of AIDS in share form can be derived from the cost function (6.2.5a) as,

$$w = \alpha + \Gamma\hat{p} + \beta \ln(y/P) \tag{6.2.6a}$$

In sum notation we have,

$$w_i = \alpha_i + \sum_j \gamma_{ij} \ln p_j + \beta_i \ln(y/P) \tag{6.2.6b}$$

where '*w*' denotes the vector of budget shares, '*p*' denotes the vector of prices, *y* is total expenditure, $\hat{p}$ denotes the vector of logarithms of '*p*', and the parameters to be estimated are α_0, the vectors α and β, and the matrix Γ.

Alternatively, inversion of (6.2.5a) yields its associated indirect utility function as,

$$u^*(y,p) = \ln(y/P)/\ln b(p) \tag{6.2.7}$$

Using Roy's identity,[10] Marshallian demand function for

*i*th commodity can be derived from the indirect utility function (6.2.7) as,

$$q_i = \frac{y}{p_i}\left(\alpha_i + \gamma_i' \hat{p} + \beta_i \ln(y/P)\right) \quad (i = 1,2,3,\ldots\ldots, n) \quad (6.2.8)$$

where γ_i' is understood as the '*i*'th column of Γ. Notice that (6.2.8) is the canonical formulation for AIDS (Deaton and Muellbauer, 1980). Multiply throughout by p_i/y to obtain the share equation of AIDS for *i*th good as,

$$w_i = \alpha_i + \gamma_i' \hat{p} + \beta_i \ln(y/P) \quad (i = 1,2,3,\ldots\ldots, n) \qquad (6.2.9a)$$

Alternatively, we have the same share equation of AIDS for *i*th commodity as in (6.2.6b),

$$w_i = \alpha_i + \sum_j \gamma_{ij} \ln p_j + \beta_i \ln(y/P) \qquad (6.2.9b)$$

where

$$\ln(P) = \alpha_0 + \sum \alpha_i \ln p_i + 1/2 \sum_i \sum_j \gamma_{ij} \ln p_i \ln p_j \,. \quad (6.2.10a)$$

and $$\gamma_{ij} = 1/2\left(\gamma_{ij}^* + \gamma_{ji}^*\right) \qquad (6.2.10b)$$

The theoretical restrictions on the cost function (6.2.3a) along with the condition (6.2.10b) translate themselves into restriction on the parameter of (6.2.9). These restrictions are[11],

Adding–up: $\iota'\alpha = 1,\ \iota'\beta = 0 \text{ and } \iota'\Gamma = 0$ (6.2.11a)

Alternatively, $\sum_{i=1}^{n} \alpha_i = 1; \quad \sum_{i=1}^{n} \beta_i = 0 \ \ and \ \sum_{i=1}^{n} \gamma_{ij} = 0$ (6.2.11b)

Homogeneity: $\iota'\Gamma = 0$ (6.2.12a)

Alternatively, $\sum_{j=1}^{n} \gamma_{ij} = 0$ (6.2.12b)

Symmetry: $\Gamma' = \Gamma$ (6.2.13a)

Alternatively, $\gamma_{ij} = \gamma_{ji} \quad i \neq j$ for all (6.2.13b)

where 'ι' is a sum vector. It is well known that the adding-up restrictions (6.2.11) are part of maintained hypothesis of any demand system because of the data construction itself, hence, needs no testing. Thus, with the help of AIDS one can test only the restrictions implied by homogeneity (6.2.12) and symmetry (6.2.13) and any other 'a priori' restrictions like implicit or explicit additivity, homotheticity etc.

In demand analysis, variables other than prices and income are often included in demand equations. For instance, in studies using cross-sectional data, demographic variables can be included and in using time-series data, trends and seasonal variables can be included in the model. One must be careful to incorporate these demand shift variables so as to maintain the theoretical properties of the model. Importantly, the estimated demand system must be 'closed under unit scaling' (CUUS), a property that ensures that estimated economic effects are invariant to scaled data.[12] In AIDS model, the intercepts of share equations are commonly expressed as linear functions of other explanatory variables, as originally suggested by Deaton and Muellbauer (1980). But the resulting model is no longer consistent with CUUS (see Appendix-A for details). We explore two specific alternative approaches for incorporating demand shifters and preserving CUUS while retaining the other desirable features of the AIDS model.

Let the intercepts (α) of the share equations are expressed as linear functions of some demand shift variables 'Z', α is then redefined as

$$\alpha = \alpha^* + \lambda Z , \qquad (6.2.14)$$

with the restrictions $\iota'\alpha^* = 1$ and $\iota'\lambda = 0$ as required for adding-up. The effects of changes in 'Z' are, thus, seen as changes in the parameters of the cost/expenditure function. The integrability is preserved in the share equations by letting each element of 'α' to vary with 'Z', while retaining the adding-up restriction. The share equations (6.2.6) incorporating demand shift variables as per (6.2.14) become

$$w=\alpha^{*}+\lambda Z+\Gamma\hat{p}+\beta\ \ln(y)-\beta\left(\alpha_{0}+\left(\alpha^{*}+\lambda\ Z\right)'\hat{p}+(1/2)\hat{p}'\Gamma\hat{p}\right) \tag{6.2.15}$$

Unfortunately, augmenting 'α' in this fashion for estimating the economic effects are not invariant to units of measurement of the prices and quantities of the goods in the model. Specifically, a disproportionate change in the units of measurement for any or all of the goods changes the estimates of Γ and β so that elasticities and consumer welfare measures also change.

Closed under unit scaling (CUUS) imposes the condition that if some parameters depend on scaling, then others may need it as well. Specifically, when we make α as a linear function of the same demand shifting variables, CUUS requires that we should also make α_0 as a linear function of the same demand shift variables. That is, if one adopts $\alpha = \alpha^{*} + \lambda Z$, then one must also adopt $\alpha = \alpha^{*}_{0} + vZ$.[13] The augmented share equations then become

$$w=\alpha^{*}+\lambda Z+\Gamma\hat{p}+\beta\ \ln(y)-\beta\left(\alpha_{0}^{*}+vZ+\left(\alpha^{*}+\lambda z\right)'\hat{p}+(1/2)\hat{p}'\Gamma\hat{p}\right) \tag{6.2.16}$$

After rescaling the quantity units (as per Appendix-A), the share equation is given by

$$\begin{aligned} w=&\tilde{\alpha}^{*}+\tilde{\lambda}Z+\tilde{\Gamma}(\hat{p}-\tilde{\pi})+\tilde{\beta}\ln(y) \\ &-\tilde{\beta}\left(\tilde{\alpha}_{0}^{*}+\tilde{v}Z+\tilde{\alpha}^{*}(\hat{p}-\tilde{\pi})'+Z\tilde{\lambda}'(\hat{p}-\tilde{\pi})+(1/2)(\hat{p}-\tilde{\pi})'\tilde{\Gamma}(\hat{p}-\tilde{\pi})\right) \end{aligned} \tag{6.2.17}$$

Collecting the terms that involve $\hat{\Pi}$ and then simplifying the above equation results in

$$w=\alpha^{*}+\lambda Z+\Gamma\hat{p}+\beta\ln(y)-\beta\left(\alpha_{0}^{*}+vZ+\left(\alpha^{*}+\lambda Z\right)'\hat{p}+(1/2)\hat{p}'\tilde{\Gamma}\hat{p}\right) \tag{6.2.18}$$

where $\alpha^* = \tilde{\alpha}^* - \tilde{\alpha}^* \tilde{\pi}; \alpha_0 = \tilde{\alpha}_0 - \alpha^{*\prime} \tilde{\pi} + (1/2)\tilde{\pi}'\tilde{\Gamma}\tilde{\pi}$ and $v = \tilde{v} - \tilde{\lambda}'\tilde{\pi}$. Notice that α^*, α_0 and v are constants and are merely rescaled, and Γ, β, and λ are unchanged (i.e. $\tilde{\Gamma} = \Gamma, \tilde{\beta} = \beta$, *and* $\tilde{\lambda} = \lambda$). The desired invariance property is achieved.

Deaton and Muellbauer (1980) pointed out that it may be difficult to estimate α_0 and such difficulties would be compounded if α_0 is a function of other variables. Hence, in many instances, it will not be feasible to estimate a model in which demand shifters augment both α and α_0, and an alternative solution must be found.

General methods for incorporating demand shifters and preserving CUUS in demand systems include scaling, translating, and other modifying functions, as described by Lewbel (1985). Among these theoretical alternatives, we would like to identify an alternative that will preserve the other desirable features of AIDS, and will also allow demand shifters to be incorporated parsimoniously and flexibly. One such alternative approach is to use a generalized version of the AIDS which is otherwise called the Generalized Almost Ideal Demand System (GAIDS) derived by Bollino (1987). The cost/expenditure function used to characterise the GAIDS model allows for a portion of total expenditures to be allocated to committed quantities which are not observed in practice but can be estimated along with the other parameters in the demand system. Generalisation of the cost/expenditure function (6.2.3) to allow 'committed quantities' is given by

$$c(u,p) = p'c + c^*(u,p) \tag{6.2.19}$$

where 'c' is the vector of 'committed quantities' and $c^*(p, u)$ is the expenditure (or cost) function for supernumerary (beyond committed) expenditures defined to be the Almost Ideal form in equations (6.2.3) and (6.2.4). The expressions for the indirect utility function corresponding to (6.2.7) derived from the generalized cost function (6.2.19) is given by

$$u^*(y,p) = \left(\ln(y - c'p)/P\right)/\ln b(p) \tag{6.2.20}$$

The Marshallian demand function and the share equation corresponding to (6.2.8) and (6.2.9b) in the GAIDS model for good '*i*' are given by

$$q_i = c_i + \left(y^*/p_i\right)\left(\alpha_i + \gamma_i'\hat{p} + \beta_i \ln(y/P)\right) \quad (i = 1,2,3,\ldots\ldots,n) \tag{6.2.21}$$

Multiplying the above equation throughout by p_i/y, we have

$$w_i = \left(p_i c_i/y\right) + (y^*/y)\left(\alpha_i + \sum_{j=1}^{n}\gamma_{ij}\ln p_j + \beta_i \ln\left(y^*/P\right)\right) \tag{6.2.22}$$

where $y^* = y - p'c$ and $\ln(P)$ as defined in (6.2.4c). The GAIDS model can of course, be viewed as a generalization of the Linear Expenditure System (LES) in which the marginal budget shares are no longer constant, but are to be the Almost Ideal form. The 'committed quantities' are independent of prices and expenditure, suggesting that augmenting the '*c*' vector by making each 'committed quantity' a function of '*Z*' can avoid the scaling problems described earlier. Such an approach is referred to as 'demographic translating'.[14] The same approach can be applied in GAIDS model to incorporate any type of demand shifter producing estimates that are invariant to changes in quantity units.[15] For this, replace each committed quantity 'c_i' with a linear function of '*Z*' as

$$c_i = c_i^* + \lambda_i Z \tag{6.2.23}$$

Then the share equations will take the form

$$w_i = \left(p_i\left(c_i^* + \lambda_i Z\right)/y\right) + (y^*/y)\left(\alpha_i + \sum_{j=1}^{n}\gamma_{ij}\ln p_j + \beta_i \ln\left(y^*/P\right)\right) \tag{6.2.24}$$

When the quantity units are redefined so that prices are rescaled, once again by dividing by π_i, the demand system becomes

$$w_i = \left((p_i/\pi_i)\left(\tilde{c}_i^* + \tilde{\lambda}_i Z\right)/y \right) + (y^*/y)\left(\tilde{\alpha}_i + \sum_{j=1}^{n} \tilde{\gamma}_{ij} \ln\left(p_j/\pi_i\right) + \tilde{\beta}_i \ln\left(y^*/P\right) \right) \tag{6.2.25}$$

The marginal budget share in parentheses is the right hand side of the share equations of the Almost Ideal Demand System shown above indicates that this term is invariant to changes in quantity units. In addition, y is y^* fixed and changes with the change in 'committed expenditures', $p'c$. To see that 'committed expenditure' doed not change when quantity units change, consider the first term on the right hand side of equation (6.2.25):

$$p_i\left(c_i^* + \lambda_i Z\right)/y = \left(p_i/\pi_i\right)\left(\pi_i\left(c_i^* + \lambda_i Z\right)\right)/y = \left(p_i/\pi_i\right)\left(\tilde{c}_i^* + \tilde{\lambda}_i Z\right)/y \tag{6.2.26}$$

Hence, the new $\tilde{c}_i^*$ is simply $c_i^*\pi_i$ and the new $\tilde{\lambda}_i$ is simply $\pi_i\lambda_i$. Thus, changing the units of measurement in the GAIDS model has no effect on its estimates. Augmenting the 'committed quantities' in this fashion does not appear to imply any restrictions on how 'Z' affects the demand for any particular commodity.

SPECIFICATION OF ESTIMABLE AIDS MODELS

Since extensive time-series of household expenditure data for India are not available to estimate the AIDS model incorporating demand shift variables and the Generalised AIDS model as discussed above, we have estimated the linear approximation of AIDS model (LA/AIDS) incorporating household size (m) as an additional explanatory variable. From the analysis of AIDS model in the previous section, it is evident that the price formulation in (6.2.10a) makes the AIDS model (6.2.9b) a nonlinear system of demand equations. To avoid nonlinear estimation, we follow the procedure of Deaton and Muellbauer (1978) of their use of Stone's index as a convenient approximation. [16] The Stone's index is given by

$$\log P \cong \log P^{*} = \alpha_0 + \sum_i w_i \log p_i \tag{6.3.1}$$

where α_0 is interpreted as the cost for an individual to subsist at reference year using the utility based PIGLOG model. On substitution of the Stone's Index (6.3.1) in the AIDS model (6.2.9b), the resulting linear approximation of AIDS (LA\AIDS)[17] model becomes

$$w_i = \alpha_i + \beta_i\left(\log Y - \alpha_0 - \sum_i w_i \log p_i\right) + \sum_j \gamma_{ij} \log p_j \tag{6.3.2}$$

The LA\AIDS (6.3.2) does not portray family size explicitly. To do so, we use the Barten (1964) type household utility function and replace '*p*' in (6.3.2) by a normalised price vector *mp* (for the scalar *m*) where '*m*' denotes family size. It must be emphasized, however, that result is not the Barten model since it involves '*m*' as a vector and includes quasi-price composition effects as the main characteristic. Now incorporating the household size '*m*' as an additional explanatory variable in the model (6.3.2), it is rewritten as

$$w_i = \alpha_i^{*} + \beta_i \log\left(\frac{y}{P^{*}}\right) + \sum_j \gamma_{ij} \log p_j + \theta_i \log m \tag{6.3.3}$$

where $a_i^{*} = a_i - a_0 \beta_i$ and y (= Y/m) is the per capita total household expenditure. Here β_i, γ_{ij} and $\theta_i \left(= \sum_j \gamma_{ij}\right)$ are the effect of per capita real total household expenditure (y/P^*), prices, and household size respectively on budget share using family size '*m*' as deflator.[18] Although, empirically the above model is not the most plausible one but our approach can be justified due to lack of published time-series data on household composition. Hence, it is better to include (average) household size as an additional explanatory variable rather than ignoring the size-effects altogether.

The LA\AIDS model (6.3.3) must satisfy the following restrictions to be consistent with utility theory:

$$\text{Adding up: } \sum_i \alpha_i^* = 1; \sum_i \beta_i = 0; \sum_i \gamma_{ij} = 0 \text{ and} \sum_i \theta_i = 0 \quad (6.3.4)$$

$$\text{Homogeneity: } \sum_j \gamma_{ij} = \theta_i = 0 \quad (6.3.5)$$

$$\text{Symmetry: } \gamma_{ij} = \gamma_{ji} \text{ for all } i \neq j \quad (6.3.6)$$

Concavity of the expenditure function- a restriction which has no obvious parametric representation.

The imposition of homogeneity in the above systems ($\theta_i = 0$) implies absence of economies of household size. Two comments are in order. First, this does not mean that there are no size effects as these effects still operate through '*y*'. Second, owing to absence of composition changes as an explicit variable and since, addition to families are more likely to be children, *m* incorporates size and composition. Hence, even if the data set are to satisfy the homogeneity restriction, a non-zero coefficients of *log*(*m*) can explain the presence of composition effects.

Recognizing $\overline{w}, \overline{y}, \overline{m}$ as the available grouped data, the distribution parameters are to be absorbed by the intercept term assuming constant expenditure and demographic distributions. The additive stochastic specification of model (6.3.3) named as AIDS-1 to be estimated in this chapter is given by[19]

$$w_{it} = \alpha_i^* + \beta_i \log\left(\frac{y_t}{P^*}\right) + \sum_j \gamma_{ij} \log p_{jt} + \theta_i \log m_t + v_{it} \quad (6.3.7)$$

Restrictions that are satisfied by the micro parameters are also satisfied by the macro-parameters of the model (6.3.7).

Now, we obtain the following elasticity formulae for the LA\AIDS model with demographic specification (AIDS-1) denoting the expenditure elasticity as η_{i0}, uncompensatory price elasticity as η_{ij} and size of elasticity as η_{im}.

$$\text{Expenditure elasticity: } \eta_{i0} = 1 + \frac{\beta_i}{w_i} \quad (6.3.8)$$

Uncompensatory price elasticity:

$$\eta_{ij} = w_i^{-1}\left\{\gamma_{ij} - \beta_i\left(\alpha_j + \sum_j \gamma_{ij}\log p_j\right)\right\} - \delta_{ij} \qquad (6.3.9)$$

Size elasticity: $\eta_{im} = \dfrac{\theta_i}{w_i}$ (6.3.10)

where δ_{ij} is Kronecker delta. Formula (6.3.8) to (6.3.10) are also appropriate for calculating micro elasticities. The use of the grouped data rests on the crucial assumption of time invariant expenditure and demographic distribution. [20]

The other estimable models are the simple LA\AIDS model which is the constraint model for (6.3.7) and unconstraint model for other variants of AIDS to be estimated imposing different theoretical restrictions, 'a priori' restriction and no cross- price effects. The second estimable model is the simple LA\AIDS model named as AIDS-2. The other variants of AIDS are AIDS-3 with homogeneity restriction imposed; AIDS-4 with both homogeneity and symmetry restrictions imposed; AIDS-5 with no economies household size and no cross price effects and finally AIDS-6 with no economies household size and no price effects (or explicit additivity restriction imposed).[21] The additive stochastic specification of all the six variants of AIDS is shown in *Table-1.*

The disturbance terms, v_{it}s in the above models (AIDS-1 to AIDS-6) are assumed to have,

$$E(v_{it}) = 0 \text{ for all i and t and } E(v_{it}v_{jt}) = \begin{cases}\Omega & \text{for } t = s\\ 0 & \text{for } t \neq s\end{cases}$$

Assuming that 'v_{it}' follows a multivariate normal distribution with mean zero and contemporaneous covariance matrix of the disturbances, $\Omega = [\sigma_{ij}]$ is singular because of the adding-up criterion. Under the assumption of multivariate normality of 'v_{it}', the log-likelihood function can be maximised by standard Non-linear Full Information Maximum Likelihood (NLFIML) method with provision of handling the singularity of Ω.

Table 1
Stochastic Specification of the Different Variants of AIDS Model

Model	*Specification of Different Models*	*Descriptions*
AIDS-1	$w_{it} = \alpha_i^* + \beta_i \log\left(\frac{y_t}{P^*}\right) + \sum_j \gamma_{ij} \log p_{jt} + \theta_i \log m_t + v_{it}$	All variables included
AIDS-2	$w_{it} = \alpha_i^* + \beta_i \log\left(\frac{y_t}{P^*}\right) + \sum_j \gamma_{ij} \log p_{jt} + v_{it}$	No economies of scale i.e. $\theta_i = 0$ (Unrestricted LA\AIDS model)
AIDS-3	$w_{it} = \alpha_i^* + \beta_i \log\left(\frac{y_t}{P^*}\right) + \sum_j \gamma_{ij} \log p_{jt} + v_{it}$ subject to	Homogeneity imposed.
	Subject to $\Sigma_j \gamma_{ij} = 0$	($\theta_i = 0$ and $\Sigma_j \gamma_{ij} = 0$)
AIDS-4	$w_{it} = \alpha_i^* + \beta_i \log\left(\frac{y_t}{P^*}\right) + \sum_j \gamma_{ij} \log p_{jt} + v_{it}$ subject to	Homogeneity & symmetry imposed.
	Subject to $\Sigma_j \gamma_{ij} = 0$ and $\gamma_{ij} = \gamma_{ji}$	($\theta_i = 0$, $\Sigma_j \gamma_{ij} = 0$ and $\gamma_{ij} = \gamma_{ji}$)

Contd.

Model	Specification of Different Models	Descriptions
AIDS-5	$w_i = \alpha_i^* + \beta_i \log\left(\frac{y_t}{P^*}\right) + \gamma_{ii} \log p_i + v_i$	No economies of HS & no cross-price effects. $\left(\theta_i = 0 \text{ and } \gamma_{ij} = 0,\ i \neq j\right)$
AIDS-6	$w_{it} = \alpha_i^* + \beta_i \log\left(\frac{y_t}{P^*}\right) + v_{it}$	No economies of HS & no price effects (Explicit additivity). $\left(\theta_i = 0 \text{ and} \gamma_{ij} = 0\right)$

Note: $y^* (= y / P^*)$ is the per capita real total household expenditure.

METHOD OF ESTIMATION

In the present exercise, we have estimated six variants of the basic AIDS model (6.2.9a). In general, estimation can be carried out by substituting the translog price index (6.2.10a) in the AIDS model (6.2.9a) which gives

$$w_i = (\alpha_i - \beta_i\alpha_0) + \sum_j \gamma_{ij} \log p_j + \beta_i \{\log y$$

$$-\sum_k \alpha_k \log p_k - \frac{1}{2}\sum_k \sum_j \gamma_{kj} \log p_k \log p_j\} \qquad (6.4.1)$$

and estimating this non-linear system of equations by maximum likelihood or other methods with and without the restrictions (6.2.12b) and 6.2.13b). Equation (6.4.1) is not particularly difficult to estimate since the first-order conditions of likelihood maximization are linear in α and γ given β and vice versa so that 'concentration' allows iteration on a subset of the parameters.[22] Although, all the parameters in (6.4.1) are identified with sufficient variation in the independent variables but practically identification of α_0 is likely to be problematical. This parameter is only identified from the α_is in (6.4.1) and stones index, log(*P*) (6.2.1b). However, in situations where individual prices are closely collinear, log(*P*) is unlikely to be very sensitive to its weights so that changes in the intercept term in (6.4.1) due to variations in α_0 can be offset in the α_is with minimal effect on log(*P*). The way to overcome problem is by assigning a value to α_0 'a priori'.[23]

However, in many situations, it is possible to exploit the collinearity of the prices to yield a much simpler estimation technique. It is to be noted from model (6.2.9b) that if *Ps* are known, the model would be linear in the parameters- α, β and γ. Given the normally distributed errors, the estimation (at least without cross-equation restrictions such as symmetry) can be done equation-by-equation by OLS which is equivalent to the maximum likelihood estimation for the system as a whole. In situations where prices are closely collinear, it may well be adequate to approximate *P* as proportional to some known index One obvious candidate in view of (6.2.9b) and (6.2.10a)) is Stone index (1953) log $P^* = \Sigma w_i \log p_i$. If $P \cong \phi P^*$ say, then (6.2.9b) can be specified as,

$$w_i = (\alpha_i - \beta_i \log\phi) + \sum_j \gamma_{ij} \log p_j + \beta_i \log\left(\frac{y}{P^*}\right) \tag{6.4.2a}$$

$$\text{or} \quad w_i = \alpha_i^* + \sum_j \gamma_{ij} \log p_j + \beta_i \log\left(\frac{y}{P^*}\right) \tag{6.4.2b}$$

Note that in this framework, the α_i parameters are identified only up to a scalar multiple of β_i. If we write, $\alpha_i^* = \alpha_i - \beta_i \log \phi$, it is easily seen that $\Sigma\alpha_i^* = 0$ is still required for adding-up, since $\Sigma\beta_i = 0$. However, it must be emphasized that (6.4.2b) exists only as an approximation to (6.4.1) and will be accurate only in specific circumstances, albeit widely occurring ones in time-series estimation.

However, in view of a large number of parameters being involved in the maximum likelihood estimation, the estimation may be computationally heavy. Indeed Deaton and Muellbauer (1980) suggested a simple equation-by-equation ordinary least squares method for the estimation of LA\AIDS model (6.4.2b). The OLS estimation of model (6.4.2b) is straightforward and one can even have the estimates of other variants of AIDS such as AIDS-3 with homogeneity and AIDS-4 with both homogeneity and symmetry restrictions imposed by restricted least squares.

THE DATA

The data used for estimating the variants of AIDS model is the time-series of estimated per capita expenditure on different commodity groups and the corresponding total consumer expenditure separately for the rural and urban households of Orissa and all India taken from the published reports of NSS 42nd to 61st rounds (excluding 49th and 60th round). The analysis thus, covers the period from July 1986 to June 2005. The nine broad specific commodity groups considered here are cereals and its substitutes; pulses and its products; milk and its products; edible oil and fats; meat, fish and egg; other food items, clothing (which including clothing and beddings); fuel and light; other non-food items. The other food items and the other non-food items are the residual categories. The analysis has been carried out at single level of aggregation with broad item-wise estimates of average per capita expenditure for all household in each period.

The retail price data used for estimating the variants of AIDS model is the time-series of consumer price indices for industrial workers and agriculture labourers complied and released by the Labour Bureau, Ministry of Labour Government of India. The consumer price indices for industrial workers are used for estimating demand pattern in urban areas and for agriculture labourer are used for estimating the demand pattern in rural areas of the state as well as the country. To maintain consistency between time-series of consumer price indices and the period of NSS round, we have not considered the consumer expenditure data for 49th and 60th rounds and the price indices of 1995-96 while deflating expenditure data. So, data on retail prices consistent with NSS commodity classification has been used in this study. Since, no other satisfactory retail price series is readily available; the series thus, constructed may be taken as a proxy for the actual retail price movements. It is also pointed out here that the price data so constructed is assumed to be applicable to households belonging to different level of real per capita expenditure, an assumption which is not strictly valid as some amount of price differentials is known to exist across households having different levels of living.

EMPIRICAL ANALYSIS

The most interesting feature of Almost Ideal Demand system from econometric view point is that it is very close to being linear. Apart from the translog price index, P used as a deflator of total expenditure in the model, the parameters can be estimated equation-by-equation using the OLS method. As regards to the translog price index (P), the restrictions on α and γ ensures that the index (P) is a linear homogeneous function in individual prices. In many practical situations where prices are nearly collinear, 'P' may be approximated by an exogenous index such as the Stone's index. We have used the Stone's index for the linear approximation of AIDS model in our empirical analysis along with its demographic specification. We have also tested the performance of this model imposing different theoretical restrictions like homogeneity, both homogeneity and symmetry, no cross-price effects and explicit additivity (no price effects). The few Indian studies[24] on the specification and estimation of AIDS model done so far vary in their nature and focus. The present exercise is an endeavour for the in-depth analysis of the six variants of AIDS model using the most recent data in the context of the backward state like Orissa and developing country like India.

GOODNESS OF FIT

For judging the goodness of fit of the estimated AIDS model under different specifications, we have used three measures such as $\bar{R}^2$ the usual adjusted squared multiple correlation coefficient); the F-ratio and the Theil's measure of information inaccuracy (TMII). The first two measures of goodness of fit is supplemented by TMII separately for each item of consumption. The only overall (or across all equations) measure of goodness of fit is the Theil's measure of average information inaccuracy (TMAII) which can be computed by lumping together the budget shares of all commodities. The different measures of goodness of fit for the six variants of AIDS model are quoted in *Tables-2 to 20* and the frequency of $\bar{R}^2$ in these models is given in *Table-21.*

Out of the 36 equations estimated under AIDS-1 model with demographic specification at nine commodity level separately for the rural and urban sectors of Orissa and all India, 9 (50 per cent) equations for India and 6 (33 per cent) equations for Orissa have $\bar{R}^2$ greater than 0.9 whereas the number of equations with $\bar{R}^2$ varies from 0.8 to 0.9 are 9 (50 per cent) for India and 6 (33 per cent) equation for Orissa. On the whole, 15 (42 per cent) equations have greater than 0.9

and another 15 (42 per cent) equations have $\bar{R}^2$ varies from 0.8 to 0.9. The F-values are highly significant for most of the equations for India and also significant for all the equations estimated for Orissa. The values of TMII are close to zero in all 36 equations. This clearly indicates that all the 36 equations estimated for India and Orissa is found to be the best fit equations to their corresponding time-series sample data. Further, AIDS-1 model fits the urban data better than the rural data as reflected by higher proportion of $\bar{R}^2$ greater than 0.8 and relatively higher F-values for urban data (*Tables-2 to 5*).

On the other hand, out of the 36 equations estimated under AIDS-2 separately for the rural and urban sectors of Orissa and all India, 12 (75 per cent) equations for India and 7 (39 per cent) of equations for Orissa are found to have $\bar{R}^2$ values greater than 0.9, but 3 (17 per cent) equations for India and 10 (56 per cent) equations for Orissa have $\bar{R}^2$ values varies from 0.8 to 0.9. The overall picture indicates that out of the 36 equations estimated, 19 (53 per cent) equations have $\bar{R}^2$ greater than 0.9 and another 13 (36 per cent) equations have $\bar{R}^2$ varying from 0.8 to 0.9. The F-values in all the 36 equations are found to be highly significant with TMII values very close to zero. This revels that AIDS-2 fits better to rural and urban sample data compared to AIDS-1. This model also fits the urban data better than the rural data as revealed by higher proportion of $\bar{R}^2$ greater than 0.8 and relatively higher F-values for urban data (*Tables-6 to 9*).

Out of the 36 equations estimated under AIDS-3 specification separately for the rural and urban sectors of Orissa and all India, 9 (50 per cent) equations for India and 9 (50 per cent) equations for Orissa have $\bar{R}^2$ values greater than 0.9, but 6 (33 per cent) equations for India and 6 (33 per cent) equations for Orissa $\bar{R}^2$ varies from 0.8 to 0.9. As a whole, out of 36 equations estimated under AIDS-3 specification, 18 (50 per cent) equations have $\bar{R}^2$ values greater than 0.9 and

Table 2

Parameter Estimates of LA\AIDS Model with Demographic Specification (AIDS-1): Rural India

				Price Related Coefficients of											
				Cereals & Subst.	*Pulses & Products*	*Milk & Products*	*Edible Oil*	*Meat, Fish & Egg*	*Other Food*	*Fuel & light*	*Clothing*	*Other Non-food*			
Commodity Group	α_i	β_i	θ_i	γ_{i1}	γ_{i2}	γ_{i3}	γ_{i4}	γ_{i5}	γ_{i6}	γ_{i7}	γ_{i8}	γ_{i9}	$\overline{R}^2$	*F-Value*	*TMII*
Cereals &	0.580	-0.097	0.007	-0.171	0.115	0.021	0.051	-0.020	-0.247	0.006	-0.014	0.086	0.976	188.09	0.00003
its substitutes		(-2.296)	(2.078)	(-2.802)	(2.639)	(1.239)	(1.891)	(-0.514)	(-2.521)	(0.062)	(-0.796)	(2.415)			
Pulses & its	0.055	-0.014	0.007	0.011	-0.022	-0.034	0.015	0.052	0.013	-0.008	-0.024	-0.003	0.951	116.55	0.00001
Products		(-2.064)	(2.064)	(1.667)	(-0.662)	(-2.094)	(1.399)	(2.621)	(2.434)	(-0.444)	(-1.801)	(-0.271)			
Milk & its	0.097	-0.004	-0.002	-0.027	-0.030	-0.046	0.029	0.093	0.077	-0.057	-0.016	-0.018	0.816	26.67	0.00004
Products		(-0.833)	(-1.168)	(-2.033)	(-0.279)	(-2.853)	(1.840)	(2.886)	(2.781)	(-1.961)	(-0.562)	(-1.478)			
Edible oil	-0.213	-0.012	0.002	-0.013	0.144	0.069	0.057	0.151	-0.247	-0.051	-0.015	-0.039	0.867	39.22	0.00007
& Fats		(-0.785)	(2.234)	(-0.273)	(2.519)	(2.466)	(1.898)	(2.647)	(-2.878)	(-1.987)	(-0.398)	(-1.223)			
Meat, Fish	0.060	-0.006	-0.004	-0.030	0.023	-0.017	0.014	0.024	0.027	-0.011	-0.032	-0.003	0.895	50.39	0.00028
& Egg		(-2.847)	(-1.104)	(-2.941)	(0.570)	(-0.825)	(1.373)	(2.609)	(1.724)	(-0.469)	(-2.927)	(-0.199)			
Other Food	0.133	-0.019	0.009	-0.072	0.078	-0.115	0.082	0.193	0.112	-0.015	-0.164	-0.080	0.844	32.40	0.00001
Items		(-2.030)	(3.060)	(-0.512)	(1.812)	(-2.393)	(1.686)	(2.072)	(1.276)	(-0.279)	(-4.186)	(-0.430)			
Fuel & Light	-0.101	-0.021	-0.004	-0.106	0.129	-0.014	0.037	0.162	0.014	-0.047	-0.081	-0.056	0.968	179.36	0.00001
		(-1.447)	(-0.634)	(-2.435)	(3.074)	(-0.460)	(1.885)	(3.690)	(0.256)	(-1.370)	(-0.192)	(-0.640)			
Clothing	0.662	0.021	-0.005	0.085	-0.299	-0.047	-0.171	-0.447	0.364	0.069	0.162	0.151	0.812	25.95	0.00013
		(2.823)	(-0.250)	(1.036)	(-2.799)	(-0.568)	(-3.243)	(-3.780)	(3.416)	(1.760)	(0.396)	(0.662)			
Other Non-	-0.274	0.151	-0.009	0.224	-0.138	0.183	-0.114	-0.207	-0.113	0.112	0.184	-0.039	0.987	469.52	0.00002
food Items		(2.026)	(-3.713)	(3.225)	(-2.978)	(2.601)	(-0.537)	(-2.517)	(-1.881)	0.456)	(3.219)	(-1.805)			

Note: Computed from the grouped consumer expenditure data collected from 42nd to 61st round NSSO Reports. Figures in the parentheses are the t-ratios.

Table 3

Parameter Estimates of LA\AIDS Model with Demographic Specification (AIDS-1): Urban India

Commodity Group	α_i	β_i	θ_i	γ_{i1} Cereals & Subst.	γ_{i2} Pulses & Products	γ_{i3} Milk & Products	γ_{i4} Edible Oil	γ_{i5} Meat, Fish & Egg	γ_{i6} Other Food	γ_{i7} Fuel & light	γ_{i8} Clothing	γ_{i9} Other Non-food	$\overline{R}^2$	F-Value	TMII
				Price Related Coefficients of											
Cereals & its substitutes	0.261	-0.063	-0.004	0.018	-0.063	0.017	-0.060	-0.022	0.050	-0.065	0.090	0.011	0.928	231.63	0.00003
		(-1.508)	(-2.050)	(0.204)	(-1.404)	(2.852)	(-1.171)	(-2.596)	(1.009)	(-1.102)	(1.214)	(2.114)			
Pulses & its Products	0.065	-0.013	0.003	0.003	-0.003	0.001	0.005	-0.006	0.009	-0.017	-0.007	0.006	0.959	407.11	0.00001
		(-2.272)	(1.057)	(2.218)	(-0.366)	(0.382)	(0.592)	(-2.823)	(2.969)	(-1.613)	(-0.521)	(0.371)			
Milk & its Products	0.137	-0.001	-0.002	-0.033	-0.046	0.004	-0.011	0.017	0.055	-0.016	0.061	-0.038	0.923	214.78	0.00001
		(-0.344)	(-1.131)	(-2.762)	(-2.105)	(2.383)	(-0.439)	(2.928)	(2.230)	(-0.553)	(1.675)	(-0.826)			
Edible oil & Fats	0.124	-0.012	0.003	-0.030	-0.019	0.019	0.023	-0.014	0.030	0.008	-0.015	-0.017	0.833	96.18	0.00007
		(-2.778)	(0.837)	(-2.399)	(-0.490)	(1.097)	(0.519)	(-2.418)	(0.702)	(0.151)	(-0.231)	(-0.207)			
Meat, Fish & Egg	0.096	-0.007	-0.004	0.021	0.009	0.002	-0.014	0.012	0.005	0.014	-0.027	-0.026	0.861	116.63	0.00002
		(-1.393)	(-2.087)	(3.723)	(2.580)	(0.341)	(-2.805)	(0.164)	(0.336)	(2.754)	(-1.132)	(-3.865)			
Other Food Items	0.254	-0.029	0.008	-0.075	-0.069	0.003	0.045	-0.048	0.013	-0.121	0.049	0.179	0.844	102.73	0.00002
		(-2.323)	(2.126)	(-0.782)	(-3.419)	(0.126)	(0.814)	(-1.183)	(2.247)	(-1.895)	(2.615)	(1.771)			
Fuel & Light	0.031	-0.019	-0.006	0.006	0.028	-0.008	-0.001	0.012	-0.021	0.056	-0.054	0.011	0.940	276.11	0.00002
		(-2.367)	(-2.353)	(0.132)	(1.153)	(-0.763)	(-0.030)	(-2.023)	(-0.762)	(1.715)	(-1.334)	(2.028)			
Clothing	0.154	0.021	-0.007	0.107	0.082	-0.019	-0.071	0.048	-0.031	0.072	-0.067	-0.141	0.802	23.57	0.00011
		(1.063)	(-1.009)	(1.101)	(0.051)	(0.023)	(0.059)	(0.043)	(2.057)	(1.067)	(2.084)	(0.107)			
Other Non-food Items	-0.162	0.123	0.008	-0.018	0.081	-0.019	0.083	0.023	-0.110	0.069	-0.029	0.025	0.976	503.82	0.00001
		(4.736)	(3.824)	(-1.137)	(2.243)	(-0.642)	(2.100)	(1.420)	(-1.522)	(2.807)	(-0.271)	(1.183)			

Note: Computed from the grouped consumer expenditure data collected from 42nd to 61st round NSSO Reports. Figures in the parentheses are the t-ratios.

Table 4
Parameter Estimates of LA\AIDS Model with Demographic Specification (AIDS-1): Rural Orissa

				Price Related Coefficients of											
				Cereals & Subst.	*Pulses & Products*	*Milk & Products*	*Edible Oil*	*Meat, Fish & Egg*	*Other Food*	*Fuel & light*	*Clothing*	*Other Non-food*			
Commodity Group	α_i	β_i	θ_i	γ_{i1}	γ_{i2}	γ_{i3}	γ_{i4}	γ_{i5}	γ_{i6}	γ_{i7}	γ_{i8}	γ_{i9}	$\bar{R}^2$	*F-Value*	*TMII*
Cereals & its substitutes	0.953	-0.138 (-2.457)	0.032 (2.848)	-0.294 (-1.148)	-0.147 (-2.776)	0.705 (1.398)	-0.321 (-0.575)	-0.178 (-2.497)	-0.181 (-2.495)	0.111 (0.671)	0.189 (1.347)	-0.012 (-2.073)	0.884	140.87	0.00005
Pulses & its Products	0.078	-0.009 (-2.865)	0.175 (0.688)	0.069 (1.282)	-0.056 (-1.405)	-0.169 (-1.593)	0.036 (0.309)	0.060 (2.802)	0.036 (3.470)	-0.013 (-0.361)	0.049 (1.672)	-0.026 (-0.744)	0.808	78.79	0.00007
Milk & its Products	-0.007	-0.002 (-2.256)	-0.025 (-2.156)	-0.042 (-1.372)	-0.026 (-1.138)	-0.017 (-0.280)	0.142 (2.140)	0.087 (2.034)	-0.101 (-2.324)	-0.037 (-1.886)	-0.018 (-1.089)	0.019 (2.964)	0.703	14.23	0.00003
Edible oil & Fats	0.047	-0.009 (-0.377)	0.047 (0.536)	0.040 (0.490)	0.051 (0.832)	-0.124 (-2.761)	-0.028 (-0.043)	0.061 (2.528)	0.007 (0.062)	-0.038 (-2.718)	-0.036 (-0.787)	0.041 (2.777)	0.714	15.00	0.00012
Meat, Fish & Egg	0.040	-0.003 (-1.466)	-0.131 (-1.580)	0.076 (2.420)	0.052 (2.263)	0.019 (0.302)	-0.167 (-2.453)	0.010 (0.232)	0.059 (1.310)	-0.018 (-2.907)	-0.040 (-2.326)	0.011 (0.543)	0.930	79.98	0.00070
Other Food Items	0.073	-0.022 (-2.398)	0.051 (2.134)	0.127 (2.541)	-0.040 (-0.232)	-0.395 (-3.851)	0.028 (0.055)	0.255 (3.775)	0.051 (1.152)	-0.048 (-0.314)	-0.016 (-0.127)	0.054 (2.358)	0.708	14.57	0.00019
Fuel & Light	0.045	-0.027 (-0.532)	-0.049 (-2.303)	-0.179 (-1.148)	0.091 (0.783)	-0.212 (-3.688)	0.436 (1.280)	0.163 (0.749)	-0.231 (-2.033)	-0.059 (-0.587)	-0.071 (-2.831)	0.069 (2.690)	0.832	76.42	0.00017
Clothing	-0.006	0.012 (2.073)	-0.081 (-0.527)	0.216 (2.771)	-0.040 (-1.194)	0.341 (3.617)	-0.378 (-2.619)	-0.171 (-2.436)	0.105 (1.262)	0.012 (0.066)	-0.029 (-0.192)	-0.036 (-0.200)	0.811	72.83	0.00090
Other Non-food Items	-0.223	0.199 (2.744)	-0.036 (-2.713)	-0.014 (-1.108)	0.116 (1.236)	-0.148 (-2.596)	0.232 (3.843)	-0.288 (-2.632)	0.255 (1.412)	0.090 (1.109)	-0.028 (-1.401)	-0.120 (-2.487)	0.933	247.63	0.00005

Note: Computed from the grouped consumer expenditure data collected from 42nd to 61st round NSSO Reports. Figures in the parentheses are the t-ratios.

Table 5

Parameter Estimates of LA\AIDS Model with Demographic Specification (AIDS-1): Urban Orissa

				Price Related Coefficients of											
				Cereals & Subst.	*Pulses & Products*	*Milk & Products*	*Edible Oil*	*Meat, Fish & Egg*	*Other Food*	*Fuel & light*	*Clothing*	*Other Non-food*			
Commodity Group	α_i	β_i	θ_i	γ_{i1}	γ_{i2}	γ_{i3}	γ_{i4}	γ_{i5}	γ_{i6}	γ_{i7}	γ_{i8}	γ_{i9}	$\bar{R}^2$	*F-Value*	*TMII*
Cereals & its	0.087	-0.083	0.005	0.132	-0.751	-0.099	0.057	0.765	0.184	-0.025	-0.205	-0.034	0.929	77.97	0.00013
substitutes		(-2.232)	(2.154)	(1.782)	(-2.197)	(-0.601)	(0.566)	(2.401)	(2.616)	(-0.139)	(-2.590)	(-0.312)			
Pulses & its	-0.056	-0.011	0.005	0.011	-0.036	-0.008	0.016	0.145	-0.024	-0.043	-0.040	-0.002	0.832	29.70	0.00007
Products		(-1.697)	(1.172)	(0.249)	(-2.407)	(-0.193)	(0.607)	(2.779)	(-0.317)	(-2.924)	(-2.201)	(-0.081)			
Milk & its	0.426	-0.005	-0.003	-0.071	-0.254	0.027	0.005	-0.134	0.293	-0.026	0.025	0.152	0.889	48.09	0.00015
Products		(-0.953)	(-0.217)	(-1.869)	(-2.536)	(0.341)	(0.105)	(-2.166)	(2.622)	(-0.304)	(0.401)	(3.004)			
Edible oil	-0.123	-0.013	-0.003	0.008	0.094	0.065	0.034	0.111	-0.233	-0.006	-0.021	-0.021	0.901	54.39	0.00009
& Fats		(-1.643)	(0.881)	(0.149)	(2.861)	(1.245)	(1.051)	(1.097)	(-2.445)	(-0.109)	(-2.121	(-0.609)			
Meat, Fish	0.025	-0.009	-0.003	-0.071	-0.254	0.027	0.005	-0.051	0.293	-0.026	0.025	0.052	0.889	48.09	0.00031
& Egg		(-1.854)	(0.217)	(-2.069)	(-2.536)	(0.341)	(0.105)	(-1.866)	(2.022)	(-0.304)	(0.401)	(1.004)			
Other Food	0.056	-0.036	0.009	0.010	-0.001	-0.090	0.126	0.339	0.048	-0.061	-0.171	-0.111	0.850	34.11	0.00005
Items		(-2.197)	(2.063)	(0.095)	(-0.005)	(-1.863)	(2.967)	(2.686)	(1.042)	(-1.535)	(-2.111)	(-2.640)			
Fuel & Light	-0.044	-0.022	0.009	-0.107	-0.031	-0.069	0.031	0.249	0.176	-0.026	-0.134	-0.060	0.941	95.94	0.00006
		(-2.619)	(2.044)	(-2.146)	(-0.247)	(-1.148)	(0.843)	(2.147)	(1.612)	(-0.400)	(-2.853)	(-1.519)			
Clothing	0.625	0.017	-0.003	-0.022	0.027	-0.021	-0.053	-0.483	-0.039	0.238	0.178	0.154	0.802	24.31	0.00024
		(2.713)	(-0.343)	(-0.199)	(2.020)	(-0.196)	(-0.792)	(-2.297)	(-1.198)	(2.013)	(2.095)	(2.766)			
Other Non-	0.004	0.162	-0.016	0.013	0.826	0.084	-0.202	-0.834	-0.133	-0.138	0.321	0.116	0.932	82.72	0.00023
food Items		(5.101)	(-3.426)	(0.046)	(3.445)	(1.006)	(-2.193)	(-3.564)	(-1.266)	(-1.460)	(2.491)	(1.646)			

Note: Computed from the grouped consumer expenditure data collected from 42nd to 61st round NSSO Reports. Figures in the parentheses are the t-ratios.

Table 6

Parameter Estimates of Unrestricted Simple LA\AIDS Model (AIDS-2): Rural India

			Price Related Coefficients of											
			Cereals & Subst.	Pulses & Products	Milk & Products	Edible Oil	Meat, Fish & Egg	Other Food	Fuel & light	Clothing	Other Non-food			
Commodity Group	α_i	β_i	γ_{i1}	γ_{i2}	γ_{i3}	γ_{i4}	γ_{i5}	γ_{i6}	γ_{i7}	γ_{i8}	γ_{i9}	$\bar{R}^2$	F-Value	TMII
Cereals & its	0.502	-0.089	0.343	-0.024	0.373	-0.613	0.566	-0.472	-0.034	0.006	-0.202	0.954	146.003	0.00003
substitutes		(-2.885)	(2.560)	(-0.075)	(1.288)	(-2.445)	(2.987)	(-2.640)	(-0.097)	(0.078)	(-1.669)			
Pulses & its	0.069	-0.011	0.043	-0.051	-0.028	0.013	0.091	-0.082	-0.011	-0.030	0.049	0.928	90.258	0.00001
Products		(-1.106)	(1.438)	(-2.981)	(-1.597)	(0.188)	(2.993)	(-2.701)	(-0.156)	(-1.218)	(1.415)			
Milk & its	0.073	-0.012	0.213	-0.231	-0.044	0.070	0.357	-0.260	-0.028	-0.016	-0.055	0.797	27.463	0.00004
Products		(-1.350)	(2.952)	(-2.925)	(-1.416)	(1.448)	(3.299)	(-2.962)	(-0.494)	(-0.509)	(-1.501)			
Edible oil	0.128	-0.013	-0.306	0.229	0.229	-0.032	-0.241	0.060	-0.010	-0.015	0.069	0.750	20.994	0.00007
& Fats		(-2.061)	(-2.965)	(2.343)	(2.521)	(-1.146)	(-2.809)	(1.156)	(-0.626)	(-0.334)	(1.440)			
Meat, Fish	0.021	-0.006	0.185	-0.008	0.028	-0.100	0.159	-0.196	0.006	-0.022	-0.050	0.835	35.533	0.00002
& Egg		(-0.692)	(2.005)	(-1.158)	(0.647)	(-2.570)	(2.843)	(-2.761)	(0.318)	(-1.728)	(-1.104)			
Other Food	0.156	-0.020	-0.008	-0.039	0.180	-0.211	0.268	-0.183	-0.008	-0.100	0.104	0.712	17.311	0.00004
Items		(-2.479)	(-0.024)	(-1.224)	(1.189)	(-2.947)	(2.890)	(-2.474)	(-0.490)	(-1.272)	(1.658)			
Fuel & Light	0.047	-0.025	-0.279	0.200	0.111	0.042	-0.207	0.081	0.023	-0.005	0.038	0.945	119.349	0.00002
		(-2.350)	(-2.414)	(2.870)	(1.180)	(1.306)	(-2.106)	(1.339)	(0.274)	(-0.166)	(1.388)			
Clothing	0.059	0.018	0.782	0.051	-0.324	-0.223	0.429	-0.598	0.157	0.183	-0.359	0.823	32.621	0.00013
		(1.485)	(3.582)	(0.193)	(-1.385)	(-0.651)	(2.226)	(-2.913)	(1.259)	(1.708)	(-2.473)			
Other Non-	-0.055	0.159	-0.972	-0.127	-0.526	1.054	-1.422	1.649	0.005	-0.004	0.206	0.980	337.596	0.00006
food Items		(3.622)	(-2.216)	(-1.539)	(-2.533)	(3.467)	(-3.458)	(3.119)	(0.237)	(-0.064)	(1.879)			

Note: Computed from the grouped consumer expenditure data collected from 42nd to 61st round NSSO Reports. Figures in the parentheses are the t-ratios.

Table 7
Parameter Estimates of Unrestricted Simple LA\AIDS Model (AIDS-2): Urban India

			Price Related Coefficients of											
			Cereals & Subst.	*Pulses & Products*	*Milk & Products*	*Edible Oil*	*Meat, Fish & Egg*	*Other Food*	*Fuel & light*	*Clothing*	*Other Non-food*			
Commodity Group	α_i	β_i	γ_{i1}	γ_{i2}	γ_{i3}	γ_{i4}	γ_{i5}	γ_{i6}	γ_{i7}	γ_{i8}	γ_{i9}	$\bar{R}^2$	*F-Value*	*TMII*
Cereals & its substitutes	0.261	-0.059 (-1.655)	0.017 (1.214)	-0.064 (-2.603)	0.017 (1.945)	-0.060 (-2.267)	-0.022 (-1.643)	0.051 (2.141)	-0.066 (-3.255)	0.091 (2.381)	0.011 (0.133)	0.975	270.117	0.00003
Pulses & its Products	0.065	0.010 (-2.472)	0.004 (0.253)	-0.013 (-0.395)	0.001 (0.449)	0.005 (0.636)	-0.006 (-0.890)	0.009 (2.066)	-0.017 (-2.796)	-0.007 (-1.604)	0.006 (1.395)	0.985	474.703	0.00000
Milk & its Products	0.136	-0.005 (-2.546)	-0.032 (-1.823)	-0.046 (-2.351)	0.004 (0.458)	-0.011 (-0.487)	0.017 (2.014)	0.054 (2.466)	-0.015 (-0.596)	0.060 (2.858)	-0.038 (-1.916)	0.973	250.293	0.00001
Edible oil & Fats	0.117	-0.012 (-0.675)	-0.017 (-1.235)	-0.009 (-0.261)	0.023 (2.427)	0.019 (1.435)	-0.014 (-0.446)	0.021 (1.517)	0.020 (1.411)	-0.029 (-2.495)	-0.027 (-2.345)	0.918	78.846	0.00008
Meat, Fish & Egg	0.097	-0.008 (-1.535)	0.020 (2.778)	0.008 (0.626)	0.002 (0.356)	-0.013 (-1.864)	0.014 (0.179)	0.006 (0.400)	0.014 (1.820)	-0.027 (-2.245)	-0.026 (-2.930)	0.951	135.883	0.00001
Other Food Items	0.296	-0.040 (-1.463)	-0.077 (-3.891)	-0.071 (-2.643)	0.002 (0.101)	0.046 (1.900)	-0.048 (-2.274)	0.015 (0.311)	-0.123 (-2.169)	0.052 (1.730)	0.181 (3.954)	0.945	119.517	0.00002
Fuel & Light	0.033	-0.021 (-2.502)	0.003 (0.065)	0.026 (2.174)	-0.009 (-1.965)	0.002 (0.611)	0.004 (-0.816)	-0.018 (-1.744)	0.052 (2.800)	-0.050 (-2.375)	0.004 (0.088)	0.978	315.445	0.00002
Clothing	0.145	0.023 (0.823)	0.122 (2.963)	0.093 (2.456)	-0.014 (-0.667)	-0.076 (-1.332)	0.047 (1.135)	-0.042 (-1.784)	0.086 (2.368)	-0.085 (-1.882)	-0.153 (-2.499)	0.863	44.044	0.00012
Other Non-food Items	-0.150	0.133 (2.706)	-0.040 (-1.323)	0.065 (2.072)	-0.026 (-1.938)	0.090 (2.231)	0.024 (1.449)	-0.095 (-2.389)	0.049 (1.614)	-0.004 (-0.043)	0.042 (1.319)	0.977	736.856	0.00002

Note: Computed from the grouped consumer expenditure data collected from 42nd to 61st round NSSO Reports. Figures in the parentheses are the t-ratios.

Table 8
Parameter Estimates of Unrestricted Simple LA\AIDS Model (AIDS-2): Rural Orissa

			Price Related Coefficients of											
			Cereals & Subst.	*Pulses & Products*	*Milk & Products*	*Edible Oil*	*Meat, Fish & Egg*	*Other Food*	*Fuel & light*	*Clothing*	*Other Non-food*			
Commodity Group	α_i	β_i	γ_{i1}	γ_{i2}	γ_{i3}	γ_{i4}	γ_{i5}	γ_{i6}	γ_{i7}	γ_{i8}	γ_{i9}	$\bar{R}^2$	*F-Value*	*TMII*
Cereals & its substitutes	0.972	-0.135 (-3.988)	-0.278 (-2.112)	-0.139 (-1.748)	0.795 (3.644)	-0.467 (-2.897)	-0.203 (-2.581)	-0.121 (-1.343)	0.151 (1.979)	0.166 (2.032)	-0.028 (-0.173)	0.954	146.008	0.00006
Pulses & its Products	0.081	-0.008 (-1.638)	0.072 (2.388)	-0.055 (-2.426)	-0.154 (-2.541)	0.011 (0.106)	0.056 (1.777)	0.047 (1.641)	-0.006 (-0.174)	0.046 (1.632)	-0.028 (-0.859)	0.839	36.448	0.00007
Milk & its Products	-0.007	-0.003 (-1.842)	-0.041 (-2.470)	-0.026 (-2.219)	-0.015 (-0.573)	0.139 (2.370)	0.086 (2.186)	-0.100 (-2.521)	-0.036 (-2.074)	-0.019 (-1.228)	0.018 (1.027)	0.802	28.386	0.00003
Edible oil & Fats	0.051	-0.009 (-2.150)	0.044 (1.559)	0.053 (2.909)	-0.106 (-2.700)	-0.037 (-1.230)	0.056 (2.512)	0.020 (0.179)	-0.030 (-1.620)	-0.040 (-1.957)	0.038 (1.762)	0.841	36.938	0.00013
Meat, Fish & Egg	0.039	-0.004 (-0.067)	0.074 (2.506)	0.052 (0.350)	0.011 (0.194)	-0.155 (-2.513)	0.012 (0.296)	0.054 (2.283)	-0.022 (-2.182)	-0.038 (-1.372)	0.012 (0.643)	0.926	87.992	0.00002
Other Food Items	0.076	-0.014 (-2.408)	0.130 (2.596)	-0.039 (-1.243)	-0.382 (-2.907)	0.007 (0.015)	0.251 (2.827)	0.060 (0.196)	-0.042 (-1.309)	-0.020 (-0.168)	0.052 (1.372)	0.877	16.925	0.00019
Fuel & Light	0.049	-0.024 (-2.473)	-0.176 (-2.211)	0.092 (1.857)	-0.192 (-2.685)	0.404 (2.337)	0.158 (2.779)	-0.218 (-0.065)	-0.050 (-1.559)	-0.076 (-1.971)	0.066 (1.708)	0.828	33.756	0.00017
Clothing	-0.019	0.011 (2.009)	0.205 (2.776)	-0.046 (-1.234)	0.280 (2.547)	-0.279 (-2.507)	-0.153 (-2.416)	0.064 (1.172)	-0.016 (-0.097)	-0.014 (-1.097)	-0.025 (-0.150)	0.779	24.678	0.00096
Other Non-food Items	-0.242	0.187 (3.059)	-0.029 (-0.205)	0.107 (1.017)	-0.238 (-0.864)	0.377 (3.275)	-0.263 (-2.323)	0.195 (2.174)	0.050 (0.564)	-0.005 (-0.066)	-0.105 (-2.154)	0.965	191.732	0.00006

Note: Computed from the grouped consumer expenditure data collected from 42nd to 61st round NSSO Reports. Figures in the parentheses are the t-ratios.

Table 9

Parameter Estimates of Unrestricted Simple LA\AIDS Model (AIDS-2): Urban Orissa

			Price Related Coefficients of											
			Cereals & Subst.	*Pulses & Products*	*Milk & Products*	*Edible Oil*	*Meat, Fish & Egg*	*Other Food*	*Fuel & light*	*Clothing*	*Other Non-food*			
Commodity Group	α_i	β_i	γ_{i1}	γ_{i2}	γ_{i3}	γ_{i4}	γ_{i5}	γ_{i6}	γ_{i7}	γ_{i8}	γ_{i9}	$\overline{R}^2$	*F-Value*	*TMII*
Cereals & its	0.078	-0.081	0.143	-0.762	-0.083	0.050	0.749	0.176	-0.023	-0.193	-0.030	0.928	90.584	0.00013
substitutes		(-2.328)	(1.007)	(-2.468)	(-1.708)	(1.606)	(2.685)	(2.645)	(-0.140)	(-2.016)	(-0.309)			
Pulses & its	-0.058	-0.010	0.014	-0.039	-0.003	0.014	0.141	-0.027	-0.042	-0.036	-0.001	0.831	34.445	0.00007
Products		(-0.360)	(0.382)	(-2.492)	(-0.115)	(1.646)	(3.966)	(-1.381)	(-2.986)	(-2.477)	(-0.052)			
Milk & its	0.432	-0.005	-0.078	-0.246	0.016	0.010	-0.123	0.299	-0.028	0.017	0.050	0.928	89.612	0.00015
Products		(-0.521)	(-1.140)	(-2.642)	(0.283)	(0.262)	(-2.905)	(2.254)	(-1.341)	(0.844)	(1.455)			
Edible oil	-0.107	-0.014	-0.012	0.115	0.036	0.048	0.141	-0.218	-0.009	-0.042	-0.027	0.899	62.167	0.00011
& Fats		(-1.905)	(-0.549)	(2.104)	(1.900)	(1.730)	(2.495)	(-2.362)	(-0.165)	(-1.305)	(-1.811)			
Meat, Fish	0.083	-0.008	-0.044	0.202	0.005	0.036	-0.055	-0.179	0.076	-0.030	-0.017	0.894	58.834	0.00029
& Egg		(-1.645)	(-1.525)	(2.106)	(0.068)	(1.734)	(-2.335)	(-3.107)	(2.773)	(-1.538)	(-0.288)			
Other Food	-0.018	0.042	0.101	-0.105	0.047	0.062	0.203	-0.061	-0.047	-0.072	-0.084	0.846	36.594	0.00009
Items		(2.590)	(2.875)	(-2.394)	(0.493)	(1.918)	(3.888)	(-1.273)	(-0.343)	(-1.618)	(-2.046)			
Fuel & Light	-0.066	-0.021	-0.080	-0.060	-0.029	0.012	0.209	0.155	-0.022	-0.105	-0.051	0.931	93.651	0.00007
		(-2.369)	(-1.431)	(-1.491)	(-0.617)	(0.377)	(2.897)	(2.439)	(-0.336)	(-2.764)	(-1.331)			
Clothing	0.612	0.028	-0.006	0.010	0.003	-0.064	-0.507	-0.051	0.241	0.195	0.059	0.808	28.688	0.00025
		(2.694)	(-0.064)	(0.047)	(0.035)	(-1.179)	(-2.732)	(-0.282)	(2.179)	(3.073)	(2.910)			
Other Non-	0.044	0.153	-0.038	0.880	0.009	-0.167	-0.758	-0.095	-0.146	0.266	0.101	0.943	99.588	0.00024
food Items		(2.192)	(-0.157)	(2.682)	(0.043)	(-2.202)	(-2.605)	(-0.205)	(-0.518)	(2.642)	(0.610)			

Note: Computed from the grouped consumer expenditure data collected from 42nd to 61st round NSSO Reports. Figures in the parentheses are the t-ratios.

another 12 (33 per cent) equations have $\bar{R}^2$ lies in between 0.8 to 0.9. Like AIDS-1 & AIDS-2, the F-values are also found to highly significant with TMII values closer to zero for all the 36 equations estimated under AIDS-3. So AIDS-3 fits well to both rural and urban data but there is no overall improvement in the goodness of fit of equations of this model compared to AIDS-2. Hence, homogeneity restriction has no impact in the improvement of goodness of fit *(Tables-10 to 13)*.

It is observed that out of the 36 AIDS-4 equations estimated separately for the rural and urban sectors of Orissa and all India, 6 (33 per cent) equations for India and only 3 (17 per cent) equations for Orissa have $\bar{R}^2$ greater than 0.9 while 8 (44 per cent) equations for India and 7 (39 per cent) equations for Orissa have $\bar{R}^2$ values lying in between 0.8 to 0.9. The overall picture reveals that out of the 36 equations estimated, 9 (25 per cent) equations have $\bar{R}^2$ greater than 0.9 and another 15 (42 per cent) equations have $\bar{R}^2$ varying from 0.8 to 0.9. The F-values like the other variants of AIDS model are found to be significant with relatively lower values in some of the 36 equations. The TMII values are found to be closer to zero in most of the cases. There is drastic reduction in the frequency of $\bar{R}^2$ greater than 0.8 due to the imposition of both symmetry and homogeneity restrictions simultaneously on AIDS-2 model. These equations have relatively poor fit to their respective sample data compared to the other variants like AIDS-2 and AIDS-3 (*Tables-14 to 17*).

Further, out of the 36 AIDS-5 equations estimated with the restriction of 'no cross-price effects' separately for the rural and urban sectors of Orissa and all India, 4 (22 per cent) equations for India and only one equation for Orissa have $\bar{R}^2$ greater than 0.9 while 6 (33 per cent) equations for India and 4 (22 per cent) for Orissa have $\bar{R}^2$ lying in between 0.8 to 0.9. On the whole, out of 36 equations estimated under AIDS-5 specification, 5 (14 per cent) equations have $\bar{R}^2$ values greater than 0.90 and another 10 (28 per cent) equations have $\bar{R}^2$ lying

Table 10
Parameter Estimates of LA\AIDS Model with Homogeneity Restriction (AIDS-3): Rural India

			Price Related Coefficients of											
			Cereals & Subst.	*Pulses & Products*	*Milk & Products*	*Edible Oil*	*Meat, Fish & Egg*	*Other Food*	*Fuel & light*	*Clothing*	*Other Non-food*			
Commodity Group	α_i	β_i	γ_{i1}	γ_{i2}	γ_{i3}	γ_{i4}	γ_{i5}	γ_{i6}	γ_{i7}	γ_{i8}	γ_{i9}	$\bar{R}^2$	*F-Value*	*TMII*
Cereals & its	0.239	-0.093	0.218	-0.395	-0.691	0.222	1.258	-0.709	-0.076	-0.017	-0.680	0.926	100.543	0.00005
substitutes		(-3.085)	(3.855)	(-1.210)	(-2.379)	(1.669)	(4.274)	(-2.820)	(-0.483)	(-1.869)	(-3.085)			
Pulses & its	0.040	-0.012	0.128	-0.094	0.004	-0.045	0.170	-0.110	-0.009	-0.039	-0.006	0.895	64.995	0.00001
Products		(-0.537)	(2.515)	(-2.994)	(0.051)	(-0.935)	(2.134)	(-0.880)	(-0.705)	(-1.101)	(-0.537)			
Milk & its	0.095	-0.010	0.149	-0.199	0.076	-0.031	0.297	-0.239	-0.030	-0.008	-0.014	0.890	64.718	0.00004
Products		(-1.526)	(2.865)	(-2.082)	(1.519)	(-1.319)	(2.831)	(-2.943)	(-1.857)	(-0.331)	(-0.526)			
Edible oil	0.046	-0.012	-0.074	0.113	-0.057	0.182	-0.025	-0.014	-0.005	-0.040	-0.080	0.795	30.997	0.00013
& Fats		(-2.058)	(-0.279)	(2.768)	(-1.251)	(3.209)	(-1.100)	(-0.036)	(-0.301)	(-1.018)	(-0.158)			
Meat, Fish	0.034	-0.006	0.149	0.010	-0.097	0.035	0.126	-0.185	0.005	-0.018	-0.027	0.882	59.722	0.00002
& Egg		(-0.049)	(2.077)	(0.248)	(-2.574)	(1.871)	(2.865)	(-2.743)	(1.232)	(-1.670)	(-1.049)			
Other Food	0.177	-0.022	-0.068	-0.008	-0.204	0.193	0.212	-0.164	-0.009	-0.093	0.143	0.778	28.015	0.00004
Items		(-2.469)	(-1.278)	(-1.062)	(-2.979)	(2.391)	(3.919)	(-2.452)	(-0.631)	(-2.559)	(2.469)			
Fuel & Light	0.074	-0.024	-0.355	0.238	0.050	0.127	-0.277	0.106	0.021	0.004	0.087	0.941	128.253	0.00003
		(-2.510)	(-2.290)	(2.756)	(0.379)	(2.440)	(-3.897)	(1.462)	(0.264)	(0.167)	(1.210)			
Clothing	0.053	0.020	0.799	0.043	-0.225	-0.327	0.445	-0.603	0.057	0.181	-0.370	0.729	30.246	0.00049
		(2.113)	(2.139)	(1.205)	(-2.704)	(-3.546)	(3.264)	(-4.095)	(1.519)	(1.257)	(-2.613)			
Other Non-	0.242	0.160	-1.816	0.293	1.144	-0.355	-2.206	1.918	-0.014	0.089	0.248	0.949	148.091	0.00008
food Items		(3.139)	(-3.450)	(1.999)	(2.541)	(-1.191)	(-4.443)	(2.471)	(-0.433)	(1.140)	(1.139)			

Note: Computed from the grouped consumer expenditure data collected from 42nd to 61st round NSSO Reports. Figures in the parentheses are the t-ratios.

Table 11
Parameter Estimates of LA\AIDS Model with Homogeneity Restriction (AIDS-3): Urban India

			Price Related Coefficients of											
			Cereals & Subst.	*Pulses & Products*	*Milk & Products*	*Edible Oil*	*Meat, Fish & Egg*	*Other Food*	*Fuel & light*	*Clothing*	*Other Non-food*			
Commodity Group	α_i	β_i	γ_{i1}	γ_{i2}	γ_{i3}	γ_{i4}	γ_{i5}	γ_{i6}	γ_{i7}	γ_{i8}	γ_{i9}	$\bar{R}^2$	*F-Value*	*TMII*
Cereals & its substitutes	0.145	-0.062 (-3.020)	0.015 (0.160)	-0.106 (-2.577)	-0.019 (-1.367)	0.010 (0.486)	-0.036 (-1.881)	0.068 (2.298)	-0.086 (-2.406)	0.165 (2.493)	-0.011 (-0.326)	0.959	186.432	0.00005
Pulses & its Products	0.031	0.011 (-0.003)	0.013 (0.143)	-0.016 (-2.598)	0.017 (2.471)	0.005 (-0.102)	-0.009 (-1.019)	0.013 (2.128)	-0.023 (-2.631)	0.014 (1.946)	0.016 (-1.003)	0.962	201.631	0.00001
Milk & its Products	0.099	-0.004 (-0.402)	-0.033 (-2.793)	-0.060 (-2.941)	0.002 (0.092)	0.002 (0.202)	0.013 (0.714)	0.060 (2.617)	-0.022 (-0.825)	0.084 (2.924)	-0.046 (-1.402)	0.963	222.337	0.00001
Edible oil & Fats	0.049	-0.012 (-2.158)	-0.018 (-1.238)	-0.034 (-2.032)	0.043 (2.036)	0.019 (1.152)	-0.022 (-1.675)	0.031 (2.738)	0.008 (0.155)	0.013 (0.254)	-0.040 (-2.158)	0.898	70.114	0.00010
Meat, Fish & Egg	0.034	-0.008 (0.081)	0.019 (2.480)	-0.015 (-2.139)	0.009 (0.405)	-0.002 (-0.172)	-0.015 (-1.308)	0.005 (0.681)	0.003 (0.113)	0.013 (1.475)	-0.038 (2.981)	0.867	52.124	0.00004
Other Food Items	0.191	-0.038 (-2.307)	-0.079 (-2.809)	-0.109 (-2.606)	0.084 (2.592)	-0.004 (-0.194)	-0.060 (-1.450)	0.031 (1.573)	-0.142 (-2.262)	0.119 (2.773)	0.160 (3.307)	0.920	91.882	0.00003
Fuel & Light	0.066	-0.019 (-1.276)	0.003 (0.076)	0.038 (2.969)	-0.012 (-1.476)	-0.008 (-0.775)	0.004 (0.187)	-0.023 (-1.947)	0.058 (2.017)	-0.071 (-2.298)	0.011 (0.276)	0.946	307.354	0.00002
Clothing	0.051	0.024 (2.080)	0.121 (2.184)	0.058 (2.332)	-0.041 (-1.751)	-0.020 (-0.882)	0.036 (1.823)	-0.028 (-1.494)	0.068 (2.044)	-0.023 (-1.332)	-0.171 (-3.080)	0.891	65.383	0.00015
Other Non-food Items	0.334	0.129 (4.015)	-0.032 (-1.117)	0.241 (2.052)	-0.083 (-1.559)	0.002 (0.037)	0.081 (1.692)	-0.167 (-2.110)	0.136 (1.770)	-0.314 (-2.660)	0.056 (1.015)	0.947	141.647	0.00009

Note: Computed from the grouped consumer expenditure data collected from 42nd to 61st round NSSO Reports. Figures in the parentheses are the t-ratios.

Table 12
Parameter Estimates of LA\AIDS Model with Homogeneity Restriction (AIDS-3): Rural Orissa

			Price Related Coefficients of											
			Cereals & Subst.	*Pulses & Products*	*Milk & Products*	*Edible Oil*	*Meat, Fish & Egg*	*Other Food*	*Fuel & light*	*Clothing*	*Other Non-food*			
Commodity Group	α_i	β_i	γ_{i1}	γ_{i2}	γ_{i3}	γ_{i4}	γ_{i5}	γ_{i6}	γ_{i7}	γ_{i8}	γ_{i9}	$\bar{R}^2$	*F-Value*	*TMII*
Cereals & its substitutes	0.396	-0.139 (-3.167)	-0.244 (-2.657)	-0.058 (-1.213)	-0.556 (-2.719)	1.461 (2.237)	-0.565 (-2.147)	0.013 (0.026)	-0.001 (-0.005)	-0.108 (-2.683)	0.059 (2.167)	0.914	96.016	0.00015
Pulses & its Products	0.028	-0.009 (-2.106)	0.075 (2.355)	-0.047 (-2.162)	0.003 (0.027)	-0.092 (-2.953)	0.023 (1.308)	0.059 (2.764)	-0.022 (-2.604)	0.020 (0.862)	-0.021 (-2.106)	0.939	107.618	0.00009
Milk & its Products	0.025	-0.003 (-1.108)	-0.043 (-0.407)	-0.030 (-1.321)	0.044 (2.248)	-0.051 (-2.953)	0.106 (2.598)	-0.107 (-2.494)	-0.028 (-1.528)	-0.004 (-0.278)	0.014 (1.108)	0.816	42.748	0.00004
Edible oil & Fats	0.034	-0.008 (-1.099)	0.045 (2.608)	0.055 (2.019)	-0.040 (-0.262)	-0.085 (-2.662)	0.045 (2.459)	0.024 (0.231)	-0.035 (-0.798)	-0.049 (-1.561)	0.041 (1.099)	0.766	26.234	0.00013
Meat, Fish & Egg	0.041	-0.003 (-0.328)	0.074 (2.676)	0.052 (2.520)	-0.155 (-2.683)	0.009 (0.184)	0.013 (0.366)	0.053 (1.368)	-0.021 (-1.293)	-0.037 (-3.151)	0.012 (0.328)	0.926	101.434	0.00002
Other Food Items	0.156	-0.012 (-2.079)	0.125 (2.603)	-0.050 (-2.330)	0.019 (0.045)	-0.474 (-3.302)	0.301 (2.097)	0.041 (1.143)	-0.021 (-0.168)	0.018 (0.207)	0.040 (1.079)	0.874	55.325	0.00019
Fuel & Light	0.084	-0.023 (-2.292)	-0.178 (-2.299)	0.088 (2.267)	0.409 (2.438)	-0.234 (-2.972)	0.180 (1.394)	-0.226 (-1.979)	-0.041 (-0.505)	-0.059 (-1.020)	0.060 (0.292)	0.724	20.936	0.00018
Clothing	0.055	0.015 (2.019)	0.201 (2.804)	-0.056 (-1.305)	-0.268 (-2.515)	0.195 (2.444)	-0.107 (-2.324)	0.047 (1.134)	0.004 (0.024)	0.021 (0.198)	-0.036 (-1.219)	0.863	50.389	0.00097
Other Non-food Items	0.181	0.183 (3.050)	-0.054 (-0.215)	0.048 (0.259)	0.443 (2.848)	-0.729 (-3.652)	0.005 (0.014)	0.096 (2.272)	0.162 (2.093)	0.197 (2.848)	-0.168 (-2.050)	0.934	105.476	0.00024

Note: Computed from the grouped consumer expenditure data collected from 42nd to 61st round NSSO Reports. Figures in the parentheses are the t-ratios.

Table 13
Parameter Estimates of LA\AIDS Model with Homogeneity Restriction (AIDS-3): Urban Orissa

			Price Related Coefficients of											
			Cereals & Subst.	Pulses & Products	Milk & Products	Edible Oil	Meat, Fish & Egg	Other Food	Fuel & light	Clothing	Other Non-food			
Commodity Group	α_i	β_i	γ_{i1}	γ_{i2}	γ_{i3}	γ_{i4}	γ_{i5}	γ_{i6}	γ_{i7}	γ_{i8}	γ_{i9}	$\bar{R}^2$	F-Value	TMII
Cereals & its	0.198	-0.083	0.160	-0.785	0.028	-0.104	0.654	0.228	0.018	-0.177	-0.021	0.927	101.095	0.00013
substitutes		(-3.362)	(2.254)	(-3.732)	(0.487)	(-2.064)	(4.884)	(2.006)	(0.149)	(-2.151)	(-1.362)			
Pulses & its	0.031	-0.010	0.027	-0.056	-0.003	-0.019	0.070	0.012	-0.011	-0.025	0.005	0.856	47.882	0.00008
Products		(-0.008)	(1.757)	(-2.704)	(-0.184)	(-1.718)	(2.890)	(0.189)	(-0.332)	(-2.082)	(0.008)			
Milk & its	0.052	-0.004	-0.133	-0.176	0.080	0.084	0.177	0.135	-0.158	-0.032	0.022	0.892	65.823	0.00028
Products		(-0.133)	(-2.555)	(-2.915)	(2.118)	(2.279)	(2.977)	(2.892)	(-2.940)	(-1.582)	(1.133)			
Edible oil	0.038	-0.012	0.019	0.088	0.021	0.010	0.026	-0.155	0.041	-0.023	-0.016	0.856	47.501	0.00013
& Fats		(-1.221)	(0.183)	(2.812)	(0.990)	(0.260)	(1.518)	(-2.811)	(1.882)	(-1.749)	(-0.221)			
Meat, Fish	0.052	-0.007	-0.048	0.208	0.041	0.010	-0.031	-0.192	0.065	-0.034	-0.019	0.912	74.761	0.00029
& Egg		(-0.236)	(-1.647)	(2.235)	(1.244)	(0.178)	(-0.393)	(-2.446)	(1.915)	(-0.712)	(-0.236)			
Other Food	0.212	-0.034	0.134	-0.142	0.019	0.006	0.021	0.038	0.033	-0.042	-0.067	0.923	78.017	0.00010
Items		(-2.206)	(2.229)	(-2.577)	(0.397)	(0.073)	(0.184)	(1.195)	(0.311)	(-1.597)	(-1.206)			
Fuel & Light	0.076	-0.019	-0.060	-0.086	-0.013	-0.053	0.099	0.215	0.026	-0.087	-0.041	0.917	88.595	0.00008
		(2.136)	(-2.108)	(-2.700)	(-0.553)	(-1.277)	(2.739)	(2.227)	(0.497)	(-2.460)	(1.136)			
Clothing	0.057	0.029	-0.085	0.113	0.038	0.102	-0.068	-0.291	0.049	0.124	0.018	0.781	28.489	0.00058
		(2.029)	(-1.708)	(2.414)	(0.708)	(2.098)	(-1.535)	(-3.354)	(0.427)	(2.582)	(0.229)			
Other Non-	0.284	0.141	-0.013	0.835	-0.211	-0.035	-0.950	0.010	-0.063	0.297	0.119	0.928	103.319	0.00023
food Items		(3.591)	(-0.014)	(4.009)	(-2.194)	(-1.208)	(-4.766)	(0.025)	(-1.301)	(2.118)	(2.591)			

Note: Computed from the grouped consumer expenditure data collected from 42nd to 61st round NSSO Reports. Figures in the parentheses are the t-ratios.

Table 14

Parameter Estimates of LA\AIDS Model with Homogeneity and Symmetry Restrictions (AIDS-4): Rural India

			Price Related Coefficients of											
			Cereals & Subst.	*Pulses & Products*	*Milk & Products*	*Edible Oil*	*Meat, Fish & Egg*	*Other Food*	*Fuel & light*	*Clothing*	*Other Non-food*			
Commodity Group	α_i	β_i	γ_{i1}	γ_{i2}	γ_{i3}	γ_{i4}	γ_{i5}	γ_{i6}	γ_{i7}	γ_{i8}	γ_{i9}	$\bar{R}^2$	*F-Value*	*TMII*
Cereals & its	0.239	-0.090	0.201	-0.395	-0.691	0.222	1.258	-0.709	-0.017	-0.076	-0.680	0.926	100.543	0.00015
substitutes		(-3.726)	(1.855)	(-2.210)	(-3.379)	(2.669)	(4.274)	(-3.820)	(-0.483)	(-1.869)	(-3.037)			
Pulses & its	0.039	-0.012	-0.395	-0.128	0.075	-0.050	0.077	0.057	-0.013	-0.043	0.420	0.878	64.861	0.00012
Products		(-1.202)	(-3.210)	(-2.882)	(2.288)	(-1.986)	(2.418)	(2.892)	(-1.716)	(-1.248)	(5.445)			
Milk & its	0.093	-0.012	-0.691	0.075	0.054	0.029	0.191	-0.219	-0.022	0.008	0.576	0.779	35.211	0.00015
Products		(-1.562)	(-4.379)	(2.288)	(2.398)	(1.234)	(2.424)	(-2.623)	(-1.173)	(0.250)	(3.581)			
Edible oil	0.047	-0.014	0.222	-0.050	0.029	0.119	0.009	-0.013	-0.011	-0.049	-0.255	0.850	62.188	0.00019
& Fats		(-2.322)	(2.669)	(-1.986)	(1.234)	(2.610)	(0.067)	(-1.086)	(-1.015)	(-1.463)	(3.970)			
Meat, Fish	0.034	-0.006	1.258	0.077	0.191	0.009	0.081	0.008	0.003	-0.016	-1.530	0.843	64.267	0.00013
& Egg		(-1.344)	(5.274)	(2.418)	(2.924)	(0.067)	(2.035)	(1.200)	(0.274)	(-1.662)	(-5.030)			
Other Food	0.176	-0.022	-0.709	0.057	-0.219	-0.013	0.008	-0.089	-0.008	-0.091	1.062	0.764	42.082	0.00014
Items		(-2.202)	(-4.820)	(1.892)	(-2.623)	(-0.086)	(0.200)	(-2.215)	(-1.139)	(-2.419)	(6.310)			
Fuel & Light	0.078	-0.025	-0.017	-0.013	-0.022	-0.011	0.003	-0.008	0.028	0.034	0.015	0.819	63.278	0.00010
		(-2.308)	(-2.483)	(-1.716)	(-2.173)	(-1.015)	(0.274)	(-1.139)	(2.754)	(2.026)	(1.673)			
Clothing	0.061	0.018	-0.076	-0.043	0.008	-0.049	-0.016	-0.089	0.034	0.101	0.131	0.726	39.705	0.00075
		(3.262)	(-2.869)	(-2.248)	(0.250)	(-2.463)	(1.662)	(-3.019)	(1.026)	(2.971)	(7.014)			
Other Non-	0.233	0.163	-0.680	0.420	0.576	-0.255	-1.530	1.062	0.005	0.131	0.272	0.912	96.581	0.00138
food Items		(5.067)	(-4.037)	(3.445)	(3.581)	(-2.970)	(6.030)	(5.310)	(0.673)	(1.014)	(2.886)			

Note: Computed from the grouped consumer expenditure data collected from 42nd to 61st round NSSO Reports. Figures in the parentheses are the t-ratios.

Table 15

Parameter Estimates of LA\AIDS Model with Homogeneity and Symmetry Restrictions (AIDS-4): Urban India

			Price Related Coefficients of											
			Cereals & Subst.	*Pulses & Products*	*Milk & Products*	*Edible Oil*	*Meat, Fish & Egg*	*Other Food*	*Fuel & light*	*Clothing*	*Other Non-food*			
Commodity Group	α_i	β_i	γ_{i1}	γ_{i2}	γ_{i3}	γ_{i4}	γ_{i5}	γ_{i6}	γ_{i7}	γ_{i8}	γ_{i9}	$\bar{R}^2$	*F-Value*	*TMII*
Cereals & its	0.145	-0.060	0.019	-0.106	-0.019	0.010	-0.036	0.068	-0.086	0.165	-0.011	0.959	186.432	0.00015
substitutes		(-3.614)	(1.160)	(-2.577)	(-1.367)	(0.486)	(-1.881)	(2.298)	(-2.606)	(3.493)	(0.794)			
Pulses & its	0.031	-0.010	-0.106	-0.017	0.018	-0.001	-0.009	0.014	-0.024	0.016	0.108	0.962	226.233	0.00014
Products		-(2.690)	(-2.577)	(-2.890)	(2.325)	(-0.302)	(-1.083)	(1.237)	(-2.850)	(1.676)	(2.864)			
Milk & its	0.097	-0.007	-0.019	0.018	-0.002	0.012	0.001	0.041	0.019	0.029	-0.099	0.916	108.614	0.00016
Products		(-0.485)	(-2.367)	(2.325)	(-0.107)	(1.375)	(0.044)	(3.346)	(0.859)	(2.361)	(-4.837)			
Edible oil	0.048	-0.013	0.010	-0.001	0.012	0.025	-0.048	0.062	0.044	0.011	-0.104	0.859	67.038	0.00052
& Fats		(-0.532)	(1.486)	(-0.302)	(1.375)	(2.195)	(-2.463)	(2.862)	(2.630)	(1.956)	(-3.982)			
Meat, Fish	0.034	-0.008	-0.036	-0.009	0.001	-0.048	-0.017	0.028	0.007	0.016	0.058	0.815	52.893	0.00012
& Egg		(-1.695)	(-2.881)	(-1.083)	(0.044)	(-2.663)	(-2.184)	(2.224)	(0.493)	(1.468)	(2.583)			
Other Food	0.180	-0.036	0.068	0.014	0.041	0.062	0.028	0.082	0.002	0.025	-0.322	0.889	104.340	0.00017
Items		(-2.188)	(3.298)	(1.237)	(2.346)	(2.862)	(2.224)	(3.073)	(0.047)	(1.619)	(-5.106)			
Fuel & Light	0.069	-0.020	-0.086	-0.024	0.019	0.044	0.007	0.002	0.034	-0.083	0.086	0.919	158.404	0.00022
		(-2.936)	(-2.406)	(-2.050)	(1.359)	(1.630)	(0.493)	(0.047)	(1.727)	(-2.681)	(2.780)			
Clothing	0.058	0.022	0.165	0.016	0.029	0.008	0.016	0.025	-0.081	0.019	-0.189	0.796	58.412	0.00047
		(2.225)	(4.493)	(0.676)	(1.361)	(0.762)	(0.468)	(1.619)	(-2.681)	(1.656)	(-4.592)			
Other Non-	0.338	0.132	-0.011	0.108	-0.099	-0.104	0.058	-0.322	0.086	-0.189	0.073	0.813	69.388	0.00023
food Items		(4.630)	(0.794)	(3.464)	(-2.537)	(-2.982)	(1.583)	(-5.106)	(1.180)	(-3.592)	(1.984)			

Note: Computed from the grouped consumer expenditure data collected from 42nd to 61st round NSSO Reports. Figures in the parentheses are the t-ratios.

Table 16

Parameter Estimates of LA\AIDS Model with Homogeneity and Symmetry Restrictions (AIDS-4): Rural Orissa

			Price Related Coefficients of											
			Cereals & Subst.	*Pulses & Products*	*Milk & Products*	*Edible Oil*	*Meat, Fish & Egg*	*Other Food*	*Fuel & light*	*Clothing*	*Other Non-food*			
Commodity Group	α_i	β_i	γ_{i1}	γ_{i2}	γ_{i3}	γ_{i4}	γ_{i5}	γ_{i6}	γ_{i7}	γ_{i8}	γ_{i9}	$\bar{R}^2$	*F-Value*	*TMII*
Cereals & its substitutes	0.396	-0.140 (-4.666)	-0.214 (-2.657)	-0.058 (-1.213)	-0.556 (-3.219)	1.461 (5.237)	-0.565 (-3.147)	0.013 (0.026)	-0.001 (-0.005)	-0.108 (-2.683)	0.059 (1.162)	0.924	102.016	0.00015
Pulses & its Products	0.030	-0.008 (-2.422)	-0.056 (-2.213)	-0.048 (-2.121)	0.058 (2.514)	-0.051 (-2.533)	0.021 (1.276)	0.030 (1.388)	-0.032 (-1.692)	0.015 (0.620)	0.066 (2.762)	0.832	34.975	0.00011
Milk & its Products	0.024	-0.003 (-0.937)	-0.556 (-4.719)	0.058 (1.514)	0.106 (2.775)	-0.080 (-2.447)	0.102 (2.320)	-0.102 (-2.327)	-0.023 (-1.232)	-0.011 (-1.057)	0.507 (4.374)	0.706	24.012	0.00026
Edible oil & Fats	0.035	-0.010 (-2.628)	1.461 (5.537)	-0.051 (-2.533)	-0.080 (-2.947)	-0.049 (-2.030)	0.051 (2.689)	0.030 (0.524)	-0.037 (-1.166)	-0.032 (-1.519)	-1.293 (5.245)	0.743	31.845	0.00015
Meat, Fish & Egg	0.043	-0.004 (-1.800)	-0.565 (-3.447)	0.021 (0.276)	0.102 (2.620)	0.053 (2.689)	0.051 (2.410)	-0.039 (-1.158)	-0.046 (-1.395)	-0.019 (-0.648)	0.410 (3.054)	0.777	41.763	0.00025
Other Food Items	0.158	-0.011 (-2.822)	0.013 (0.026)	0.030 (1.388)	-0.102 (-2.327)	0.030 (1.524)	-0.005 (-0.158)	-0.039 (-2.311)	-0.012 (-1.151)	0.026 (1.484)	0.188 (3.524)	0.857	77.851	0.00028
Fuel & Light	0.182	-0.027 (-2.009)	-0.011 (-0.005)	-0.032 (-1.692)	-0.023 (-1.232)	-0.037 (-1.866)	-0.046 (-2.395)	-0.141 (-2.851)	0.012 (0.345)	-0.011 (-0.716)	0.136 (3.812)	0.816	31.124	0.00027
Clothing	0.062	0.015 (2.246)	-0.108 (-3.683)	0.015 (1.620)	-0.011 (-1.057)	-0.032 (-2.519)	-0.019 (-1.648)	0.026 (2.484)	-0.012 (-1.316)	-0.011 (-1.315)	0.153 (5.834)	0.896	29.203	0.00119
Other Non-food Items	0.070	0.189 (3.630)	0.059 (2.162)	0.066 (2.062)	0.507 (4.574)	-1.293 (-5.245)	0.410 (3.654)	0.188 (2.524)	0.280 (3.312)	0.153 (2.834)	-0.136 (-2.368)	0.935	102.059	0.00112

Note: Computed from the grouped consumer expenditure data collected from 42nd to 61st round NSSO Reports. Figures in the parentheses are the t-ratios.

Table 17

Parameter Estimates of LA\AIDS Model with Homogeneity and Symmetry Restrictions (AIDS-4): Urban Orissa

			Price Related Coefficients of											
			Cereals & Subst.	Pulses & Products	Milk & Products	Edible Oil	Meat, Fish & Egg	Other Food	Fuel & light	Clothing	Other Non-food			
Commodity Group	α_i	β_i	γ_{i1}	γ_{i2}	γ_{i3}	γ_{i4}	γ_{i5}	γ_{i6}	γ_{i7}	γ_{i8}	γ_{i9}	$\bar{R}^2$	*F-Value*	*TMII*
Cereals & its	0.198	-0.082	0.198	-0.785	0.028	-0.104	0.654	0.228	0.018	-0.177	-0.021	0.927	101.095	0.00013
substitutes		(-3.423)	(2.254)	(-3.732)	(1.487)	(-2.064)	(3.484)	(2.406)	(0.149)	(-2.151)	(-1.334)			
Pulses & its	0.032	-0.010	-0.385	-0.014	0.003	-0.030	0.080	0.004	-0.011	-0.032	0.384	0.885	69.297	0.00028
Products		(-1.124)	(-3.732)	(-1.112)	(0.231)	(-2.483)	(2.392)	(0.070)	(-0.335)	(-1.631)	(3.999)			
Milk & its	0.052	-0.005	0.028	0.003	0.033	0.133	-0.065	-0.168	0.013	0.067	-0.043	0.808	42.029	0.00057
Products		(-0.535)	(1.487)	(0.231)	(2.267)	(2.725)	(-2.824)	(-3.456)	(1.184)	(2.117)	(-2.732)			
Edible oil	0.037	-0.013	-0.104	-0.030	0.133	0.010	0.088	-0.047	-0.023	-0.026	0.007	0.786	39.426	0.00018
& Fats		(-2.081)	(-2.064)	(-1.283)	(2.725)	(0.283)	(2.980)	(-2.966)	(-1.794)	(-1.077)	(-0.685)			
Meat, Fish	0.049	-0.007	0.654	0.080	-0.065	0.088	0.044	-0.008	-0.012	-0.028	-0.754	0.854	70.004	0.00039
& Egg		(-1.616)	(4.884)	(2.392)	(-2.024)	(3.180)	(1.581)	(-2.910)	(-0.291)	(-1.869)	(-6.944)			
Other Food	0.217	-0.028	0.228	0.004	-0.168	-0.047	-0.008	0.055	-0.056	0.016	-0.124	0.798	51.385	0.00022
Items		(-2.822)	(3.206)	(0.070)	(-2.456)	(-1.966)	(-0.910)	(2.731)	(-2.594)	(1.032)	(2.886)			
Fuel & Light	0.074	-0.020	0.018	-0.011	0.013	-0.023	-0.012	-0.056	0.122	-0.088	0.038	0.798	47.842	0.00025
		(-2.565)	(1.149)	(-0.335)	(0.184)	(-1.794)	(-0.291)	(-2.594)	(3.013)	(-2.859)	(1.627)			
Clothing	0.066	0.028	-0.177	-0.032	0.067	-0.026	-0.028	0.016	-0.088	0.129	0.099	0.734	41.479	0.00107
		(2.527)	(-3.151)	(-1.631)	(2.117)	(-1.077)	(-1.869)	(0.232)	(-2.859)	(3.298)	(-2.361)			
Other Non-	0.275	0.137	-0.021	0.784	-0.043	0.005	-0.754	-0.124	0.038	0.220	-0.099	0.794	61.635	0.00287
food Items		(5.871)	(-0.834)	(3.799)	(-1.732)	(-0.368)	(-3.744)	(2.886)	(1.627)	(-3.361)	(-2.636)			

Note: Computed from the grouped consumer expenditure data collected from 42nd to 61st round NSSO Reports. Figures in the parentheses are the t-ratios.

in between 0.8 to 0.9. So, most of the equations estimated under AIDS-5 have poor fit to the simple data indicating that imposition of the assumption of 'no cross-price effects' have drastically reduced the frequency of $\bar{R}^2$ greater than 0.8 as prices of other commodities are the important determinants in a demand system. Most of the F-values are relatively small but are found to be significant compared to its other variants. Some of the TMII values are not closer to zero which further strengthens the argument not in favour of imposing the more restrictive assumption like 'no cross-price effects' on model AIDS-2 model (*Tables-18 and 19*).

Finally, it is noticed that out of the 36 equations estimated under AIDS-6 separately for the rural and urban sector of Orissa and all India, 12 (33 per cent) equations have $\bar{R}^2$ lying in between 0.8 to 0.9 and for the rest 24 equations have $\bar{R}^2$ less than 0.8. Most of the F-values of these equations are relatively small but found to be significant compared to its other variants. So the drastic reduction in the frequency $\bar{R}^2$ of greater than 0.8 under AIDS-6 compared to the other variants (AIDS-2 and AIDS-3) is due to the imposition of the more restrictive assumption like explicit additivity. Most of the equations under AIDS-6 have poor fit to the simple data indicating that the imposition of the restrictive assumption like explicit additivity is not desirable while estimating AIDS. Some of the TMII values are not closer to zero which further strengthen the argument not in favour imposing the more restrictive assumption like explicit additivity (no price effect) in model AIDS-2 model (*Table-20*).

Imposition of neo-classical and a priori restrictions seems to affect the goodness of fit of the model adversely. The effect of explicitly additivity seems to be the largest. More specifically, the frequency of $\bar{R}^2$ greater than 0.9 decreases as we move from an unconstrained model to an explicitly additive model in both rural and urban India. It is also noticed that the explanatory power of the model either falls or remain constant in some cases with the imposition of different restrictions.

Table 18

Parameter Estimates of LA\AIDS Model with No Cross-price Effects (AIDS-5): Rural and Urban India

	Rural India						*Urban India*					
	Intercept	*Income Coefficient*	*Own Price Effect*	*Adj.* R^2			*Intercept*	*Income Coefficient*	*Own Price Effect*	*Adj.* R^2		
Commodity Group	α_i	β_i	γ_{ii}	$\bar{R}^2$	*F-value*	*TMII*	α_i	β_i	γ_{ii}	$\bar{R}^2$	*F-value*	*TMII*
Cereals & its substitutes	0.524	-0.922 (-8.433)	-0.145 (-2.826)	0.841	79.169	0.00028	0.382	-.064 (-.878)	-0.185 (-3.201)	0.874	103.751	0.00015
Pulses & its Products	0.072	-0.012 (-5.964)	-0.018 (-1.476)	0.727	50.042	0.00024	0.087	-.012 (-.849)	-0.060 (-4.153)	0.871	101.056	0.00024
Milk & its Products	0.115	-0.014 (-2.869)	-0.021 (-2.919)	0.740	53.655	0.00038	0.225	-.009 (-.240)	-0.114 (-3.846)	0.853	87.089	0.00036
Edible oil & Fats	0.097	-0.015 (-3.396)	-0.043 (-2.123)	0.735	57.245	0.00022	0.141	-.015 (-.451)	-0.032 (-1.876)	0.725	39.599	0.00052
Meat, Fish & Egg	0.044	-0.004 (-3.310)	-0.064 (-2.118)	0.776	61.263	0.00022	0.083	-.008 (-.653)	-0.029 (-2.722)	0.924	101.696	0.00022
Other Food Items	0.157	-0.024 (-2.466)	-0.050 (-2.821)	0.732	56.740	0.00023	0.352	-.037 (-.141)	-0.099 (-1.831)	0.833	74.754	0.00017
Fuel & Light	0.020	-0.021 (-6.087)	-0.071 (-3.409)	0.785	64.859	0.00028	-0.044	-.018 (-.013)	-0.133 (-5.132)	0.919	169.435	0.00027
Clothing	0.057	0.021 (2.426)	-0.030 (-1.412)	0.727	49.961	0.00029	0.076	0.027 (3.475)	-0.016 (-0.817)	0.829	72.534	0.00047
Other Non-food Items	-0.072	0.163 (9.761)	-0.073 (-3.473)	0.905	142.129	0.00075	-0.155	0.136 (8.781)	-0.223 (-3.905)	0.929	173.914	0.00043

Note: Computed from the grouped consumer expenditure data collected from 42nd to 61st round NSSO Reports. Figures in the parentheses are the t-ratios.

Table 19

Parameter Estimates of LA\AIDS Model with No Cross-price Effects (AIDS-5): Rural and Urban Orissa

	Rural India						*Urban India*					
	Intercept	*Income Coefficient*	*Own Price Effect*	*Adj.* R^2			*Intercept*	*Income Coefficient*	*Own Price Effect*	*Adj.* R^2		
Commodity Group	α_i	β_i	γ_{ii}	$\bar{R}^2$	*F-value*	*TMII*	α_i	β_i	γ_{ii}	$\bar{R}^2$	*F-value*	*TMII*
Cereals & its substitutes	0.640	-0.136	-0.164	0.826	71.421	0.00024	0.532	-0.082	-0.191	0.647	27.488	0.00090
		(-3.061)	(-3.638)					(-0.023)	(-4.847)			
Pulses & its Products	0.054	-0.009	-0.016	0.716	34.078	0.00017	0.082	-0.010	-0.030	0.892	86.781	0.00016
		(-2.834)	(-2.228)					(-0.023)	(-1.842)			
Milk & its Products	0.021	-0.004	-0.018	0.621	25.304	0.00029	0.122	-0.006	-0.078	0.912	102.002	0.00068
		(-2.413)	(-1.550)					(-0.308)	(-3.592)			
Edible oil & Fats	0.087	-0.011	-0.033	0.664	29.629	0.00026	0.127	-0.014	-0.027	0.707	35.277	0.00026
		(-2.743)	(-0.970)					(-0.918)	(-1.211)			
Meat, Fish & Egg	0.079	-0.006	-0.045	0.724	35.523	0.00016	0.096	-0.010	-0.028	0.867	82.618	0.00039
		(-2.678)	(-1.887)					(-0.018)	(-1.954)			
Other Food Items	0.080	-0.017	-0.108	0.747	38.488	0.00036	0.299	-0.035	-0.067	0.729	38.958	0.00019
		(-0.688)	(-3.365)					(-0.125)	(-3.090)			
Fuel & Light	0.094	-0.028	-0.174	0.758	42.941	0.00028	0.028	-0.021	-0.072	0.786	42.717	0.00033
		(-0.561)	(-3.443)					(-0.273)	(-2.085)			
Clothing	0.060	0.017	-0.071	0.791	47.690	0.00120	0.076	0.032	-0.024	0.723	36.426	0.00119
		(2.416)	(-3.991)					(2.003)	(-1.367)			
Other Non- food Items	0.082	0.194	-0.085	0.850	84.018	0.00033	-0.189	0.146	-0.062	0.774	41.053	0.00083
		(6.124)	(-3.084)					(5.102)	(-3.416)			

Note: Computed from the grouped consumer expenditure data collected from 42nd to 61st round NSSO Reports. Figures in the parentheses are the t-ratios.

Table 20

Parameter Estimates of LA\AIDS Model with Explicit Additivity (AIDS-6): Rural and Urban Sectors of Orissa and India

	Rural India			*Urban India*			*Rural Orissa*			*Urban Orissa*		
	Intercept	*Adj. Income Coefficient*	*Adj. R^2*	*Intercept*	*Adj. Income Coefficient*	*Adj. R^2*	*Intercept*	*Adj. Income Coefficient*	*Adj. R^2*	*Intercept*	*Adj. Income Coefficient*	*Adj. R^2*
Commodity Group	α_i	β_i	$\bar{R}^2$	α_i	β_i	$\bar{R}^2$	α_i	β_i	$\bar{R}^2$	α_i	β_i	$\bar{R}^2$
Cereals & its substitutes	0.211	-0.087	0.888	0.131	-0.059	0.821	0.397	0.129	0.818	0.203	0.076	0.858
		(-3.886)			(4.159)			(6.382)			(4.497)	
Pulses & its Products	0.036	-0.012	0.781	0.029	-0.011	0.849	0.032	0.009	0.761	0.033	0.009	0.584
		(-4.714)			(-3.411)			(4.523)			(2.774)	
Milk & its Products	0.088	-0.023	0.853	0.092	-0.011	0.767	0.023	0.005	0.615	0.046	-0.007	0.761
		(-4.448)			(-4.578)			(2.126)			(-2.696)	
Edible oil & Fats	0.045	-0.013	0.621	0.042	-0.015	0.784	0.036	0.009	0.645	0.037	-0.012	0.701
		(-3.626)			(-3.873)			(2.581)			(-3.274)	
Meat, Fish & Egg	0.035	-0.006	0.775	0.033	-0.008	0.613	0.041	-0.006	0.601	0.049	0.010	0.646
		(-2.452)			(-2.079)			(-2.273)			(3.589)	
Other Food Items	0.174	-0.021	0.782	0.177	-0.036	0.894	0.155	-0.017	0.784	0.201	0.038	0.772
		(-3.856)			(-4.843)			(-4.743)			(3.784)	
Fuel & Light	0.088	-0.024	0.655	0.074	-0.017	0.681	0.081	0.005	0.743	0.068	-0.023	0.874
		(-3.511)			(-3.847)			(2.363)			(-5.747)	
Clothing	0.061	0.021	0.722	0.058	0.022	0.745	0.061	0.019	0.791	0.061	0.031	0.713
		(4.164)			(4.040)			(3.929)			(4.107)	
Other Non- food Items	0.262	0.165	0.824	0.364	0.136	0.813	0.174	0.402	0.875	0.302	0.144	0.864
		(4.199)			(5.030)			(3.805)			(4.549)	

Note: Computed from the grouped consumer expenditure data collected from 42nd to 61st round NSSO Reports. Figures in the parentheses are the t-ratios.

Among the hypotheses, homogeneity restrictions seem to cause less reduction in $\bar{R}^2$ compared to homogeneity and symmetry, 'no cross-price effects' and explicit additivity at nine commodity level in both rural and urban sectors of Orissa as well as India. The F-values values and the Theil's Measure of Information Inaccuracy also confirm this. Thus, broadly we notice a trade off between theoretical consistency and statistical goodness of fit. The neo-classical restrictions may be desirable on theoretical grounds, but the same are less acceptable statistically. This is in conformity with earlier studies using other flexible models (e.g. Murty, 1989)

PARAMETER ESTIMATES

The parameter estimates of AIDS model under various specifications separately for rural and urban sectors of Orissa and all India are presented in *Tables-2 to 20* and the frequency of the t-ratios of these estimates are presented in *Table-21*. Here, we have examined the statistical significance of income coefficients (β_i), own-price coefficients (γ_{ii}), cross-price coefficients (γ_{ij}) and size coefficients (θ_i). The impact of neoclassical restrictions on income coefficients is marginal because income variable is a passive participant in those restrictions. It also appears that the proportion of statistically significant cross-price coefficients is larger for disaggregated models than the aggregated models. It is a common belief that there will be higher price response for disaggregated commodities. With commodity aggregation some valuable price information may be smoothened or lost resulting less price variability and hence, insignificant price coefficients. It is generally, expected that the number of statistically significant price coefficients may increase but the number of statistically significant income coefficients will decrease with the imposition of these restrictions.

The parameter estimates of AIDS model with demographic specification (AIDS-1) separately for the rural and urban sectors of Orissa and all India are presented in *Tables-2 to 5*. The individual statistical significance of the income coefficients

Table 21
Frequency of t-ratios of Income, Price, Size Coefficients and Range of Variation Adj. R^2 for different Variants of AIDS: Orissa and all-India

MODELS	*AIDS-1*						*AIDS-2*						*AIDS-3*					
Parameters	*R.I.*	*U.I.*	*R.O.*	*U.O.*	*Total*	*Prop.*	*R.I.*	*U.I.*	*R.O.*	*U.O.*	*Total*	*Prop.*	*R.I.*	*U.I.*	*R.O.*	*U.O.*	*Total*	*Prop.*
$\beta_i \geq 2$	6	5	6	5	22	0.61	5	4	6	5	20	0.56	6	5	6	5	22	0.61
$1 \leq \beta_i < 2$	1	3	1	2	6	0.17	3	3	2	2	10	0.28	2	1	2	2	7	0.19
$\beta_i < 1$	2	1	2	2	8	0.22	1	2	1	2	6	0.17	1	3	1	2	7	0.19
Total	9	9	9	9	36	1.00	9	9	9	9	36	1.00	9	9	9	9	36	1.00
$\tilde{a}_{ij}$ ep 2	33	29	35	33	130	0.40	34	32	36	33	135	0.42	38	35	42	36	151	0.47
1dp $\tilde{a}_{ij}$ <2	22	20	22	19	83	0.26	28	26	25	22	101	0.31	24	24	19	18	85	0.26
$\tilde{a}_{ij} < 1$	26	32	24	29	111	0.34	19	23	20	26	88	0.27	19	22	20	27	88	0.27
Total	81	81	81	81	324	1.00	81	81	81	81	324	1.00	81	81	81	81	324	1.00
	Adjusted R^2 (AIDS-1)						*Adjusted R^2 (AIDS-2)*						*Adjusted R^2 (AIDS-3)*					
Adj. $R^2 \geq 0.9$	4	5	2	4	15	0.42	4	8	3	4	19	0.53	3	6	4	5	18	0.50
$0.8 \leq$ Adj. $R^2 < 0.9$	5	4	4	5	18	0.50	2	1	5	5	13	0.36	3	3	3	3	12	0.33
Adj. $R^2 < 0.8$	0	0	3	0	3	0.08	3	0	1	0	4	0.11	3	0	2	1	6	0.12
Total	9	9	9	9	36	1.00	9	9	9	9	36	1.00	9	9	9	9	36	1.00
MODELS	*AIDS-4*						*AIDS-5*						*AIDS-6*					
Parameters	*R.I.*	*U.I.*	*R.O.*	*U.O.*	*Total*	*Prop.*	*R.I.*	*U.I.*	*R.O.*	*U.O.*	*Total*	*Prop.*	*R.I.*	*U.I.*	*R.O.*	*U.O.*	*Total*	*Prop.*
$\beta_i \geq 2$	6	6	7	6	25	0.69	9	7	9	6	31	0.86	9	9	9	9	36	1.00
$1 \leq \beta_i < 2$	3	1	1	2	7	0.19	0	2	0	2	4	0.11	0	0	0	0	0	0.00
$\beta_i < 1$	0	2	1	1	4	0.11	0	0	0	1	1	0.03	0	0	0	0	0	0.00
Total	9	9	9	9	36	1.00	9	9	9	9	36	1.00	9	9	9	9	36	1.00
													Adjusted R^2 (AIDS-6)					
$\gamma_{ij} \geq 2$	48	42	46	44	180	0.56	7	6	6	5	24	0.66	0	0	0	0	0	0.00
$1 \leq \gamma_{ij} < 2$	23	23	24	21	91	0.28	2	2	2	4	10	0.28	3	4	2	3	12	0.33

Contd.

$\gamma_{ij} < 1$	10	16	11	16	53	0.16	0	1	1	0	2	0.06	6	5	7	6	24	0.67
Total	81	81	81	81	324	1.00	9	9	9	9	36	1.00	9	9	9	9	36	1.00
	Adjusted R^2 (AIDS-4)						*Adjusted R^2 (AIDS-5)*						*Household size coefficient-$\grave{e}_i$ (AIDS-1*					
Adj. $R^2 \geq 0.9$	2	4	2	1	9	0.25	1	3	0	1	5	0.14	5	5	5	4	19	0.53
$0.8 \leq$ Adj. $R^2 < 0.9$	4	4	4	3	15	0.42	1	5	2	2	10	0.28	2	3	1	1	7	0.19
Adj. $R^2 < 0.8$	3	1	3	5	12	0.33	7	1	7	6	21	0. 66	2	1	3	4	10	0.28
Total	9	9	9	9	36	1.00	9	9	9	9	36	1.00	9	9	9	9	36	1.00

(β_i), price coefficients (γ_{ii}) and size coefficients (θ_i) are judged on the basis of t-ratios. It is found that out of the 36 income coefficients, 22 (61 per cent) income coefficients are statistically significant with t-ratios exceeding 2 and for another 6 (17 per cent) income coefficients, the t-ratios vary in between 1 and 2. But out of the 36 size coefficients, 19 (53 per cent) size coefficients are found to be statistically significant with t-ratios greater than 2. For another 7 (17 per cent) size coefficients, t-ratios are found to vary from 1 to 2 and it is less than unity for the rest of the 10 coefficients. It is further observed that out of 324 own-price and cross-price coefficients estimated under AIDS-1 model, 130 (40 per cent) price coefficients are statistically significant with t-ratios greater than 2; for another 83 (26 per cent) price coefficients the t-ratios vary in between 1 to 2 and for the rest of the price coefficients the t-ratios are less than unity.

The parameter estimates of the unconstrained simple LA\AIDS model (AIDS-2) separately for the rural and urban sectors of Orissa and all India are presented in *Tables-6 to 9*. On perusal of the results, it is observed that out of 36 income coefficients, only 20 (56 per cent) income coefficients have t-ratios greater than 2 and the t-ratios for another 10 (28 per cent) income coefficients vary between 1 and 2. But out of 324 price coefficients, 135 (42 per cent) price coefficients are found to significant with t-ratios greater than 2. The rest of the price coefficients are found to be insignificant. The t-ratios of 101 (31 per cent) price coefficients are found to vary between 1 and 2. The number of statistically significant price coefficients in rural areas of both the state and the country are 70 (21 per cent) which is much greater than the number of statistically significant price coefficients in urban areas (55 i.e. 17 per cent).

The parameter estimates from the constrained LA\AIDS model with homogeneity restriction imposed (AIDS-3) are noted separately for the rural and urban areas of the state and the country in *Tables-10 to 13*. On review of these results, it is noticed that out of 36 income coefficients estimated, 22 (61 per cent) are found to be significant with t-ratios greater than 2. The t-ratios of 7 (19 per cent) income coefficients vary in between 1 and 2. On the other hand, out of 324 own-price and cross-price coefficients estimated from this model, only 151 (56 per cent) price coefficients are found to be significant with t-ratios greater than 2 and for another 85 (56 per cent) price coefficients have t-ratios vary between 1 and 2. In this model, the number of statistically significant income and price coefficients is marginally higher in the rural sector than that of the urban sector of the state and the country. Further, imposition of homogeneity restriction enhances the number of statistically significant income and price coefficients in both the sectors of the state as well as the country.

The parameter estimates from another specification of LA\AIDS model with both homogeneity and symmetry imposed (AIDS-4) separately for the rural and urban sectors of the state and the country are presented in *Tables-14 to 17.* The results noted in these tables reveals that out of 36 income coefficients, 25 (69 per cent) income coefficients have t-ratios greater than 2. The t-ratios of 7 (19 per cent) income coefficients vary between 1 and 2. For the rest four coefficients, the t-ratios are less than unity. Further, out of 324 own-price and cross-price coefficients estimated under this model, 180 (56 per cent) price coefficients have t-ratios exceeding 2; 91(28 per cent) price coefficients have t-ratios vary from 1 to 2. Imposition of these two restrictions together has enhanced the number of statistically significant parameters compared to AIDS-2 and AIDS-3 in both the sectors of the state and the country. Further, like the other variants, the statistically significant parameters of this model in rural areas are found to marginally higher than urban areas.

Further, the parameter estimates of LA/AIDS model with 'no cross price effects' (AIDS-5) separately for the rural and urban sectors are presented in *Table-18* for India and in *Table-19* for Orissa. The 'no cross price effect' restriction forces all cross-prices to zero. Hence, intercept, own-price and income coefficients are estimated in each equation. The results of this model reveals that out of 36 income coefficients, the t-ratio of 31 (86 per cent) of the income coefficients are found to be significant with t-ratios exceeding 2. The t-ratios of 4 (11 per cent) income coefficients vary from 1 to 2. But out of 36 own-price coefficients, 25 (69 per cent) own-price coefficients have t-ratios greater than 2 and for only 10 (28 per cent) price coefficients, the t-ratios vary from 1 to 2. Unlike other models, most of the price and income coefficients are found to be statistically significant. The own- price coefficients in rural areas (13) is marginally higher than urban areas (12).

Finally, the parameter estimates of the more restricted specification of LA\AIDS model with explicit additivity imposed (AIDS-6) separately for the rural and urban sectors of the state and the country are presented in *Table-20*. This restriction forces all price coefficients to zero. Therefore, only intercept and income coefficients are estimated in each equation. The results have revealed that all the 36 income coefficients are found to be highly significant with very high values of t-ratios.

INCOME RESPONSE COEFFICIENTS

To facilitate comparison, the income coefficients under various specifications are reproduced in *Table-22*. It is clear that the income coefficients are sensitive to model specification. Further, it is interesting to note a systematic pattern of variation in these coefficients across different model specifications as well as in the rural and urban sectors of the state and the country at nine commodity levels. The absolute values of income coefficients seem to increase for some commodities and decrease for others with the imposition of different restrictions. In some cases, the sign of the coefficients has changed as well implying the change in the nature of commodity from necessity to luxury types or vice-versa.

Different food items in all the models have negative income coefficients implying their necessity nature. Clothing and other non-food item have positive income coefficients in all models implying their luxury nature. Fuel and light also have a negative sign implying its necessity nature in most of the cases except in rural Orissa under explicit additivity restriction. The magnitude of these coefficients indicates the relative degree of necessity or luxury nature of an item. For example, cereals

Table 22
Estimates of Income Coefficients of Different Variants of AIDS Model for Nine Commodity Groups: Orissa and all-India

	AIDS-1	*AIDS-2*	*AIDS-3*	*AIDS4*	*AIDS-5*	*AIDS-6*	*AIDS-1*	*AIDS-2*	*AIDS-3*	*AIDS4*	*AIDS-5*	*AIDS-6*
Commodity Groups			*Rural India*						*Urban India*			
Cereals & its substitutes	-0.0965	-0.0890	-0.0931	-0.0899	-0.0922	-0.0871	-0.0626	-0.0590	-0.0616	-0.0596	-0.0642	-0.0585
Pulses & its products	-0.0142	-0.0113	-0.0118	-0.0115	-0.0122	-0.0117	-0.0125	-0.0100	-0.0105	-0.0101	-0.0121	-0.0114
Milk & its products	-0.0043	-0.0115	-0.0104	-0.0124	-0.0138	-0.0232	-0.0013	-0.0050	-0.0042	-0.0072	-0.0088	-0.0106
Edible oil & fats	-0.0122	-0.0127	-0.0119	-0.0136	-0.0147	-0.0125	-0.0120	-0.0121	-0.0117	-0.0132	-0.0145	-0.0149
Meat, fish & egg	-0.0055	-0.0059	-0.0056	-0.0062	-0.0040	-0.0057	-0.0072	-0.0084	-0.0079	-0.0081	-0.0083	-0.0084
Other food items	-0.0189	-0.0204	-0.0223	-0.0221	-0.0236	-0.0217	-0.0292	-0.0403	-0.0384	-0.0361	-0.0371	-0.0360
Fuel & light	-0.0213	-0.0253	-0.0241	-0.0253	-0.0213	-0.0241	-0.0190	-0.0205	-0.0188	-0.0195	-0.0175	-0.0173
Clothing	0.0215	0.0176	0.0195	0.0184	0.0209	0.0213	0.0210	0.0226	0.0242	0.0224	0.0267	0.0216
Other non-food items	0.1514	0.1586	0.1598	0.1627	0.1628	0.1648	0.1228	0.1328	0.1288	0.1315	0.1358	0.1356
Commodity Groups			*Rural Orissa*						*Urban Orissa*			
Cereals & its substitutes	-0.1382	-0.1352	-0.1391	-0.1399	-0.1364	-0.1294	-0.0829	-0.0814	-0.0832	-0.0817	-0.0822	-0.0763
Pulses & its products	-0.0092	-0.0081	-0.0093	-0.0082	-0.0092	-0.0088	-0.0105	-0.0098	-0.0104	-0.0099	-0.0103	-0.0092
Milk & its products	-0.0023	-0.0032	-0.0028	-0.0032	-0.0038	-0.0049	-0.0046	-0.0049	-0.0041	-0.0052	-0.0062	-0.0069
Edible oil & fats	-0.0087	-0.0093	-0.0084	-0.0099	-0.0105	-0.0094	-0.0134	-0.0138	-0.0119	-0.0129	-0.0139	-0.0121
Meat, fish & egg	-0.0032	-0.0042	-0.0032	-0.0043	-0.0059	-0.0057	-0.0086	-0.0082	-0.0071	-0.0070	-0.0100	-0.0101
Other food items	-0.0222	-0.0142	-0.0121	-0.0106	-0.0171	-0.0168	-0.0361	-0.0422	-0.0339	-0.0282	-0.0349	-0.0381
Fuel & light	-0.0271	-0.0243	-0.0233	-0.0271	-0.0275	0.0054	-0.0218	-0.0205	-0.0189	-0.0202	-0.0205	-0.0226
Clothing	0.0119	0.0112	0.0153	0.0145	0.0167	0.0194	0.0169	0.0276	0.0285	0.0278	0.0323	0.0309
Other non-food items	0.1991	0.1871	0.1830	0.1887	0.1938	0.1502	0.1612	0.1532	0.1409	0.1372	0.1457	0.1444

Note:

1. Computed from the grouped consumer expenditure data collected from 42nd to 61st round NSSO Reports.
2. AIDS-1: Simple AIDS; AIDS-2: AIDS with Demographic specification; AIDS-3: AIDS with Homogeneity Restriction; AIDS-4: AIDS with Homogeneity and symmetric restriction; AIDS-5: AIDS with no cross price effects and AIDS-6: AIDS with explicit additivity.

and other food items as a whole is more of a necessity item than milk & its products and meat, fish & egg; pulses & its products are a higher necessity than milk & its products, edible oil and meat, fish & egg both in rural and urban areas of the state and the country and so on. The rural-urban variations are also clearly visible from these estimates.

It is also observed from *Table-22* that the absolute values of the income coefficient in rural India are greater for most of the food items except meat, fish & egg and other food item and smaller for most of the non-food items except fuel and light than urban India. No such definite pattern is observed for fuel and light. The rural-urban variation of income coefficients is quite different in Orissa. The absolute values of these coefficients in rural Orissa are greater for most of the food and non-food items except cereals & its substitutes and pulses & its products than its urban counterparts. On the other hand, the income coefficients among different food items across the model specifications indicate that it is the highest for cereals followed by other food item but among different non-food items, it is the highest for other non-food item followed by clothing.

Imposition of homogeneity restriction on AIDS-2 enhances the absolute value of income coefficients of essential food items like cereals & its substitutes; pulses & its products and non-food items like clothing and other non-food item in the both the sectors of the state and the country but it reduces the absolute value of income coefficients of the delicious food items like milk and its products and meat, fish and egg and essential non-food item like fuel and light. But imposition of both homogeneity and symmetry together on AIDS-2 enhances the absolute value of income coefficients of most of the food and non-food items except other food items in rural sector and edible oil; meat, fish and egg and other food item in the urban sector of the state as well as the country. The restriction of no cross price effects on AIDS-2 enhances the absolute value of income coefficients of most of the food items except other food and reduces its value for most of the non-food items except fuel and light in both the sectors of Orissa. But it enhances the value absolute of income coefficients of most of the food and non-food items except edible oil; meat, fish and egg and other food item in rural India and with the exception of other food and other non-food item in urban India. On the other hand, the imposition of the more restrictive assumption like explicit additivity (no price effects) on AIDS-2 enhances the absolute value of income coefficients of most of the food and non-food items except cereals & its substitutes; edible oil and fuel and light in both sectors of the India with the exception of cereals & its substitutes; clothing and other non-food in rural Orissa and cereal & its substitutes, pulses and its products, other-food item and other non-food in urban Orissa.

At nine commodity levels, the magnitude of income coefficients for different food items except milk & its products, meat, fish & eggs and fuel and light in rural India; and the magnitude of these coefficients for other food, clothing, and other non-food item tend to increase when we move from a less restrictive model to a more restrictive type. In other cases, there is no such systematic pattern. The magnitude of income coefficients across model specifications in Orissa follows almost the same pattern as that of all-India. Neo-classical restrictions seem to increase the importance of commodities with larger budget share and reduce that of minor items i.e. results in polarization of commodities.

PRICE RESPONSE COEFFICIENTS

Generally, the proportion of the own-price and cross-price coefficients statistically significant is larger for disaggregated than aggregated models. This result is in conformity with the common belief that there will be higher price response for disaggregated commodities. With commodity aggregation some valuable price information may be smoothened or lost resulting in less price variability and thereby insignificant coefficients. Some of the own-price coefficients are also insignificant. Even then for systemic reasons, we do not omit those variables form the analysis. Due to the complex nature of the models, we can not infer the substitutability/ complementarity of commodities based on the signs of γ_{ij}

coefficients alone. Therefore, this aspect will be considered later. The magnitude of t-ratios for γ_{ij} coefficients may indicate the relative significance of price variables. The price variables may also be ranked on the basis of their t-ratios. The statistical significance of individual price variables along with other parameter estimates judged on the basis of the 't' ratios is presented in *Table-2 to 20.*

Despite this, inclusion of all price variables in complete demand system is quite justified because out of 180 own-price coefficients, 120 (67 percent) own-price coefficients and out of 1152 cross-price coefficients, 501 (43 percent) cross-price coefficients are found to be statistically significant in both the rural and urban areas of the state and the country. Due to highly aggregated nature of commodity groups, many cross-price effects are not significant. By these criteria, among the cross-price effects, food prices significantly influence the demand for clothing and other non-food item which seem to be most dominant and negative in both rural and urban areas. This implies that the budget share on clothing and other non-food item will decline with increase in food price. Consumer may withdraw expenditure from clothing and other non-food items to meet the increased cost of food. The same is true with fuel and light as well.

Since, the explicit additivity assumption forces all price coefficients (γ_{ij}) to zero; the demand relations reduce themselves to simple Engle curves under AIDS-6. Therefore, price responses are not estimated under this specification. Hence, the own-price coefficients of five variants of AIDS model (except AIDS-6) separately for the rural and urban sectors of the state and the country are reproduced in *Table-23*. From the figures quoted in the table, it is noticed that the own-price coefficients neither follow any definite pattern across the model specifications nor across the sectors. But these coefficients are negative in AIDS-5 (model with no cross-price effects) as expected. It is also observed that these coefficients are positive for most of the food items and negative for most of the non-food items.

Table 23
Estimates of Own-price Coefficients of Different Variants AIDS Model for Nine Commodity Groups: Orissa and all-India

	AIDS-1	*AIDS-2*	*AIDS-3*	*AIDS4*	*AIDS-5*	*AIDS-1*	*AIDS-2*	*AIDS-3*	*AIDS4*	*AIDS-5*
Commodity Groups			*Rural India*					*Urban India*		
Cereals & its substitutes	-0.1712	0.3427	0.2181	0.2012	-0.1452	0.0180	0.0171	0.0153	0.0193	-0.1855
Pulses & its products	-0.0217	-0.0513	-0.0938	-0.1277	-0.0177	-0.0029	-0.0128	-0.0149	-0.0174	-0.0598
Milk & its products	-0.0460	-0.0441	0.0763	0.0540	-0.0209	0.0038	0.0040	0.0021	-0.0024	-0.1138
Edible oil & fats	0.0568	-0.0322	0.1817	0.1185	-0.0431	0.0231	0.0188	0.0191	0.0251	-0.0320
Meat, fish & egg	0.0242	0.1595	0.1263	0.0814	-0.0635	0.0122	0.0140	-0.0153	-0.0170	-0.0285
Other food items	0.1116	-0.1831	-0.1639	-0.0887	-0.0501	0.0133	0.0150	0.0306	0.0820	-0.0998
Fuel & light	-0.0466	0.0231	0.0214	0.0278	-0.0707	0.0555	0.0523	0.0583	0.0338	-0.1326
Clothing	0.1617	0.1829	0.1810	0.1005	-0.0304	-0.0674	-0.0847	-0.0234	0.0194	-0.0161
Other non-food items	-0.0386	0.2064	0.2477	0.2719	-0.0735	0.0248	0.0418	0.0558	0.0726	-0.2233
Commodity Groups			*Rural Orissa*					*Urban Orissa*		
Cereals & its substitutes	-0.2935	-0.2779	-0.2443	-0.2136	-0.1635	0.1317	0.1426	0.1598	0.1983	-0.1906
Pulses & its products	-0.0561	-0.0547	-0.0472	-0.0477	-0.0163	-0.0356	-0.0390	-0.0556	-0.0138	-0.0299
Milk & its products	-0.0168	-0.0149	0.0439	0.1058	-0.0177	0.0272	0.0161	0.0802	0.0327	-0.0783
Edible oil & fats	-0.0277	-0.0374	-0.0854	-0.0487	-0.0326	0.0339	0.0479	0.0096	0.0096	-0.0273
Meat, fish & egg	0.0101	0.0122	0.0134	0.0510	-0.0450	-0.0506	-0.0553	-0.0309	0.0444	-0.0277
Other food items	0.0512	0.0600	0.0414	-0.0394	-0.1082	0.0480	-0.0612	0.0380	0.0548	-0.0665
Fuel & light	-0.0591	-0.0502	-0.0408	0.0118	-0.1743	-0.0261	-0.0220	0.0259	0.1220	-0.0723
Clothing	-0.0295	-0.0139	0.0210	-0.0112	-0.0711	0.1780	0.1954	0.1236	0.1291	-0.0239
Other non-food items	-0.1201	-0.1047	-0.1683	-0.1356	-0.0845	0.1162	0.1011	0.1189	-0.0992	-0.0622

Note:
1. Computed from the grouped consumer expenditure data collected from 42nd to 61st round NSSO Reports.
2. AIDS-1: Simple AIDS; AIDS-2: AIDS with Demographic specification; AIDS-3: AIDS with Homogeneity Restriction; AIDS-4: AIDS with Homogeneity and symmetric restriction; AIDS-5: AIDS with no cross price effects and AIDS-6: AIDS with explicit additivity.

As expected, imposition of neoclassical restrictions seems to increase the number of statistically significant price coefficients. Among the restrictions, under homogeneity and symmetry, a large number of price coefficients are statistically significant in both the rural and urban sectors of the state and the country. Prices of food items continue to play an important role in determining the demand for food as well as non-food items. The cross-price effects of cereals and its substitutes; milk and its products; edible oil; meat fish and egg and other non-food items are prominent. The demand for other non-food items is sensitive to the price of cereals & its substitutes; pulses & its products and edible oil in addition to its own price in some specifications. Most of the income coefficients are significant. These results under-score the use of estimating flexible complete demand system like AIDS.

INCOME AND PRICE ELASTICITIES

Estimates of income, price and size elasticities at mean level of the variables are presented in *Appendix Tables-1 to 10*. Here, we may recall that the phrase 'income elasticity' actually means demand elasticity with respect to consumer's total expenditure; the latter is taken as a proxy for income. Since, the elasticities are non-linear functions of parameter estimates and variables (at their mean level), we can not infer anything about the sampling distributions of different elasticities and hence, it is not possible know their statistical significance. In this section we, therefore, examine only the signs and magnitudes of these elasticities and interpret their implications in demand analysis.

Income Elasticities

To facilitate comparison, the estimates of income elasticities are reproduced for the six variants of AIDS model together in Table-24. By and large, the magnitudes of these income elasticities are quite plausible for most of the commodities in all model specifications. For time series models, these estimates are immensely satisfactory. But for mean level data, these values seem to be some what puzzling. Income elasticities exhibit a pattern similar to that of income coefficients. It is

Table 24
Estimates of Income Elasticities of different Variants of AIDS Model for Nine Commodity Groups: Orissa and all-India

	AIDS-1	AIDS-2	AIDS-3	AIDS4	AIDS-5	AIDS-6	AIDS-1	AIDS-2	AIDS-3	AIDS4	AIDS-5	AIDS-6
Commodity Groups	*Rural India*						*Urban India*					
Cereals & its substitutes	0.5808	0.6137	0.5956	0.6095	0.5649	0.6217	0.5261	0.5533	0.5339	0.5491	0.5145	0.5571
Pulses & its products	0.6209	0.6983	0.6852	0.6927	0.6748	0.7569	0.5718	0.6579	0.6395	0.6540	0.5857	0.6768
Milk & its products	0.9530	0.8726	0.8854	0.8627	0.9358	0.7435	0.9860	0.9465	0.9548	0.9227	0.8831	0.8640
Edible oil & fats	0.7319	0.7206	0.7485	0.7011	0.6906	0.7252	0.7206	0.7170	0.7264	0.6910	0.6619	0.6631
Meat, fish & egg	0.8375	0.8250	0.8336	0.8147	0.8817	0.7031	0.7827	0.7454	0.7620	0.7548	0.7312	0.7467
Other food items	0.8880	0.8787	0.8677	0.8687	0.9784	0.8712	0.8360	0.7735	0.7847	0.7972	0.9038	0.7979
Fuel & light	0.7288	0.6778	0.6929	0.6780	0.7291	0.6931	0.7430	0.7222	0.7464	0.7358	0.7632	0.7661
Clothing	1.3320	1.2715	1.3015	1.2848	1.4786	1.4842	1.3608	1.3887	1.4164	1.3855	1.6306	1.5432
Other non-food items	1.6036	1.6323	1.6349	1.6487	1.5192	1.3875	2.0511	1.9879	1.9661	1.9436	2.0120	1.9910
Commodity Groups	*Rural Orissa*						*Urban Orissa*					
Cereals & its substitutes	0.6233	0.6317	0.6208	0.6459	0.6084	0.6474	0.5638	0.5716	0.5625	0.5757	0.5678	0.5987
Pulses & its products	0.6842	0.7217	0.6814	0.7184	0.7169	0.7675	0.6561	0.6786	0.6571	0.6750	0.6607	0.6978
Milk & its products	0.8986	0.8612	0.8767	0.8592	0.9764	0.7849	0.9124	0.9083	0.9227	0.9014	0.8297	0.8451
Edible oil & fats	0.7537	0.7395	0.7628	0.7221	0.6807	0.7353	0.6422	0.6320	0.6836	0.6572	0.6172	0.6934
Meat, fish & egg	0.9231	0.8994	0.9222	0.8966	0.7946	0.7407	0.8125	0.8215	0.8453	0.8480	0.7825	0.7807
Other food items	0.8634	0.9129	0.9254	0.9347	0.8963	0.8354	0.8149	0.7837	0.8263	0.8554	0.8210	0.8046
Fuel & light	0.6910	0.7228	0.7344	0.6906	0.7066	1.0620	0.7165	0.7335	0.7547	0.6463	0.7339	0.7063
Clothing	1.1854	1.1744	1.2384	1.2260	1.3615	1.4569	1.2674	1.4380	1.4523	1.4359	1.5114	1.4899
Other non-food items	1.3415	1.3693	1.3581	1.3656	1.3015	1.3479	1.5233	1.4973	1.4575	1.4661	1.4837	1.4711

Note:
1. Computed from the grouped consumer expenditure data collected from 42nd to 61st round NSSO Reports.
2. AIDS-1: Simple AIDS; AIDS-2: AIDS with Demographic specification; AIDS-3: AIDS with Homogeneity Restriction; AIDS-4: AIDS with Homogeneity and symmetric restriction; AIDS-5: AIDS with no cross price effects and AIDS-6: AIDS with explicit additivity.

found that income elasticities are les than unity for all food items and hence, different food items are necessity items in both rural and urban sectors of the state and the country. Therefore, the results satisfy the Engel's law. The income elasticities are fairly sensitive to model specification. For some items, rural-urban variations are quite striking. There is no uniform pattern of these estimates across rural and urban sectors for some items. Different food items have lower estimates in urban sector while the opposite in true for clothing and other non-food items. These estimates do not differ much for fuel and light across model specifications but differ across rural and urban sectors.

The income elasticities are fairly sensitive to model specifications. For some commodities rural-urban variations are quite striking. On perusal of the figures quoted in *Table-24*, it is noticed that income elasticities are less than unity for different food items and greater than unity for different non-food items except fuel and light. It is interesting to note that fuel and light which is a necessity item in most of the model specifications changes into a luxury item when explicit additivity restriction is imposed on AIDS-2 in the rural sector of Orissa. It is further noticed that rural elasticities are greater than urban elasticities for most of the food items except milk and its products. This pattern is reversed for various non-food items except fuel and light across different model specifications. It is also found that inclusion of household size as an additional explanatory variable in the AIDS model (AIDS-1) tends to increase these elasticities for most of the food items except cereal and its substitutes and pulses and its products, and tends to decrease for most of the non-food items except fuel and light in both the sectors of Orissa and all India. Imposition of homogeneity restriction also enhances the value of these elasticities for most of the food items except cereals and its substitutes; pulses and its products and all non-food items. No such definite pattern is observed when homogeneity and symmetry restrictions are imposed together. On the other hand, imposition of explicit additivity restriction enhances the elasticities for various food items and reduces the elasticities for various non-food items.

The estimated rural-urban variations in income elasticities for some items do not follow the expected pattern i.e. these elasticities of demand for necessity items such as food items are likely to be higher in rural sector (under-developed region) compared to that of urban sector (developed region). The higher income elasticities for meat, egg & fish and other food item in rural areas compared to urban areas is some what puzzling. This may be due to the aggregated data used here. Instead of mean level data, expenditure class-wise data may provide more convincing results.

Uncompensatory own-price elasticities

It may be mentioned at the outset that the explicit additivity assumption forces all γ_{ij} coefficients to zero and the demand relations reduce themselves to simple Engel function. Therefore, price responses are not estimated under this specification. The matrix of the estimates of own-price and cross-price elasticities form the first four specifications of AIDS model on nine broad commodity groups separately for the rural and urban sectors of Orissa and all India are presented in *Appendix Tables-1 to 8* and only the own-price elasticities of the fifth specification (AIDS-5) are presented in *Appendix Table-9*. As expected from the flexible demand system like AIDS, the own-price and cross-price elasticities are more sensitive to the model specification. The estimates do not follow any systematic pattern across models with different restrictions imposed, and also across rural and urban sectors. The utmost erraticness of even the own-price elasticities is perhaps the (unreliable) price variables in the specification of the fully flexible model like AIDS. Further, the use of mean level data might have also contributed to this erratic behaviour. Such data is known to contain cyclical movement for some durable goods (like clothing) which are difficult to model.

The estimates of own-price elasticities (η_{ii}) for five different specifications of AIDS model on nine broad commodity groups separately for the rural and urban sectors of Orissa and all India are reproduced in *Tables-25*. On perusal of the figures quoted in the table, it is noticed that all the own-price

Table 25

Estimates of Uncompensated Own-price Elasticities of different Variants of AIDS Model for Nine Commodity Groups: Orissa and all-India

	AIDS-1	*AIDS-2*	*AIDS-3*	*AIDS4*	*AIDS-5*	*AIDS-1*	*AIDS-2*	*AIDS-3*	*AIDS4*	*AIDS-5*
Commodity Groups			*Rural India*					*Urban India*		
Cereals & its substitutes	-0.7459	-0.7763	-0.7022	-0.6554	-0.6473	-0.6554	-0.5513	-0.5198	-0.5152	-0.5773
Pulses & its products	-0.5539	-0.6814	-0.6293	-0.6750	-0.6585	-0.5219	-0.5494	-0.5420	-0.5345	-0.4732
Milk & its products	-1.0313	-0.9507	-0.9205	-0.9063	-0.9268	-0.7177	-0.7216	-0.7016	-0.6294	-0.8132
Edible oil & fats	-0.3342	-0.6591	-0.6387	-0.6305	-0.6223	-0.5952	-0.5608	-0.5545	-0.5343	-0.5104
Meat, fish & egg	-0.7835	-0.7182	-0.7038	-0.6830	-0.7489	-0.9652	-0.9655	-0.8572	-0.7940	-1.0431
Other food items	-0.6837	-0.4916	-0.5205	-0.5093	-0.4603	-0.9935	-1.0005	-0.8606	-0.9189	-0.8335
Fuel & light	-0.5551	-0.6754	-0.7813	-0.0646	-0.7622	-0.8221	-0.8727	-0.8582	-0.9734	-1.0530
Clothing	-1.0887	-1.0709	-1.1298	-0.9956	-0.9793	-1.4276	-1.4068	-1.3702	-0.9989	-1.0694
Other non-food items	-1.2320	-1.2024	-1.2883	-0.9746	-0.9813	-0.6580	-0.6972	-0.6271	-0.5819	-0.6715
Commodity Groups			*Rural Orissa*					*Urban Orissa*		
Cereals & its substitutes	-0.6125	-0.6826	-0.6412	-0.3026	-0.6497	-0.4517	-0.3801	-0.3671	-0.3417	-0.5743
Pulses & its products	-0.8303	-0.7564	-0.6330	-0.6467	-0.7868	-0.3023	-0.3905	-0.4577	-0.5675	-0.3714
Milk & its products	-0.7274	-0.7988	-0.7220	-0.5966	-0.9842	-0.6965	-0.4471	-0.5178	-0.4968	-0.5416
Edible oil & fats	-0.4214	-0.4185	-0.4072	-0.3732	-0.2886	-0.2511	-0.3475	-0.3821	-0.3406	-0.3917
Meat, fish & egg	-0.6711	-0.7260	-0.6423	0.5673	-0.4836	-0.9640	-1.2568	-1.2367	-1.2595	-1.2465
Other food items	-0.5755	-0.6206	-0.6484	-0.5954	-0.7702	-0.8901	-0.9791	-0.9017	-0.9817	-1.1750
Fuel & light	-0.5123	-0.5933	-0.6783	-0.8111	-0.8708	-0.7020	-0.7034	-0.6887	-0.7686	-0.6661
Clothing	-1.1717	-1.4767	-0.9892	-0.9341	-0.9280	-1.0811	0.9440	-0.8666	-0.8981	-1.0286
Other non-food items	-1.5463	-1.7168	-1.5916	-1.6695	-1.6157	-0.8459	-0.8087	-0.8460	-0.9526	-0.8655

Note:
1. Computed from the grouped consumer expenditure data collected from 42nd to 61st round NSSO Reports.
2. AIDS-1: Simple AIDS; AIDS-2: AIDS with Demographic specification; AIDS-3: AIDS with Homogeneity Restriction; AIDS-4: AIDS with Homogeneity and symmetric restriction; AIDS-5: AIDS with no cross price effects and AIDS-6: AIDS with explicit additivity.

elasticities are negative as expected. The correct sign for all the estimates is indicative of the fulfillment of second order conditions which require the negative semi-definiteness of the Slutsky substitution matrix. The estimates of own-price elasticities in rural sector for most of the food items except meat, fish and egg and other food item, and some non-food items like clothing (except India) and other non-food item are grater than those of the urban sector. The rural-urban pattern of own-price elasticities is reversed for clothing in India and fuel and light both in Orissa and India. The magnitude of most of food items are less than unity indicating price inelastic in both the sector. But most of the food items are highly inelastic in rural sector than that of the urban sector. It seems that the order of magnitude of these estimates is quite plausible in contrast to other flexible models.

It is interesting to note that most of the commodities are price inelastic under different specifications, more so in urban areas. Food items are generally part of this group, with the exception of meat, fish and egg and other food in the state as well as in the country. Neo-classical restrictions of homogeneity and symmetry seem to reduce (increase) the own-price elasticity when it is inelastic (elastic), with some exceptions. Thus, restrictive models may under (over) estimates own-price elasticity of inelastic (elastic) commodities.

Uncompensatory Cross-Price Elasticities

The cross-price elasticities (η_{ii}) are uncompensated in nature and therefore, the classification of commodity pairs are considered as gross substitutes/complements (but not termed as net substitutes/complements). Further, $\eta_{ij} \gtrless 0$ if need not imply $\eta_{ji} \lessgtr 0$. Therefore, substitutability or complementarity need not be symmetric. The numerical values of η_{ij}s once again indicate the appropriateness of using a more flexible model like AIDS even for aggregated commodity classification as is done in the study. A perusal of the figures in *Appendix Tables-1 to 8* indicates that most of the estimates of cross-price elasticities are numerically large and negative implying considerable cross-price responses. It also follows that several pairs of goods are gross complements as demand for pairs of goods move together.

It is well known that for a price inelastic good, an increase in its price would lead to an increase in the budget allocation on it (i.e. increase in the price can not be offset by the decline in quantity purchased) while the opposite is true for an elastic good. Most of the food items are found to be price inelastic i.e. increase in their prices should result in reallocation of expenditures in their favour, implying gross complementarity. For most of the non-food items, the opposite is true. This is may be due to the low levels of income wherein consumer has to buy some quantity of each commodity and may imply less scope for substitutability.

Among the cross-price estimates obtained here, quite a few are large and negative and a majority of the large and negative estimates belong to that of food items and its constituents. The positive estimates are mostly located above the principal diagonal in the matrix of price elasticities. This implies that increase in the prices of some food and non-food items leads to increase in the consumption of the former. The money so saved through the reduction in the demand for non-food items due to increase in their price is spent on food items.

The cross-price elasticities are sensitive to the imposition of restrictions and rural-urban variations. The degree of substitutability varies with the model specifications but does not show any systematic pattern. For some pairs of commodities, the estimates are much more divergent. No systematic pattern could be seen across models. Thus, flexibility of the AIDS model has the adverse effect of erratic cross-price responses as well.

HOUSEHOLD SIZE COEFFICIENT AND SIZE ELASTICITY

Size effects (expressed in person) along with size elasticities (η_{im}) are reproduced in *Table-26*. As pointed out earlier 19 (53 percent) of size coefficient are found to be significant with t-ratios greater than 2. One striking feature of size coefficient

Table 26

Estimates of Household Size Coefficients and Size Elasticities of AIDS-1 Model for Nine Commodity Groups: Orissa and all-India

	Household Size				*Household Elasticity*			
	India		*Orissa*		*India*		*Orissa*	
Commodity Groups	*Rural*	*Urban*	*Rural*	*Urban*	*Rural*	*Urban*	*Rural*	*Urban*
Cereals & its substitutes	0.0074	-0.0041	0.0094	0.0049	0.032	-0.031	0.075	0.026
Pulses & its products	0.0066	0.0029	0.0072	0.0054	0.175	0.099	0.245	0.178
Milk & its products	-0.0022	-0.0015	-0.0026	-0.0034	-0.025	-0.016	-0.114	-0.064
Edible oil & fats	0.0021	0.0033	0.0056	-0.0028	0.047	0.077	0.157	-0.074
Meat, fish & egg	-0.0044	-0.0036	-0.0023	-0.0034	-0.131	-0.109	-0.085	-0.073
Other food items	0.0086	0.0078	0.0040	0.0093	0.051	0.044	0.024	0.048
Fuel & light	-0.0038	-0.0056	0.0060	0.0092	-0.049	-0.075	0.068	0.119
Clothing	-0.0052	-0.0068	-0.0066	-0.0032	-0.081	-0.116	-0.103	-0.051
Other non-food items	-0.0090	0.0076	-0.0206	-0.0161	-0.036	0.021	-0.109	-0.052

Note: Computed from the grouped consumer expenditure data collected from 42nd to 61st round NSSO Reports.

estimated from AIDS-1 model is that most of the coefficients are relatively much smaller in magnitude than the income and price coefficients. The size coefficients for most of the food items are positive exhibiting economies of scale and most of non-food items are negative indicating the operation of diseconomies of scale. It is observed that different food items except other food item (in both the sectors); milk and its products and meat, fish and egg (only in the rural sector) exhibit economies of scale while different non-food items except clothing (in both the sectors of India) exhibit diseconomies of scale.

Like size coefficient, the negative size elasticity shows the operation of diseconomies of scale and positive elasticities indicate the operation of economies of scale in household consumption which has a direct bearing on the demand for different commodities. On the other hand, the absolute value of size elasticities shows a definite rural-urban pattern for most of the food items and no such pattern for various non-food items. The magnitude of these elasticities is less than unity in both the sectors of the state and country. The absolute values of these elasticities in rural areas for most of the food items except edible oil and meat, fish and egg are higher than urban areas of the state as well as the country. Similar pattern is also observed for other non-food items. But no such definite pattern is observed for fuel and light and clothing.

The effect of changes in household size on demand pattern can be known by comparing AIDS-1 and AIDS-2. At the all India level, increase in household size, ceteris paribus, seems to decrease the money income allocated to cereals and its substitutes at the margin, implying economies of scale. The opposite namely diseconomies of scale seems to happen in case of non-food items. The direction of change for most of the delicious food items like milk and its products and meat, fish and egg is similar like non-food items. Milk and its products; meat, fish & egg; other non-food items and clothing are probably given lesser priority by rural households compared to cereals & its substitutes and pulses its products in event of increase in household size. By virtue of budget constraint, every household reduce expenditure on some items in order to buy more of other items. For rural households, addition of an extra member to the family causes reduction in per capita expenditure on milk and its products, meat, fish and egg, clothing and other non-food items. The money so saved is spent on cereals and its substitutes, pulses and its products, edible oil and other food items. The magnitude of this effect may decline with the rise in income.

TESTS OF HYPOTHESES

Flexible models like the AIDS permit us to test the empirical validity of neo-classical and other 'a priori' restrictions by comparing a restricted model with an unrestricted one. The statistical test of different hypothesis can be done in various ways. One can use the likelihood ratio test based on the concentrated log likelihood function which is computed for each estimated model. Another way is to compare the item-wise residual sum squares of the unrestricted model with the restricted model using F-statistic. In this section, we have used the latter method to test different hypothesis formulated on the basis of different restrictions imposed on AIDS model (AIDS-2).

In any complete demand system, due to the budget constraint, only (n-1) equations, *n* being the number of commodities in the model are estimated and the parameters in the deleted equation are estimated using the implied restrictions. In the AIDS model, budget constraint implies (n+2) restrictions. Therefore, for the model without constraints, the number of independent parameters is (n-1)(n+2). Under homogeneity, another (n-1) restrictions are imposed and therefore the number of independent parameters is reduced to (n-1)(n+1). There will be (n-1)(n-2)/2 symmetry restrictions which will further reduce the number of independent parameters under homogeneity and symmetry to (n-1)(n+4)/2. Thus, the hypotheses, homogeneity and both homogeneity & symmetry are nested to the unconstrained model. However, a priori restrictions like 'no cross-price effects' and explicit additivity (no price effects) are not nested. The 'no cross price effect' restriction forces all cross-prices (γ_{ij}) to zero. Hence, intercept, own-price and income coefficients are estimated in each equation. So there are only 3(n-1) independent parameters under this hypothesis. On the other hand, explicit additivity forces all price coefficients to zero. Therefore, only intercept and income coefficients are estimated in each equation and hence there are only 2(n-1) independent parameters under this hypothesis. Thus, the number of parameters to be estimated declines as we move from unconstrained model to different constrained models in a sequence from AIDS2 to AIDS6.

The empirical validity of the different hypotheses formulated viz., no household size effect, homogeneity, homogeneity and symmetry, 'no cross-price effects' and explicit additivity has been tested in this section using the F-statistic[25]. As expected, the F-values show almost a rising trend as we move from a less restrictive model to a more restrictive one. The F-test can be applied to verify the empirical validity of a more restrictive null hypothesis against a less restrictive alternative. The F-values along with the theoretical (critical) values of F-statistic at 1 and 5 per cent level of significance (in the two bottom rows) and the numerator and denominator degrees of freedom in the parenthesis (in the second row) are given in *Table-27.* If the calculated value of F-statistic exceeds the corresponding theoretical value, we reject the null hypothesis (more restrictive model) in favour of the less restrictive alternative at the chosen level of significance. In the reverse case, we do not reject the null hypothesis.

The empirical validity of the first null hypothesis of no economic and diseconomies of scale from household size (i.e. $\theta_i = 0$) as implied from AIDS-2 has been tested against AIDS-1 (with $\theta_i \neq 0$) as the maintained hypothesis. The F_1-statistic has been estimated from the error sum of squares and the degrees of freedom associated with AIDS-1 and AIDS-2 and the results are quoted in the 2nd and 8th columns of *Table 27* separately for the rural and urban sectors of Orissa and all India. The results reveal the acceptance of the null hypothesis for all food and non-food items in the rural and urban sectors of the state and the country. It clearly indicates the less relevance of including

Table 27

Testing of restrictions in different formulations of LA\AIDS Model for Nine Commodity Groups: Orissa and all-India

	AIDS-1 vs AIDS-2	AIDS-2 vs AIDS-3	AIDS-2 vs AIDS-4	AIDS-3 Vs AIDS-4	AIDS-2 vs AIDS-5	AIDS-2 vs AIDS-6	AIDS-1 vs AIDS-2	AIDS-2 vs AIDS-3	AIDS-2 vs AIDS-4	AIDS-3 Vs AIDS-4	AIDS-2 vs AIDS-5	AIDS-2 vs AIDS-6
	F_1 (1,6)	F_2 (1, 7)	F_3 (2,7)	F_4 (1,8)	F_5 (8,7)	F_6 (9,7)	F_1 (1,6)	F_2 (1, 7)	F_3 (2,7)	F_4 (1,8)	F_5 (8,7)	F_6 (9,7)
Commodity Group			*Rural India*						*Urban India*			
Cereals & its substitutes	4.0061	7.5817	8.7227	5.1283	9.5817	10.7227	3.0025	5.6721	5.8611	5.0126	7.8405	8.4135
Pulses & its products	3.2584	6.1856	7.8524	4.2978	8.9856	9.3524	4.0033	7.3829	7.7149	4.6204	8.9074	10.8787
Milk & its Products	4.3632	5.9439	7.0467	4.6516	7.6039	8.6367	3.0065	5.9362	6.3458	4.8190	5.8505	7.3328
Edible oil & Fats	2.0550	3.4031	3.6367	3.9637	3.1631	2.6467	2.7013	2.8919	3.5503	3.7106	2.4192	2.7859
Meat, Fish & Egg	4.2192	4.8715	5.1702	5.6134	5.7247	5.8702	3.0076	7.0119	7.7109	5.1180	8.2872	8.8556
Other Food Items	2.3621	3.6481	4.8530	5.0304	5.8481	6.1530	3.0158	9.1409	9.8964	3.0188	10.7680	11.9523
Fuel & Light	4.4025	6.2207	7.7574	4.3597	8.2207	8.7574	4.1244	11.1799	12.0920	5.1082	12.4836	14.0307
Clothing	5.0627	5.7282	6.6210	4.7396	3.7982	3.9210	4.2368	4.7218	5.7673	4.2714	6.9492	7.3453
Other Nonfood Items	3.7833	8.0045	9.1786	5.2749	9.7645	10.5427	5.6797	22.7659	24.5414	5.2936	25.0924	26.5647
Commodity Group			*Rural Orissa*						*Urban Orissa*			
Cereals & its substitutes	4.7193	6.4447	7.0167	4.0553	7.4447	7.8167	3.0236	5.7559	6.0780	4.8726	6.6513	7.4333
Pulses & its products	3.4737	5.7766	6.1210	4.8366	6.4166	7.3210	2.0296	5.8136	5.9542	3.1724	6.2377	6.8239
Milk & its Products	3.0242	6.0018	6.7934	3.6913	7.0018	8.7934	2.0470	6.6030	7.9089	3.1241	8.5132	9.2446
Edible oil & Fats	1.2868	1.9845	2.3040	3.0976	3.8545	4.2840	1.7765	1.9924	3.3045	2.1071	3.8406	4.1457
Meat, Fish & Egg	3.3360	5.6492	5.7659	5.9824	6.1499	6.9124	5.3055	7.0295	8.6590	4.3922	5.7427	5.2372
Other Food Items	3.0181	3.7790	4.9120	3.6642	2.1792	2.9859	4.1753	5.6517	5.8875	5.0917	2.7619	2.9256
Fuel & Light	4.0918	5.8737	6.5291	5.0083	6.5737	6.9291	4.0898	6.3359	7.8929	3.8675	8.9804	9.4633
Clothing	2.2783	5.4480	5.8127	4.8128	6.2280	8.2027	3.1175	5.0426	6.5126	4.5171	4.3626	5.9257
Other Nonfood Items	2.9338	8.8506	10.2014	5.1213	9.8506	10.3137	4.1818	8.2202	8.8382	5.1843	9.8155	10.3418
F-VALUE (5% level of sign.)	5.99	5.59	4.25	5.32	3.73	3.08	5.99	5.59	4.74	5.32	3.73	3.08
F-VALUE (1% level of sign.)	13.70	12.20	9.55	11.30	6.84	6.72	13.70	12.20	12.20	9.55	11.30	6.84

Note: Computed from the grouped consumer expenditure data collected from 42nd to 61st round NSSO Reports.

average household size as an explanatory variable in the simple AIDS model (AIDS-2).

The empirical validity of the second null hypothesis of homogeneity i.e. absence of money illusion ($\sum_j r_{ij} = 0$) has been tested with AIDS-3 (homogeneity imposed) as against AIDS-2 (without homogeneity i.e. $\sum_j r_{ij} \neq 0$) as the maintained hypothesis. To test this hypothesis, F_2-statistic is estimated from the error sum of squares from AIDS-2 and AIDS-3 models and the results are given in 3rd and 9th columns of the above table. The results indicate the rejection of this null hypothesis for most of the food and non-food items with the exception of edible oil and other food item in rural sector and edible oil and clothing in the urban sector of Orissa and India.

The empirical validity of the third null hypothesis of both homogeneity and symmetry i.e. absence of money illusion along with symmetry of cross-substitution effects of the Slutsky substitution matrixis ($\sum r_{ij} = 0$ and $r_{ij} = r_{ji}$) is tested using AIDS-4 against AIDS-2 (without homogeneity and symmetry) as the maintained hypothesis. To test this hypothesis, the F_4-statistic is estimated using the error sum of squares of AIDS-2 and AIDS-4 and the results are presented in 4th and 10th columns of *Table 27* separately for the rural and urban sectors of Orissa and all India. The results clearly indicate the rejection of this hypothesis for all food and non-food items except edible oil in both the sectors of Orissa and India.

The empirical validity of the fourth null hypothesis with both homogeneity and symmetry imposed as implied by AIDS-4 model is tested against AIDS-3 model (with only homogeneity imposed) as the maintained hypothesis. Otherwise, this hypothesis is meant to test symmetry against homogeneity. The F_4-statistic is estimated using error sum of squares of AIDS-3 and AIDS-4 with AIDS-3 as the maintained hypothesis and the results are noted in the 5th and 11th columns of the table separately for the rural and urban sectors of the state and the country. The results reveal the acceptance of this hypothesis for all food and non-food items in both the sectors of Orissa and all India.

The empirical validity of the fifth null hypothesis with no cross price effects ($\gamma_{ij} = 0, i \neq j$) as implied by AIDS-5 is tested against AIDS-2 with all price effects are non-zero ($\gamma_{ij} \neq 0$) as the maintained hypothesis. To test this hypothesis, we have estimated F_5-statistic using the error sum of squares and degrees of freedom associated with AIDS-2 and AIDS-5 and the results are quoted in the 6th and 12th columns of the table separately for the rural and urban sectors of the state and the country. The results reveal the rejection of this hypothesis for all food and non-food items except edible oil in both the sectors of India and except other food item in both the sectors of Orissa. It indicates the relevance of including all other prices as explanatory variables in the simple AIDS model (AIDS-2).

Finally, the empirical validity of the sixth null hypothesis with all price effects are zero ($\gamma_{ij}= 0$) as implied by AIDS-6 model is tested against AIDS-2 with all price effects are non-zero ($\gamma_{ij} \neq 0$) as the maintained hypothesis. To test this null hypothesis, we have estimated the F_6-statistic separately for the rural and urban areas of the state and the country and the results are presented in the 7th and 13th columns of *Table 27*. The results reveal the rejection of this hypothesis for all food and non-food items except edible oil in both the sectors of India and except other food item in both the sectors of Orissa. It indicates the relevance of all prices i.e. own- and cross-prices as explanatory variables in a demand system.

Comparison of homogeneity and symmetry against unrestricted model reveals the rejection of both restrictions for most of the food and non-food items in the rural and urban sectors of Orissa as well as all India. Thus, there seems to be similarity in the behaviour of rural and urban consumers with regard to the validity of neo-classical postulates. Clearly, a priori restrictions like explicit additivity (no price effects) and 'no cross price effects' are too restrictive and rejected at nine commodity level for all food and non-food items except edible oil and other food item in both the sectors when tested against unconstrained model. The validity of homogeneity and symmetry and the rejection of homogeneity postulate in both the sectors of Orissa and India at nine commodity level also reveals that imposition of homogeneity (absence of money illusion) itself seems to cause much damage and Slutsky symmetry may not be a severe restriction.

Thus, neo-classical restrictions are theoretically sound but empirically not valid at broad commodity level for the developing country like India and the backward region like Orissa. All neo-classical as well as a priori hypotheses are rejected in both rural and urban areas conclusively at conventional 5 per cent level of significance using the AIDS model and the observed household expenditure data. This kind of summary rejection of neo-classical hypotheses is not uncommon for India. Similar conclusion has been drawn by Deaton (1974) using another flexible demand model on British data and Ray (1980) using AIDS model on Indian data.

CONCLUSION

The different variants of AIDS model have been estimated using time-series NSS data (mean level per capita monthly expenditures) from 42nd to 61st round (excluding 49th and 60th rounds) at the level of nine commodity classifications separately for rural and urban sectors of Orissa and all India. The retail price data used for estimating the variants of AIDS model is the time-series of consumer price indices for industrial workers and agricultural labourers compiled and released by the Labour Bureau, Ministry of Labour (GoI) separately for Orissa and all India. The variants of AIDS model are estimated by imposing neo-classical restrictions and two 'a priori' restrictions such as 'no cross-price effects' and explicit additivity (no price effects). The unconstrained model along with its demographic specification is also estimated to ascertain the effect of household size on the budget share and the economies and diseconomies of scale exhibited in the consumption of different items which has a direct bearing on the demand for different commodities. The empirical analysis led to the following broad conclusions:

Most of the estimated models show good fit to the sample observations and amply demonstrate the usefulness of the variants AIDS model for quantifying consumer behaviour in

India. The models seem to perform better for urban data as compared to rural data. The performance of AIDS model also varied across model specifications, across rural-urban sectors and also across commodities. Imposition of neo-classical restrictions leads to decline in $\bar{R}^2$ value. The reduction in $\bar{R}^2$ varied as we move from an unconstrained model to an explicitly additive model. Homogeneity restrictions seem to cause less reduction in $\bar{R}^2$ compared to homogeneity and symmetry, 'no cross-price effects' and 'explicit additivity' at nine commodity levels. The effect of explicit additivity seems to be the largest. We notice a trade-off between theoretical consistency and statistical goodness of fit. Neo-classical restrictions may be desirable on theoretical grounds, but these are less acceptable statistically. However, as expected, precision of estimates increased with the imposition of restrictions.

The results indicate a high frequency of significant income and size response coefficients but a moderate frequency of significant price response coefficients in different demand equations. Most of the income and size coefficients are statically significant at 5 per cent level of significance. But a large number of own-price and cross-price coefficients are not statically significant which may be due to overwhelming income rather than price information contained in the budget data. Despite this, inclusion of all price variables in the demand system is quite justified because 67 percent of own-price coefficients and 43 percent of cross-price coefficients are found to be statistically significant in all model specifications in both the sectors of the state and the country. Due to highly aggregated nature of commodity groups, many cross-price effects are not significant.

The impact of neo-classical restrictions on income coefficients is some what moderate and the coefficients exhibit a systematic pattern across model specifications. The absolute values increased for some items and decreased for others as we move from unconstrained model to more restrictive models like 'no price effects' and explicit additivity. Thus, the neo-classical restrictions change the degree of necessity/luxuries and in some case the nature of the item itself. Fuel and light which is a necessity item in most of variants of AIDS model changes into luxury item with the imposition of explicit additivity in rural Orissa. However, imposition of these restrictions reveals that all food items remained as necessity items while most of non-food items except edible oil seem to be luxury items. These results seem to be consistent with the backward region like Orissa and the developing country like India. Neo-classical restrictions also seem to increase the importance of commodities with larger budget and reduce that of minor items.

Generally, the proportion of statistically significant own-price and cross-price coefficients is larger for disaggregated than aggregated models. This result is in conformity with the common belief that there will be higher price response for disaggregated commodities. With commodity aggregation some valuable price information may be smoothened or lost resulting in less price variability and thereby insignificant coefficients. As expected, the effects of neo-classical restrictions on price coefficients are quite strong and vary across model specifications and also in the rural and urban sectors. Price coefficients do not exhibit any systematic pattern across model specifications. Among the cross-price effects, those relating to food items especially cereals and its substitutes; milk and its products and other food item are prominent. The prices of these items will exert decisive negative influence on the demand for non-food items as well.

The estimated income elasticities are quite plausible for most of the commodities in all model specifications. There are sectoral variations both in their magnitude as well as pattern across model specifications. The estimates are not very sensitive to the level of commodity aggregation. Income elasticities exhibit a pattern similar to that of income coefficients. It is found that income elasticities are less than unity for all food items and hence, different food items are necessity items and greater than unity for clothing and other non-food items indicating their luxury nature. It is also noticed that rural elasticities are greater than urban elasticities for most of the food items except milk and its products. This pattern is reversed for various non-food items except fuel and light across different model specifications. Unlike in rural areas, the income elasticities for urban India do not exhibit any systematic pattern as we move from unconstrained model to more restrictive models like 'no price effects' and explicit additivity.

The estimated rural and urban income elasticities for some items do not follow the expected pattern viz. the income elasticities of demand for necessity items like food found to be higher in rural areas (under-developed region) compared to that of urban area (developed region). The high income elasticity for meat, egg, fish in rural areas (between 0.703 – 0.923) compared to urban areas (between 0.731-0.848) is some what puzzling. These exceptions may be due to aggregation of data over commodities. Instead of mean level data, expenditure class-wise data may provide more convincing results.

The price elasticities are quite sensitive to model specification. The estimates do not show any violation of convexity conditions. It is interesting to note that most of the commodities are price inelastic under different model specifications, more so in urban areas. Food items are generally part of this group, with the exception of meat, egg and fish in urban Orissa. Clothing and other non-food items are price elastic in the rural areas but price inelastic in urban areas whereas fuel and light is price inelastic in both the sectors of Orissa and all India. Neo-classical restrictions of homogeneity and symmetry seem to reduce (increase) the own-price elasticities when demand is inelastic (elastic) with some exceptions. Thus, restrictive models may under (over) estimate own-price elasticity of inelastic (elastic) commodities. The flexibility of the AIDS model has adverse effect on the erratic cross-price responses.

Like size coefficient, the negative size elasticity shows the operation of diseconomies of scale and positive elasticities indicate the operation of economies of scale in household consumption which has a direct bearing on the demand for different commodities. On the other hand, the absolute values of size elasticities show a definite rural-urban pattern for most of the food items and no such pattern is observed for various non-food items. The magnitude of these elasticities is small but less than unity in both the sectors of the state and country. The absolute values of these elasticities in rural areas for most of the food items except edible oil and meat, fish and egg are higher than urban areas of the state as well as the country. Similar pattern is also observed for other non-food items. But no such definite pattern is observed for fuel and light and clothing.

Using the F-test, the neo-classical hypotheses like homogeneity and symmetry and 'a priori' restrictions like 'no cross-price effects' (absence of other price variables in the demand functions) and explicitly additivity (absence of all price variables in the demand functions) are tested for their empirical validity. At the level of nine commodity aggregation, homogeneity and both homogeneity & symmetry seem to be empirically invalid for most of the food and non-food items with exception of edible oil and other food item in the rural sector and edible oil and clothing in the urban sector of Orissa and all-India. Likewise, when homogeneity is taken as a maintained hypothesis, symmetry could not be rejected for all the food and non-food items in both the sectors of Orissa and India. But the restrictive hypotheses such as 'no cross-price effects' and 'explicitly additivity' are rejected for most of the food and non-food items except edible oil in both the sector of all India and other food items in both the sectors of Orissa. Thus, neo-classical hypotheses may be theoretically desirable but their empirical validity is frequently in doubt. These results are in conformity with the earlier studies using the AIDS model and also for other flexible demand models.

NOTES

1. See Martinez-Garcia (2005) for a proof of this result and a detailed explanation of the properties of this class of cost/expenditure functions.
2. A demand system is said to flexible if it is capable of providing a second order approximation to an unknown preference structure at the point of price- expenditure space.
3. For AIDS and LA\AIDS refer the studies of Deaton and Muellbauer (1980) Blanciforte and Green (1983), Buse (1994), Alston, Foster and green

(1994), Lewbel (1985) and Asche and Wessells (1997). For QAIDS refer the studies of Blundell, Pashardes and Weber (1993); Dickens, Fry and Pashardes (1993) and Meenakshi and Ray (1999) and Alston, Chalfant and Piggott (2001). For GAIDS refer the studies of Bollino (1987); Bollino and Violi (1990) and Pollak and Wales (1992). For GQAIDS see Banks, Blundell and Lewbel (1992); Ray (1996); and Meenakshi and Ray (1999). For EQAIDS see Banks, Blundell and Lewbel (1992); Ray (1996) and Meenakshi and Ray (1999). For DAIDS see Pollak (1970); Blanciforte and Green (1983); Alessi and Kapteyn (1991) and Heien and Durham (1991).

4. For details refer Blundell et al. (1993); Meenakshi and Ray (1999); Banks et al. (1992); Dickens et al. (1993) and Murty (2005).
5. For details refer the studies of Blundell et al. (1999); Bollino (1987); and Bollino and Violi (1990).
6. In a series of articles, Lewbel (1987, 1991, and 1995) has extended the Gorman's concept of 'rank' of an Engel curve to any demand system. He has introduced the idea of a fractional demand systems expressed in budget share form. According to this approach, the rank of any demand system is defined as the minimum number of function in income (including the constant term) required such that all of the Engel curves can be expressed as linear combination of these income functions. The rank of a demand function is also equal to the minimum number of functions in prices required to express the cost or indirect utility function. Based on these definitions, the LES and its variants and AIDS have rank two and the quadratic extensions of the LES and AIDS have rank three. Rank three demand systems are supposed to extract all the information available in budget data.
7. For details refer Blanciforte and Green (1983); Alessi and Kapteyn (1991) and Heien and Durham (1991).
8. Interpretation of $a(q)$ and $b(q)$ are analogous to those of $a(p)$ and $b(p)$ for the AIDS model. If utility is scaled such that $0 \leq u \leq 1$, then $a(q)$ gives the value by which q must be divided to reach subsistence ($u = 0$) and $b(q)$ is the value by which q must be divided to achieve bliss ($u = 1$).
9. As per Shephard's lemma, the price derivatives of the cost function are the quantities demanded i.e. $\delta c(u, p)/\delta p_i = q_i$; multiply both sides of this equation by $p_i / c(u, p)$ will provide $\delta \log c(u, p)/\delta \log p_i = p_i q_i / c(u, p) = p_i q_i / y = w_i$.
10. See for details Deaton and Muellbauer (1999 reprint)
11. See Deaton and Muellbauer (1980) and Blanciforte and Green (1983).
12. See Pollak and Wales (1992), pp.70 and also Alston, Chalfant and Piggott pp.75.
13. The two versions of the model are equivalent only if the scale factor π_i does not vary across the goods, so that $\pi_i = \pi$ for all 'i' which implies that $\lambda'\bar{\pi} = 0$ since, $\iota'\lambda = 0$ for adding-up.
14. Pollak and Wales (1992) have used the concept of demographic scaling while incorporating demographic variables in LES.
15. The more appealing approach from an empirical view is that using

GAIDS and allowing its committed quantities to be linear function of demand shift variable. This approach allows the demand shifter to be included in a fashion that is flexible, parsimonious and maintains the models invariance to changes in units of measurement.

16. For the implication of different price indices in AIDS refer the study of Asche and Wessells (1997) and Pashardes (1993).
17. Deaton and Muellbauer (1980) with British data have found that the parameter estimates did not very much between the non-linear and the linear version of AIDS (i.e. LA\AIDS). Pashardes (1993) argued that Stone's approximation of the price index leads to bias in parameter estimates of AIDS. The bias will be more serious for micro-level data than the aggregate time series data like ours.
18. The use of family size, *'m'* as deflator for *'Y'* follows Houthakker (1957), Weisskoff (1971), Sener (1977), Ray(1980) and Murty (2005).
19. See Ray (1980) for details.
20. For example, η_{i0} is the change in the average quantity demanded per unit change in average expenditure with no change in other distributional aspects.
21. The adding-up constraints (6.2.11b) will be automatically satisfied by these estimates by virtue of data construction, hence needs no testing.
22. For details see Deaton, 1975, pp. 46-69.
23. The parameter, α_0 can be interpreted as the outlay required for a minimal standard of living when prices are unity. So choosing a plausible value for the parameter α_0 is not difficult.
24. Earlier applications of this model to Indian data include Ray (1980, 1982); Majumder (1986); Ravi (1989); Murty (1997, 1999 & 2005); Radhakrishna and Ravi (1992); Meenakshi (1996); Meenakshi and Ray (1999); and Radhakrishna and Murty (1999).
25. One of the appropriate statistics for the joint test on several regression coefficients is the F-test on residual sum of squares. The F-statistic is as follows:

$$F = \frac{\left(ESS_R - ESS_{UR}\right)/p}{ESS_{UR}/(N-k)}$$

where ESS_R is the error sum of squares of the restricted model, ESS_{UR} is the error sum of squares of the unrestricted model, p and $(N\text{-}K)$ are the numerator and denominator degrees of freedom of the F-statistic. The numerator degrees of freedom of the F-statistic is the difference in the number of parameters of the two models-unrestricted and restricted, which is also equal to the number of additional restrictions. The denominator degree of freedom of the F-statistic is the difference between the number of observations and the number of parameters of the unrestricted model (for details see Pindyck and Rubinfeld, 1998, pp. 128-30).

APPENDIX-A

Consider the change in the units of measurement for quantities, using $\tilde{q}_i = q_i\pi_i$ *and* $\tilde{p}_i = p_i/\pi_i$ $(\pi_i > 0)$. Let us substitute $\hat{p}$ with $(\hat{p}-\hat{\pi})$ [where $\hat{\pi}_i = \ln\pi_i$] in the share equations (without 'Z') i.e. $w=\alpha+\Gamma\hat{p}+\beta\ \ln(y/P)$ which become

$$w=\tilde{\alpha}+\tilde{\Gamma}(\hat{p}-\hat{\pi})+\tilde{\beta}\ \ln(y/\tilde{P}) \tag{6.1}$$

where $In\ (P)=\alpha_0+\alpha'\hat{p}+(1/2)\hat{p}'\,\Gamma\,\hat{p}$ (6.2)

Substituting (6.2) into (6.1) and then $\hat{p}$ with $(\hat{p}-\hat{\pi})$, the equation (6.1) is rewritten as

$$w=\tilde{\alpha}+\tilde{\Gamma}(\hat{p}-\hat{\pi})+\tilde{\beta}\ \ln(y)-\tilde{\beta}\left(\tilde{\alpha}_0+\tilde{\alpha}'(\hat{p}-\hat{\pi})+(1/2)(\hat{p}-\hat{\pi})'\,\tilde{\Gamma}(\hat{p}-\hat{\pi})\right)$$

$$=\tilde{\alpha}-\tilde{\Gamma}\hat{\pi}+\tilde{\Gamma}\hat{p}+\tilde{\beta}\ \ln(y)-\tilde{\beta}\left(\tilde{\alpha}_0-\tilde{\alpha}'\hat{\pi}+(1/2)\hat{\pi}'\tilde{\Gamma}\hat{\pi}+\tilde{\alpha}'\hat{p}+(1/2)\hat{p}'\tilde{\Gamma}\hat{p}-\hat{\pi}'\tilde{\Gamma}\hat{p}\right)$$

$$=\tilde{\alpha}-\tilde{\Gamma}\hat{\pi}+\tilde{\Gamma}\hat{p}+\tilde{\beta}\ \ln(y)-\tilde{\beta}\left(\tilde{\alpha}_0-\tilde{\alpha}'\hat{\pi}+(1/2)\,\hat{\pi}'\,\tilde{\Gamma}\hat{\pi}+\left(\tilde{\alpha}-\tilde{\Gamma}\hat{\pi}\right)'\hat{p}+(1/2)\,\hat{p}'\tilde{\Gamma}\hat{p}\right)$$

$$=\alpha+\Gamma\hat{p}+\beta\ \ln(y)-\beta\left(\alpha_0+\alpha'\hat{p}+(1/2)\,\hat{p}'\Gamma\,\hat{p}\right), \tag{6.3}$$

provided that $\alpha=\tilde{\alpha}-\tilde{\Gamma}\hat{\pi}$ and $\alpha_0=\tilde{\alpha}_0-\tilde{\alpha}'\hat{\pi}+(1/2)\hat{\pi}'\Gamma\hat{\pi}$. Hence, rescaling leaves $\tilde{\Gamma}=\Gamma$ and $\tilde{\beta}=\beta$, and α and α_0 adjust to changes in units of measurement, a familiar result when constants are added to regressors. Predicted shares, elasticities, and welfare measures are, thus, invariant to such scaling choices.

The same invariance is not achieved when a similar rescaling is done in the augmented demand system such as

$$w=\alpha^*+\lambda Z+\Gamma\hat{p}+\beta\ \ln(y)-\beta\left(\alpha_0+\left(\alpha^*+\lambda\ Z\right)'\hat{p}+(1/2)\,\hat{p}'\Gamma\,\hat{p}\right) \tag{6.4a}$$

Substituting $\hat{p}$ with $(\hat{p}-\hat{\pi})$ in the above augmented demand system, it becomes

$$w = \tilde{\alpha}^* + \tilde{\lambda} Z + \tilde{\Gamma}(\hat{p} - \hat{\pi}) + \tilde{\beta}\ln(y)$$
$$-\tilde{\beta}\left(\tilde{\alpha}_0 + \tilde{\alpha}^*(\hat{p} - \hat{\pi}) + Z\tilde{\lambda}'(\hat{p} - \hat{\pi}) + (1/2)(\hat{p} - \hat{\pi})'\tilde{\Gamma}(\hat{p} - \hat{\pi})\right) \tag{6.4b}$$

Collecting the terms that involve $\hat{\pi}$ and then simplifying, the above the share equations become

$$w = \bar{\alpha}^* + \tilde{\lambda} Z + \tilde{\Gamma}\hat{p} + \tilde{\beta}\ln(y) - \tilde{\beta}\left(\bar{\alpha}_0 + \left(\bar{\alpha}^* + \tilde{\lambda} Z\right)'\hat{p} + (1/2)\,\hat{p}'\tilde{\Gamma}\hat{p}\right) \tag{6.5}$$

where,.

$$\bar{\alpha}^* = \tilde{\alpha}^* - \tilde{\Gamma}\hat{\pi} \text{ and } \bar{\alpha}_0 = \tilde{\alpha}_0 - \tilde{\alpha}^{*\prime}\hat{\pi} + (1/2)\hat{\pi}'\tilde{\Gamma}\hat{\pi} - Z\tilde{\lambda}'\hat{\pi}$$

Note that since $\bar{\alpha}_0$ is not constant and the term, $Z\tilde{\lambda}'\hat{\pi}$ varies across the data, so the model (6.5) with the prices rescaled is not equivalent to the original model. As a result, the parameters Γ, β and λ are affected by the scaling, and hence, the price and income elasticities and consumer welfare measures now depend on the units chosen for measuring quantities. This implies that any empirical results from an Almost Ideal Demand System augmented in this way are conditioned on some choice of quantity units.

Appendix Table 1
Uncompensatory Own-price, Cross-price, Income and Size Elasticities Estimated from LA\AIDS Model with Demographic Specification (AIDS-1): All-India

Commodity Group	Cereals & its substitutes	Pulses & its products	Milk & its Products	Edible oil & Fats	Meat, Fish & Egg	Other Food	Fuel & Light	Clothing	Other Non-food	Income Elasticity	H-Size Elasticity
Rural India											
Cereals & its substitutes	-0.7459	0.4416	-0.0354	0.1753	-0.1496	-1.2338	-0.0624	-0.1378	0.1370	0.5808	0.032
Pulses & its products	0.2810	-0.5539	-0.9192	0.3869	1.3719	0.3399	-0.2150	-0.6425	-0.0883	0.6209	0.175
Milk & its Products	-0.2861	-0.3296	-1.0313	0.3208	1.0270	0.8560	-0.6214	-0.1708	-0.1791	0.9530	-0.025
Edible oil & Fats	-0.2231	3.1676	1.5478	-0.3342	3.3231	-5.3849	-1.1011	-0.3197	-0.8124	0.7319	0.047
Meat, Fish & Egg	-1.0575	0.6631	-0.5763	0.3984	-0.7835	0.7080	-0.3638	-0.9980	-0.2201	0.8375	-0.131
Other Food Items	-0.6019	0.4286	-0.7670	0.4582	1.1058	-0.6837	-0.1450	-1.0220	-0.6275	0.8880	0.051
Fuel & Light	-1.2951	1.6544	-0.1564	0.4822	2.0748	0.2155	-0.5551	-1.0119	-0.6642	0.7288	-0.049
Clothing	2.0198	-4.4796	-0.3928	-2.5265	-6.7507	6.0530	1.3009	-1.0887	2.9523	1.3320	-0.081
Other Nonfood Items	1.0621	-0.5148	0.8124	-0.4240	-0.7852	-0.3475	0.5043	0.7837	-1.2320	1.6036	-0.036
Urban India											
Cereals & its substitutes	-0.6554	-0.5008	0.0717	-0.4863	-0.1919	0.2741	-0.5406	0.6412	-0.1604	0.5261	-0.031
Pulses & its products	0.0107	-0.5219	-0.0229	0.1521	-0.2162	0.1655	-0.6414	-0.2800	-0.0820	0.5718	0.099
Milk & its Products	-0.4522	-0.5267	-0.7177	-0.1512	0.1614	0.4731	-0.2263	0.6149	-0.6709	0.9860	-0.016
Edible oil & Fats	-0.8274	-0.4740	0.3620	-0.5952	-0.3459	0.5565	0.1111	-0.3924	-0.7169	0.7206	0.077
Meat, Fish & Egg	0.5229	0.2280	-0.0017	-0.4437	-0.9652	0.0364	0.3775	-0.8660	-1.0835	0.7827	-0.109
Other Food Items	-0.4806	-0.4031	-0.0249	0.2350	-0.2858	-0.9935	-0.7120	0.2495	0.8333	0.8360	0.044
Fuel & Light	0.2222	0.4214	-0.0253	0.0325	0.0274	-0.1177	-0.8221	-0.6749	0.3912	0.7430	-0.075
Clothing	1.8808	1.4226	-0.2959	-1.1985	0.8347	-0.4822	1.2573	-1.4276	-2.2997	1.3608	-0.116
Other Nonfood Items	0.0362	0.2487	0.0036	0.2576	0.0853	-0.2033	0.2402	-0.0453	-0.6580	2.0511	0.021

Note: Uncompensatory Own and Cross-price Elasticities With Respect to Price of the column commodity groups.

Note: Computed from the grouped consumer expenditure data collected from 42nd to 61st round NSSO Reports. H.Size - Household Size

Appendix Table 2

Uncompensatory Own-price, Cross-price, Income and Size Elasticities Estimated from LA\AIDS Model with Demographic Specification (AIDS-1): All-Orissa

Commodity Group	Cereals & its substitutes	Pulses & its products	Milk & its Products	Edible oil & Fats	Meat, Fish & Egg	Other Food	Fuel & Light	Clothing	Other Non-food	Income Elasticity	H-Size Elasticity
Rural Orissa											
Cereals & its substitutes	-0.6125	-0.4138	1.9157	-0.9103	-0.4923	-0.5302	0.2743	0.4967	-0.0858	0.6233	0.075
Pulses & its products	2.7708	-0.8303	-2.7505	1.4163	2.1028	1.4194	-0.2918	1.7855	-0.6116	0.6842	0.245
Milk & its Products	-2.6155	-1.2454	-0.7274	1.9040	1.7205	-1.7901	-1.8845	-0.9802	0.3235	0.8986	-0.114
Edible oil & Fats	1.3659	1.4695	-3.4711	-0.4214	1.7364	0.3056	-1.0018	-0.9528	1.3022	0.7537	0.157
Meat, Fish & Egg	2.1204	1.3152	0.4737	-1.9301	-0.6711	1.5462	-0.3477	-0.9014	0.4481	0.9231	-0.085
Other Food Items	0.9307	-0.2264	-2.4121	0.2362	1.5790	-0.5755	-0.2429	-0.0662	0.4268	0.8634	0.024
Fuel & Light	-1.7977	1.0712	-2.3991	1.0751	1.8886	-2.5264	-0.5123	-0.7563	0.9448	0.6910	0.068
Clothing	1.2712	-0.6379	1.2905	-1.9124	-2.6590	1.5974	0.1570	-1.1717	-0.6100	1.1854	-0.103
Other Nonfood Items	-0.2007	0.5917	-0.7936	1.1701	-1.5316	1.2904	0.4338	-0.1763	-1.5463	1.3415	-0.109
Urban Orissa											
Cereals & its substitutes	-0.4517	-1.1080	-1.0317	0.4722	1.1311	0.9365	-0.0440	-1.8406	-0.1842	0.5638	0.026
Pulses & its products	0.3437	-0.3023	-0.3324	0.5401	1.7891	-0.8034	-1.3865	-1.3997	-0.0742	0.6561	0.178
Milk & its Products	-1.3334	-1.7899	-0.6965	0.0850	-2.5322	2.5419	-0.5056	0.5302	0.9885	0.9124	-0.064
Edible oil & Fats	0.1517	2.3623	1.3126	-0.2511	1.0534	-1.2365	-0.0936	-1.1894	-0.5619	0.6422	-0.074
Meat, Fish & Egg	0.4254	2.3995	1.3264	0.0559	-0.9640	-2.1138	2.0666	-0.5979	0.0792	0.8125	-0.073
Other Food Items	0.0081	-0.1007	-0.7649	0.7472	1.8008	-0.8901	-0.2590	-1.3353	-0.5750	0.8149	0.048
Fuel & Light	-1.4241	-0.4725	-1.1268	0.4818	1.2865	2.2688	-0.7020	-2.0850	-0.7770	0.7165	0.119
Clothing	-0.4341	0.2444	-0.9247	-0.6433	-1.5335	-0.6590	3.8792	-1.0811	0.8522	1.2674	-0.051
Other Nonfood Items	0.1701	2.9621	1.1716	-0.9571	-2.8914	-0.3723	-0.6019	2.3858	-0.8459	1.5233	-0.052

(Uncompensatory Own and Cross-price Elasticities With Respect to Price of: Cereals through Other Non-food columns.)

Note: Computed from the grouped consumer expenditure data collected from 42nd to 61st round NSSO Reports. H.Size - Household Size

Appendix Table 3
Uncompensatory Own-price, Cross-price and Income Elasticities Estimated from Unrestricted Simple LA\AIDS Model (AIDS-2): All-India

Commodity Group	Cereals & its Substitutes	Pulses & its Products	Milk & its Products	Edible Oil & Fats	Meat, Fish & Egg	Other Food	Fuel & Light	Clothing	Other Non-food	Income Elasticity
	Uncompensatory Own and Cross-price Elasticities With Respect to Price of									
Rural India										
Cereals & its substitutes	-0.7763	0.4127	0.0095	0.1543	-0.1962	-1.2539	-0.0577	-0.1038	0.1493	0.6137
Pulses & its products	0.7190	-0.6814	-0.3088	0.1171	0.7671	0.0978	-0.1406	-0.1848	0.1074	0.6983
Milk & its Products	0.0503	-0.6155	-0.9507	0.1138	0.5628	0.6703	-0.5642	0.1806	-0.0287	0.8726
Edible oil & Fats	-0.3444	3.2713	1.3783	-0.6591	3.4915	-5.3171	-1.1216	-0.4468	-0.8663	0.7206
Meat, Fish & Egg	-0.7225	0.3764	-0.1078	0.1908	-0.7182	0.5209	-0.3072	-0.6467	-0.0712	0.8250
Other Food Items	-0.1678	0.0575	-0.1603	0.1894	0.5034	-0.4916	-0.0715	-0.5669	-0.4344	0.8787
Fuel & Light	-1.1765	1.5542	0.0083	0.4096	1.9120	0.1506	-0.6754	-0.8884	-0.6109	0.6778
Clothing	1.8229	-4.3041	-0.6741	-2.3993	-6.4665	6.1706	1.2687	-1.0709	2.8677	1.2715
Other Nonfood Items	0.5464	-0.0743	0.0920	-0.1051	-0.0702	-0.0603	0.4170	0.2434	-1.2024	1.6323
Urban India										
Cereals & its substitutes	-0.5513	-0.5035	0.0703	-0.4853	-0.1919	0.2760	-0.5442	0.6451	-0.1588	0.5533
Pulses & its products	0.0215	-0.5494	-0.0194	0.1489	-0.2166	0.1588	-0.6318	-0.2915	-0.0889	0.6579
Milk & its Products	-0.4403	-0.5184	-0.7216	-0.1548	0.1610	0.4658	-0.2158	0.6023	-0.6783	0.9465
Edible oil & Fats	-0.4957	-0.2449	0.4721	-0.5608	-0.3552	0.3646	0.4029	-0.7353	-0.9053	0.7170
Meat, Fish & Egg	0.5101	0.2192	-0.0060	-0.4402	-0.9655	0.0433	0.3664	-0.8531	-1.0771	0.7454
Other Food Items	-0.4931	-0.4117	-0.0291	0.2385	-0.2855	-1.0005	-0.7229	0.2622	0.8399	0.7735
Fuel & Light	0.1661	0.3825	-0.0438	0.0487	0.0291	-0.0848	-0.8727	-0.6165	0.4239	0.7222
Clothing	2.1595	1.6150	-0.2033	-1.2776	0.8270	-0.6428	1.5022	-1.4068	-2.4569	1.3887
Other Nonfood Items	-0.0319	0.2016	-0.0190	0.2771	0.0873	-0.1637	0.1803	0.0252	-0.6972	1.9879

Note: Computed from the grouped consumer expenditure data collected from 42nd to 61st round NSSO Reports.

Appendix Table 4
Uncompensatory Own-price, Cross-price and Income Elasticities Estimated from Unrestricted Simple LA\AIDS Model (AIDS-2): All-Orissa

Commodity Group	*Cereals & its Substitutes*	*Pulses & its Products*	*Milk & its Products*	*Edible Oil & Fats*	*Meat, Fish & Egg*	*Other Food*	*Fuel & Light*	*Clothing*	*Other Non-food*	*Income Elasticity*
	Rural India									
	Uncompensatory Own and Cross-price Elasticities With Respect to Price of									
Cereals & its substitutes	-0.6826	-0.4020	2.1519	-1.3343	-0.5676	-0.3985	0.3605	0.4186	-0.1738	0.6317
Pulses & its products	2.7083	-0.7564	-1.2356	0.4932	1.9390	1.7075	-0.1030	1.6157	-0.8015	0.7217
Milk & its Products	-2.6280	-1.2424	-0.7988	1.7737	1.6973	-1.7517	-1.8595	-1.0047	0.2946	0.8612
Edible oil & Fats	1.3040	1.4949	-2.9678	-0.4185	1.5762	0.5870	-0.8175	-1.1190	1.1160	0.7395
Meat, Fish & Egg	2.1432	1.3067	0.3019	-3.6209	-0.7260	1.4508	-0.4101	-0.8442	0.5128	0.8994
Other Food Items	0.9213	-0.2222	-2.3319	0.0925	1.5535	-0.6206	-0.2133	-0.0926	0.3974	0.9129
Fuel & Light	-1.8242	1.0825	-2.1786	0.6800	1.8185	-2.4029	-0.5933	-0.8289	0.8636	0.7228
Clothing	3.3862	-0.6842	1.3679	-1.2565	-2.3651	1.0822	-0.1804	-1.4767	-0.2676	1.1744
Other Nonfood Items	-0.1437	0.5685	-1.2537	1.9956	-1.3851	1.0333	0.2655	-0.0243	-1.7168	1.3693
	Urban Orissa									
Cereals & its substitutes	-0.3801	-1.2969	-0.5096	0.2401	1.0192	0.7119	-0.1792	-1.1273	-0.5479	0.5716
Pulses & its products	0.4410	-0.3905	-0.1192	0.4448	1.6287	-0.8926	-1.3861	-1.1996	-0.0708	0.6786
Milk & its Products	-1.4798	-0.6503	-0.4471	0.1966	-2.3150	1.6457	-0.5204	0.3195	0.9455	0.9083
Edible oil & Fats	-0.5526	2.7352	0.8614	-0.3475	3.8444	-1.0572	-0.3136	-1.2541	-1.1670	0.6320
Meat, Fish & Egg	-1.5642	3.5218	-0.1213	0.7080	-1.2568	-1.5333	1.4794	-1.0000	-1.5379	0.8215
Other Food Items	0.4490	-0.6131	0.2163	0.3087	1.0690	-0.9791	-0.2601	-0.4093	-0.5681	0.7837
Fuel & Light	-1.0952	-0.8564	-0.3908	0.1529	2.7392	1.9605	-0.7034	-1.3891	-0.7739	0.7335
Clothing	-0.3070	-0.1460	-0.0342	-1.0402	-1.9503	-1.0372	3.7582	0.9440	0.5308	1.4380
Other Nonfood Items	0.2258	3.3528	0.1552	-0.5047	-2.5976	0.0633	-0.3755	1.0574	-0.8087	1.4973

Note: Computed from the grouped consumer expenditure data collected from 42nd to 61st round NSSO Reports.

Appendix Table 5
Uncompensatory Own-price, Cross-price and Income Elasticities Estimated from LA\AIDS Model with Homogeneity Restriction (AIDS-3): All-India

Commodity Group	Cereals & its Substitutes	Pulses & its Products	Milk & its Products	Edible Oil & Fats	Meat, Fish & Egg	Other Food	Fuel & Light	Clothing	Other Non-food	Income Elasticity
Rural India										
	Uncompensatory Own and Cross-price Elasticities With Respect to Price of									
Cereals & its substitutes	-0.7022	0.7659	0.4161	0.3537	1.0975	-2.0135	-0.5897	-0.3133	0.0307	0.5956
Pulses & its products	0.7005	-0.6293	0.1506	-0.2993	0.8586	0.0436	-0.1808	-0.2041	0.0932	0.6852
Milk & its Products	0.0893	-0.6695	-0.9205	-0.0893	0.3655	0.7860	-0.4840	0.2109	-0.0128	0.8854
Edible oil & Fats	0.5386	2.0637	0.2725	-0.6387	-0.9439	-2.7085	0.7305	0.3200	-0.3964	0.7485
Meat, Fish & Egg	-0.8175	0.5074	0.2869	0.0207	-0.7038	0.2393	-0.5043	-0.7241	-0.1148	0.8336
Other Food Items	-0.0951	-0.0407	0.0819	-0.2228	0.1410	-0.5205	0.0834	-0.4982	-0.3880	0.8677
Fuel & Light	-0.8071	1.0483	-0.0244	-0.4280	0.0545	1.2428	-0.7813	-0.5704	-0.4182	0.6929
Clothing	0.3940	-2.3578	-0.5459	0.8290	0.6928	1.9562	-1.7450	-1.1298	2.0553	1.3015
Other Nonfood Items	0.8267	-0.4586	-0.4278	-0.2461	-1.4805	0.7688	1.0034	0.4829	-1.2883	1.6349
Urban India										
Cereals & its substitutes	-0.5198	-0.8121	-0.1650	0.0654	-0.2826	0.4722	-0.6709	1.2390	-0.1729	0.5339
Pulses & its products	0.0684	-0.5420	0.5675	-0.0284	-0.3342	0.4140	-0.7967	0.4782	-0.1086	0.6395
Milk & its Products	-0.4277	-0.6680	-0.7216	-0.0032	0.1170	0.5563	-0.2739	0.8925	-0.6756	0.9548
Edible oil & Fats	-0.4277	-0.7902	0.9940	-0.5545	-0.5155	0.7162	0.1754	0.3118	-0.9402	0.7264
Meat, Fish & Egg	0.5928	-0.4341	0.2720	-0.0425	-0.8572	0.4659	0.0929	0.4009	-1.1215	0.7620
Other Food Items	-0.4691	-0.6212	0.4548	-0.0316	-0.3471	-0.8606	-0.8088	0.6655	0.8309	0.7847
Fuel & Light	0.1543	0.5512	-0.0907	-0.0684	0.0787	-0.1846	-0.8582	-0.9446	0.4162	0.7464
Clothing	2.2433	1.0607	-0.6094	-0.2833	0.6642	-0.2710	1.2606	-1.3702	-2.5222	1.4164
Other Nonfood Items	-0.0907	0.6699	-0.2312	0.0055	0.2249	-0.4661	0.3760	-0.8739	-0.6271	1.9661

Note: Computed from the grouped consumer expenditure data collected from 42nd to 61st round NSSO Reports.

Appendix Table 6

Uncompensatory Own-price, Cross-price and Income Elasticities Estimated from LA\AIDS Model with Homogeneity Restriction (AIDS-3): All-Orissa

Commodity Group	Cereals & its Substitutes	Pulses & its Products	Milk & its Products	Edible Oil & Fats	Meat, Fish & Egg	Other Food	Fuel & Light	Clothing	Other Non-food	Income Elasticity
Rural Orissa										
Uncompensatory Own and Cross-price Elasticities With Respect to Price of										
Cereals & its substitutes	-0.6412	-0.2310	-1.6933	1.9174	-1.5847	-0.1692	-0.1617	-0.3876	-0.1400	0.6208
Pulses & its products	2.4226	-0.6330	0.0629	-1.1707	0.7586	1.9652	-0.7116	0.6671	-0.7686	0.6814
Milk & its Products	-2.4780	-1.3919	-0.7220	-2.3301	1.6009	-1.9371	-1.3901	-0.2604	0.2781	0.8767
Edible oil & Fats	1.2271	1.5484	-1.1383	-0.4072	1.2559	0.6568	-0.9827	-1.3766	1.1249	0.7628
Meat, Fish & Egg	2.1894	1.3011	-3.6212	0.2641	-0.6423	1.4378	-0.3972	-0.8314	0.5070	0.9222
Other Food Items	1.0199	-0.2756	0.2018	-2.8785	1.8700	-0.6484	-0.0513	0.1560	0.3858	0.9254
Fuel & Light	-1.7338	1.0380	1.7684	-2.6294	2.0812	-2.4648	-0.6783	-0.6250	0.8529	0.7344
Clothing	1.6054	-0.8085	-1.9985	3.0891	-1.6267	0.9141	0.1983	-0.9892	-0.2933	1.2384
Other Nonfood Items	0.2451	0.3247	2.5151	-3.7841	0.0683	0.7098	1.0129	1.1339	-1.5916	1.3581
Urban Orissa										
Cereals & its substitutes	-0.3671	-1.3701	0.1280	-0.5807	1.5874	0.9400	0.0129	-1.0412	-0.4490	0.5625
Pulses & its products	0.8492	-0.4577	-0.0967	-0.6430	2.3192	0.3570	-0.3788	-0.8251	0.1302	0.6571
Milk & its Products	-2.4757	-3.2875	-0.5178	1.5883	3.3285	2.5913	-2.9811	-0.5928	0.4654	0.9227
Edible oil & Fats	-0.0194	2.0552	0.5440	-0.3821	0.8786	-1.4586	0.9840	-0.7557	-0.8422	0.6836
Meat, Fish & Egg	-1.6671	3.7915	0.8451	0.1266	-1.2367	-1.9439	1.1740	-1.0682	-1.4117	0.8453
Other Food Items	0.6118	-0.8209	0.0927	0.0196	0.1630	-0.9017	0.1363	-0.2570	-0.4690	0.8263
Fuel & Light	-0.8451	-1.1870	-0.1788	-0.7031	1.3350	2.7190	-0.6887	-1.1577	-0.6376	0.7547
Clothing	-1.5335	1.5768	0.5871	1.5879	-0.9504	-1.8316	0.7101	-0.8666	0.0003	1.4523
Other Nonfood Items	0.3404	3.1225	-0.6572	-0.0584	-3.3296	0.4692	-0.0630	1.1476	-0.8463	1.4575

Note: Computed from the grouped consumer expenditure data collected from 42nd to 61st round NSSO Reports.

Appendix Table 7
Uncompensatory Own-price, Cross-price and Income Elasticities Estimated from LA\AIDS Model with Homogeneity & Symmetry Restrictions (AIDS-4): All-India

Commodity Group	Cereals & its Substitutes	Pulses & its Products	Milk & its Products	Edible Oil & Fats	Meat, Fish & Egg	Other Food	Fuel & Light	Clothing	Other Non-food	Income Elasticity
Rural India										
Uncompensatory Own and Cross-price Elasticities With Respect to Price of										
Cereals & its substitutes	-0.6554	0.8077	0.4273	0.3525	1.0860	-2.0386	-0.5774	-0.3340	-0.0179	0.6095
Pulses & its products	0.9180	-0.6752	0.2746	-0.5726	1.1685	-0.1292	-0.2341	-0.4183	-1.0310	0.6927
Milk & its Products	1.2795	0.1130	-0.9063	-0.1120	0.0742	0.1701	-0.2052	0.2908	-1.5326	0.8627
Edible oil & Fats	2.2649	-0.4819	-0.1382	-0.6305	0.5620	0.3510	-0.7860	0.2184	-0.7930	0.7011
Meat, Fish & Egg	1.2106	1.3001	0.2170	0.8293	-0.6830	0.3920	-0.1986	-0.3801	-1.5317	0.8147
Other Food Items	-0.1215	0.0015	-0.0169	-0.0072	0.0117	-0.5093	-0.0359	-0.0319	-0.0387	0.8687
Fuel & Light	-0.1456	0.0034	-0.0363	-0.0159	0.0191	-0.1535	-0.0646	-0.0514	-0.1433	0.6780
Clothing	0.0145	0.0001	0.0026	0.0011	-0.0015	0.0158	0.0079	-0.9956	0.0097	1.2848
Other Nonfood Items	0.0309	-0.0160	-0.0049	-0.0019	-0.0298	0.0569	0.0267	0.0224	-0.9746	1.6487
Urban India										
Cereals & its substitutes	-0.5152	-0.8075	-0.1658	0.0670	-0.2841	0.4780	-0.6700	1.2346	-0.1904	0.5491
Pulses & its products	-1.6520	-0.5345	0.6063	-0.0431	-0.3371	0.4288	-0.8481	0.5281	1.5772	0.6540
Milk & its Products	-0.2236	0.1937	-0.6294	0.1232	0.0045	0.4224	0.1909	0.3032	-1.1318	0.9227
Edible oil & Fats	0.2961	-0.0075	0.3229	-0.5943	-1.0958	1.5128	1.0561	0.0212	-2.2215	0.6910
Meat, Fish & Egg	-1.0360	-0.2734	0.0690	-1.4266	-0.9940	0.9180	0.2285	0.5094	1.9243	0.7548
Other Food Items	0.0672	0.0164	0.0475	0.0257	0.0251	-0.9189	0.0324	0.0242	0.1656	0.7972
Fuel & Light	0.0402	0.0099	0.0336	0.0166	0.0170	0.0547	-0.9734	0.0115	0.1613	0.7358
Clothing	0.0000	0.0007	0.0025	0.0014	0.0012	0.0048	0.0047	-0.9989	0.0210	1.3855
Other Nonfood Items	-0.1572	-0.0302	-0.1206	-0.0571	-0.0527	-0.2147	-0.0780	-0.0715	-0.5819	1.9436

Note: Computed from the grouped consumer expenditure data collected from 42nd to 61st round NSSO Reports.

Appendix Table 8
Uncompensatory Own-price, Cross-price and Income Elasticities Estimated from LA\AIDS Model with Homogeneity & Symmetry Restrictions (AIDS-4): All Orissa

Commodity Group	*Cereals & its Substitutes*	*Pulses & its Products*	*Milk & its Products*	*Edible Oil & Fats*	*Meat, Fish & Egg*	*Other Food*	*Fuel & Light*	*Clothing*	*Other Non-food*	*Income Elasticity*
	Uncompensatory Own and Cross-price Elasticities With Respect to Price of									
					Rural Orissa					
Cereals & its substitutes	-0.3026	-0.2097	-1.5616	3.9558	-1.6005	-0.2158	-0.1909	-0.4016	-0.1206	0.6459
Pulses & its products	-2.1942	-0.6467	1.9581	-1.7607	0.7031	0.9511	-1.1640	0.4790	2.1684	0.7184
Milk & its Products	-2.0763	2.4789	-0.5966	-3.5439	1.4057	-1.7354	-1.2066	-0.6108	1.9705	0.8592
Edible oil & Fats	1.1041	-1.4464	-2.2586	-0.3732	1.4397	0.8146	-1.0432	-0.9120	-3.4309	0.7221
Meat, Fish & Egg	-1.3812	0.5370	2.4908	1.2561	0.5673	0.0096	-1.0122	-0.4167	1.0852	0.8966
Other Food Items	0.5288	0.0453	0.0259	0.0254	0.0489	-0.5954	0.1386	0.0922	0.2547	0.9347
Fuel & Light	0.6383	0.0486	0.0448	0.0244	0.0572	0.2448	-0.8111	0.1071	0.2976	0.6906
Clothing	0.3915	0.0303	0.0284	0.0170	0.0370	0.1533	0.1149	-0.9341	0.1670	1.2260
Other Nonfood Items	0.8229	0.0701	0.1002	-0.0709	0.1100	0.3395	0.2640	0.1505	-1.6695	1.3656
				Urban Orissa						
Cereals & its substitutes	-0.3417	-0.3701	0.0922	-0.5951	1.5702	1.0022	-0.0174	-1.0383	-0.4202	0.5757
Pulses & its products	-2.8833	-0.5675	0.0758	-0.9919	2.7006	0.0478	-0.4157	-1.1151	2.6042	0.6750
Milk & its Products	0.4586	-0.0079	-0.4968	2.4917	-1.1921	-3.2213	0.2176	1.2303	-0.8960	0.9014
Edible oil & Fats	-2.7608	-0.7661	3.5392	-0.3406	2.3220	-1.2417	-0.6033	-0.6736	0.0276	0.6572
Meat, Fish & Egg	1.0389	1.5677	-1.4493	1.8666	-1.2595	-0.3108	-0.3446	-0.6866	-1.5977	0.8480
Other Food Items	0.0270	0.0003	-0.0201	-0.0057	-0.0008	-0.9817	-0.0068	0.0018	-0.0151	0.8554
Fuel & Light	-0.3593	-0.3778	-0.0815	-0.0734	0.1990	-0.3093	-0.7686	-0.1680	-0.4753	0.6463
Clothing	0.2334	0.2400	0.0503	0.0464	-0.1258	0.1936	0.1139	-0.8981	0.2967	1.4359
Other Nonfood Items	0.0401	0.1074	0.0061	0.0084	-0.0843	0.0255	0.0235	0.0368	-0.9526	1.4661

Note: Computed from the grouped consumer expenditure data collected from 42nd to 61st round NSSO Reports.

Appendix Table 9

Uncompensatory Own-price and Income Elasticities Estimated from LA\AIDS Model with No Cross-price Effects (AIDS-5): All-Orissa and All-India

	Rural India		*Urban India*		*Rural Orissa*		*Urban Orissa*	
	Own-price	*Income*	*Own-price*	*Income*	*Own-price*	*Income*	*Own-price*	*Income*
Commodity Group	η_{ij}	η_{oj}	η_{ij}	η_{oj}	η_{ij}	η_{oj}	η_{ij}	η_{oj}
Cereals & its substitutes	-0.6473	0.5649	-0.5773	0.5145	-0.6497	0.6084	-0.5743	0.5678
Pulses & its products	-0.6585	0.6748	-0.4732	0.5857	-0.7868	0.7169	-0.3714	0.6607
Milk & its Products	-0.9268	0.9358	-0.8132	0.8831	-0.9842	0.9764	-0.5416	0.8297
Edible oil & Fats	-0.6223	0.6906	-0.5104	0.6619	-0.2886	0.6807	-0.3917	0.6172
Meat, Fish & Egg	-0.7489	0.8817	-1.0431	0.7312	-0.4836	0.7946	-1.2465	0.7825
Other Food Items	-0.4603	0.9784	-0.8335	0.9038	-0.7702	0.8963	-1.1750	0.8210
Fuel & Light	-0.7622	0.7291	-1.0530	0.7632	-0.8708	0.7066	-0.6661	0.7339
Clothing	-0.9793	1.4786	-1.0694	1.6306	-0.9280	1.3615	-1.0286	1.5114
Other Nonfood Items	-0.9813	1.5192	-0.6715	2.0120	-1.6157	1.3015	-0.8655	1.4837

Note: Computed from the grouped consumer expenditure data collected from 42nd to 61st round NSSO Reports.

Appendix Table 10
Income Elasticities Estimated from LA\AIDS Model with Explicit Additivity (AIDS-6): All-Orissa and All-India

	Rural India	*Urban India*	*Rural Orissa*	*Urban Orissa*
Commodity Group	η_{oj}	η_{oj}	η_{oj}	η_{oj}
Cereals & its substitutes	0.6217	0.5571	0.6474	0.5987
Pulses & its products	0.7569	0.6768	0.7675	0.6978
Milk & its Products	0.7435	0.8640	0.7849	0.8451
Edible oil & Fats	0.7252	0.6631	0.7353	0.6934
Meat, Fish & Egg	0.7031	0.7467	0.7407	0.7807
Other Food Items	0.8712	0.7979	0.8354	0.8046
Fuel & Light	0.6931	0.7661	1.0620	0.7063
Clothing	1.4842	1.5432	1.4569	1.4899
Other Nonfood Items	1.3875	1.9910	1.3479	1.4711

Note: Computed from the grouped consumer expenditure data collected from 42nd to 61st round NSSO Reports.

7

SUMMARY AND FINDINGS

Current research in applied demand analysis has been addressing the twin issues of degree of non-linearity of the Engel curves and the ability to capture price effects approximately by the demand system. In addition to income and prices, the role of demographic variables like household size, composition etc. and dynamic aspects like past level of consumption, tastes and preferences of the consumer over time etc. are also being emphasized in some recent studies. Continuous efforts are being made to modify and generalize the existing models and propose new models to incorporate the above developments. The widely used demand systems like the Linear Expenditure System (LES) and the Almost Ideal Demand System (AIDS) can be made flexible by incorporating household size as an additional explanatory variable through demographic translation procedure. Even though the use of family size, '*m*' as a deflator for the total expenditure, (Weisskoff, 1971 and Sener, 1977) is empirically not plausible (Prais and Houthakker,1971), its inclusion is justified due to lack of published NSS data on household composition. It is, therefore, better to incorporate household size as an additional explanatory variable in the demand equations rather than ignoring the household size effects altogether.

The basic objective of the study is to estimate the Linear Expenditure System and the Almost Ideal Demand System and their variants. The LES has been made flexible by incorporating household size and time trend where the later is used as a proxy for examining the shift in the consumers taste and preferences for various commodity groups over time while the former as a proxy for analysing the operation of economics and diseconomies of scale in household consumption. The LES models estimated are the simple Linear Expenditure System named as LES-1; a flexible form of LES by incorporating household size in its budget share parameters named as LES-2; and another flexible form of LES obtained by replacing its budget share parameters by linear time trend which has been abbreviated as LES-3. The fourth flexible form is the non-additive variant of LES popularly known the Nasse Expenditure System (NES), which allows specific substitution between commodity groups. We have also estimated LES-2 and LES-3 by incorporating the household size and time trend separately in the vectors of β_i and γ_{ij} parameters and found that the results are better with appropriate signs when the above two variables (household size and time trends) are incorporated in the budget share parameters of LES. We have also estimated all the four models using both expenditure equations and budget share equations of these models and found better results when the parameters are estimated from the budget share equations. To make the analysis simpler, we have not analysed the estimates obtained from the expenditure equations of LES and its variants and also the estimates obtained from the LES-2 and LES-3 incorporating household size and time trend in the committed quantity parameters of LES.

Six variants of the AIDS model have been estimated imposing neo-classical restrictions such as homogeneity and both homogeneity and symmetry; imposing two 'a priori' restrictions such as 'no cross-price effects' and 'no price effects' (explicit additivity) and also incorporating household size as an additional explanatory variable. So the variants of AIDS model estimated in the study are the LA\AIDS model with demographic specification which is abbreviated as AIDS-1 to examine the operation of economies and diseconomies of scale in the consumption of different items which has a direct bearing on the demand for different commodities. The second estimable model is the simple LA\AIDS model named as AIDS-2 with no household size. The other variants of AIDS are AIDS-3 with only homogeneity restriction imposed; AIDS-4 with both homogeneity and symmetry restrictions imposed; AIDS-5 with 'no household size' and 'no cross price effects' and finally, AIDS-6 with explicit additivity restriction imposed i.e with 'no household size' and 'no price effects'.

The consumer expenditure data used for the estimation of the LES and AIDS and their variants consist of all-Orissa and all-India average monthly per capita consumer expenditure (MPCE) on nine broad commodity groups and the corresponding monthly per capita total consumer expenditure (MPTCE) separately for rural and urban households. The expenditure data has been taken from the published NSS reports of different rounds form 42nd round (July,1986-June,1987) to 61st round (July,2004-June,2005) on consumer expenditure excluding the 49th and 60th rounds for which the consumer price indices are not compatible. The period covered is, therefore, from July 1986 to June 2005. To examine the inter-sectoral variations in consumption pattern in the state and the country, the expenditure class-wise grouped data of the 61st round (the 7th quinquennial round of consumer expenditure survey of NSSO, 2004-05) has been further aggregated into three income/expenditure groups viz. low income group (bottom 30 per cent of the population), middle income group (middle 40 per cent of the population), and high income group (top 30 per cent of the population). The expenditure data of the first group consisting of aggregation over the first four expenditure classes; second group consisting of aggregation over the middle four expenditure classes; and third group consisting of aggregation over the last four expenditure classes of the item-wise twelve expenditure classes of consumer expenditure data published by NSSO. To analyse the inter-temporal variation in the consumption patterns separately for the rural and urban sectors of the state as well as the country, broad items-wise grouped time-series data of NSSO has been used.

Prices of different commodity groups are the important determinants in a demand system. The retail price data used for estimating demand systems is the time-series of consumer price indices for industrial workers and agriculture labour compiled and released by the Labour Bureau, Ministry of Labour (GoI). The Labour Bureau compiles the state-wise and all India consumer price indices for these three categories of workers such as industrial workers, agricultural labourers and rural labourers for different financial years and calendar years. We have further compiled both the calendar year and financial year consumer price indices of industrial workers and agricultural labourers separately for Orissa and all India for nine commodity classifications which can be used as the proxy variables for retail prices of these commodities. The calendar year consumer price indices are used if the period of the NSS round coincides with a calendar year (from January to December) and financial year consumer price indices are used as an approximation for agricultural-year price indices if the period of the NSS round coincides with a agricultural-year (form July to June) as agricultural-year price indices over the period of analysis for all items are not available. Further, the consumer price indices for industrial worker are used for estimating demand systems for the urban sector and agricultural labourers are used for estimating the demand systems for the rural sector. To maintain consistency between time-series of consumer price indices and the period of NSS round, we have not considered the consumer expenditure data for 49th and 60th rounds and the price indices of 1995-96 while compiling these indices so data the retail price-series consistent with NSS rounds can be obtained. The retail price-series so compiled has been used for estimating the LES and AIDS models and their variants.

The nine broad specific items considered in this study are cereals and substitutes; pulses and its products; milk and its products; edible oil and fats; meat, fish and egg; other food items, clothing; fuel and light; other non-food items. The other food items and other non-food items are the residual categories. The former includes vegetables and fruits; sugar and gur; salt and spices; beverages and processed food etc. while the latter consists of expenditures on pan, tobacco and intoxicants; alcoholic beverages; transport; medical care; education; recreation; rents and taxes etc. and also expenditure on durables. It should be mentioned that the groups other than the residual groups are fairly standard items for which the NSSO regularly publishes expenditure estimates. However, for some commodity groups like pulses and its products; meat, fish and egg; edible oil and fats; salt; spices etc.; the observed budget shares are frequently small. Yet, this grouping of items has been retained essentially because of the fact that such a grouping is considered in most of the disaggregated studies based on consumer expenditure data.

Stone (1954) has suggested a two-stage iterative procedure for estimating the parameters of LES. Since LES is quadratic in parameters, it becomes linear if one set of parameters is assumed to be known. The second set of parameters can be estimated by ordinary least squares. Using this estimated second set of parameters as given, the first set can be estimated again by ordinary least squares. The new set of parameters is used as the initial set and the procedure is repeated until two successive iterations give approximately identical estimates for the parameters. This procedure, in practice is very slow and may require a large number of iterations. The non-linear estimation procedure followed in some studies is the maximum likelihood method, the modified version of the Guass-Newton method, the steepest descent method and the Park's method. Park's method is essentially a two stage iterative procedure to maximise the concentrated log likelihood function w.r.t. the two set of parameters of LES. Another method is the linearization method (Slater, 1972) which yields maximum likelihood estimates has been used for estimating LES in the study (Solari, 1971 and Slater, 1972). However, in view of a large number of parameters being involved in the maximum likelihood estimation, the estimation may be computationally heavy. The linearization procedure is relatively simple for computation. The quickness of convergence of this procedure depends on the initial guess solution and the degree of non-linearity of the demand system. So, we have used the linearised iterative procedure for the estimation of LES and its variants. Some of the variants of the AIDS model are estimated by simple equation-by-equation ordinary least squares method (Deaton and Muellbauer, 1980). The OLS estimation of this model is straightforward and one can even have the estimates of other variants of AIDS such as AIDS-3 with homogeneity and AIDS-4 with both homogeneity and symmetry restrictions imposed by restricted least squares method (Majumder, 1980).

The choice of a most plausible demand system among the various alternatives is quite difficult because some equations in the system are likely to be better determined than others and there is no unique measure which can determine the goodness of fit of a system to another. However, some traditional goodness-of-fit measures like adj. $R^2\left(\overline{R}^2\right)$, quasi, R^2, F-statistic, distance measures like D^2 etc. has been used in earlier demand studies. But some of these measures, in practice are not quite sensitive to the performance of the model and many lead to different conclusions altogether. So, we have used adj., R^2, the F-statistic and the correlation coefficients (R_w^2) between the observed and predicted budget shares to examine the goodness-of-fit of the demand equations. The above goodness-of-fit measures are supplemented by Theil's measure of information accuracy (π_i) separately for each item. The only overall (or across all equations) measure of goodness of fit used here is the Theil's measure of average information inaccuracy (π) which can be computed by lumping together the budget shares of all items.

MAIN FINDINGS

The review on complete demand systems in chapter-2 reveals that the Indian studies on demand systems are scanty. These studies differ not only in their scope but also in their sources of the database. Most of the consumer studies in India are based on cross-section NSS data on consumer expenditure collected by NSSO during its various rounds. Non-availability of continuous time-series of consumer expenditure data during 29th to 41st rounds and also non-availability of satisfactory consumer price indices has discouraged researchers to work on complete demand systems, generally, based on time-series data. However, very few researchers have estimated different complete demand systems either from time-series or pooled time-series of cross-section data on consumer expenditure collected by the NSSO during its 1st to 28th rounds using wholesale price indices at different levels of commodity aggregation. The regional/state level studies on complete demand system are scanty in India. Particularly for the state like Orissa, no such study on complete demand system has been done so far as evident from the literature. Recently Murty (2005) has estimated the LES and AIDS models with their few variants for all-India using five quinquennial rounds of consumer expenditure data from 27th to 50th NSS rounds at seven levels of broad commodity aggregation. No such specific study on complete demand system has been done so far either using the time-series or time-series of cross-section data from the recent rounds of NSS consumer expenditure data (i.e. 42nd to 61st rounds). Considering such aberrations, the present study is the modest attempt to bridge this gap by estimating the most popular complete demand systems like the Linear Expenditure System and the Almost Ideal Demand System along with some of their variants to explore the patterns of demand in the backward state like Orissa and in the developing country like India.

From Chapter-3, it is concluded that even though the introduction of theoretical restrictions reduce the number of parameters to be estimated in demand systems, severe limitations still stem from the large number of parameters contained in these systems. The assumptions of additivity (Houthakker, 1960) and separability (Sono, 1960 and Leontief, 1947) provide a means of alleviating these limitations. The additive utility function, in spite of its restrictive consequences, has been very popular, particularly for broad commodity groups, because of its simplicity of specification and estimation as well as less demanding of data requirements. Further restrictions on the additive utility functions with Frisch's want independence assumption enables us for estimating a complete set of direct and cross-price elasticities from income elasticities, expenditure weights, and money flexibility (Frisch, 1959). The money flexibility coefficient can be computed if the direct price elasticity for a want-independent commodity or group of commodities is reliably known. The assumption of separability is more popular in complete demand systems that encompass a large number of commodities.

Chapter-4 provides a brief description of a variety of complete demand systems which has been proposed for econometric use. All pay strong allegiance to the neo-classical demand theory. Most of the demand systems introduce restrictions in order to simplify the model and to reduce the number of parameters to be estimated. The models based on well behaved utility functions automatically satisfy the theoretical restrictions such as adding-up, homogeneity and the Slutsky symmetry conditions but the later two restrictions must be imposed while estimating the non-utility based demand systems. A large number of parameters in demand systems offer more descriptive flexibility but this advantage must be weighed against the advantages of simplicity offered by other models.

The linear, double-log and Rotterdam demand systems can be dubbed as a priori or statistical models. These models are neither theoretically consistent nor can be integrated with larger economic tools like general equilibrium. The other category of theoretically consistent but highly restrictive demand systems obeying this additivity assumption is the Linear Expenditure System, the Direct and Indirect Addilog Systems. The additive preferences do not allow inferior goods into the analysis. In LES, commodities can only be gross substitutes but not complements. Hence, the additive models are unrealistic for empirical use and also need non-linear estimation. In spite of its limitations viz., linearity of the Engel curves, and inelasticity of the price-quantity demand curves, incapability of incorporating complementary and inferior commodities, the Linear Expenditure System has found extensive empirical applications. This is essentially due to its relative simplicity from the point of view of estimation and interpretation. In some applications, the LES model can be made flexible by allowing its parameters to change with the change in the level of income, demographic features, and dynamic behavior related to past levels of consumption, shift in the consumer's taste and preference etc.

Due to these limitations of the early demand models, recent effort in applied demand analysis have centered around specifying demand systems that allow non-linear Engel curves and non-separable preferences. It aggregates perfectively over consumers without forcing linearity on the Engel curves. The Almost Ideal Demand System proposed by Deaton and Muellbauer (1980) is one such functional form. This model overcomes most of the limitations of additive models and hence, the adjective 'almost ideal'. This model has been extensively estimated and has also been used to test neoclassical restrictions like homogeneity and symmetry and the 'a priori' restrictions like explicit additivity (no price effects) and 'no cross-price effects'. On theoretical grounds, however, none of the demand systems dominates its competitors. The choice of specification of the demand systems for empirical work must then be made on an empirical basis as the models differ in their computational problems and also in their empirical performance. Comparisons of the model's predictive abilities on non-sample data would be desirable. The models can also be compared on the basis of their goodness-of-fit to the sample data for each commodity separately; the concept of average information accuracy is generally applied to evaluate the overall fit of the model to the sample data. The elasticity estimates at mean level expenditure shares are also contrasted for such comparison.

The analysis in Chapter-5 reveals distinct rural-urban and income-group variations in consumption pattern of different food and non-food items. The low and middle-income groups in rural India spend a very high proportion of 64.4 and 62 per cent of their budget on food items respectively; while the high income group allocates only 44.5 per cent to food items. The corresponding figures for the rural Orissa are 69.3 and 62.6 per cent for low and middle income brackets; 46 per cent for high income bracket. On the other hand, the low and middle-income groups in urban India spend 60.7 and 50.4 per cent of their budget on food items respectively while the high income group allocates only 32.1 per cent to food items. But these figures are on the higher side in urban Orissa. The corresponding figures for the urban Orissa are 63.9 and 52.7 per cent for low and middle income brackets; 45.6 per cent for high income bracket. Within food item, cereals and its substitutes occupy a predominant position with relatively higher share in the respective budgets of rural and urban sectors of Orissa and all-India. The share of cereals and its substitutes is much higher for the low income group compared to high income group and also much higher for all income brackets in the rural sector than their counter parts in the urban sector of the state as well as the country. The budget shares of most of the food items except milk and its products and meat, fish and eggs decline uniformly as we move up the income ladder. But the budget shares of different non-food items rise uniformly as we move up the income ladder. The existence of distinct inter-income group variations in the consumption patterns of different food and non-food items confirms the acceptance of hypothesis-1

The analysis also reveals distinct rural-urban (or inter-sectoral) variations in the consumption patterns of different food and non-food items in the state as well as in the country. When we compare the rural-urban consumption pattern in India, non-food expenditure is much higher than food expenditure in urban sector where as food expenditure is much higher than non-food expenditure in rural sector. Almost the same pattern rural-urban variation in the consumption of different food and non-food expenditure is observed in Orissa with marginally higher share of expenditure on non-food items compared to food items in the urban areas of the state. Thus, the above analysis portrays wide rural-urban variations in the consumption patterns that still exist in the state and the country which leads to the acceptance of hypothesis-2.

The analysis of inter-temporal variations in consumption patterns reveals that in rural India the percentage share of expenditure of different food items except other food items has declined and the share of expenditure of different non-food items except pan, tobacco and intoxicants has increased during the period from 1986-87 to 2004-05. This is an important indication in the improvement in the standard of living of the rural population of the country. Another important feature of the consumption pattern in rural India is that the percentage share of food expenditure (60.4 per cent) is much higher than the percentage share of non-food expenditure (39.6 per cent). On the other hand, the pattern of food and non-food expenditure in urban India is quite different from that of rural India. In rural India, food expenditure is much higher than non-food expenditure over the period 1986-87 to 1995-96. During the period 1997-98, the non-food expenditure was marginally higher than food expenditure thereafter non-food expenditure was much higher than food expenditure till 2004-05. The expenditure on different food items like cereals and its substitutes; pulses and its products; milk and its products; edible oil; meat, fish and egg; other food items and all food items have a downward trend and different non-food items except clothing have an upward trend during the period from 1986-87 to 2004-05. The sharp decline in food expenditure especially after 1998 is due to the sharp rise in expenditure on other non-food items.

But the average percentage of MPCE on different food items like pulses and its products; milk and its products; edible oil and other food items are much lower in the rural Orissa as compared to its counterparts in the country. This clearly reveals the variation in the consumption pattern in rural Orissa from rural India. Like urban India, the share of food expenditure exhibits an overall downward trend while the share of non-food expenditure exhibits an overall upward trend in rural Orissa. The share of food expenditure exhibits an overall downward trend while the share of non-food expenditure exhibits an overall upward trend in urban Orissa. The trend of different food items indicates that the decline in food expenditure is mainly due to the decline in the share of cereals and its substitutes; milk and its products; edible oil and other food items in urban Orissa. This indicates the inter-temporal as well as inter-sectoral variation in consumption patterns in the state and the country. Therefore, hypothesis-3 is accepted.

It is evident from the empirical analysis of the Linear Expenditure System (LES) in chapter-5 that although NES is a non-additive variant of LES, its performance is relatively poor compared to the other three variants. But when we compare the performance of LES-2 with LES-1 and LES-3, the performance of LES-2 is relatively better than the performance of both LES-1 and LES-3 with a large number of significant estimates of γ_{ij} and also relatively better fit of demand equations to the sample data which is evident from $\overline{R}^2$ and F-values. The Theil's measure of information inaccuracy (π) values are also confirms this. Hence, on the basis of the statistical criteria, performance of LES-2 is found to be better compared to the other three variants. However, to judge the most suitable function form of the LES and AIDS models, we have applied the economic 'a priori' criteria for which we have to examine the sign and magnitude of the estimates of β_i, γ_{ij}, θ_i and θ^*_i along with the different elasticities estimated from these models to see how far these estimates and elasticities are theoretically meaningful.

It is noticed that the marginal budget shares (MBS) are somewhat 'robust' across model specifications. However, minor differences do exist between the model specifications of LES-2 and LES-3. The NES underestimates most of the food and non-food items where as LES-1 and LES-3 overestimates few staple food items like cereal and its substitutes; pulses and its products and other non-food items in both the rural and urban sectors of Orissa and all India. Further, LES-1 seems to overestimate the own-price effects for some items and underestimate for some other items of consumption compared to other flexible model specifications. The estimates of marginal budget shares and expenditure elasticities obtained from LES-2 for most of nutritious food items like milk and its products, meat, fish and egg and other food items as well as the staple food items like cereal and its substitutes and pulses and its products seems to have reasonable values compared to its other variants. The estimates of marginal budget shares and expenditure elasticities obtained from LES-2 for most of the food and non-food items also follow certain definite patterns in Orissa and all India. But the estimates of own-price coefficients obtained from LES-2 for most of the food and non-food items seem to be plausible compared to other model specifications judged on the basis of their sign and magnitude. Hence, the performance of LES-2 is better than the other variants of LES.

The marginal budget shares of different food and non-food items exhibit a well known pattern in the state as well as in the country. The estimated marginal budget shares of LES and its variants have the expected positive sign. It is very interesting to note that the estimated marginal budget shares (MBS) of cereals and its substitutes; other food and other non-food items are much higher compared to other six commodity groups in both rural and urban sectors of Orissa and all India. The marginal budget shares of cereals and its substitutes, and milk and its products are much higher but that of other food items these shares are marginally higher for the rural households than their urban counterparts in the country. In case of non-food items, the budget shares of other non-food items and clothing are much lower but for fuel and light, these shares are marginally lower for the rural households than their urban counterparts in the country. In Orissa, the behaviour of marginal budget shares is quite different. The estimated marginal budget shares of cereals and its substitutes are much higher and that of pulses and its products and edible oil are marginally higher for the rural households than their urban counterparts in the state. But this pattern is reversed for other food items. On the other hand, the marginal budget shares of milk and its products and other food items are much higher and that of meat, fish and egg are marginally higher for the urban households than their rural counterparts in the state. Among different non-food items, marginal budget shares of other non-food items are much higher for the urban households than their rural counterparts but for clothing and fuel & light, these shares are marginally higher for the rural households than their urban counterparts in the state. Thus, the above results indicate a distinct rural-urban variation in marginal budget shares which is typical for the undeveloped state like Orissa and for the developing country like India. Hence, hypothesis-4 relating to the pattern of inter-sectoral variations in MBS estimated from LES and its variants is accepted for India but rejected for Orissa.

From the empirical analysis of LES, it is also observed that for some food items like cereals and its substitutes; pulses and its products and edible oil (except for rural Orissa) and for some non-food items like fuel and light, the expenditure elasticities are less than unity indicating that these items are necessity items in both rural and urban sectors of Orissa and India. The expenditure elasticities are more than unity for milks and its products; meat, fish and egg; clothing and other non-food items indicating that these items are luxury items in both rural and urban sector of the state and the country. The expenditure elasticities for other food items are greater than unity in the rural sector and less than unity in the urban sector of the country. But it is greater than unity in both rural and urban sectors of the state. It indicates that other food item group is a luxury item in the rural sector and a necessity item in the urban sector of the country but it is a luxury item in both the sectors of the state. Further, expenditure elasticities for edible oil are greater than unity in rural sector and less than unity in the urban sector of the state but it is less than unity in both the sectors of the country. Hence, edible oil is a necessity item in both the sectors of the country but it is a necessity item in the rural sector and luxury item in the urban sector of the state. This leads to the partial acceptance of hypothesis-5 since the magnitude of expenditure elasticities follow a definite rural-urban pattern for most of the food and non-food items estimated from LES and its variants.

The empirical analysis of LES also reveals a distinct rural-urban variation in the expenditure elasticities of different food and non-food items. For most of the food items, rural expenditure elasticities are higher than urban expenditure elasticities and it is reversed for most of the non-food items. Almost the same pattern of rural-urban variation of these elasticities is observed in Orissa for most of the food items except milk and its products and meat, fish and egg for which rural expenditure elasticities are higher than urban expenditure elasticities. This is a clear indication of higher standard of living of the urban households than their rural counterparts in Orissa and all India. Further, the expenditure elasticities for most of the food items are higher and most of the non-food items are lower in the state as compared to the all-India level. It clearly indicates lower standard of living of the people in the state compared to the all India level. Hence, hypothesis-6 is accepted for India but partially accepted for Orissa since the pattern of rural-urban variation is true for most of the food and non-food items in the state.

The estimates of own price elasticities of LES are theoretically meaningful with appropriate negative sign. It is well known that simple LES (i.e.LES-1) allows only price inelastic items in its fold, as long as committed quantity parameters are non-negative. Apparently, this limitation seems to hold here. Quite a few values of own-price elasticities are found to be closer to unity in magnitude. Probably, the situation would have been different if the γ_{ij} parameters are allowed to vary across rural and urban sectors. Thus, LES and its variants (except NES) tried here could not capture the full price effects. Further, to capture price responses adequately, the simple generalization of the LES namely, the NES has a good claim. It may be necessary to restrict the utility interaction or specific substitution between commodities to get empirically meaningful own-price and cross-price elasticities of demand. In this sense, the restrictive LES model is easy to handle. The own-price effects vary across rural and urban sectors in a way similar to the expenditure elasticity of demand. Broadly, the income and own price responses seems to obey a proportionality relationship as suggested by Deaton (1976). Acceptance of hypothesis-7 is confirmed.

The empirical analysis of LES also reveals that the urban households are less responsive to price changes for most of the food items and more responsive to price changes for most of the non-food items than their rural counterparts in the state and the country. The own-price elasticities of rural households are uniformly higher for cereals and its substitutes; pulses and its products; edible oil; meat, fish and egg and other food items and smaller for clothing and other non-food items than their urban counterparts across all the model specifications. But no such definite pattern of rural-urban variation in own-price elasticities is observed for milk and its products and fuel and light across different model specifications. This pattern is reversed for most of the non-food items. This indicates that the urban households are less responsive to price changes for most of the food items and more responsive to price changes for most of the non-food items than their rural counterparts in the state and the country. When we compare the own-price elasticities of the households in Orissa with their counterparts in India, it is observed that these elasticities are higher for most of the food and non-food items except meat, fish and egg in Orissa compared to all India level indicating that these items are relatively inelastic in the country than that of the state. Hence, hypothesis-8 is partially accepted.

Among food items, cereals and its substitutes; pulses and its products and edible oil seem to exhibit economies of scale where as other food items exhibit diseconomies of scale in both the sectors but milk and its products and meat, fish and egg seem to exhibit diseconomies of scale only in the rural sector of the state and the country. This shows a marked hierarchy in the consumer basket. Milk and its products, meat, fish and egg and other food item are probably given lesser priority in rural household compared to cereals and its substitutes & pulses and its products in the event of increase in household size. Also, due to budget constraint, every household has to reduce expenditure on some items in order to buy more of others. In rural areas, an extra person in the family will cause reduction in per capita expenditures on milk and its products; meat, fish and egg and all non-food items. The money so saved is spent on cereals and substitutes; pulses and products and edible oil. The magnitude of these effects decline as income level rises. On the other hand, other non-food items and fuel and light seem to exhibit diseconomies of scale in both the sectors where as clothing exhibits economies of scale in the both sectors in the country and diseconomies of scale in the both sectors in the state. Hence, hypothesis-9 is partially accepted since it is true for most of the food and non-food items.

The taste and preference coefficients have significant effect on the budget shares of cereals and its substitutes; milk and its products, other food items, clothing and other non-food items in both the sectors of Orissa and all-India. The marginal effect of taste changes are negative for most of the food items except meat, fish and egg and other food items (only in rural India) but positive for most of the non-food items except clothing in both the sector of India. On the other hand, the pattern of taste changes are little different for Orissa. The marginal effect of taste changes are also negative for most of the food and non-food item except cereals and its substitutes, edible oil and clothing in rural Orissa and except other food items only in urban Orissa. Almost similar rural-urban variation in demand pattern due to change in taste over time is also noticed from the estimated preference elasticities. This implies that at the margin, taste and preferences seem to reduce the money income allocated to most of the food items thereby increasing its allocation to different non-food items both in the rural and urban sectors of the state as well as the country. Hence, hypothesis-10 is partially accepted since it is true for most of the food and non-food items.

The empirical analysis of Almost Ideal Demand System in chapter-6 reveals that the estimated models show good fit to the sample observations and amply demonstrates the usefulness of the variants of AIDS model for quantifying consumer behaviour in India. The models seem to perform better for urban data compared to rural data. The performance of AIDS model also varied across model specifications, across rural-urban sectors and also across commodities. Imposition of neoclassical restriction led to the decline in $\overline{R}^2$ values. The reduction in values $\bar{R}^2$ varied as we move from an unconstrained model to an explicitly additive model. Homogeneity restrictions seem to cause less reduction in $\bar{R}^2$ values compared to both homogeneity and symmetry, 'no cross-price effects' and explicit additivity at nine commodity level. The effect of explicitly additivity seems to be the largest. Further, the F-values and the Theil's measure of information inaccuracy (π_i) values also confirm this. We notice a trade-off between theoretical consistency and statistical goodness-of-fit. Neo-classical restrictions may be desirable on theoretical grounds, but these are less acceptable statistically. However, as expected, precision of estimates increased with the imposition of restrictions.

The impact of neo-classical restrictions on income coefficients is some what moderate and the coefficients exhibit a systematic pattern across model specifications. The absolute values of income coefficients increased for some items and decreased for others as we move from unconstrained model to more restrictive models like 'no cross-price effects' and explicit additivity (no price effects). Thus, the neo-classical restrictions change the degree of necessity/luxury and in some case the nature of the item itself. Fuel and light which is a necessity item in most of variants of AIDS model changes into luxury item with the imposition of explicit additivity in rural Orissa. However, imposition of these restrictions reveals that most of the food items remained as necessity items while most of non-food items except edible oil seem to be luxury items. These results seem to be consistent with the backward region like Orissa and the developing country like India. Neo-classical restrictions also seem to increase the importance of commodities with larger budget share and reduce that of minor items. So, the income response coefficients of the variants of LA\AIDS model confirm the acceptance of hypothesis-4 for different food and non-food items except fuel and light in the state and the country.

Generally, the proportion of statistically significant own-price and cross-price coefficients is larger for disaggregated than aggregated models. This result is in conformity with the common belief that there will be higher price response for disaggregated commodities. With commodity aggregation some valuable price information may be smoothened or lost resulting in less price variability and thereby insignificant coefficients. As expected, the effects of neo-classical restrictions on price coefficients are quite strong and vary across model specifications and also in the rural and urban sectors. Price coefficients do not exhibit any systematic pattern across model specifications. Among the cross-price effects, those relating to food items especially for cereals and its substitutes; milk and its products and other food item are prominent. The prices of these items will exert decisive negative influence on the demand for non-food items as well.

The estimated income elasticities are quite plausible for most of the food and non-food items in all model specifications. There are sectoral variations both in their magnitude as well as pattern across model specifications. Income elasticities exhibit a pattern similar to that of income coefficients. It is found that income elasticities are less than unity for all food items and hence, different food items are necessity items and greater than unity for clothing and other non-food items indicating their luxury nature. But the elasticities are less than unity for fuel and light in both the sectors of the state and the country indicating its necessity nature. So, the income elasticities estimated from the variants of LA\AIDS model confirm the acceptance of hypothesis-5 for different food and non-food items except fuel and light in the state as well as in the country.

It is also noticed that rural income elasticities are greater than urban elasticities for most of the food items except milk and its products. This pattern is reversed for various non-food items across most of the model specifications. Unlike rural India, the income elasticities for urban India do not exhibit any systematic pattern as we move from unconstrained model to more restrictive models like 'no cross-price effects' and explicit additivity (no price effects). The estimated rural and urban income elasticities for some items do not follow the expected pattern viz. the income elasticities of demand for different food items are found to be higher in rural areas (under-developed region) compared to that of urban area (developed region). These exceptions may be due to aggregation of data over commodities. Instead of mean level data, expenditure class-wise data may provide more convincing results. So, hypothesis-6 relating to the pattern of rural-urban variations in income elasticities is accepted for different food and non-food items except milk and its products both in the state and the country.

The own-price elasticities are negative as expected. The correct sign for all the estimates is indicative of the fulfillment of second order conditions which require the negative semi-definiteness of the Slutsky substitution matrix. Hence, hypothesis-7 is accepted. The estimates of own-price elasticities in rural sector for most of the food items except meat, fish and egg and other food item, and some non-food items like clothing (except India) and other non-food item are grater than those of the urban sector. The pattern of rural-urban variation in the own-price elasticities is reversed for clothing in India and fuel and light both in Orissa and India. The magnitude of most of the food items are less than unity indicating price inelastic in both the sectors. But most of food items are highly inelastic in rural sector than that of the urban sector. It seems that the order of magnitude of these estimates is quite plausible in contrast to other flexible models. The own-price and cross-price elasticities are more sensitive to the model specification. The estimates do not follow any systematic pattern across model specifications with different restrictions imposed, and also across rural and urban sectors. The utmost erraticness of even the own-price elasticities is perhaps the (unreliable) price variables in the specification of the fully flexible model like AIDS. Further, the use of mean level data might have also contributed to this erratic behaviour. Therefore, hypothesis-7 relating to the pattern of rural-urban variations in the own-price elasticities estimated from the variants of LA\AIDS model is rejected for most of the food and non-food items in the state and also in the country.

Most of the estimates of cross-price elasticities are numerically large and negative implying considerable cross-price responses. It also follows that several pairs of goods are gross complements as demand for pairs of goods move together. It is well known that for a price inelastic good, an increase in its price would lead to an increase in the budget allocation on it (i.e. increase in the price can not be offset by the decline in quantity purchased) while the opposite is true for an elastic good. Most of the food items are found to be price inelastic i.e. increase in their prices should result in reallocation of expenditures in their favour, implying gross complementarity. For non-food items, the opposite is true. This may be due to the low levels of income wherein consumer has to buy some quantity of each commodity and with less scope for substitutability. The cross-price elasticities are sensitive to the imposition of restrictions and rural-urban variations. The degree of substitutability varies with the model specifications but does not show any systematic pattern. For some pairs of commodities, the estimates are much more divergent. No systematic pattern could be seen across model specifications. Thus, flexibility of the LA\AIDS model has the adverse effect on erratic cross-price responses as well.

Like size coefficient, the negative size elasticity shows the operation of diseconomies of scale and positive elasticities indicate the operation of economies of scale in household consumption which has a direct bearing on the demand for different commodities. The absolute values of size coefficients and elasticities show a definite rural-urban pattern for most of the food items and no such pattern for various non-food items. The magnitude of these elasticities is small but less than unity in both the sectors of the state and country. Most of the food items except other food item (in both the sectors); milk and its products and meat, fish and egg (only in the rural sector) exhibit economies of scale while different non-food items except clothing (in both the sectors of India) exhibit diseconomies of scale. The absolute value of these elasticities in rural areas for most of the food items except edible oil and meat, fish and egg are higher than urban areas of the state as well as the country. Similar pattern is also observed for other non-food items. But no such definite pattern is observed for fuel and light and clothing. So, hypothesis-9 is partially accepted since the size elasticities follow a definite pattern among food and non-food items estimated form the LA\AIDS model.

Flexible models like the AIDS permit us to test the empirical validity of neo-classical and other 'a priori' restrictions by comparing a restricted model with it's unrestricted form. The statistical test of different hypothesis can be done in various ways. One can use the likelihood ratio test based on the concentrated log likelihood function which is computed for each estimated model. Another way is to compare the item-wise residual sum squares of the unrestricted model with the restricted model using F-statistic. In this section, we have used the latter method to test different hypothesis formulated on the basis of different restrictions imposed on AIDS model (AIDS-2). The empirical validity of the different hypotheses formulated viz., no household size effect, homogeneity, both homogeneity and symmetry, 'no cross-price effects' and explicit additivity (no price effects) has been tested in this section using the F-statistic. As expected, the F-values are almost rising as we move from a less restrictive model to a more restrictive one. The F-test can be applied to verify the empirical validity of a more restrictive null hypothesis against a less restrictive alternative. Comparison of homogeneity and symmetry against unrestricted model reveals the rejection of both restrictions for most of the food and non-food items in the rural and urban sectors of Orissa as well as all India. Thus, it reveals the similarity in the behaviour of rural and urban consumers with regard to the validity of neoclassical postulates. Clearly, the 'a priori' restrictions like explicit additivity (no price effects) and 'no cross-price effects' are too restrictive and rejected at nine commodity level for all food and non-food items except edible oil and other food item in both the sectors when tested against unconstrained model. The validity of both homogeneity and symmetry and the rejection of homogeneity postulate in both the sectors of Orissa and India at nine commodity level also reveals that imposition of homogeneity (absence of money illusion) itself seems to cause much damage and Slutsky symmetry may not be a severe restriction.

Thus, neoclassical restrictions are theoretically sound but empirically not valid at broad commodity level for the developing country like India and the backward region like Orissa. All neoclassical as well as a priori hypotheses are rejected in both rural and urban sectors conclusively at conventional 5 per cent level of significance using the AIDS model and the observed household expenditure data. This kind of summary rejection of neo-classical hypotheses is not uncommon for India. Similar conclusion has been drawn by Deaton (1974) using another flexible demand model on British data and Ray (1980) using AIDS model on Indian data.

The additive models like LES and its variants even though consistent with theory are highly restrictive because of their additive features which do not allow inferior and complement gods. On the other hand, the variants of AIDS model correspond to a well defined flexible preference structure consistent for aggregation from micro to macro level and allow non-linear Engel curves which is also theoretical consistent. But the additive models like LES and its few variants though theoretically consistent are unrealistic for empirical use while the variants of AIDS model are both theoretically consistent and more reliable for empirical use. The LES and variants require non-linear estimation whereas the variants of AIDS model can be estimated through equation-by-equation least squares either or ordinary restricted least square or by restricted least square . Hence, the variants of AIDS model have a lot of advantage over the LES and its variants from the point of view of estimation, interpretation of result and empirical performance.

When we compare the goodness-of-fit of the demand equations of the simple LES (LES-1) with LA/AIDS (AIDS-2) and LES-2 with AIDS-1 (both with demographic specification), the fit is relatively better with high $\overline{R}^2$ and F values and low values π_i for AIDS-2 and AIDS-1 compared to the corresponding models such as LES-1 and LES-2. The number of significant price, income and size coefficients are also more for the variants of AIDS model than LES and its variants. Further, most of the variants of LES model seem to over-estimate the price coefficient for some items and under-estimate for some other items since the LES models could not capture the full price effects while the variants of AIDS model provides plausible price coefficients for most of the food and non-food items which capture the price-effects to a maximum extent. The income and size co-efficient estimated from variants of AIDS model show a definite rural and urban pattern judged on the basis of their sign and magnitude compared to the LES and its variants.

The income, price and size elasticities estimated from the variants of AIDS model follow a definite pattern of rural-urban variation with appropriate sign and magnitude but these elasticities estimated from LES and its variants follow a quite different pattern of rural-urban variation across different commodities and also across their model specifications. On the other hand, the compensatory own-price elasticities of LES and its variants are erratic across different commodities and also across their model specifications. But these elasticities show a definite rural-urban pattern across commodities and no such definite pattern across model specifications in case of the variants of AIDS model. Further, the flexible model like AIDS permits us to test the empirical validity of neo-classical and other 'a priori' restrictions which are not possible under LES and its variants since LES models is derived from a well-behaved utility function which satisfies the neoclassical restrictions automatically. So, it is concluded that the performance of the variants of AIDS model is much better than the LES and its variants on the basis of their theoretical consistency and empirical performance in both the rural and urban sectors of the state as well as the country.

POLICY IMPLICATIONS

Demand analysis in general and complete demand systems in particular is the rich areas for the development and testing of new tools of econometrics. There are several uses of the estimated demand parameters for economic policy and planning. Thus, current interest in demand analysis extends to welfare application and other diverse areas such as demand projections, computation of true cost of living indices, measurement of inequality, measurement of poverty, calculation of optimal commodity taxes, estimation of cost of a child etc. All these are very useful for current and future policy formulations. As the demand systems are, generally, derived from a utility function, there is a close link between the behavioral and welfare aspect of demand. Even if the demand systems are estimated using cost function approach, there is welfare implication of changes in cost as a consequence of changes in prices of commodities over a period of time.

An important application of complete demand systems is the projection of future consumer demand for various commodities in the economy. This involves a number of steps. First, we need to identify the appropriate model to be used for making demand projections. If a particular demand model is not plausible, we may try for other alternative models to see the sensitivity of demand projection to model specifications. Secondly, we need to assume values for the exogenous variables, viz. income and prices of different commodities appearing in the demand model. It is desirable to have alternative scenarios for these variables because it would be impossible to predict the future with certainty. Several approaches are available to project future demand depending on the assumptions made on income growth, income distribution etc.

Another important area in which complete demand systems are found useful is for deriving true cost of living index. The true cost of living index is derived by comparing the minimum cost, $c(p, u^r)$ for attaining a given level of utility, (u^r) at different prices. If the preferences are homothetic, price would be independent of (u^r) and we have a unique cost of living index. Unlike the conventional (Statistical) Laspeyre and Passche indices which are based on fixed quantity bundles, the true cost of living index is based on fixed utility which allows for substitution among commodities whenever prices change. The base weighted (Laspeyre) true cost of living index associated with linear expenditure system turned out to be

$$P(p^1, p^0; u) = \left(\sum_j p_j^1 \gamma_j + \left(y^0 - \sum_j p_j^0 \gamma_j \right) \prod_k (p_k^1)^{\beta_k} \right) \Big/ y_0$$

where '*P*' is the price index; are the reference (base) and current period prices respectively.

The incidence of under-nutrition and mal-nutrition is very high in the state of Orissa. A large section of the population is deprived of the minimum calorie intake in the state. The total quantity of different food items consumed by the households does not meet its minimum calorie requirement (under-nutrition). The real problem appears to be the distributional imbalance in the cereals consumption, since cereals is the major source of calorie intake. What then are the policies to alleviate the caloric deprivation of the poor? The redistribution strategy of limiting the consumption of the high income (top 30 per cent of the population) group and transferring the purchasing power to the poor has received wide attention in Indian plan formulations. Simple calculations using the caloric elasticity would show that in order to eradicate caloric deficiency, it would be necessary to increase the per capita expenditure of the low income (bottom 30 per cent of the population) group through slicing the expenditures of the high income group. However, such consumption transfers would result in additional demand for cereals, since the cereal group takes a comparatively greater share in the marginal rupee spent by the low income group. If the excess demand for cereals is not eased through supply expansion, cereal price tends to rise, and the impact of the price rise would be heaviest on the poorest section of the population not covered by purchasing power transfers.

It is, thus, clear that meeting the caloric deficiency by consumption transfers presupposes stepping up of the aggregate cereal consumption. On the other hand, a number of schemes have been proposed for nationwide public distribution which is workable with the existing supply. The implementation of the schemes is still a hope. The rural population, especially their vulnerable sections had little access to the public distribution system. Such inadequate coverage would be worse than no rationing at all, since the vulnerable population outside the rationed areas may then be without assured supplies.

The presence of inter-regional and inter-community variations in the consumption patterns in Orissa reveals that southern region and particularly ST households of this region have the lowest per capita expenditure with the highest Engel ratio for food (Panda, 2006). This supports the view that the incidence of poverty in Orissa is the highest among tribal households. Adequate attention must be given in planning and allocation of resources for tribal development in general and development of the Southern region in particular.

Yet, another important area in which complete demand systems are found useful is nutrition. From the estimated demand system, nutrition consumption functions can be derived by assuming constant nutrient-food conversion factors. Notice that different food and non-food prices influence nutrient prices. The nutrition consumption function has been used in many poverty studies in India. In many other Indian poverty studies, the total expenditure corresponding to a given minimum desirable level of calories intake is also considered for the estimation of poverty line.

Money metric utility is concerned with expressing the preferences of an individual for different goods and services in money terms. Hence, it is used for welfare measurement of an individual. It considers the minimum cost, c (p, u^r) for attaining a given level of 'u' at a fixed base (reference) period price vectors, p^r as the measure of welfare of an individual. The money metric utility gives the minimum expenditure required in each year at the base (or reference) period prices to achieve the same utility level for different set of current total expenditures and current prices. It is clear that in the base year the value of money metric coincides with the actual expenditure. The relative welfare index, $c(u^1, p^r)/c(u^0, p^r)$ is used as a measure of welfare. If the relative welfare index ratio is greater (less) than 1, it indicates an increase (decrease) in welfare for the transition from u^0 to u^1. It can be seen that money metric utility values indicate exactly the same pattern as that of real expenditure obtained by deflating nominal expenditure by base weighted true cost of living index. Note that the two will coincide exactly if the nominal expenditure is deflated by current weighted true cost of living index (Deaton, 1980).

The household size economies of scale from cereals and its product; pulses and its product; edible oil and other food items for both rural and urban households suggests greater increase in demand for these food items in future. Hence, further diversification of agriculture in the state as well as in the country is necessary to meet the growing demand of these food items. There is clear evidence of diseconomies of scale in the consumption of milk and its products, meat, fish and egg and clothing for both rural and urban households which indicates less demand for these items in future as the state is lagging behind in the production of milk and its products, meat, fish and egg and textile products. The Government of Orissa has initiated its efforts to increase the production of milk and its products and meat, fish and egg. But there is urgent need for development of textile industry in Orissa to restrict the outflow of greater proportion of state income to other textile producing states of western India.

These days' econometrics studies on household consumption expenditure occupy prime of place in the formulation of perspective plan and government policy making. Demand forecasting for various items of consumption is made, given a certain growth pattern of the economy, a projected growth in population, its rural-urban consumption patterns and the distribution consumer expenditure on different good and services. While estimating the demand for different goods and services, estimation of their income/ expenditure elasticities become an imperative necessity. The success of government programmes depend on correct specification and estimation of the various demand functions for different good and services. For estimation of poverty line, determination of consumption baskets at different levels of expenditure is essential. It must now be mentioned that the theoretical restrictions are far more relevant for time-series based demand analysis than for cross-sectional analysis. The time-series data depict simultaneous variation in quantities, prices and income and hence, provide a scope for checking whether the theoretical restrictions are valid or not. Cross-sectional studies, on the other hand, are usually based on the assumption that variation of prices in cross-section data are negligible and as such only income responses may be computed from such studies. Thus, most of the theoretical restrictions find little importance in cross-section studies.

BIBLIOGRAPHY

Aasnes, J. E., Bierens, H. and Skjerpen T. (1993), "Engel Functions, Panel Data, and Latent Variables", Econometrica, Vol. 61, No. 6, pp.1395-1422.

Abdulai, A. and Aubert, D. (2002), "A Cross-section Analysis of Household Demand for Food and Nutrients in Tanzania", Agricultural Economics, Vol.31, pp.67-79.

Abdulai, A. (2001), "Economies of Scale and Demand for Food in Switzerland: Parametric and Non-Parametric Analysis", Journal of Agricultural Economics, Vol.54, No.2, pp. 247-67.

Abdulai, A. (2002), "Household Demand for Food in Switzerland: A quadratic Almost Ideal Demand System", Swiss Journal of Economics and Statistics, Vol.138, No.1, pp.1-18.

Adrian M, Ferguson, B.S (1987), "Demand for Domestic and Imported Alcohol in Canada" Applied Economics, Vol. 19, pp-531-540.

Agbola, F.W. (2001), "Estimation of Food Demand Patterns in South Africa based on a Survey of Households", Journal of Agricultural and Applied Economics, Vol.35, No.3, pp.662-70.

Aguero, J.M. and Gould, B.W. (2001), "Household Composition and Brazilian Food Purchases: An Expenditure System Approach", Canadian Journal of Agricultural Economics, Vol. 51, pp.323-45.

Acharya. Lalita (2000), "Effect of the Age of the head on household consumption pattern" an Unpublished M.Phil. Thesis Submitted to Berhampur University, Orissa.

Ahmad, E. and Ludlow, S. (1987), "Aggregate and Regional Demand Response Pattern in Pakistan", Pakistan Devolvement Review, Vol.26, pp. 645-55.

Ahmad, E. and Ludlow, S. (1988), "Demand Response in Pakistan: A Modification of Linear Expenditure System", Pakistan Development Review, Vol.27, No.3, pp.293-308.

Ahtola. O.T. (1986), "Effects of Cost-related Feedback on Consumer Knowledge and Consumption", Journal of Economic Psychology, Vol. 23, pp 48-61.

Alston, J.M Foster, K.A and Green, R.D. (1994), "Estimating Elasticity with the Linear Approximate Almost Ideal Demand System: Some Monto Carlo Results", Review of Economics and Statistics, Vol.74.

Amemiya, T. (1974), "Multivariate Regression and Simultaneous Equation Models When the Dependent Variable are Truncated Normal", Econometrica, Vol. 42, pp. 999-1012.

Amemiya, T. (1985), "Instrumental Variable Estimator for the Non-Linear Errors in Variables Model", Journal of Econometrics, Vol.28, pp.273-90.

Amemiya, T. (1999), Advanced Econometrics. Cambridge: Harvard University Press.

Arndt, C. (1985), "Demand for Herbicide Use in Corn: An Entropy Approach Using Micro-Level Data" Journal of Agricultural and Resource Economics, Vol. 24, No.1, pp. 4-22.

Anderson, G.J. and Blundell, R. (1983), "Testing Restrictions in a Flexible Demand System: An Application to Consumer's Expenditure in Canada", Review of Economic Studies, Vol.50, pp.397-410.

Anderson, R.W. (1979), "Perfect Price Aggregation and Empirical Demand Analysis", Econometrica, Vol. 47, pp. 1209-30.

Anderson, R.W. (1980), "Some Theory of Inverse Demand for Applied Demand Analysis", European Economic Review, Vol.14, pp. 281-90.

Anderson, G.J. and Blundell, R.W. (1982), "Estimation and Hypothesis Testing in Dynamic Singular Equation Systems", Econometrica, Vol.50, No.6, pp.1559-79.

Arndt, C., Liu, S. and Preckel, P.V. (1999), "On Dual Approaches to Demand Systems Estimation in the Presence of Binding Quantity Constraints", Applied Economics, Vol.31, pp. 999-1008.

Asche, F, and Wessells, C.R.(1997),"On Prices Indices in the Almost Ideal Demand System", American Journal of Agricultural Economics, Vol. 79, pp.1182-85.

Ashley, R. Granger C.W.J. and Schmalensee R. (1980), "Advertising and Aggregate Consumption: An Analysis of Causality", Econometrica, Vol.48, pp.1149-68.

Attfield, C.L.F. (1997), "Estimating a Co-integrating Demand System", European Economic Review, Vol. 41, pp. 61-73.

Bachmeier, L. and Li, Q. (2002), "Is the Disturbance Term Structure Non-linear? A Semi-Parametric Investigation", Applied Economics Letters, Vol.9, pp.151-51.

Balcombe, K.G, and Davis, J.R. (1996), "An Application of Co-integration Theory in the Estimation of the Almost Ideal Demand System for Food Consumption in Bulgaria", Agricultural Economics, Vol.15, pp. 47-60.

Banerjee, A., Dolado, J. and Smith, G. (1986), "Exploring Equilibrium Relationships in Econometrics through Static Models: Some Monte Carlo Evidence", Oxford Bulletin of Economics and Statistics, Vol. 48, pp. 253-78.

Banks, J., Blundell, R. and Lewbel, A. (1996), "Tax Reform and Welfare Measurement: Do We Need Demand System Estimates?", The Economic Journal, Vol. 106, pp. 1227-41.

Banks, J., Blundell, R. and Lewbel, A. (1997), "Quadratic Engel Curves and Consumer Demand", Review of Economics and Statistics, Vol.79, pp. 527-39.

Barens, Rand, and Gillingham, R. (1984), "Demographic Effects in Demand Analysis: Estimation of the Quadratic Expenditure System using Micro Data", Review of Economics and Statistics, Vol.66, No.4, pp.591-601.

Barnett, W.A. (1979), "Theoretical Foundation for The Rotterdam Model", Review of Economic Studies, Vol.46, pp. 109-30.

Barten, A. P. (1964), "Consumer Demand Functions under Conditions of Almost Additive Preferences", Econometrica, Vol.32, pp.1-38.

Barten, A.P. (1964), "Family Composition, Price and Expenditure Patterns" in Hart, P.E., G. Mills, and J.K. Whittaker (eds.), Econometric Analysis for National Planning, Butterworth, London.

Barten, A. P. (1967), "Evidence on the Slutsky Conditions for Demand Equations", Review of Economics and Statistics, Vol.49, pp.77-84.

Barten, A.P. (1968), "Estimating Demand Equations", Econometrica, Vol.36, No.2, pp.213-51

Barten A. P. (1969), "Maximum Likelihood Estimation of a Complete System of Demand Equations", European Economic Review, Vol. 1, pp. 7-73.

Becketti, S, W., Lillard, Gould L. and Welch, F. (1988), "The Panel Study of Income Dynamics after Fourteen Years: An Evaluation", Journal of Labor Economics, Vol.6, No.4, pp. 472-92.

Bhargava, A. (1991), "Identification and Panel Data Models with Endogenous Regressors", Review of Economic Studies, Vol.58, pp. 129-40.

Bhattacharya, N. (1978), "Studies on Consumer Behavior in India", in N. Bhattacharya and N.S. Iyengar (eds.), A Survey of Research in Economics: Econometrics, Vol.7, ICSSR, pp.176-232.

Bierens, H, and Pott-Buter H. A. (1990), "Specification of Household Expenditure Functions and Equivalence Scales by Nonparametric Regression", Econometric Reviews, Vol.9, pp.123- 210.

Biswas, A. K. (1959), "Estimation of the Increase in the Demand for Food and Cereals during the Third Five Year Plan", ISI, Planning Division, Working Paper No.167.

Blackorby, Charles, Boyce Richard, and Russell, Robert R. (1978), "Estimation of Demand Systems Generated by the Gorman Polar Form: A Generalization of the S-Branch Utility Tree", Econometrica, Vol.46, pp. 345-362.

Blanciforti, L, and Green, R. (1983), "The Almost Ideal Demand System: A Comparison and Application to Food Groups", Agriculture Economics Research, Vol. 35, No.3, pp.1-10.

Blaylock, J. and Blisard, W. (1992), "U.S. Cigarettes Consumption: The Case of Low- Income Women", American Journal of Agricultural Economics, Vol. 74, pp. 698-705.

Blaylock, J. and Blisard, W. (1993), "Women and the Demand for Alcohol: Estimating Participation and Consumption", The Journal of Consumer Affairs, Vol. 27, pp. 48-89.

Blaylock, J., and Blisard, W. (1993), "Wine Consumption by US Men", Applied Economics 24: 645-651

Blundell, R.W. and C. Meghir. (1987), "Bivariate Alternatives to the Tobit Model", Journal of Econometrics, Vol. 34, pp. 179-200.

Blundell, R. (1988), "Consumer Behaviour: Theory and Empirical Evidence: A Survey", The Economic Journal, Vol. 98, pp.16-65.

Blundell, R., Duncan, A. and Pendakur, K. (1998), "Semi-parametric Estimation of Consumer Demand, Journal of Applied Econometrics, Vol.13, pp. 435-461.

Blundell, R.W. and Robin, J.M. (1999), "Estimation in Large and Disaggregated Demand Systems: An Estimator for Conditionally Linear Systems", Journal of Applied Econometrics, Vol. 14, pp.209-32.

Blundell, R. and Robin, J.M. (2000), "Latent Separability: Grouping Goods without Weak Separability", Econometrica, Vol. 68, pp. 53-84.

Blundell, R. and Powell, J.L. (2002), "Endogeneity in Semi-parametric Binary Response Models", Review of Economic Studies, Vol.71, pp. 655-79.

Bollino, C.A. and Violi, R. (1990), "A Generalized Version of the Almost Ideal System and Translog Demand System" , Economics Letters, Vol. 34, pp. 127-29.

Boroah, V.K. (1985),"Consumer Expenditure Using Rotterdam Model", Applied Econometrics,Vol.17, No4, pp. 675-88.

Bouis, H. and Haddad, L. (1992), "Are Our Estimates of Calorie-Income Elasticities too High? A Recalibration of the Plausible Range" Journal of Development Economics, Vol.39, No.2, pp. 333-64.

Bouis, H. (1994), "The Effect of Income on Demand for Food in Poor Countries: Are our Data Bases Giving us Reliable Estimates?", Journal of Development Economics, Vol. 44, pp.199-226.

Bowmaker, P.A, and Nieuwoudt, W.L (1990), "Demand Equations for Selected South African Agricultural Commodities", Agrekon, Vol.29, No.1, pp. 46–50.

Bradly, D.S. and Barber, H.A. (1948), "The Pattern of Food Expenditures", Review of Economics and Statistics, Vol.30, pp. 198-206.

Brian W. Gould and Villarreal, Hector J. (2006), "An assessment of the Current Structure of Food Demand in Urban China", Agricultural Economics, International Association of Agricultural Economists, Vol. 34 (1), pp 1-16.

Brian W. Gould & Villarreal, Hector J.(2006), "An Assessment of the Current Structure of Food Demand in Urban China", Agricultural Economics, Vol.34(1), pp 1-16.

Brown, J.A.C. and Deaton, A.S. (1972), Models of Consumer Behaviour: A Survey", Economic Journal, Vol. 82, pp. 1145-1236.

Browning, R, and M, Collado. (2001), "The Response of Expenditures to Anticipated Income Changes: Panel Data Estimates", American Economic Review, Vol. 91, No.3, pp.681-92.

Browning, R. and Collado, M. (2002), "Habits and Heterogeneity in Demands: A Panel Data Analysis", Centre for Applied Micro Econometrics, Institute of Economics, Working Paper No. 2002-18, University of Copenhagen, Copenhagen.

Burney, N. and Akmal, M. (1991), "Food Demand in Pakistan: An Application of the Extended Linear Expenditure System", Journal of Agriculture Economics, Vol.27, No-4, pp. 28-52.

Buse, A. (1992), "Aggregation, Distribution and Dynamics in the Linear and Quadratic Expenditure System", Review of Economic and Statistics, Vol.74, pp. 45-53.

Buse, A. (1994), "Evaluating the Linearized Almost Ideal Demand System", American Journal of Agricultural Economics, Vol.76, pp. 781-93.

Byrne, P, Capps, O., and Saha, A. (1996), "Analysis of food-away from home expenditure patterns for U.S. households, 1982-89", American Journal of Agricultural Economics, Vol.78, pp.614- 27.

Byron, R.P. (1968), "Methods of Estimating Demand Equation Using Prior Information," Australian Economics Papers, Vol.7, pp. 76-232.

Byron, R.P. (1984), "On the Flexibility of the Rotterdam Model", European Economic Review, Vol.24, No.3, pp.273-83.

Carpentier, A. and Guyomard, H. (2001), "Unconditional Elasticities in Two-Stage Demand Systems: An Approximate Solution", American Journal of Agricultural Economics, Vol. 83, No.1, pp.222-29

Carter, M.R, and May J.(1999), "Poverty, Livelihood and Class in Rural South Africa", World Development Report, Vol. 27, No.1, pp.1-20.

Carter, M.R, and May, J. (2001), "One Kind of Freedom: Poverty Dynamics in Post-Apartheid South Africa", World Development, Vol.29, No.12, pp. 1987-2002.

Chalfant, J.A.(1987), "A globally flexible, almost ideal demand system", Journal of Business and Economic Statistics, Vol. 5, pp.233-42.

Chambers, M.J. (1990), "Forecasting with demand systems", Journal of Econometrics, Vol.4, pp.363-76.

Chambers, M.J. and Nowman, K.B. (1997), "Forecasting with the Almost Ideal Demand System: Evidence from Some Alternative Dynamic Specifications", Applied Economics, Vol. 29, pp. 935- 43.

Charlier, E. Melenberg, B. and Van Soast, A.H.O. (2000), "An Analysis of Housing Expenditure Using Semi Parametric Cross-Section Models", Empirical Economics, Vol.25, pp. 437-62.

Chavas, J.P. (1983), "Structural Change in the Demand for Meat", American Journal of Agricultural Economics, Vol.65, pp.148-54.

Chern, Wen S (2000), "Assessment of Demand Factors Affecting Global Food Security," in W.S. Chern, C.A. Carter, and S.Y. Shei (eds.), Food Security in Asia: Economics and Policies, Edward Elgar, 2000.

Christensen, L.R., Jorgenson, D.W. and Lau, L.J.(1975), "Transcendental Logarithmic Utility Functions.", American Economic Review, Vol. 65, No. 3, pp. 367-83.

Christensen, M.L. (2002), "Heterogeneity in Consumer Demands and the Income Effect" Institute of Economics, University of Copenhagen, mimeo.

Chung, C.F. (2001), "Modeling Demand Systems with Demographic Effects Based on the Modifying Function Approach" Economics Letters, Vol.73, pp. 269-74.

Clarkson, G.P.E. (1963), "The Theory of Consumer Demand", Prentice Hall, U.S.A.

Clements, K., Selvanathan, E. and Selvanathan, S. (1996), "Applied Demand Analysis: A Survey", Economic Record, Vol.72, No. 216, pp. 63-82.

Cleveland, W.S. and Devlin, S.J. (1988), "Locally Weighted Regression: An approach to Regression Analysis by Local Fitting.", Journal of the American Statistical Association, Vol.83, pp.596- 610.

Coondoo, D. (1975), "Contribution to the Analysis of Consumer Behaviour", Unpublished Ph.D. Thesis, Indian Statistical Institute, Calcutta.

Coondoo, D. and Majumder, A. (1985), "Performance of the Linear Expenditure System and its Modification with Non-Linear Price Functions on the Indian Data , Journal of Quantitative Economics, Vol.1, No.12, pp. 299-313.

Coondoo, D. and Majumder, A. (1987), "A System of Demand Equations based on Price Independent Generalized Linearity", International Economic Review, Vol.28, pp. 213-28.

Cox, T. L. and Wohlgenant, M. K. (1986), "Prices and Quality Effects in Cross-Sectional Demand Analysis", American Journal of Agricultural Economics, Vol.68, No.4, pp. 908-19.

Craig, J.G. (1971), "Some Statistical Models for Limited Dependent Variables with Applications to the Demand for Durable Goods", Econometrica, Vol. 39, pp.829-844.

Daniel, Rubinfeld and Roy Epstein, (2002), "Merger Simulation with Brand-Level Margin Data: Extending PCAIDS with Nests", Berkeley Olin Program in Law and Economics, Working Paper Series.

Dax, P. (1987), "Estimation of Income Elasticities from Cross-section Data", Applied Economics, Vol.19, No.11, pp. 1471-82.

Deaton, A. (1972), "The Estimation and Testing of Systems of Demand Equations: A Note", European Economic Review, Vol.3, pp.399-411.

Deaton, A. (1974), "The Analysis of Consumer Demand in the United Kingdom", Econometrica, Vol. 42, pp.341-366.

Deaton, A. (1978), "Specification and Testing in Applied Demand Analysis", Economic Journal, Vol.88, pp.524-36.

Deaton, A. (1987), "Estimation of Own-and Cross-Price Elasticity from Household Survey Data", Journal of Econometrics, Vol. 36, pp. 7-30.

Deaton, A. (1988), "Quality, Quantity and Spatial Variation of Price" American Economic Review, Vol.78, No.3, pp.18-430.

Deaton, A. (1997), "The Analysis of Household Surveys: A Microeconomic Approach to Development Policy", Baltimore, John Hopkins University Press.

Deaton, A., and Muellbauer, J. (1980), "An Almost Ideal Demand System", American Economic Review, Vol. 70, No.3, pp.312-36.

Deaton, A. and Irish, M. (1984), "A Statistical Model for Zero Expenditures in Household Budgets", Journal of Public Economics, Vol. 23, pp.312-26.

Deaton, A. and Muellbauer, J. (1999), "Economies of Consumer Behaviour", Cambridge University Press, Cambridge, U.K.

Decoster, Andre and Schokkaert, Erik, (1996), "Tax Reform Results with Different Demand Systems", Journal of Public Economics, Elsevier, Vol. 41(3), pp. 277-296,

Dhar, T., Chavas, J.P. and Gould, B.W. (2001), "An Empirical Assessment of Endogeneity Issues in Demand Analysis for Differentiated Products", American Journal of Agricultural Economics, Vol.85, No.3, pp. 605-17.

Dickey, D.A. and Fuller, W.A. (1981), "Likelihood Ratio Statistics for Autoregressive Time- series with a Unit Root", Econometrica, Vol. 49, pp.1057–72.

Diewert, W. E. (1981), "The Economic Theory of Index Numbers: A Survey", in Angus Deaton (ed.), The Theory and Measurement of Consumer Behaviour, Cambridge University Press, Cambridge, London, New York

Diewert, W.E and Wales, T.J. (1993), "Linear and Quadric Spine Model For Consumer Demand Functions", Canadian Journal of Economics, Vol.26, No.1, pp.77-106.

Döckel, J.A. and Groenewald, J.A. (1970), "The demand for food in South Africa" Agrekon, Vol. 9, No.4, pp.15-20.

Dong, D, Shonkwiler, J.S. and Capps, O. (1998), "Estimation of Demand Functions using Cross-sectional Household Data: The Problem Revisited", American Journal of Agricultural Economics, Vol.80, pp.466–73.

Dong, D., Gould, B.W. and Kaiser, H.M. (2002), "Food demand in Mexico: An application of the Amemiya-Tobin Approach to the Estimation of a Censored Food System", American Journal of Agricultural Economics, Vol. 86, pp.1094-1107.

Douglas Fisher, Fleissig, Adrian R. and Serletis A.(2001), "An Empirical Comparison of Flexible Demand System Functional Forms", Journal of Applied Econometrics, John Wiley & Sons, Ltd., Vol. 16(1), pp 59-80.

Duffy, M. (2002), "Advertising and Food, Drink and Tobacco Consumption in the United Kingdom:A Dynamic Demand System", Agricultural Economics, Vol.37,pp.1-20.

Dynan, K.E. (2000), "Habit Formation in Consumer Preferences: Evidence from Panel Data", American Economic Review, Vol. 90, No.3, pp. 391-406.

Eales, J.S. and Unnevehr, L.J. (1988), "Demand for Beef and Chicken Products: Separability and Structural Change", American Journal of Agricultural Economics, Vol.70, pp.521- 532.

Eales, J.S and Unnevehr, L.J (1994), " The Inverse Almost Ideal Demand System", European Economic Review,Vol.38, No.1, pp-101-15.

Eales, J.S., and Unnevehr, L.J. (1993), "Simultaneity and structural change in U.S. meat demand", American Journal of Agricultural Economics, Vol.75, pp. 259-68.

Edgerton, D.L. (1997), "Weak Separability and the Estimation of Elasticities in Multistage Demand Systems", American Journal of Agricultural Economics, Vol. 79, pp. 62-79.

Elliot, M.B. and Van Z.J. (1991), "The Effect of Income on the Market for Carbohydrates in South Africa", Agrekon, Vol. 30, No.4, pp-269-71.

Engle, R.F. and Granger, C.W.J. (1987),"Cointegration and Error Correction: Representation, Estimation and Testing", Econometrica, Vol.55, pp. 251-76.

Evert, V.I. (1984), "Estimation of Demand System using both Time-series Data and Cross- section Data", De Economist, Vol.132, No.4, pp.419-39.

Fan, J. X., Lee, J. and Hanna, S. (1996), "Household Expenditures on Apparel: A Complete Demand System Approach", Consumer Interests Annual, Vol.42, pp.173-180.

Feenstra, R. and Rose, A. K. (1997), "Putting Things in Order: Patterns of Trade Dynamics and Macroeconomics", CEPR Discussion Paper No.1629, C.E.P.R.

Fitsgerald, J. P and Moffitt, R. (1998), "An Analysis of Sample Attrition in Panel Data: The Michigan Panel Study of Income Dynamics", Journal of Human Resources, Vol. 33, No. 2, pp. 251-99.

Fraser, I, and Moosa, I.A. (2002), "Demand Estimation in the Presence of Stochastic Trend and Seasonality: The Case of Meat Demand in the United Kingdom", American Journal of Agricultural Economics, Vol.84, pp. 83-89.

Frisch, R. (1936), "Annual Survey of General Economic Theory: The Problem of Index Numbers", Econometrica, Vol. 4, pp.1-39.

Ganguly, A. (1960), "Consumption Pattern of Different Occupation Groups, in A. Ganguly (ed.), Studies on Consumer Behaviour", Asia Publishing House, Bombay.

Gao, X., and Spreen, T. (1994), "A. Micro-econometric Analysis of U.S. Meat Demand", Canadian Journal of Agricultural Economics. Vol.42, pp.397-412.

Ghysels, E, Lee, H.S, and Noh, J. (1994) "Testing for Unit Roots in Time-series: Some Theoretical Extensions and A Monte Carlo Investigation", Journal of Econometrics, Vol. 62, pp. 415– 42

Goldberger, A.S. (1970), "Functional Form and Utility: A Review of Consumer Demand Theory, Westview Press, London.

Goldman, S. and Uzawa, H. (1964), "A Note on Separability in Demand Analysis", Econometrica, Vol. 32, pp.387-98.

Gorman, W.M. (1953), "A Revision of Demand Theory", Oxford University Press.

Gorman, W.M. (1976), "Tricks with Utility Functions", in M. Artis and R. Nobay (eds.), Essays in Economic Analysis, Cambridge University Press, Cambridge, U.K.

Gorman, W.M. (1981), "Some Engel Curves", in A.Deaton (ed.), The Theory and Measurement of Consumer Behaviour, Cambridge University Press, Cambridge.

Gould, W, and Villarreal, H.J. (2002),"An Assessment of the Current Structure of Food Demand in Urban China", Agricultural Economics, Vol. 34, pp.1-16.

Government of India (2006), "Level and Pattern of Consumer Expenditure", National Sample Survey Organisation, Ministry of Statistics and Programme Implementation, Delhi.

Green, R., and Alston, J.M. (1990), "Elasticities in AIDS Models", American Journal of Agricultural Economics, Vol. 72, pp.442-445.

Greene, William H. (1993), "Econometric Analysis" Second Edition, Macmillan Publishing Company, New York.

Gujarati, D. (2000), "Basic Econometrics", Mc-Graw Hill, Kogakusha Ltd. ,Tokyo, Japan.

Gupta, D. B. (1968), "A Comparison of Consumption Pattern in Uttar Pradesh and Madras: A Study of Inter Regional Variation with Reference to India", Indian Economic Review, Vol.5, pp.193-205.

Gupta, D.B. (1968), "Consumption Pattern in India: A Study of Inter Regional Variation", Ph.D. Dissertation, University of Birmingham.

Gupta, D.B. (1972), "Some International Comparison of Consumption Pattern: A Study with Reference to India", Presented to the 11th Econometric Conference, Hyderabad.

Haines,P.S., Guilkey, D.K. and Popkin, B.M. (1988), "Modeling Food Consumption Decisions as a Two-step Process" American Journal of Agricultural Economics, Vol. 70, pp.543-52.

Hancock, P.J., Nieuwoudt, W. L. and Lyne, M.C. (1984), "Demand Analysis of Meats in South Africa", Agrekon, Vol. 23, No.3, pp.26–29.

Hausman, J.A. and Taylor, W. E. (1986), "Panel Data and Unobservable Individual Effects" Econometrica, Vol. 31, pp. 93-118.

Hausman, J.A. (1978), "Specification Tests in Econometrics", Econometrica, Vol.46, pp.1251- 71.

Heckman, J.J. (1979), "Sample Selection Bias as a Specification Error", Econometrica, Vol. 47, pp. 153-62.

Heien, D. and Wessells, C.R. (1990), "Demand Systems Estimation with Micro Data: A Censored Regression Approach", Journal of Business and Economic Statistics, Vol. 8, pp.365-71.

Hogarty, T. and Elzinga, K. (1972), "The Demand for Beer", Review of Economics and Statistics, Vol. 54, pp. 195–198.

Houthakker, H. S. (1951), "Compensated Changes In Quantities And Qualities Consumed", The Review of Economic Studies, Vol.19, pp.155-64.

Houthakker, H.S.(1965), "New Evidence on Demand Elasticities", Econometrica, Vol.33, pp.277-88.

Howe, H., Pollak, R. A. and Wales, T. J. (1979), "Theory and Time-series Estimation of the Quadratic Expenditure System", Econometrica, Vol. 47, pp.1231-43.

Huang, K.S. and Haidacher, R. (1983), "Estimation of a Composite Food Demand System for the United States", Journal of Business and Economic Statistics, Vol.1, pp.285-91.

Hylleberg, S, Engle, R.F, Granger, C.W.J, and Yoo, B.S. (1990), "Seasonal Integration and Cointegration", Journal of Econometrics, Vol.44, pp.215–38.

Iyengar, N.S. (1960), "On a Problem of Estimation of Increase in Consumer Demand", Sankhya, Vol. 22, pp.379-90.

Iyengar. N.S. (1964), "Contribution to the Analysis of Consumer Behavior", Unpublished Thesis, Indian Statistical Institute, Calcutta.

Jaffry, S, Taylor, G. and Pascoe, S. (2005), "An Inverse Demand System for Fish Species in Spain, Working paper, Centre for the Economics and Management of Aquatic Resources.

Jain, L.R. and Minhas, B.S. (1991), "Rural and Urban Consumer Price Indices by Commodity Groups", Sarvekshana, Vol. 15, pp.1-21.

Johansen, S. (1988), "A Statistical Analysis of Cointegrating Vectors." Journal of Economic Dynamics and Control, Vol.12, pp.231-54.

Johnston, J. (1972), "Econometric Methods", 2nd Ed., Mc-Graw Hill New York.

Jones, A. (1989), "A Systems Approach to the Demand For Alcohol and Tobacco", Bulletin of Economic Research, Vol.41. No.2, pp. 85-101.

Jonson, S.R, Hussian, Z.A and Green, R.D. (1986),"Demand System Estimation: Methods and Applications", The Lowa University Press, Amsterdam.

Jorgenson, D.W, Lau, L.J. and Stoker, T.M. (1982),"The Transcendental Logarithmic Model of Aggregate Consumer Behavior." in R. Basman and G. Rhodes (eds.), Advances in Econometrics, Vol.1, Greenwich, Ct. JAI Press.

Jospeh, P. (1968), "Application of the Linear Expenditure System to NSS Data", Some Further Result", Economic and Political Weekly, Vol.13, pp. 609-15.

Karagiannis, G. and Mergos, G. J. (2002),"Estimating Theoretically Consistent Demand Systems using Cointegration Techniques with Application to Greek Food data" , Economics Letters, Vol. 74, pp.37-43.

Karagiannis, G., Katranidis, S. and Velentzas, K. (2000), "An Error Correction Almost Ideal Demand System for Meat in Greece", Agricultural Economics, Vol. 22, pp.29-35.

Kastens, T.L. and Brester, G.W. (1996), "Model Selection and Forecasting Ability of Theory: Constrained Food Demand Systems", American Journal of Agricultural Economics, Vol.78, pp.301-13.

Kebede (2003), "Decomposition of Household Expenditure and Child Welfare in Rural Ethiopia", Bereket Working Paper.

Kesavan, T., Hassan, Z.A., Hensen, H. H. and Johnson, S.R. (1993), "A Dynamic and Long-run Structurein U.S. Meat Demand", Canadian Journal of Agricultural Economics, Vol. 41, pp.139-53.

Klevmarken, A. (1979), "A Comparative Study of Complete Demand Functions", Journal of Econometrics, Vol.10, No.2 , pp. 165-91.

Koch, S.F. (2002), "South African Households: Are Expenditure Patterns Almost Ideal?" Paper Presented at the 9th Annual Conference on Econometric Modeling for Africa, Cape Town, South Africa.

Kremers, J., Ericsson, N. and Dolado, J. (1992), "The Power of Cointegration Tests", Oxford Bulletin of Economics and Statistics, Vol.54, pp. 325-48.

Krishnamurthy, K. (1965), "Consumption Function for India: A Macro Time-series Study", The Indian Economic Journal, Vol.13, No.2, pp.218-31.

Labeaga, J.M. and López, A. (1997), "A Study of Petro Consumption Using Spanish Panel Data", Applied Economics, Vol.29, No.6, pp.795-802.

LaFrance, J.T.(1991), "When is Expenditure Exogenous in Separable Demand Models", Western Journal of Agricultural Economics, Vol.16, pp. 49-62.

Lamm, R.M. (1982), "A System of Dynamic Demand Functions for Food", Applied Economics, Vol.14, No.4, pp.375-89.

Laurent, C. and Comon, E. (2001), "Behavioral Heterogeneity and the Income Effect", The Review of Economics and Statistics, Vol.85, No.3, pp. 653-69.

Lecocq, S. and Robin, J. (2002), "Estimating Demand Response with Panel Data", Empirical Economics, Vol. 27, pp. 65-74.

Lee, L. and Pitt, M. M. (1986), "Micro econometric Demand System with Binding Non-negativity Constraints: The Dual Approach", Econometrica, Vol.54, No.5, pp.1237-42.

Lesser, C.E.V. (1963), "Forms of Engel Functions", Econometrica, Vol.31, No.4, pp. 694-03

Lewbel, A. (1985), "A Unified Approach to Incorporating Demographic and Other Effects into Demand Systems", Review of Economic Studies, Vol.52, No.1, pp.1-18.

Lewbel, A. (1996), "Aggregation without Separability: A Generalized Composite Commodity Theorem", The American Economic Review, Vol.86, No.3, 524-43.

Lewbel, A. (1997),"Constructing Instruments for Regressions with Measurement Error When no Additional Data are Available: With an Application to Patents and R&D" Econometrica , Vol.65, pp. 93-118.

Lewis, P. and Andrews, N. (1989), "Household Demand in China", Applied Economics, Vol. 21, pp.793-807.

Liu, K.E (2001), "Food Demand in Urban China: An Empirical Analysis using Micro Household Data", Unpublished Ph.D. Dissertation, Ohio State University, Columbus, Ohio,

Liu, Kang E. and Wen S. Chern (2002), "Food Demand in Urban China and its Implications for Agricultural Trade: Model Selection Based on Forecasting", Journal of Agricultural Economics, Vol. 29, pp. 75-100.

Ljung, G. and Box, G. (1978), "On a Measure of Lack of Fit in Time-series Models", Biometrika, Vol. 67, pp. 297-303.

Lluch, C. (1973), "The Extended Linear Expenditure System", European Economic Review, Vol4, pp. 21-32.

Lluch, C. (1971), "Consumer Demand Functions", European Economic Review, Vol.2, pp. 272-302.

Loubser, M. (1990), "Income Elasticities of the Demand for Consumer Goods and Services", Bureau of Market Research, No. 175, University of South Africa, Pretoria.

Lubbe, W.F. (1990), "Decomposition of Price Time-series Components of the Red Meat Industry for Efficient Policy and Marketing Strategies", Agrekon, Vol.29, No.4, pp. 296 - 304.

Majudar, A. (1986), "Statistical Models of Consumer Behavior", Ph.D. Thesis, Indian Statistical Institute, Calcutta.

Majumdar, A. (1986), "Consumer Expenditure Pattern in India: A comparison of the Almost Ideal Demand System and The Linear Expenditure System", Sankhya, Series-B, Vol.48, pp.115-43.

Majumder, A. (1991), "Use Pooled Data: An Empirical Note on Demand Model for Consumers in India", Empirical Economics, Vol.17, No.2, pp.315-21.

Marnett, W. A. (1984), "On the Flexibility of The Rotterdam Model : A First Empirical Look", European Economic Reviews, Vol.24, No.3, pp.285-89

Mattei, A. (1971), "A Complete System of Dynamic Demand Functions", European Economic Review, Vol.2, pp.251-76.

Meenakhi. J.V and Ray, Ranjan (1999), "Regional Differences in India's Food Expenditure Pattern: A Complete Demand System

Approach", Journal of International Development, Vol.11, pp. 47-74.

Meenakshi et. al. (2002), "Impact of Household Size and Family Composition on Poverty", Journal of Policy Modeling, Vol.24, pp.539-59.

Meenakshi, J.V. and Ray, R. (1999), "Regional Differences in India's Food Expenditure Pattern: A Complete Demand Approach", Journal of International Development, Vol.2, pp.47-74.

Meghir C. and Robin, J.M. (1991), "Frequency of Purchase and the Estimation of Demand Systems", Journal of Econometrics, Vol.53, pp.53-85.

Meyerhoefer, C.D. (2002), "The Econometrics of Non-Standard Structural Demand Modeling: Applications to Transition Country Data", Unpublished Ph.D. Dissertation, Cornell University, Ithaca, New York,

Meyerhoefer, C.D., Ranney, C.K. and Sahn, D.E. (2001), "Consistent Estimation of Censored Demand Systems using Panel Data", American Journal of Agricultural Economics, Vol. 87, No.3, pp. 660-72.

Michalek, J. and Keyzer, M.A.(1992), "Estimation of a Two-Stage LES and AIDS: Consumer Demand System for Eight Countries", European Review of Agricultural Economics, Vol. 19, pp.137-163.

Moffit, R., Fitzgerald, J. and Gottschalk, P. (1999), "Sample Attrition in Panel Data: The Role of Selection on Observables",Annale d'Economie et de Statistique,pp.55-56.

Molina, J.S. and Gil, A. I. (2001), "The Demand Behavior of Consumers in Peru: A Demographic Analysis using the QUAIDS", Journal of Developing Areas, Vol. 39, No.1, pp.191-206.

Moro, D. and Sckokai, P. (2000), "Heterogeneous Preferences in Household Food Consumption in Italy", European Review of Agricultural Economics, Vol. 27, No.3, pp. 305-323.

Moschini, G. (1992), "A Non-nested Test of Separability for Flexible Functional Forms", The Review of Economics and Statistics, Vol. 74, No.2, pp.365-369.

Moschini, G. (1993), "Units of Measurement and the Stone Price Index in Demand System Estimation", American Journal of Agricultural Economics, Vol.77, pp. 63-68.

Moschini, G. and Daniele, M.(1994), "Maintaining and Testing Separability in Demand Systems." American Journal of Agricultural Economics, Vol.76, pp.61-74.

Moschini, G., Moro.D and Green R.D. (1994), "Maintaining and Testing Separability in Demand Systems", American Journal of Agricultural Economics, Vol.76, pp.61-73.

Moschini, G., and Vissa, A. (1995), "Food demand in Spain: An Application of the Almost Ideal System", Journal of Agricultural Economics, Vol. 45, No. 2, pp. 252-58.

Moschini, G. (1998), "The Semi Flexible Almost Ideal Demand System", European Economic Review , Vol.42, pp. 349-64.

Muellbauer, J. (1974), "Household Composition, Engel Curves and Welfare Comparisons Between Households: A Duality Approach", European Economic Review, Vol.5, pp.103-122

Muellbauer, J. (1976), "Community Preferences and the Representative Consumer," Econometrica, Vol. 44, pp. 525-43.

Muellbauer, J. (1977), "Testing the Barten Model of Household Composition Effects and the Cost of Children", Economic Journal, Vol. 87, No.347, pp.800-08.

Muellbauer, J. (1974), "Household Composition, Engel Curves and Welfare Comparisons between Households: A Duality Approach", European Economic Review, Vol.5, pp.103-122

Mukhatar. K.N. (1985), "Essays in Consumer Behavior: Evidence from Pakistan", Unpublished Ph.D. Thesis, Boston University, USA.

Murty, G.V.S.N and Murty, K.N. (1980), "On a Linear Demand System", Indian Economic Journal, Vol.27, pp118-24.

Murty, K.N. (1977), "Estimation of the Linear Expenditure System", A FORTAN-IV, Computer Algorithm, Anvesak,Vol.7, pp.181-93.

Murty, K.N. (1982), "Theoretical Restriction on the Parameter of Indirect Addilog Demand Equation: A Comment", Econometrica, Vol.50, pp. 225-37.

Murty, K.N. (1978), "Econometrics of Consumer Behaviour in India: A Study of Complete Demand Systems", Unpublished Ph.D. Thesis, Gujarat University, Ahmedabad.

Murty, K.N. (1980), "Consumer Behaviour in India: An Application of the Rotterdam Demand System", European Economic Review, Vol.14, pp.221-35.

Murty. K.N (1998), "Complete Demand System: A Compendium Occasional Paper No.3, University of Hyderabad, Hyderabad.

Murty. K.N. (2000), "Effects of Changes in Household Size, Current Taste and Preferences on Demand Pattern in India", Working Paper No.72, Center of Development of Economics, Delhi School of Economics, Delhi.

Nayga, Jr. R. M. and Capps, Jr. O. (1994), "Tests of Weak Separability in Disaggregated Meat Products", American Journal of Agricultural Economics, Vol.76, No.4, pp. 800-08.

Nayga, J.R.N. (1995), "Testing for Homogeneity in Demand Systems When the Regressors are Non-Stationary", Journal of Applied Econometrics , Vol.10, pp.147-63.

Nayga, Jr. R.M. (1996), "Sample Selectivity Models for Away From Home Expenditures on Wine and Beer", Applied Economics, Vol. 28, pp. 1421-25.

Nelson, J. (1992), "Methods of Estimating Household Equivalence Scales: An Empirical Investigation", Review of Income and Wealth, Vol. 38, No.3, pp.295-310.

Nelson, J. (1993), "Household Equivalence Scales: Theory Versus Policy?", Journal of Labour Economics, Vol.11, No.3, pp.471-93.

Nelson, J.A. (1991), "Quality Variation and Quantity Aggregation in Consumer Demand for Food", American Journal of Agricultural Economics, Vol.73, No.4, pp. 1204-12.

Nicol, C. (2000), "The Rank and Model Specification of Demand Systems: An Empirical Analysis using United States Micro Data", Canadian Journal of Economics, Vol. 34, No.1, pp.259- 89.

Nieuwoudt, W.L.(1998), "The Demand for Livestock Products in South Africa for 2000, 2010 and 2020", Part 1", Agrekon, Vol. 37, No.2.

Orcutt, G.H., Watts, H.W. and Edwards, J.B. (1968), "Data Aggregation and Information Loss", American Economic Review, Vol. 58, No.4, pp.773-87.

Panda, B. K. (1996), "Consumption Pattern in Orissa: An Econometric analysis", An Unpublished Ph.D. Thesis Submitted to Berhampur University, Berhampur.

Panda, B.K, Panda, R. K. and Sarangi. P. (2002), "Impact of Watersheds on Dry Land Farming in KBK Districts of Orissa", Journal of Rural Development, Vol. 26. No.2, pp.189-206.

Panda, B.K, Panigrhi, S and Sarangi, P. (2005), "Level of Living of Tribals in Orissa", PSE Economic Analyst, Vol.25, No.2.

Panda, B.K, and Dash M. K. (2002), "Determinants of Tribal Poverty in Orissa", Prajnanubhuti, Journal of Social Science and Humanities, Vol. 15, No. 2, pp.20-34.

Panda, B.K, and Sarangi, P. (2002), "Incidence of Poverty among Tribal in Orissa: An Empirical Analysis", Studies in History and Culture, Vol.9, No.2.

Panda, B.K, and Sarangi, P. (2002), "Spatial and Social Differentiation and the Level of Poverty in Orissa", in S.N. Mishra and B.K. Sahu (eds.), Globalisation: Economic Growth and Human Development, Anmol Publications, New Delhi..

Panda, B.K, and Sarangi. P. (2002), "Variation in the Level of Poverty among Social Classes", Indian Journal of Regional Science, Vol. 38, No.1.

Panda, B.K, and Sarangi. P and S. Patnaik (2002), "Impact of Economic Reforms on Employment in Orissa", Pratibimba, Vol.6, No.2

Panda, B.K, and Sarangi. P. (2001), "A Comparative Analysis of Growth of Employment in Different Sectors of Orissa", Strategy, Vol. 9, No.1.

Panda, B.K, and Sarangi. P. (2002), "Pattern of Employment in Orissa", in K.K.Bagchi (ed.) Employment and Poverty Alleviation Programmes in India: An Appraisal, Vol. 2, Abhijeet Publications, Delhi, pp. 504-544.

Panda, B.K, and Sarangi, P. and Pothal, S.P. (2005) , "Level of Living of Tribals in Southern Orissa", Adivasi Journal, Vol.46, No.1.

Panda, B.K, Panigrhi. S and Sarangi, P. (2007), "Estimation of Engel Elasticity from Different Specifications of Engel Function," Finance India, Vol.12, No.1, pp.105-32 (Forthcoming).

Panda, B.K. (2005), "Economic Reforms and Emerging Patterns of Employment", Mayur Publication, Bhubaneswar.

Panda, B.K. (2005), "Ownership and Diffusion of Household Durables", Productivity, Vol.48, No 2-3.

Panda, B.K. and Sarangi, P. (2004), "Inter-sectoral Variation in Household Consumption Pattern in Orissa", Studies in History and Culture, Vol.10, No.2.

Pandey. R. K and Sarin, B.S. (1984), "Estimation of Demand for Food Grains in UP, Margin, Vol.16, No.3,, pp.70-76.

Panigarhi, S.K. (2006), "Econometric Analysis of Household Consumption in Orissa" an Unpublished Ph.D. Thesis Submitted to Berhampur University.

Panigrahi. S.K. (1998), "Variation in Consumption Pattern of Affluent and Non-affluent Rural Households in Orissa: An Econometric Analysis", Unpublished M.Phil. Dissertation submitted to Berhampur University.

Park, J. and Rodney, H.B. (1996), "A Demand Systems Analysis of Food Commodities by U.S. Households Segmented by Income", American Journal of Agricultural Economics, Vol. 78, pp. 290-301.

Park, J. and Davis, G.C. (2001), "The Theory and Econometrics of Health Information in Cross-Sectional Nutrient Demand Analysis." American Journal of Agricultural Economics, Vol. 83, No.4, pp. 840-51.

Park, T. (1990), "Forecast Evaluation for Multivariate Time-series Models: The U.S. Cattle Market", Western Journal of Agricultural Economics, Vol. 15, pp. 133-43.

Parks, R. W. and Barten, A. P. (1973), "A Cross-Country Comparison of the Effects of Prices, Income and Population Composition on Consumption Patterns", The Economic Journal, Vol. 83, pp.834-52.

Parks, R. W. (1969), "Systems of Demand Equations: An Empirical Comparison of Alternative Functional Forms", Econometrica , Vol.37, pp.629-50.

Pashardes, P. (1993), "Bias in Estimating the Almost Ideal Demand System with the Stone Index Approximation, Economic Journal, Vol.103, pp.908-15.

Pearce, I .F. (1964), "A Contribution to Demand Analysis", Oxford University Press.

Pendakur, K. (1999), "Estimates and Tests of Based on Independent Equivalence Scales", Journal of Econometrics, Vol. 88, pp.1-40.

Perali, F.P., and Chavas, J.P. (2000), "Estimation of Censored Demand Equations" American Journal of Agricultural Economics, Vol. 82, pp.1022-37.

Perron, P.P. (1988), "Trends and Random Walk in Macroeconomic Time-series: Further Evidence and Implication", Journal of Economic Dynamics Control, Vol. 12, pp. 279-332.

Phillips, P.P. (1987), "Time-series Regression with a Unit Root", Econometrica, Vol. 55, pp.277-301.

Phlips, L. (1972), "A Dynamic Version of the Linear Expenditure Model", Review of Economics and Statistics, Vol. 54, pp.450-58.

Piggot, N.E. (2001), "The Nested PIGLOG Model: An Application to U.S. Food Demand" American Journal of Agricultural Economics, Vol. 85, No.1, pp.1-15.

Piggott, N.E., and Marsh, T.L. (2002), "Does Food Safety Information Impact US Meat Demand?", American Journal of Agricultural Economics, Vol. 86, pp. 154-74.

Pitt, M.M, Rosenzweig, M. R. and Hassan, Md. N.(1990), "Productivity, Health, and Inequality in the Intra-Household Distribution of Food in Low-income Countries", American Economic Review, Vol. 80, No.5, pp.1139-56.

Pollak, R. A. and Wales, T. J. (1969), "Comparison of the Quadratic Expenditure System and Translog Demand Systems with Alternative Specifications of Demographic Effects", Econometrica, Vol. 78, pp. 575–612.

Pollak, R.A. and Wales, T.J. (1980), "Comparison of the Quadratic Expenditure System and Translog Demand Systems with Alternative Specifications of Demographic Effects", Econometrica, Vol. 48, No.3, pp. 595-612.

Pollak, R.A. and Wales, T.J. (1981), "Demographic Variables in Demand Analysis", Econometrica, Vol. 49, No.6, pp.1533-51.

Pollak, R.A. and Wales, T.J. (1992), "Demand System Specification and Estimation", Oxford University Press, New York.

Pollak, R.A., and Wales, T.J. (1978), "Estimation of Complete Demand Systems from Household Budget Data: The Linear and Quadratic Expenditure Systems", American Economic Review, Vol. 68, No.3, pp.348-59.

Pollak. A, and Wales, T.J. (1969), "Estimation of the Linear Expenditure System." Econometrica, Vol. 37, No.4, pp. 611-27.

Poonyth, D., Hassan, R. and Kirsten, J.F. (2001), "Random Coefficients Analysis of Changes in Meat Consumption Preferences in South Africa", Agrekon, Vol. 40, pp.426-37.

Pradhan, N.B and Panda, B.K. (2000), "Economies of Scale in Household Consumption: An Econometric Analysis, in V.V.N. Somayajulu (ed.), Econometric Studies of Economic Reforms in India, Academic Foundation, Delhi.

Pradhan. N.B.(1979), "Economic Backwardness and Development of Orissa" , Unpublished Ph.D. Thesis Submitted to Berhampur University.

Prais, S.J, and Houthakker, H.S. (1955), "The Analysis of Family Budgets", Cambridge University Press, Cambridge, U.K.

Radhakrishna, R. and Mishra, G. K. (1970), "A Regional Approach to the Consumption Patterns in India", Arthavijnan, Vol.12, pp. 523-63.

Radhakrishna, R. Murty, G.V.S.N and N.C Saha. (1973), "Estimation of Complete Demand System under Two Stage Consumer Budgeting", Paper Presented at the 14th Indian Econometrics Conference, Indian Statistical Institute, New Delhi.

Radhakrishna. R, Murty. G.V.S.N and Saha. N.C. (1979), "Models of Consumer Behavior for Indian Economy", Sardar Patel Institute of Economic and Social Research, Ahmedabad.

Radhakrishna, R. and Murty, G.V.S.N. (1981), "An Application of Indirect Addilog Demand System to Consumer Behaviour in India", Indian Economic Journl, Vol.27, pp. 28-52.

Radhakrishna, R. and Murty. K.N. (1999), "Econometrics of Complete Demand System with Illustration for India", in K.L Krishna (ed), Econometric Application in India, Oxford University press, Delhi.

Raper, K.C., Wanzala, M. N. and Nayga, Jr. R.M. (2002), "Food Expenditures and Household Demographic Composition in the US: A Demand Systems Approach", Applied Economics, Vol. 34, pp. 981- 92.

Ravi. C. (1980), "Complete Demand System for India", M.Phil. Dissertation, Centre of Economic and Social Studies, Hyderabad.

Ray, R. (1982), "The Testing and Estimation of Complete Demand System on Household Budget Survey: An Application of Almost Ideal Demand System", European Economic Review, Vol.17, pp348-69.

Ray, R.(1985), "A Dynamic Analysis of Expenditure Pattern in Rural India", Journal of Development Economics, Vol.-19, No.-3, pp.283-97.

Ray, R. (1991), "Complete Demand System and Recent Welfare Application in India A Review", Journal of Quantitative Economics, Vol.7, pp.1-22.

Reed, A.J., Levendahl, J.W. and Hallahan, C. (1987), "The Generalized Composite Commodity Theorem and Food Demand Estimation",

American Journal of Agricultural Economics, Vol. 87, No.1, pp.28-37.

Robinson, P. (1988), "Root-N-Consistent Semi-parametric Regression", Econometrica, Vol.56, pp. 931-54.

Roy. J. and Laha. C.G. (1960), "Preliminary Estimates of Relative Increase in Consumer Demand in Rural and Urban India, in A. Ganguly (ed), Studies on Consumer Behavior, Asia Publishing House, Bombay.

Ornstein, S.I and Hanssensn, D.M. (1985) "Alcohol Control Laws and the Consumption of Distilled Spirits and Beer", Journal of Consumer Research, Vol.45, pp. 45-64.

Sahabuddin. S. (1989), "Pattern of Food Consumption in Bangladesh", Bangladesh Development Studies, Vol.17, No. 3, pp. 101-17.

Sandhu, H.S. (1984), "Methods of Consumer Demand Projection: A Survey", Asian Economic Review, Vol26, pp. 87-96.

Sandhu. H.S. (1985), "A Review of Models on Consumer Demand Analysis", The Asian Economic Review, Vol. 27, pp. 45-75.

Sarangi. P. (2002), "Consumption and Poverty in Orissa: An Econometric Analysis", Unpublished M.Phil. Dissertation submitted to Berhampur University.

Sarangi. P., and Panda, V.K. (2008), "Consumption, Poverty & Inequility in Orissa", Discovery Publishing House Pvt. Ltd., New Delhi.

Schultz, H. (1938), "The Theory and Measurement of Demand", Chicago University Press, Chicago, Illinois.

Selvanathan, E. (1991), "Cross-Country Alcohol Consumption Comparison: An Application of the Rotterdam Demand System", Applied Economics, Vol.23, No.10, pp. 1613-23.

Shonkwiler, J. S. and Yen, S.T. (1999), "Two-step Estimation of a Censored System of Equations", American Journal of Agricultural Economics, Vol. 81, No.4, pp. 972-82.

Siddiqui. R (1982), "An Analysis of Consumption Pattern in Pakistan", Pakistan Development Review, Vol.21, No.4, pp. 275-96.

Stone, J.R.N. (1954), "Linear Expenditure Systems and Demand Analysis: An Application to the Pattern of British Demand", Economic Journal, Vol.64, pp. 511-27.

Subramanian, S. and Deaton, A. (1966), "The Demand for Food and Calories", Journal of Political Economy, Vol. 104, No.1, pp. 133-62.

Taljaard, P.R., Alemu, Z.G. and Schalkwyk, H.D. Van (2002), "The Demand for Meat in South Africa: An Almost Ideal System Estimation", Agrekon, Vol. 43, No.4, pp. 430-43.

Taylor, J. Edward and Mora, Jorge (2006), "Does Migration Reshape Expenditures in Rural Households?-Evidence from Mexico", Policy Research, Working Paper Series 3842, World Bank, New York.

Teklu, T. and Johnson, S.R. (1988), "Demand Systems from Cross-section Data: An Application of the Indian Data", Canadian Journal of Agriculture Economics, Vol.51, pp. 83-101.

Theil, H. (1951), "Compensated Changes in Quantities and Qualities Consumed", The Review of Economic Studies, Vol.19, pp. 155-64.

Theil, H. (1965), "The Information Approach to Demand Analysis", Econometrica, Vol. 33, pp. 67-87.

Theil, H. (1975), "Theory and Measurement of Consumer Demand", Vol.1, North Holland Publishing Company.

Tobin, J.(1958), "Estimation of Relationships for Limited Dependent Variables" Econometrica, Vol. 26, No.1, pp. 24-36.

Verma, R. (1959), "Income Elasticity of Demand for Food grains", Arthavigyan, pp.271-80.

Wales T.J. and Woodland A.D.(1983), "Estimation of Consumer Demand Systems with Binding Non-negativity Constraints", Journal of Econometrics, Vol. 21, pp. 263-85.

Wooldridge, J.M. (2002), "Econometric Analysis of Cross-section and Panel Data". Cambridge, MIT Press.

Yen, S.T., Kan, K. and Su, S. (2002), "Household Demand for Fats and Oils: Two-step Estimation of Censored Demand System", Applied Economics, Vol. 34, No.14, pp. 1799-06.

Yen, S.T., Lin, B.H and Smallwood, D.M. (2001), "Quasi and Simulated Likelihood Approaches to Censored Demand Systems: Food Consumption by Food Stamp Recipients in the United States", American Journal of Agricultural Economics, Vol. 85, pp. 458-91.

Yen, Steven T. and Wen S. Chern (1992), "Flexible Demand Systems with Serially Correlated Errors: Fat and Oil Consumption in the U.S", American Journal of Agricultural Economics Vol.74, No.3, pp. 689 - 697.

Yen, T. S. and Helen, J.H. (1996), "Determinant of Household Expenditure on Alcohol", Journal of Consumer affair, Vol. 30, pp. 121-146.

Yoshihara, K. (1969), "Demand Functions: An Application to the Japanese Expenditure Pattern", Econometrica, Vol. 37, pp. 257-74.

Zellener, A. (1962), "An efficient Method of Estimating Seemingly Unrelated Regressions and Tastes for Aggregation Bias", Journal of American Statistical Association, Vol. 57, pp. 348-68.